Sir Walter Ralegh

John Winton

What is our life? a play of passion,
Our mirth the musicke of division,
Our mothers wombes the tyring houses be,
Where we are drest for this short Comedy,
Heaven the Judicious sharpe spectator is,
That sits and markes still who doth act amisse,
Our graves that hide us from the searching Sun,
Are like drawne curtaynes when the play is done,
Thus march we playing to our latest rest,
Onely we dye in earnest, that's no Jest.

Ralegh: On the Life of Man.

Sir Walter Ralegh

John Winton

COWARD, McCANN & GEOGHEGAN, INC.

NEW YORK

Contents

Illustrations

7

ACKNOWLEDGEMENTS

My grateful thanks are due to Juliet Brightmore, for her research into pictures of the Elizabethan era; to the late Marquess of Salisbury, K.G., P.C., and Miss Clare Talbot, Librarian at Hatfield House, for allowing me to examine the MS in Ralegh's handwriting of *The Ocean to Scinthia*; and to Mr Simon Wingfield Digby, M.P., and Mr P. A. Howe, Curator, for the opportunity to examine Ralegh's will, and pictures, furnishings and other items of Raleghana at Sherborne Castle.

I . 'A Bare Gentleman'

'SIR WALTER RAWLEIGH,' wrote Sir Robert Naunton, in what is still the best thumb-nail sketch of Ralegh's career, 'was one, that (it seems) Fortune had pickt out of purpose, of whom to make an example, or to use as her Tennis-Ball, thereby to shew what she could doe; for she tost him up of nothing, and too and fro to greatnesse, and from thence down to little more than to that wherein she found him, (A bare Gentleman).'

Walter Ralegh's provocative personality always stimulated such vivid comment from his contemporaries. Queen Elizabeth and King James both punned on his name. The Queen called him her dear 'Water'. James said, ominously, 'I have heard rawly of thee, mon.' Ralegh's friend and fellow-poet Edmund Spenser praised him as 'thee that art the sommers Nightingale' but Sir John Harington's epigram accused him as 'You that will lose a friend, to coine a jest.' Sir Edward Coke, who prosecuted Ralegh for high treason, called him 'a spider of hell' and Sir Anthony Bagot said that Ralegh was 'the best hated man in the world; in court, city and country.' Even Ralegh's long-time friend Henry Percy, Earl of Northumberland, admitted that he 'desired to seem to be able to sway all men's fancies, all men's courses'. But when Ralegh was imprisoned in the Tower by King James, Henry Prince of Wales remarked that 'Only my father would keep such a bird in a cage.'

Ralegh was courtier, soldier, sailor, explorer, poet, parliamentarian, patron of the arts, falconer, gardener, botanist, chemist, historian, war reporter and antiquary. He tried his hand at so many things, and everything he touched seemed to glow. Yet, ultimately, his record is one of paradoxes and failures. He always promised more than he achieved. He pioneered, but seldom profited. None of his settlements in Virginia took permanent root. His estates in Ireland were unprofitable. His expeditions left him out of pocket. His great long poem to the Queen, and his *History of the World* were both unfinished. He might have had the Queen's heart, as a courtier, but he never had her ear, as a politician. He meddled in affairs of state, and was convicted of high treason. He twice tried to find Eldorado, and twice failed. He once tried to commit suicide, and failed. His wit was always keen, but his judgment was often faulty. He could make friends, and fail to recognize his enemies. He wrote the most delicious poetry, and committed the most savage atrocities. His marriage with Elizabeth Throckmorton was long and successful, but his writings show him as curiously impersonal towards women. He wrote poems recommending chastity, but himself begot illegitimate children. He had a great reputation as an admiral, but his chief services to his country were on land. He sailed across the Atlantic, but preferred to cross the Thames 'by the bridge'. He was accused of atheism, but wrote in his *History of the World* a majestic exposition of the providential view of history. He was 'the embodiment of Tudor England,

Sir Walter Ralegh. From the frontispiece of 1736 edition of Ralegh's *History of the World*, Vol. I

but he survived into the seventeenth century, and was not out of place in it. He served as a soldier in France and Ireland, possibly also in the Low Countries; he sent his ships both to North and South America, and himself sailed to Guiana, to Cadiz and to the Azores; the ambassadors of Spain, France and Venice reported constantly on his doings; the King of Spain regarded him as the greatest menace to his realm, after Drake; the King of Denmark wanted to employ him as his admiral; he spoke all his life with a provincial English accent, but he was possibly the most international Elizabethan of them all.

Ralegh was sensitive about his family background. At Court he soon overheard, as he was doubtless meant to, the malicious murmurings (many instigated by the Earl of Oxford) about 'upstarts' and 'Jacks'. He was sufficiently concerned to have the College of Heralds and local genealogists in Devon fully investigate his family history. The result of their researches, relayed through Ralegh's fellow-Devonian John Hooker, could hardly have been more flattering. In the 'epistle dedicatorie' to his continuation of Holinshed's *Chronicles*, published in October 1586, Hooker traced Ralegh's descent to 'D'Amerie of Clare, Clare of King Edward the First; which Clare, by his father, descended of King Henry the First'. Thus Ralegh was supposed to have Plantagenet blood like the Queen herself. This family tree was subsequently challenged by other genealogists; but its importance lies in the fact that Ralegh needed its reassurance, not its accuracy.

Tudor society was moderately flexible, and it was quite possible for a man to rise solely through administrative ability, as the Cecils had; but to make his way into the Queen's favour as he eventually did, Ralegh had to be of gentle birth. As Naunton says, significantly, 'It is a certain note of the times that the Queen in her choice, never took into her favour a meer new man, or a Mechanick.' In fact, Ralegh had nothing to worry about on the score of breeding. He was 'well descended and of good alliance'. The Raleghs, though quite unknown at Court, were a prominent family of West-Country gentry, known in Devon since the Norman Conquest. During the reign of Edward III the Devon Raleghs branched into five separate families, who all lived at different places within the county. Ralegh's father was Walter Ralegh (1496?–1581) of Fardell, near Dartmoor, in the parish of Cornwood, a few miles outside Plymouth.

In 1497 Ralegh's grandfather Wimund Ralegh had been forced by Henry VII's lawyers to sell a family estate at Smallridge, near Axminster, to pay a fine for misprision (i.e. concealment) of treason. However, in 1518 Walter Ralegh of Fardell still owned the manors of Collaton Ralegh, Wythecombe Ralegh and Bollams, in addition to Fardell.

Walter Ralegh of Fardell's first wife was Joan, daughter of John Drake of Exmouth, and a relative of Sir Francis. They had two sons: George Ralegh, who is said to have furnished one of the ships which defeated the Spanish Armada, and John Ralegh, who succeeded to Fardell and died at a great age in 1629. Walter's second wife was Isabel, the daughter of a merchant, Darrell or Dorrell, by whom he had a daughter, Mary, who married Hugh Snedall of Exeter. His second wife died some time before 1549 and Walter Ralegh married again. His third wife was Katherine, daughter of Sir Philip Champernoun or Champernowne of Modbury, and widow of Otho Gilbert of Compton. Katherine already had three sons

Ralegh's birthplace: Hayes Barton, near East Budleigh in Devon. In 1584, Ralegh tried unsuccessfully to buy it, saying that he would 'rather seat myself there than anywhere else'

by her first marriage: Sir John Gilbert of Greenway, Sir Humphrey Gilbert of Compton, and Adrian Gilbert. By Walter Ralegh Katherine had two more sons, Carew and Walter, and a daughter Margaret. Through his mother Sir Walter Ralegh was related to the most distinguished families of the west, not only the Gilberts and the Champernownes, but the Carews, the Grenvilles, the St Legers, the Tremaynes, the Courtenays, and the Russells. These kinships had a considerable effect upon his career.

The Raleghs, Walter and Katherine, were, in historical terms, an obscure West-Country gentleman and his wife, yet they were widely known as staunch Protestants in a predominantly Roman Catholic county. Walter Ralegh was never afraid to proclaim his faith, and his standing in the county was such that he was never arrested or punished for stating his beliefs even when the Marian persecutions were at their height. The young Ralegh's earliest memories must have been imbued with his parents' antipathetic feelings towards the Church of Rome, and thus towards Spain and her king. The Spaniards were the bogeys of his childhood.

In 1520 Walter Ralegh of Fardell bought from the Duke family of Otterton the remainder of an eighty-year lease of a farm or 'barton' at Hayes, in the parish of East Budleigh, near

Budleigh Salterton in Devon. Here, at the farmhouse of Hayes Barton, his second son by Katherine, Walter Ralegh was born in 1552 or 1554 — the date of birth is not definitely known. The existing register of births for the parish begins in April 1555. Portraits of Sir Walter give some information on his age. One is inscribed 'aetatis suae 34 1588'. Another, '1598 aet. 44'. A miniature of him is captioned 'Aetatae Sue. 65 Anno. Do. 1618'. Thus 1554 seems the more probable year.

Hayes Barton is a solid, substantial farmhouse with a thatched roof, two gabled wings and a central porch, forming an E-shape. It stands today, looking much as it did in Ralegh's day, in a shallow valley, facing south, with the land rising to woods behind and in front of it. To the south is Hayes Wood, which had the same name in the sixteenth century. Beyond the wood, just over two miles away, lies the sea. Hayes Barton is almost exactly halfway between the two Ralegh manors of Wythecombe and Collaton.

Ralegh himself left evidence of his birth at Hayes Barton and of his sentimental attachment to the place in a letter he wrote in 1584 trying, in vain, to buy back the place: 'being born in that house I had rather seat myself there than anywhere else.'

Of Ralegh's early education nothing is known except by inference. He may have gone to a local school or have been taught privately at home. Possibly Walter Ralegh Senior was not able to afford a tutor for his family, and young Ralegh may have boarded with relatives, and shared their tutor. Besides learning to read and write, he would have learned Latin, both grammar and translation, and possibly some Greek, although it was still a comparatively new study in schools. Ralegh's prose writings display a sound knowledge of the classics; his *History of the World*, for instance, is studded with translations and well-turned quotations from classical authors. He may also have learned some French and Italian. He was the sort of man who continued to educate himself, long after he had left school and university. As Naunton says, he 'had the adjuncts of some generall Learning, which by diligence he enforced to a great augmentation, and perfection; for he was an indefatigable Reader, whether by Sea or Land.'

Occasionally young Ralegh accompanied his father on business to Exmouth and Sidmouth and Budleigh Salterton. At that time every town on the Devon coast was full of sailors, only too ready to hold an eager audience of small boys with their tales of fierce storms, shipwrecks and tidal waves, of desperate sea-fights and struggles with sea-monsters, of exotic birds and beasts in faraway lands and, above all, of the cruelties of the iniquitous Spaniards and the terrible tortures inflicted upon those unfortunate enough to fall into their hands.

The county families of Devon formed almost an exclusive warrior caste, like a band of brothers bred for war and conflict, who followed the fighting wherever a battle-cry was raised. Ralegh's cousins, the Tremayne brothers Nicholas and Andrew, went to France under the Earl of Warwick in 1562, and were both killed in the defence of Le Havre, on the same walls where, in September of the following year, Ralegh's half-brother Humphrey Gilbert was severely wounded. During a temporary lull in the French religious wars in 1567, a party of Ralegh's relatives and family friends, including Richard Grenville, Henry Champernowne, Philip Budockshide, William Gorges and Thomas Cotton, went to Hungary

As a very young man, Ralegh served with the Protestant side in the French religious wars. He may have been one of a party of Englishmen, including Sir Philip Sidney, sheltered in the English Ambassador's house during the Massacre of St Bartholomew's Day, August 1572

to fight for the Emperor Maximilian against the Turks under their great sultan Suleiman the Magnificent. Young Walter Ralegh was of this same breed, and it was a question only of time before he joined their ranks.

As the fifth son, Ralegh could not expect much of a patrimony. His father could give him little more than his education, and he duly sent him up to Oxford. Anthony à Wood, in the biography of Ralegh in his *Athenae Oxonienses*, says that 'in 1568, or thereabouts, he became a commoner of Oriel coll. at what time C. Champernoon his kinsman, studied there, where his natural parts being strangely advanced by academical learning, under the care of an excellent tutor, became the ornament of the juniors, and was worthily esteemed a proficient in oratory and philosophy.'

Ralegh did not stay long enough at Oxford to get a degree. In 1569 he went to France to serve on the Huguenot side in the French religious wars. In his *Annals* of Elizabeth's reign, published in 1615, the historian William Camden records for the year 1569 that, the Protestants in France being 'now in a distressed and almost desperate condition', Queen Elizabeth sent them money and 'permitted Henry Champernowne (whose cousin-german Gawen had married the Earl of Montgomery's daughter) to carry into France a troup of a hundred volunteer gentlemen on horseback . . . Amongst these volunteer gentlemen, who arrived in France in October 1569, were Philip Budockshide, Francis Berkely, and Walter Raleigh, a very young man, who now first began to be of any note.'

It is not clear how long Ralegh served in France. Richard Hakluyt the younger, Ralegh's friend and contemporary at Oxford, suggests that it was more than five years. It does seem probable that Ralegh spent only one year, 1568–9, up at Oxford, followed by some five years, 1569–74, serving in France. (The appearance of his name on the Oriel College register for 1572 is no definite evidence that he was still at the university.)

The French wars of religion, which for the last forty years of the sixteenth century set province against province and brother against brother, witnessed some of the bloodiest and bitterest fighting in European history. In one of the rare personal references in the *History* Ralegh recalls seeing fire used to force entry into defended caves in Languedoc. The effect of such terrible events on the young Ralegh can only be guessed. Such experiences were normal for his times and he himself seems to have taken it for granted that he should serve such an apprenticeship. In France Ralegh gained his lifelong horror of civil war, by which, as he wrote in his *Discourse of War in General,* 'the condition of no nation was ever bettered'. But it was in France, too, that a certain latent strain of savagery in Ralegh's own nature emerged.

In June 1574 the Huguenot Count of Montgomery, with whose cause Ralegh's Champernowne relatives were linked, was captured and beheaded. Ralegh himself probably returned to England later that same year. He was in London early in 1575. The Register of the Middle Temple for 27th February has the entry 'Walter Rawley, late of Lyons Inn, [an Inn of Chancery off Drury Lane] Gent. Son of Walter R. of Budleigh, Co Devon, Esq.'. In fact, Ralegh never seems to have had any intention of following a legal career. When Sir Edward Coke taunted him at his trial for his lack of legal expertise, Ralegh retorted, 'If I ever read a word of the law or statutes before I was a prisoner in the Tower, God confound me!' In Ralegh's day the Inns of Court were almost a third, metropolitan, university where young men about town could consort with their equals, acquire some culture, learn to sing and dance and generally make themselves agreeable in company without any need to study law.

Here, Ralegh showed that there was a gentler side to his nature, and tried his hand at poetry, with some success. Some verses headed 'Walter Rawely of the middle Temple, in commendation of the Steele Glasse' were bound into the first edition of George Gascoigne's *The Steele Glas* published in April 1576. The poem was a satire in blank verse, the conceit implicit in the title being the fact that an old-fashioned metal mirror was supposed to give a less distorted reflection than the flattering Venetian crystal used by gallants and ladies of the poet's day. Ralegh must already have had some little reputation as a man about town and as a poet for Gascoigne to notice him. Soldier, adventurer, poet and literary figure, George Gascoigne was a friend of Humphrey Gilbert, having served with him in Flanders, and also of Robert Dudley, the great Earl of Leicester and favourite of the Queen. It was possibly Gascoigne who first introduced Ralegh to Leicester.

Ralegh's poem for *The Steele Glas* reads as though it had been written with short, sharp jabs of the pen, with lines of spiked monosyllables. But the tone is confident, and the poem

is clearly an attack on the envious. One couplet has often been regarded as prophetic in Ralegh's own case:

> For whoso reapes renowne above the rest,
> With heapes of hate shal surely be opprest.

His position was almost certainly that of an Esquire of the Body Extraordinary, a member of a reserve or 'pool' of unemployed and unpaid young men who waited about the threshold of the Court, literally on the fringe of affairs. They were available to take letters, escort visitors, and generally to run minor Court errands. Meanwhile they hoped to be noticed and given preferment and offices. An unlucky or unliked Esquire could wait years without employment.

Ralegh does not seem to have made much impression at Court in these early days, although he must have stood out from the crowd by his appearance alone. He was a seasoned veteran soldier, with his experiences stamped in his face, in his mid-twenties, six foot tall, handsome and bold. He had, as Naunton says, 'in the outward man, a good presence, in a handsome and well compacted person, a strong natural wit, and a better judgement, with a bold and plausible tongue, whereby he could set out his parts to the best advantage'. He had what Aubrey called 'a most remarkable aspect, an exceeding high forehead, long-faced, and sour eie-lidded, a kind of pigge-eie'. With his dark, brooding good looks, swarthy complexion, black hair and beard which 'turned up naturally', he looked more like a Spaniard than an Englishman. His voice was 'small' but he spoke 'broad Devonshire to his dying day'. He had the capacity for both melancholy introspection and violent physical activity typical of his age. He was a man of dreams and ideas, who longed to put his thoughts into action. He was proud, quarrelsome, and quick to defend his honour. Insults and injustices rankled with him. He had a talent for acquisition, with a jackdaw's eye for bright colours and ornaments, as well as for new ideas. His companions were kindred spirits. Aubrey describes them as 'boysterous blades, but generally those that had wit'.

Naunton mentions that Ralegh 'cast a new chance, both in the Low-Countries and in a Voyage to Sea'. He could have been one of the English contingent who went to the Low Countries under Sir John Norris, to fight on the side of the Prince of Orange. But there is no other evidence that he did. He was certainly in England on 11th April 1578, to sign his name 'Walter Rauleygh' on a document with his father and his brother Carew renouncing a tithe of fish and larks to William Peryam for £60 (the Raleghs had leased this tithe from Thomas Baron and John Leigh of the manor of Sidmouth, Devon, since 10th September 1560). It has been said that Ralegh was present at the defeat of Don John of Austria at the battle of Rimenant on 1st August 1578. Again, although it is possible, there is no evidence for it, nor any reference in Ralegh's own writings. Besides, by August 1578, Ralegh was much involved with Humphrey Gilbert in an exciting plan of their own – the Voyage to Sea.

Robert Dudley, Earl of Leicester, the Queen's 'sweet Robin', probably sponsored Ralegh at Court, but soon found that this young man was 'an apprentice as well enough knew how to set up for himself'

2. To Sea and to Ireland

HUMPHREY GILBERT was some thirteen or fourteen years older than Ralegh; he seems always to have treated his younger half-brother as his favourite – he gave him advice, lent him money, dropped his name in the right places, and introduced him to the right people. Gilbert went to Eton and Oxford. Although a second son, he inherited some money, and married more. His family hoped he would become a lawyer, but Gilbert chose a life of action as an adventurer and soldier; in France, in the Low Countries, and in Ireland. As Governor of Munster in 1569–70 he treated the Irish with a severity unusual even in Elizabethan Ireland. He was knighted in 1570, but replaced in Ireland by Sir John Perrot, a more lenient man.

For years, Humphrey Gilbert dreamed of finding a north-west passage by sea to China. In 1576 George Gascoigne published, possibly without its author's consent, Gilbert's *Discourse to prove a Passage, by the North-west, to Cataia, and the East Indies*, in which he set out to prove, first, the existence of such a passage; second, its feasibility for traffic; and third, the immense trading advantages that would accrue if it were ever established.

The best way to prove the passage was to make it. But first, in 1577, Gilbert proposed a way of damaging Spanish interests and at the same time making some money: he would sail to Newfoundland and capture foreign (meaning Spanish) ships, bring them back to Dutch ports, and sell them. From the proceeds, he intended to fit out a full expedition to attack Spanish possessions in America. The Queen's name would not be involved in the venture. Those taking part would claim they were servants of William of Orange.

The Queen received the scheme coolly. Her Privy Council treated it with open suspicion. However, Gilbert also continued to press his schemes for the exploration of Norumbega, which was the name given to the North American coastline approximately from Long Island northward to Cape Breton Island. Eventually, on 11th June 1578, the Queen signed letters patent, valid for six years, granting Sir Humphrey Gilbert 'free libertie and licence from time to time and at all times for ever hereafter, to discover, finde, search out, and view such remote, heathen and barbarous lands, countreys and territories not actually possessed by any Christian prince or people'.

At once, according to the account by Edward Hayes in Hakluyt, 'very many gentlemen of good estimation drew unto him, to associate him in so commendable an enterprise, so that the preparation was expected to grow into a puissant fleet, able to encounter a kings power by sea.' The 'puissant fleet' actually consisted of eleven vessels (four of them very small), some to be fitted out in Devon and some in London.

The project was bedevilled by difficulties throughout. There was a shortage of money,

Sir Humphrey Gilbert of Compton, Ralegh's half-brother, with whom he went privateering in 1578. Gilbert colonized Newfoundland in 1583; he was later drowned

although Gilbert sold some of his own and his wife's possessions. There were clashes of personality, and four ships withdrew from the expedition before it had begun. There were further delays due to the weather. The ships starting from London were held up for a time, set sail, were driven back up Channel, set out again, and were again driven back.

At last, on 19th November 1578, the seven remaining ships, with a total force of 365 men, set sail westwards, with Sir Humphrey himself in the admiral, 250 tons, and Ralegh's brother Carew in the vice-admiral. Ralegh commanded the old and somewhat leaky ship *Falcon*, of 100 tons, armed with fifteen cast pieces, four fowlers, and twelve double bases. Ferdinando the Portugal was his sailing-master, and there were on board seventy mariners, soldiers and gentlemen, including Ralegh's kinsman Charles Champernowne. Their motto was *Nec mortem peto, nec finem fugio* – I neither seek death, nor flee mine end.

Falcon was a Queen's ship, which suggests that Elizabeth, even if she had not met Ralegh by this date, must at least have known his name and something about him. The Queen did not lend her property, even an ancient ship, to anybody. Perhaps this was one more occasion on which Humphrey Gilbert (who had been page to Elizabeth before her accession) put in a good word for his young half-brother.

It is hard to see what the purpose of Gilbert's expedition was, other than pure privateering. *Falcon* was very heavily armed, as indeed was the whole flotilla, for ships which were ostensibly on an innocent trading or exploratory voyage. Winter was imminent, and it was far too late in the year to attempt the north-west passage or to land settlers, or even to intercept a Spanish treasure fleet: the second of them (there were normally two a year) would have reached the safety of Cadiz by the end of October at the latest. Gilbert may have intended to sail down the coast of Africa, and then across to the West Indies. He may have done so.

22

THE

Irish historie com-
posed and written by Gi-
raldus Cambrensis, and translated into English (with scho-
lies to the same) by Iohn Hooker of
the citie of Excester gentleman; to-
gither with the supplie of the said historie, from the death of king Henrie
the eight, vnto this present yeere
1 5 8 7, doone also by
the said Iohn
Hooker:

And dedicated to the ho-
norable sir Walter Ralegh
knight, lord warden of
the stannarie in the
counties of Deuon
and Cornwall.

1. Eldras. 4.
And king Artaxerxes commanded the
chronicles to be searched whether it were
true that had béene informed.

Act. 17.
And they dailie searched the scrip-
tures whether the things taught were true
or not.

Historie placeant nostrates ac peregrinæ.

FINIS

But he certainly met misfortune. Edward Hayes puts his sad fate in one sentence. 'Others failed of their promises contracted, and the greater number were dispersed, leaving the General with few of his assured friends, with whom he adventured to sea: where having tasted of no less misfortune, he was shortly driven to retire home with the loss of a tall ship, and (more to his grief) of a valiant gentleman Miles Morgan.' For all his talents and his hopes, Humphrey Gilbert had one fatal flaw as an admiral. He was unlucky. One by one his ships returned until, by about February 1579, only the *Falcon* was still at sea.

Falcon sailed on alone, and did not return for nearly six months, while Ralegh presumably hoped for some adventure or exploit to turn up. Edward Hayes did not mention Ralegh as one of the 'assured friends' of Gilbert, and gives no information about his voyage, but Ralegh did encounter at least one adversary. In this supplement to Holinshed, John Hooker writes of 'one ship wherein his [Gilbert's] brother Walter Ralegh was captain, who being desirous to do somewhat worthy of honour, took his course for the West Indies, but for want of victuals and other necessaries (needful in so long a voyage) when he had sailed as far as the islands of Cape Verde upon the coast of Africa, was enforced to set sail and return for England. In this voyage he passed many dangerous adventures, as well by tempests as fights on the sea; but lastly he arrived at Plymouth in the west country in May next following.'

Hooker's account was probably taken first-hand from Ralegh himself. It has the ring of truth about it. It can be imagined that Ralegh, being separated through circumstances from the main body of the fleet, was too proud to return home without trying to accomplish *something*. He was willing to stay at sea throughout the winter in the attempt.

Ralegh arrived home in the middle of an altercation between Sir Humphrey Gilbert and the Privy Council. The previous month, April 1579, Gilbert had been about to put to sea again, possibly to try to recoup by piracy his expedition's losses. Bernardino de Mendoza, the Spanish Ambassador, had been complaining vigorously about Gilbert's expedition. Reacting to Spanish pressure, the Privy Council had forbidden Gilbert to sail again without giving sureties for his good behaviour. By the end of May Gilbert and Ralegh were not allowed to put to sea, even though they had promised to behave themselves. They were 'to desist from any such enterprise, upon pain of Her Majesty's indignation'.

The sanction of the Queen's indignation was effective. The next time Sir Humphrey Gilbert put to sea, it was by command of their Lordships, who had ordered him to try to prevent James Fitzmaurice, cousin of the Irish Earl of Desmond, landing a force of Spanish and Italian soldiers in south-west Ireland. Gilbert failed to intercept them, and on 17th July 1579 the force landed at Dingle Bay and built a fort at Smerwick – a name which Ralegh and others were shortly to make notorious. Gilbert's ships were engaged by the Crown and given to the command of Sir John Perrot. Gilbert did not get any of them back except the smallest, the eight-ton *Squirrel*.

For the last half of 1579 and the first months of 1580, Ralegh was in London, again a hanger-on at Court. But, this time, he was at last beginning to be noticed. His letters from Ireland written a year later show that, during this period of 1579–80, he must have made the acquaintance of Burghley, possibly also of Walsingham, and he must certainly have achieved some form of familiarity with Leicester. On 25th August 1581 Ralegh wrote to Leicester from his campaign headquarters at Lismore, in terms which suggest that some kind of bargain had been struck between them. It is a letter from client to patron. Ralegh has, apparently, publicly allowed it to be known that he is Leicester's man. Now he asks Leicester to fulfil his side of the bargain. 'I may not forgett continually to put your Honor in mind of my affection unto your Lordshipe, havinge to the worlde bothe professed and protested the same. Your Honor, havinge no use of such poore followers, hathe utterly forgotten mee. Notwithstandinge, if your Lordshipe shall please to thinke mee your's, as I am, I wilbe found as redy, and dare do as miche in your service, as any man you may cummande.'

Ralegh himself was as hot-tempered as any young gentleman at Court. Such records as there are of him at this time are all of his getting into trouble. On 7th February 1580 he and Sir Thomas Perrot were called before the Privy Council and committed to the Fleet Prison for 'a fray made betwixt them'. Six days later, after a cooling-off period, both men were summoned before the Council again and released on bond, provided they demeaned themselves quietly. On 17th March Ralegh was in trouble again, for fighting on the tennis court at Westminster with Mr Wingfield. Both were committed to the Marshalsea Prison, where, as it happened, Ralegh's cousin Arthur Gorges arrived the next day, for giving the lie to Lord Windsor and 'other speeches made in the Presence Chamber'. Ralegh was clearly spoiling for some sort of action, and at last he got his desire – in Ireland.

The landing at Dingle in July 1579 had sparked off a rebellion in Munster. The Geraldines, as the Fitzgerald family were known, had been compromised by the murder of an English officer, in bed, while a guest of the family. Sir Nicholas Maltby and Sir Warham St Leger (kinsman and friend of Ralegh's) attempted to put down the rebellion with fire and sword, but in November the rebel Earl of Desmond and his kinsman the Seneschal of Imokilly took and sacked the town of Youghal. By December St Leger was writing to London asking for urgent reinforcements.

In fact, Ralegh did not take his place amongst the new levies for service in Ireland until July 1580. On the 11th a letter from the Privy Council authorized the Lord Treasurer to pay to Walter Ralegh, gentleman, the sum of one hundred pounds as imprest, as he had been appointed by Lord Grey (who had been Gascoigne's old patron and was now the new Lord Deputy of Ireland) to have the charge of one hundred of the men then being levied within the City of London to be transported for her Majesty's service into Ireland. On the same day their Lordships issued a 'placard' for Walter Ralegh, 'being to repair for her Majesty's service into Ireland, for one cart, five post horses, and to be provided of convenient shipping where he shall think meet to embark'.

Ralegh had wages for his men for six days, by which time they had reached the Isle of Wight, by way of Portsmouth. They waited there for fifteen days for a ship. Their voyage to Cork took a further seventeen days. Ralegh himself drew his pay and allowances as a captain from 13th July; he was paid four shillings a day; his lieutenant, Michael Butler, two shillings; his officers (NCOs), fourteen pence each; and the soldiers eightpence a day. The exchequer in Munster evidently moved very slowly, and these details, with those about his journey to

Ireland, are included in a letter dated 22nd February 1581, in which Ralegh writes from Cork to Lord Burghley to complain that he had received victuals at the rate of only sixpence a day per man for the thirty-two days of the journey, and asking that he should be reimbursed.

On 27th July 1580 Sir James Fitzgerald, younger brother of the rebel Earl, had been captured by the Sheriff of Cork, and almost Ralegh's first duty on arrival in the town was to assist at his trial. Fitzgerald was sentenced to be hanged, drawn and quartered. His dismembered body was then hung in chains above the main gate of Cork. For Ralegh it was a grim initiation into the campaign to come.

The problems of pacifying, colonizing, and converting the Catholic Irish had been beyond the capacity of the Tudors to solve. Ireland was a widow-maker, a breaker of hopes and health and reputations. The Irish would neither be governed, nor govern themselves. For the English, the trouble with Ireland was the Irish. It was hard for the English even to look upon the Irish as fellow human beings. They looked and lived like animals. Often their only garment was a large enveloping cloak, which served in turn as swaddling cloth, pillow, and shroud. They never washed. They wore their unkempt hair long over their eyes, so that a man could not tell if they were lying – which they almost always were. They lived on sour milk, butter, oat-bread and, occasionally, fish or meat. They got drunk whenever they could, swore all the time, and tied their ploughs to the tails of their horses which, like themselves, were small and hairy.

When Ralegh arrived, Cork was garrisoned by nearly a thousand men, with more arriving

26

from England every month. The English were preparing themselves for yet another punitive lunge across the Irish countryside. In September there were rumours that a Spanish fleet was cruising off the west coast and that another force of Spaniards had landed. Early in October, the English army marched out of Cork, led by an Anglo-Irishman, Thomas Butler, Earl of Ormond, Lord General of Munster. Ralegh's company went with them, into a devastated land of green hills and greener bogs, few roads and fewer hopes. Ormond camped at Rathkeale, where Lord Grey eventually joined him. A fresh force of some 600 Italian troops with Spanish officers had indeed landed in September and occupied the Dingle peninsula. After one brush with Ormond's forces, the invaders retreated to Fort Smerwick where Grey followed them. John Hooker, in his *Irish Chronicles*, tells a rather unpleasant propagandist story of how Ralegh stayed behind to await the Irish peasant soldiers come to scavenge the English camp. They were trapped and their leader hanged.

Ralegh was harsher yet in his next undertaking, at Fort Smerwick, which by the beginning of November 1580 was under siege by Lord Grey's army. The fort was called Castell del Oro, the 'Fort of Gold', supposedly because a shipload of black ore, thought to be gold-bearing, had been wrecked nearby during one of Sir Martin Frobisher's voyages. The fort had been strengthened since Fitzmaurice's day and was now defended by about 600 men. Even so, the garrison commander had written to Philip of Spain for help, although his main present hope was in the Earl of Desmond, who was approaching by land.

Lord Grey had no artillery, and to reduce the fort needed the assistance of the guns of the Queen's ships under Sir William Winter and Vice-Admiral (later Sir Richard) Bingham – 'A great jewel of Captain Bingham', as Lord Grey called him in his report.

The ships arrived on 27th October, before Desmond. Their field pieces were landed and the bombardment began. The position of the Smerwick garrison was seen to be hopeless. By 10th November they had surrendered unconditionally, having first asked for a parley, which was not granted by Grey. Hooker, again, has the story: 'When they saw that they could not prevaile anie waie, then at the length they hanged out a white flag, and with one voice they all cried out *Misericordia, misericordia*, and offered to yeeld both themselves and the fort, without anie condition at all . . . When the capteine had yeelded himselfe, and the fort appointed to be surrendered, capteine Ralegh together with capteine Macworth, who had the ward of that daie, entered into the castell, & made a great slaughter, manie or the most part of them being put to the sword.'

Lord Grey, in his dispatches of 12th November (written by his secretary, the poet Edmund Spenser), wasted no words on his account of the great slaughter: 'The Coronell [Colonel Sebastiano di San Joseppi] comes forth with x or xij of his chief ientlemen, trayling theyr ensignes rolled up, and presented them unto mee with theyr lives and the Forte . . . Then putt I in certeyn bandes, who streight fell to execution. There were 600 slayne; munition and vittaile great store, though much wasted through the disorder of the Souldiers, which in that furie could not bee helped.' When the news of the massacre reached England, Mendoza wrote to Philip that 507 men had been put to the sword, along with some pregnant women, besides which seventeen Irish and Englishmen were hanged.

By the standards of Elizabethan Ireland, Lord Grey's conduct was unexceptionable: the massacre at Smerwick was typical of the age. The Queen did not censure Grey, nor Ralegh, nor Macworth. If she had a quibble, it was that she might possibly have been consulted beforehand about who was to be slain and who spared.

Nor did Ralegh ever feel the need to excuse himself or experience any misgivings about the part he played at Fort Smerwick. He had, in any case, a very low opinion of Ireland and the Irish. As Naunton says, 'The Land service of Ireland, then did not yield him food or rayment for it was ever very poor, nor had he the patience to stay there.' There was little hope of money or glory in Ireland, and after a year's service Ralegh grew very impatient. In his letter of August 1581 to Leicester he wrote, 'I have spent some time under the Deputy, in suche poor place, as, were it not for that I knew him to be on of yours, I would disdayn it as miche as to keep sheepe.'

That was indeed a disdainful way for a penniless captain of infantry to speak of the general who had appointed him. The inference is that Ralegh had accepted his Irish commission only as a first step to better things. He now looked to Leicester to improve his lot, thus fulfilling a previous understanding between them. He continued: 'I will not troble your Honor with the business of this loste lande; for that Sir Warram Sentleger can best of any man deliver unto your Lordshipe the good, the badd, the mischeifs, the meanes to amend, and all in all of this common welthe, or rather common woo.' To substitute *woe* for *wealth* was perhaps the nearest Ralegh ever came to a joke, but common woe was a fair description of Ireland under Lord Grey de Wilton.

Lord Grey was a good soldier, an able commander, an enlightened patron of letters, a religious man and a zealous Puritan. It could well be that Grey was so upright, so God-fearing, so estimable, so conscientious, so *unyielding*, that in the end the Irish fared worse under him than they might have done with a less worthy Lord Deputy. To Grey, the chief trouble with the Irish was the Roman Catholic Church. In his view, the Irish were offenders against God and the Queen. They were damned, body and soul, in this world and the next. He had hesitated before taking on the task of Lord Deputy. He knew (who at Court did not?) that Ireland had been the graveyard of so many reputations, and he feared (justifiably, as it turned out) that that terrible country would damage his own. He knew, too, that the Queen did not like him much, and his position at Court was not strong. He asked again and again to be allowed to come home. Meanwhile, in his two years as Lord Deputy, he dealt with the Irish efficiently, energetically and mercilessly, having '1485 chief men and gentlemen slain, not accounting those of the meaner sort, nor yet executions by law, which were innumerable'. Lord Grey believed that nothing could be done with Ireland 'before force have planed the ground for the foundation'. The government at home professed to dislike Grey's cruelty. In fact, they only deplored the expenses he incurred.

Edmund Spenser recommended the winter as the best time for Lord Grey's 'planing' operation: 'It is not with Ireland as with other Countries, wheare the warrs flame most in Sommer, and the helmetes glister brightest in the faire sunshine. But in Ireland the winter yeildeth best services for then the trees are bare and naked, which use both to Cloath and

Lord Grey of Wilton, Ralegh's superior officer in Ireland. 'I must be plain', he wrote of Ralegh, 'I like neither his carriage nor his company.' Portrait by Gerlach Flicke

howse the kerne. The ground is could and wett which useth to bee his beddinge, the ayre is sharp and bytter which useth to blowe thorowe his naked sydes and legges, the kyen are barren and without milke which useth to bee his onelie foode.' It took a poet of genius to describe a faultless strategy of genocide: 'Townes there are none of which he maye get spoyle, they are all burnt, Country howses and farmers there are none, they bee all fledd, breed he hath none he plowed not in somer, fleshe he hath, but yf he kyll yt in winter he shall want milke in sommer. Therefore yf they bee well followed but one winter ye shall have lyttle worke with them in the next sommer.'

The Irish were 'well followed' by Lord Grey during the Desmond rebellion. Famines were promoted by destroying crops and slaughtering livestock. The people were subdued by putting large numbers of them to death. There were, at least at this time, no schemes for resetting the Irish, no plans for educating them or improving their land or their way of life. The Irish were to be pacified, which meant the peace imposed by Sir Humphrey Gilbert, the quiet of the grave.

Ralegh wholeheartedly approved of this policy; indeed in a letter to Sir Francis Walsingham, written at Cork and dated 25th February 1581, he complained bitterly that Ormond was being too soft on the Fitzgeralds, and compared his régime unfavourably with Sir Humphrey Gilbert's: the Geraldines, wrote Ralegh, in what was already becoming his characteristically vigorous prose,

will rather dy a thowsand deathes, entre into a million of mischeifes and seek soccor of all nacions, rather than they will ever be subdued by a Butler – that aftre Her Majesty hathe spent a hundred thowsand pound more she shall at last be driven by to dere experience to send an Inglishe Presedent to follow thes mallicious traytors with fier and sword, nether respectinge the aliance nor the nacion. Would God your Honor and Her Majesty, as well as my poore selfe, undrestoode how pitifully the service here goethe forward! Considering that this man, havinge now byn Lord Generall of Munstre now about too yeares, theire ar at this instant a thowsand traytors more then ther were the first day. Would God the service of Sir Humfry Gilbert might be rightly lokt into; who, with the third part of the garreson now in Irland, ended a rebellion not miche inferior to this, in to monethes!

Evidently Ralegh disliked or envied Ormond and, naturally, he was anxious to put in a good word for his half-brother. This letter, and one written to Walsingham two days earlier, seem to suggest that Ralegh was on unexpectedly familiar terms with the head of the Queen's secret service. Ralegh writes of having just had a letter from Walsingham, wherein he found 'Your Honor's disposicion and oppinion more favorable then I can any way deserve'. The language, on both sides, may have been mere polite finery, but it is not impossible that Ralegh had been engaged by Walsingham to provide him with private intelligence on the state of affairs in Ireland.

Ralegh's derogatory comments on Ormond, made by a junior officer about a senior to a third party, were startlingly disloyal, but there was little service protocol and few official channels of communication in the Elizabethan army and Ralegh was not one to suffer inefficiency if he thought a well-directed letter could remove it, especially if that inefficiency stood in the way of his own interests. In this case Ralegh's own interests were most definitely engaged. A landless man, he now had the offer of a 'little old castle' – his first estate – and Ormond, through apathy or malice, was threatening to deprive him of it. A month earlier, in January 1581, Ralegh had ridden to Dublin to complain to Lord Grey of Ormond's inactivity. He knew there was another rebellion afoot, plotted by David Barry, son of Lord Barry, and other young Irishmen. He was commissioned by Lord Grey to fight Barry and put down his rebellion, and also to take possession of Barry Court and Barry Island (the site of the present town of Cobh). Unfortunately Barry was given time to carry out a form of 'scorched earth' policy and burn the castle down. Ralegh suspected Ormond, believing he either meant to keep the castle for himself, or anyway to prevent an Englishman from possessing it.

Riding back to Cork from Dublin, Ralegh had a narrow escape. He had come through Youghal, and was approaching a river ford in Barry country, when he and his small party were ambushed by John Fitzedmond FitzGerald, the Seneschal of Imokilly, with six horse-men and some Irish kerns.

In Hooker's opinion, telling the story in his *Chronicles*, Ralegh's was too small a force in so doubtful and dangerous times. Ralegh compounded the danger by riding alone some way ahead of the rest. He was surprised by the Seneschal and his men and pursued to the ford, which he succeeded in crossing safely. Meanwhile, the guide had taken to his heels, and the next man, Henry Moile, who was also riding about a bow's shot in front of the others, reached the middle of the ford when his horse foundered under him. Afraid that he might be surrounded and killed by the Seneschal's men, Moile called out for help. Ralegh went back and recovered horse and man. In his haste Moile overleapt his horse, (which bolted and was captured by the enemy) and landed in a bog. Once more Ralegh helped him out. Ralegh then sat on horseback, staff in one hand and loaded pistol in the other, while the rest of his party, including his man Jenkin who had two hundred pounds in money on him, crossed safely. The Seneschal had been reinforced with more horsemen and kerns, but although he outnumbered Ralegh's force by twenty to one, he merely shouted what Hooker called 'hard speeches' at Ralegh before riding off. Ralegh later wrote modestly of the affair to Walsingham: 'The manner of myne own behavior I leve to the report of others, but the escape was strange to all men.'

From a professional viewpoint, Ralegh had behaved with almost criminal carelessness, not only by riding so far ahead himself, but by allowing the rest of his party to straggle. The incident was typical of Ralegh's behaviour in Ireland. He seems to have been indifferent to his personal safety, to have delighted in physical danger and personal combat. It was almost as though he wished to be ambushed at that ford, so that he could pit himself to the limit, and then extricate himself from a dangerous situation. He set his life at hazard again and again. Later in the year, during a search for David Barry, Ralegh and five horse charged a troop of infantry, who retaliated with unexpected vigour. Ralegh's horse was shot under him and if it had not been for the assistance of Nicholas Wright and an Irishman called

Patrick Fagaw, Ralegh would probably have been killed.

The image of Ralegh in his days in Ireland (an image perhaps cultivated by Ralegh himself) is a romantic one, of a young hero, reckless of his own life, riding across a wild, green romantic countryside in search of knightly exploits.

To physical courage, Ralegh added considerable physical presence and powers of leadership. He brought off one of his most famous feats by sheer force of personality. Lord and Lady Roche were suspected of plotting rebellion, and Ralegh was ordered by Ormond to bring them from their seat at Castle Bally-in-Harsh to Cork. The Irish intelligence was good, as it often was, and the Seneschal and David Barry lay in wait for Ralegh, with some seven or eight hundred men.

Ralegh was well aware of the danger, and set off with a force of some ninety men, both horsemen and foot, late at night, between ten and eleven o'clock. He reached Bally-in-Harsh, which was about twenty miles from Cork, early the next morning. He went straight to the castle gate. The townsmen of Bally were roused, and about five hundred of them armed themselves, whereupon Ralegh disposed his own men in strategic positions around the town, before going back to the gate, taking with him Michael Butler, James Fulford, Nicholas Wright, Arthur Barlow, Henry Swain and Pinking Hughes. Ralegh demanded admittance. Three or four of Lord Roche's gentlemen asked his business. Ralegh replied that he had come to speak with my Lord. He was allowed to enter, on condition he brought only two or three of his men with him. Ralegh agreed, but somehow managed to infiltrate the whole of his party into the castle.

Once in the castle, and talking to Lord Roche, Ralegh 'so handled the matter by devises and meanes, that by little and little, and by some and some, he had gotten in within the iron doore or gate of the courtlodge all his men. And then having the advantage he commanded his men to stand and gard the said gate, that no man should passe in or out: and likewise charged everie man to come into the hall with his peece well prepared, with two bullets.'

When he realized what had happened, Lord Roche 'was suddenlie amazed & stricken at the harte with feare'. However, he put a good face on it, called for meat and asked Ralegh and the gentlemen with him to keep him company at dinner. After dinner, Ralegh explained the purpose of his visit, told Lord and Lady Roche they were suspected of treason, and showed them his commission which was his authority to take them to Cork. Lord Roche tried to make excuses. Ralegh replied that Roche was going to Cork, if not with a good will, then if need be against his will. Roche gave up, and he and Lady Roche set out with Ralegh that evening. The ways were so foul, so 'full of balks, hillocks, pits, and rocks, that the souldiers thereby were marvellouslie troubled and incombred'. But the night was so stormy and black that it actually helped them, hiding them from Barry's ambushes. They all arrived safely in Cork except 'one soldier named John Phelium, who by his often falling and stumbling among the rocks and stones, did so hurt one of his feet, that he could never recover the same, but did in the end consume and rot awaie'. Early the next morning, Ralegh presented his prisoners to Ormond, 'with no little admiration that he had escaped so

Hibernia, Elizabethan Ireland: a country which Ralegh described as 'not a Common wealth but a Common woe'. Notes in bottom left hand of map by William Cecil, Lord Burghley

dangerous a iorneie, being verelie supposed of all men that he could never have escaped'. If Ormond had ever nursed the unworthy hope that he might get rid of an awkward subordinate by setting him an impossibly dangerous task, he was disappointed. For all his physical exploits in the field, Ralegh kept a close eye on his political chances. In May 1581 he was again complaining of Ormond's conduct of the campaign, this time in a letter to Lord Grey, written from Cork. Ralegh complained of unpardonable inactivity. The Irish were not being followed enough: 'The bandes of Sir Georg Bowser, Edward Barkley, Captayne Dowdall, and of my self, have bine ever since the seconde weeke of Lente remayning in Cork.' Meanwhile, all the county of Limerick and the whole country between Dingle and Kilkenny was left defenceless. The garrison of Cork was in a parlous condition. The stores were all spent, except for small amounts of wheat and butter. Worse still, the wives of Desmond and of Barry had come openly to Cork and left again without their baggage being searched. In short, things were going from bad to worse under Ormond.

Oddly enough, and no doubt to Ralegh's great joy, Ormond was soon to be dismissed as Lord General of Munster, although probably not through any direct connection with Ralegh's complaints. He fell out with Lord Grey and returned to England. He was replaced as Lord General jointly by Ralegh, a Captain Piers, and Sir William Morgan (who had served as long as Ralegh had in Ireland, and who had also served with him in France). The triumvirate acted until Colonel John Zouch's arrival in Munster in August 1581. This was Ralegh's first political appointment. It was shared with two others, and it lasted only a short time. But it was a beginning.

In the same letter of 1st May in which he had complained of Ormond, Ralegh reminded Lord Grey of Barry's Court and Island 'which your Honour willed me to keepe'. The castle was in ruins, and the island spoiled and devastated. Nevertheless, Ralegh had 'by great perswacion of the Commissioners, gott leve to edifie the same, and leve a ward therin; and if it shall please your Honor to thinke mee woorthie the keeping and custodie thereof I will at myne owne coast buyld it up agayne and defend it for her Maiestie.'

Ralegh writes like an eager and importunate child claiming a promised present, but one wonders how he came to have the money to rebuild a castle at his own expense and defend it for the Queen. He may have picked up loot, even in ravished Ireland, or reward or ransom of some kind. Just possibly, he may have inherited a little money, for his father Walter Ralegh of Fardell had died. He was buried in St Mary Major, Exeter, on 23rd February 1581. (Katherine Ralegh lived on until 1594, and was buried with her husband.) Lord Grey confirmed Ralegh as custodian of Barry in September 1581, but the Queen did not sanction the appointment, being dissuaded for some reason, possibly by Lord Burghley.

Lord Grey never recommended Ralegh in any of his dispatches from Ireland, nor even mentioned him by name, but there is no doubt, from his own writings and from the opinions of others, that Ralegh emerged from his service during the Desmond Rebellion as a most competent soldier and an unusually well-equipped military thinker. He was no mere hewer of limbs and drawer of swords, and there were depths to him not to be expected in a crude campaign company commander. He was the man of action perpetually driven onwards by the quality of his thought. All his life he suffered under, and was inspired by, the divine tension between ideas and deeds. He had the vision to see at last that Lord Grey's methods in Ireland, the methods used by Gilbert and all the others, could never bring about a lasting solution. In December 1581 Ralegh was sent back to London with Lord Grey's dispatches. It was only natural that one or more of the Lords of the Privy Council should draw aside a soldier so recently returned from Ireland, and one who was Lord Grey's representative, and ask him, privately, about the course of the campaign. Ralegh put forward a proposal that promised to be quicker, more humane and more economical (the last a consideration which would appeal powerfully to the Queen). He suggested a way of transferring a large part of the expense of policing the Irish territories from the Crown to the Irish chieftains. The way, Ralegh said, lay through the hearts and purses of the minor Irish chieftains, most of whom were far more hostile to Desmond than to Elizabeth. Their main fear was that Desmond would be restored to favour once the rebellion had been crushed. His hand would lie far more heavily upon them than would the Queen of England's.

In January 1582 Lord Burghley wrote to Lord Grey to tell him of these new and subtler policies which had impressed the Queen. The expense of providing and maintaining 500 soldiers could be transferred from the Crown to the nobles of the Province of Munster.

Lord Grey must often have been annoyed by Ralegh – that self-assured, self-opinionated, self-confident, argumentative junior officer, who was 'perpetually differing' and always thought he knew best. Lord Grey conceded that at first sight the 'plott delivered by Captain Rawley unto Her Majesty' offered a very plausible show of thrift. But, he went on,

I doubt not but you will soone discerne a difference between the judgments of those which with grownded experience and approved reason looke into the condicion of things, and those which upon no grownd but seeming fancies, and affecting creditt with profitt, frame 'Plotts' upon impossibilities, for others to execute.

Later, in March 1582, when there was some question of another appointment for Ralegh in Ireland, lest anybody should be any longer in any doubt about his opinion of the man, Lord Grey wrote, 'for myne own part, I must bee playne: I nether like his carriage nor his company.'

But by that time it no longer mattered what Lord Grey liked or disliked. The Queen had had a good look at Walter Ralegh.

3. *The Queen's Favour*

WALTER RALEGH may or may not have spread his splendid new cloak over a puddle for the Queen to walk on, but the anecdote is in character for them both. Ralegh probably did first catch the Queen's eye with some strikingly gallant appearance or gesture which took her fancy. The story of the cloak first appears some forty years after Ralegh's death, in the Reverend Thomas Fuller's *History of the Worthies of England* of 1662:

This captain Raleigh coming out of Ireland to the English court in good habit (his clothes then being a considerable part of his estate) found the queen walking, till, meeting with a plashy place, she seemed to scruple going thereon. Presently Raleigh cast and spread his new plush cloak on the ground; whereon the queen trod gently, rewarding him afterwards with many suits, for his so free and seasonable tender of so fair a foot cloth.

From the moment the Queen noticed him, Ralegh's career leaped from shadow into sunlight. It was as though Ralegh as a personality suddenly emerged from behind curtain-veils and stepped forward to the front of a brightly-lit stage upon which he was to lead a public life, when his every action, gesture, look or remark would be noticed, examined and remembered. In an age which rewarded precocity, Ralegh's talents and character remained, astonishingly, virtually unknown until he was twenty-eight years old. Perhaps his very obscurity was an important ingredient in his powerful attraction for the Queen. Here was a new face, a new voice, a new entertainment, perhaps even a new suitor and adoring swain to replace the ageing Leicester. He had no political, religious or family associations. He was simply himself – a romantic-looking, witty, bold soldier, dandy and poet, with a hint of mystery in his background, and an intriguing record of violence and cruelty. The Queen delighted in him. He was to be her creature. His future lay utterly in her favour. For any courtier, the Queen's displeasure would have been a severe professional setback. For Ralegh, in his special case, it would be the end, like being consigned to those outer deserts of darkness beyond the known world.

Ralegh's patroness, then nearly fifty years old, was one of the most remarkable people ever to rule England. Vain, autocratic, quick-tempered, almost rough, Elizabeth never left anybody in any doubt as to whose daughter she was. She swore by God's death. She publicly picked her teeth with a gold toothpick. She relished risqué songs and jokes. She made political capital of her sex, wielding that long-preserved virginity as a powerful weapon of foreign policy. She was never daunted by detail, always read the small print, and counted the small change. When frightened, she could turn vindictive, and afterwards pretend

Elizabeth I, from a frontispiece to a poem by George de la Motthe, c. 1586, French

SEMPER

EADEM

Qui voudra figurer, d'vn ouurage parfaict,
La beauté, la Vertu, l'Ornement, et les graces,
De Nature, des Dieux, de l'vniuers, des Graces,
A coure contempler la grand d'ELIZABETH.

regret, as with Mary Stuart. She loved dancing, and spring flowers, and pearls, and playing cards, and silk stockings. She was an excellent horsewoman and a very competent musician on the virginal. She had famous red hair, and was noted for the very white skin which she maintained with a great variety of cosmetics. She had a marvellous smile, and a cruel wit. She disliked married clergy. She loved the conversation and company of men, loved to have them compete for her approval. She was a 'blue-stocking', more than intelligent enough to follow the 'New Learning' and to dispute with the best brains in her kingdom. She probably did love Leicester, her 'Robin', and went to the brink of sexual intercourse with him, but only to the brink. The malicious said she had 'a membrane on her which made her incapable of man', though for her delight she tried many'. She vacillated and hesitated, drove her Ministers wild with impatience and exasperation. She screamed abuse at Mendoza, flung her slippers at Walsingham, and boxed the ears of William Killigrew, her Groom of the Chamber. She was a good judge of a minister, knew how to pick him, and how to get the last ounce of work and devotion out of him. She summed up Ralegh, and realized his brilliance and his versatility, but she never admitted him to her Privy Council and thus, ultimately, deprived him of the chance to play the role he later in life came to long for above all else, that of a statesman.

Someone must have sponsored Ralegh at Court, before he could ever have reached a position where he could lay his cloak before the Queen. The probability, and some contemporary evidence, is that it was Leicester. In his *Reliquiae Wottoniae* (1641) Sir Henry Wotton suggests, somewhat maliciously, that Leicester promoted Ralegh at Court to take some of the burden off himself, 'to bestow handsomely upon another some part of the pains, and perhaps of the envy, to which long indulgent fortune is obnoxious'. Naunton also mentions Leicester, wondering 'whether Leicester had then cast in a good word for him to the Queen, which would have done no harm'. It is not impossible that Burghley or Walsingham, who both recognized Ralegh's talents, put in a word for him. It has also been suggested that the Earl of Sussex introduced Ralegh as a counter-balance to Leicester.

Whoever was the sponsor amongst them, they must all have been taken aback by the speed with which the protégé advanced. Very soon there was nobody at Court unaware that a new star was rapidly rising. 'But true it is,' wrote Naunton. 'He had gotten the Queen's eare at a trice, and she began to be taken with his elocution, and loved to hear his reasons to her demands: and the truth is, she took him for a kind of Oracle, which netled them all.'

This new man Ralegh, this flashy provincial, patently out for what he could get, also had valuable experience of military matters. He was for a time one of the Queen's main advisers on Irish affairs. It was his knowledge of Ireland which had first brought him into the Queen's councils. The contemporary story was that he had got the better of Lord Grey in an argument on the conduct of Irish affairs before the Queen and the Privy Council. 'It drew them both over the Council table,' Naunton wrote, 'there to plead their cause, where (what advantage he had in the cause, I know not) but he had much better in the telling of his tale; and so much, that the Queen and the Lords took no slight mark of the man, and his parts.' Certainly the Queen took no slight mark of the man, but Lord Grey was not there. He did not return from Ireland until August 1582. A document, written jointly by Ralegh and Burghley, dated 25th October 1582 and entitled 'The Opinion of Mr Rawley upon motions made to him for the means of subduing the Rebellion in Monster', is probably the minutes of a policy meeting, which Lord Grey may well have attended. Possibly the meeting was held earlier in the year, in Lord Grey's absence. But in either case Ralegh had clearly gained the Queen's ear on Irish affairs long before Lord Grey's return. In April 1582 the Queen wrote out a curiously contradictory warrant appointing Ralegh to the command of a company of footmen of a Captain Appesley, lately deceased. 'Our pleasure is to have Our servant Walter Rawley trained some time longer in that Our realm [of Ireland] for his better experience in martial affairs.' However, the Queen continued, 'he is, for some considerations, by Us excused to stay here'. Ralegh was to depute a lieutenant to take his place. The Queen did not wish her favourite to leave her side. The appointment to 'Appesley's bande' was most probably a quick and convenient way of increasing Ralegh's income.

There is no evidence that Ralegh returned to Ireland in 1582. The last reference to his Irish service is in a minute of the Privy Council of 1st February 1582, authorizing the Lord Treasurer to pay £200 to Walter Rawley and Edward Denny 'upon the entertainment due to them in that realm'. On that day, Ralegh was on other business for the Queen. He was one of the hundred gentlemen, including Leicester and Sidney, who escorted the Duc d'Alençon, known as the Queen's 'Frog', back to the Continent when he had finally been turned down after wooing the Queen for six years.

By the beginning of 1583, Ralegh's standing at Court had improved so much that it was he who was able to intercede with the Queen on behalf of his half-brother Humphrey Gilbert. The years of Sir Humphrey's patent of exploration were running out – there were only two left. He still had not made another voyage and he was chronically short of money. In July 1582 he entered into an agreement with Sir George Peckham and Sir Thomas Gerard for the financing of a colony of English Catholics in North America. Ralegh took shares in the company and he also provided a ship of his own new design, the *Bark Ralegh*, of 200 tons, costing £2,000. But Ralegh's ship, commanded by his lieutenant in Ireland, Michael Butler, returned empty-handed early on, and the rest of the voyage was a disaster. Although Sir Humphrey Gilbert took possession of Newfoundland in the Queen's name – the first Englishman to do so for an English sovereign in North America – he himself was drowned on the way back.

In April 1583 the Queen had given Ralegh the manors of Stolney and Newland, formerly owned by All Souls College, Oxford. But these gifts were just the beginning of her favours. On 4th May she made Ralegh a rich man by granting him the 'Farm of Wines', the patent under which every vintner in the Kingdom had to pay Ralegh, during his lifetime, an annual retail licence fee of one pound. This monopoly brought in an income of about £1,000 a year. The Farm of Wines did Ralegh's reputation in the country no good. It was a very unpopular monopoly, 'a thing extracted of the subject upon a nice point of statute law', and it needed a very tender hand to administer it, avoiding 'noise and clamour'. He himself seems to have applied his patent moderately, but the annoyance of an already unpopular monopoly was probably aggravated by the behaviour of his agents. It could well be that the general dislike in which Ralegh was held was the result, not of any misdoings of his own, but of those of his servants.

As an Esquire, Ralegh travelled with the Court, from Richmond to Greenwich, or from Whitehall to Somerset House, or on a Royal Progress in the country, sharing accommodation with other courtiers. He appears not to have had any other London base but his dwelling in Islington until the beginning of 1584, or perhaps the year before, when the Queen leased to him the greater part of Durham House (Sir Edward and Lady Darcy occupied the rest of the property).

Durham House, or Duresme Place as it used to be called, belonged to the See of Durham but was transferred to the Crown by Bishop Tunstall at the end of Henry VIII's reign. Edward VI gave it to his sister the Princess Elizabeth for life, but Mary returned it to the Bishop of Durham, who once again lost it when Elizabeth came to the throne. The house was off the Strand, on the north bank of the Thames, at a point where the river turns almost through a right angle. About a quarter of a mile downstream were Russell House, the Savoy Palace and Somerset House. Just upstream was the Palace of Westminster. Across the river on the opposite bank were Lambeth marshes. It was a great rambling edifice, with Norman foundations and fourteenth-century towers rising sheer out of the water. The main entrance was surrounded by mean tenement buildings and led through gateways to an outer and an inner courtyard. There was a water-gate, with steps leading to the river, a main hall with marble pillars, and a chapel. On the east side there were gardens and orchards sloping down to the water's edge. John Aubrey evidently visited the place and was impressed.

Durham-house was a noble palace; after [Ralegh] came to his greatnes he lived

40

there, or in some apartment of it. I well remember his study, which was a little turret that looked into and over the Thames, and had the prospect which is pleasant perhaps as any in the world, and which not only refreshes the eie-sight but cheeres the spirits, and (to speake my mind) I beleeve enlarges an ingeniose man's thoughts.

Although he was only a tenant (and an insecure one at that, as James I very quickly proved when he came to the throne), Ralegh claimed that he spent some £2,000 of his own money in repairing and rebuilding Durham House over a period of about twenty years; it was his London headquarters from about 1584 until his downfall in 1603. He had stabling for twenty horses there, and kept an establishment of about forty people. He did not live in extravagant style. He gave dinner-parties, but there were no armies of servants, grand furniture, elaborate meals, or lavish and luxurious living. The gentlemen and friends of Ralegh's establishment also lived at Durham House when they were in London – men like the mathematician Thomas Hariot, Ralegh's lieutenant Michael Butler, his sea captains Laurence Keymis, Philip Amadas, Arthur Barlow, Charles Thynne and Jacob Whiddon, and his manuscript-copier John Pearson. Lady Ralegh called it 'a rotten house'.

In March 1584 the Queen further increased Ralegh's income by granting a licence to export undyed woollen broadcloths, subject to paying a rent to the Crown. Concessions to

Durham House, Ralegh's London home for twenty years. He spent £2,000 on it. His wife called it 'a rotten house'

Durham

Elizabeth's courtiers were often so hedged about with conditions and reservations that they proved to be far less profitable than expected, but the broadcloth licence was a lucrative one, and it was renewed for Ralegh in subsequent years. Lord Burghley considered Ralegh's profits excessive. In 1591 he calculated that Ralegh made £3,950 from his wool-cloth patent in his first year alone, of which he paid to the Crown a rent of only £700, and Burghley recommended that the rent be increased.

Ralegh spent money on the same scale as he earned it, especially upon clothes and jewels. Ralegh's clothing was no more extravagant than that of many other gallants of the Court, but the expense of clothing an Elizabethan courtier can be judged by the case brought against Mr Hugh Pugh, a Welsh gentleman, on 26th April 1584. He was charged with stealing at Westminster a jewel worth £80, a hatband of pearls worth £30, and five yards of damask silk worth £3, all 'the property of Walter Rawley'. This was at a time when a considerable household with servants could be kept up for the sum of £50 a year.

Ralegh's clothes attracted especial attention because of his position in the public eye. Surviving portraits show him as a figure of pale, elegant magnificence, in white satin pinked vest, close-sleeved to the wrist, brown doublets of velvet, finely flowered and embroidered with pearls, double pearl ear-drops, a fine white hat worn with a flourish and a feather secured with a ruby, trunk hose and white satin fringed garters, buff-coloured shoes tied with fine white ribbons. Often he holds the jewelled pommel of a dagger at his hip, and he has a cloak worked with an intricate design of pearls, and edged with brown fur. His armour is solid silver, inlaid with pearls, rubies and diamonds. He has the same jewels in the sword-belt across his chest. His favourite colours seem to be white and silver, and his favourite jewels were pearls (although his brother's servants told Aubrey that the pearls were actually not so big as they were painted).

Court life was an extravagant and elaborate game in which the main rule was that every courtier should profess himself hopelessly and endlessly in love with Gloriana, that radiant centre from which emanated all light, all warmth, all beauty – and all wealth. Elizabeth required her man to submit to her, not just as Queen, but as a woman. The Court conceit of love unattainable, love unapproachable, love eternally sought after and eternally unconsummated, suited Ralegh's position in regard to the Queen very appropriately. The lady was always supreme, so high above her adoring suitor that the gulf could never be bridged, except in the poet's imagination. The poet must worship his Queen and Empress in silence and from afar:

> Our Passions are most like to Floods and streames;
> The shallow Murmure; but the Deep are Dumb.
> So when Affectiones yeeld Discourse, it seems
> The bottom is but shallow whence they come.
> They that are Rich in Words must needs discover
> That they are Poore in that which makes a Lover.

Unlike Edmund Spenser, who was in a sense a professional poet who hoped to advance

Sir Philip Sidney, the flower of Elizabethan chivalry with all the advantages of rank and birth Ralegh lacked

himself in life through his poetry, Ralegh was an amateur. To write such poetry was part of the accomplishment of being a gentleman and courtier. He was careless of publication, and later actually discouraged it. In his circle, poems were read in manuscript by a few friends. They were slipped into a lady's pocket. It is not easy to decide which of the poems attributed to Ralegh, in their stylized genres – pastoral, question-and-answer poetry – are truly his. One example of pastoral traditionally attributed to Ralegh, 'The Shepheards description of Love', certainly gives the flavour:

> Melibeus. Sheepheard, what's Love, I pray thee tell?
> Faustus. It is that Fountaine, and that Well,
> Where pleasure and repentance dwell.
> It is perhaps that saucing bell,
> That toules all into heaven or hell,
> And this is Love as I heard tell.
>
> Meli. Yet what is Love, I pre-thee say?
> Fau. It is a worke on holy-day,
> It is December match'd with May,
> When lustie-bloods in fresh aray,
> Heare ten moneths after of the play,
> And this is Love, as I heare say.
>
> Meli. Yet what is Love, good Sheepheard saine?
> Fau. It is a Sun-shine mixt with raine,
> It is a tooth-ach, or like paine,
> It is a game where none dooth gaine,
> The Lasse saith no, and would full faine:
> And this is Love, as I heare saine.

We do know that it was Ralegh who complained:

> Fortune hath taken the away my love
> my lives soule and my soules heaven above
> fortune hath taken the away my princess
> my only light and my true fancies mistres.

And that it was the Queen, with her fondness for this game of poem and answer-poem, who replied:

> Ah silly pugge wert thou so sore afraid,
> mourne not (my Wat) nor be thou so dismaid,
> it passeth fickle fortunes powere and skill,
> to force my harte to thinke thee any ill.

Ralegh's most famous answer-poem was 'The Nimphs Reply to the Sheepheard', his reply to Marlowe's 'The passionate Sheepheard to his love'. To Marlowe's invitation, 'Come

Duc d'Alençon, the Queen's 'Frog'. Ralegh escorted him back to the Continent

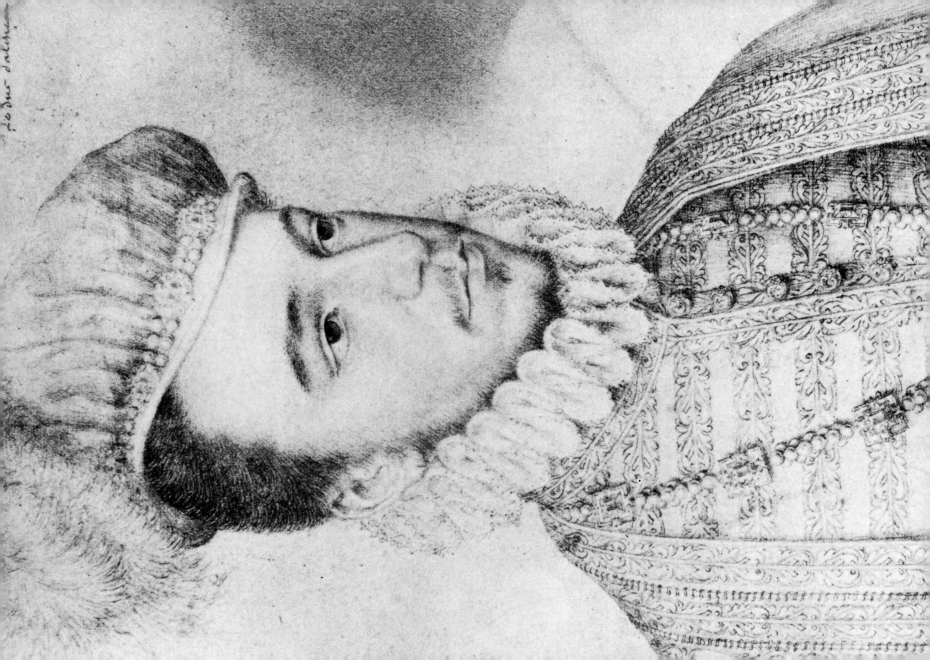

live with mee, and be my love', **Ralegh** begins with a question, '*If all the world and love were young*'. Marlowe's poem is a light-hearted celebration of love, a recital of love's delights. **Ralegh**'s poem, like much of his work, shows a depth of personal feeling uncommon in Elizabethan poetry. He takes a sadder, graver view of life. Love fades, flowers wither, winter comes, youth gives way to age:

If all the world and love were young,
And truth in every Sheepheards tongue,
These pretty pleasures might me move,
To live with thee, and be thy love.

Time drives the flocks from field to fold,
When **Rivers** rage, and **Rocks** grow cold,
And **Philomell** becommeth dombe,
The rest complaines of cares to come.

The flowers doe fade, & wanton fieldes,
To wayward winter reckoning yeeldes,

A honny tongue, a hart of gall,
Is fancies spring, but sorrowes fall.

Thy gownes, thy shooes, thy beds of **Roses**,
Thy cap, thy kirtle, and thy poesies,
Soone breake, soone wither, soone forgotten:
In follie ripe, in reason rotten.

Thy belt of straw and Ivie buddes,
Thy **Corall** claspes and Amber studdes,
All these in mee no meanes can move,
To come to thee, and be thy love.

But could youth last, and love still breede,
Had joyes no date, nor age no neede,
Then these delights my minde might move,
To live with thee, and by thy love.

In his critical opinion of **Ralegh**'s poetry, given in *The Arte of English Poesie*, George Puttenham very aptly describes **Ralegh**, as a poet and as a man: 'For dittie and amorous Ode I finde Sir Walter **Rawleyghs** vayne most loftie, insolent, and passionate.'

4. The New World

I N 1584 Ralegh appears to have decided that his name 'should henceforth always be spelled Ralegh, the signature his father used. Until then, he had sometimes used Ralegh but more often Rauley, and, on the deed renouncing the tithe of fish and larks in 1578, Rauleygh. He used Rauley twice, early in 1584, but from the date of a letter to the Vice-Chancellor and Senate of Cambridge of 9th July 1584 he wrote his name Ralegh on all surviving correspondence, and it was also the spelling used in his books. He does not seem ever to have used the common modern version Raleigh. He pronounced his name as 'rawly' and this pronunciation seems to have been generally used. The two syllables of his name, raw and lie, are punned and given double meanings in a contemporary couplet (Aubrey gives one version of it) 'The foe to the stommacke, and the word of disgrace Shewes the gentlemans name with the bold face.' (Traditionally, this was the answer of a gentleman called Noel to a couplet Ralegh composed on his name: 'The word of deniall, and the letter of fifty Makes the gentlemans name that will never be thrifty.' Noe L.)

Ralegh was the spelling the Queen used in the letters patent she signed for him on 25th March 1584. Sir Humphrey Gilbert's patent was due to expire in June. Ralegh was just about to assume Gilbert's mantle, and take on the task of exploring the West. His patent conferred on him new and even wider powers of discovery and possession, for a further six years – although, in the small print, the Queen reserved to the Crown 'the fift part of all the oare and silver' that might be found.

Ralegh gave English exploration and colonization in America a powerful stimulus which had far-reaching and long-lasting effects. Until then, the English had tended to look upon America as an obstacle, a great land mass which had somehow to be sailed around in order to reach the riches of the East. Ralegh concentrated English attention upon America itself and its possibilities. John Cabot and his men of Bristol had reached Newfoundland as early as 1497, but there had been no thought of establishing a colony. While Spain and Portugal had built empires, England had no colonies abroad except in Ireland and no settlements in America except the seasonal occupations by the Newfoundland fishermen. Ralegh was to change all that.

His own motives for undertaking his expeditions were complex. There was, of course, always the chance of finding treasure, gold, silver and precious stones, but any explorer who hoped to get rich in that way had before him the awful example of the 'gold-bearing' ore which Sir Martin Frobisher had brought home by the ton in 1577 and 1578; it proved useful for making roads. That débâcle made the Elizabethans sceptical of stories about gold and gold-mines for many years afterwards. There was Ralegh's own intellectual curiosity, his

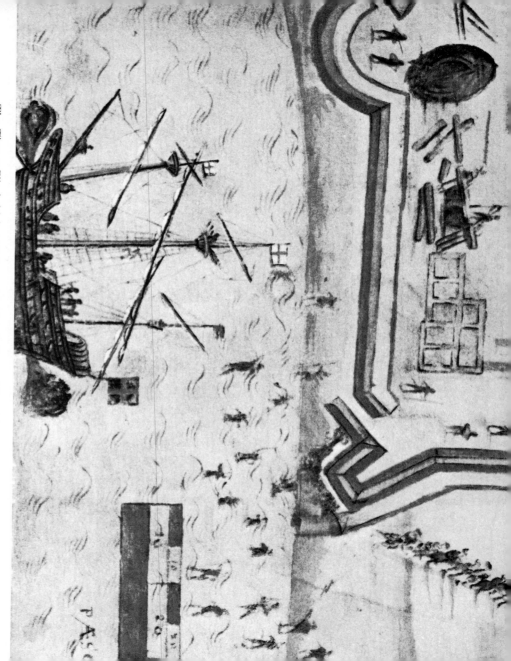

The *Tiger* or *Elizabeth* lying off-shore at anchor in Puerto Rico, May 1585. Drawing by John White

need to know what lay out there. As he said himself, 'There are stranger things to be seen in the world than are between London and Stanes.' He might even hope to discover a new Garden of Eden, where men lived in innocent harmony, like Adam and Eve before the Fall. There was also the prospect of riches by means of trade and agriculture. A colony might be a useful base from which to launch raids against the Spaniards. Exploration, colonization and aggression all played their parts in the formation of Ralegh's plans, but the main driving force was his personal ambition. He would be the courtier to lay before his Queen a new, rich and vast empire. He saw himself as viceroy in the Queen's name of this land beyond the sunset.

At the beginning of 1584 Ralegh had formed a 'College of the Fellowship for the Discovery of the North-west Passage' with Adrian Gilbert and the experienced seaman John Davis. But he seems soon to have dropped all ideas of trying for the north-west passage, in favour of new plans. These did not clash directly with Spanish interests. The Spaniards, after one

48

abortive attempt, had established settlements in Florida. But further north along the coast of America was virgin territory, so far unexplored and, in the words of the Queen's patent, 'not actually possessed of any Christian prince, nor inhabited by Christian people'. It was on these lands that Ralegh's hopes were fixed.

He must have anticipated his patent and had preparations for a preliminary voyage of reconnaissance already in hand, because by the middle of April two of his ships – which may have been the *Bark Ralegh*, saved from Gilbert's expedition, and the smaller *Dorothy* – had been fitted out in the Thames. They were commanded by Philip Amadas, a young man from Plymouth, in his early twenties, and Arthur Barlow, who emerges from his writings as a very capable seaman and much-travelled man. Both were members of Ralegh's household.

The ships were, as Arthur Barlow wrote, well furnished with men and victuals. They would also have had on board Thomas Hariot's navigational instruction manual *Articon* and the first of several sets of new navigation tables, drawn up from calculations and observations (some made from the roof of Durham House) in which Hariot made suns and stars, chart and compass, staff and astrolabe, all agree in what he himself called 'Three sea marriadges':

Three new Marriadges here are made
one of the staffe & sea astrolabe
card & compasse is another
one is sister thothers a brother.

Of the Sunne & starre is another
Which now agree like sister & brother.
And the carde & compasse which were at bate
will now agree like master & mate.

If you voyage well in this your iourney
They will be the Kinge of Spaynes Atomy
To bringe you to silver and Indian gold
which will kepe you in age from hunger and cold
God spare you well & send you fayre wether
And that agayne we may meet to gether.

The first expedition to the coast of America shows the range of Ralegh's interests and abilities. It was no ordinary man, and certainly a very unusual Court favourite, who could organize and equip an expedition of exploration, using a ship probably of his own design, providing captains from his domestic establishment, and charts, navigational tables and instruments whose design and manufacture he had sponsored.

The ships called at a West-Country port, probably Plymouth, for final letters of instruction from Ralegh before sailing on 27th April 1584. They reached the West Indies by way of the Canaries and took on food and fresh water at Puerto Rico before sailing northwards to the eastern coast of North America. They sailed along the coast for 'a hundred and twenty English miles' before they found an entrance, probably that now called Port Ferdinando. On 13th July a landing party went ashore on the island of Hatarask, one of a chain off the coast of what is now the state of North Carolina. Arthur Barlow's beautifully vivid account presents a picture of an idyllic country:

We viewed the land about us, being, whereas we first landed, very sandie and low towards the waters side, but so full of grapes, as the very beating and surge of the Sea overflowed them, of which we found such plentie, as well there as in all places else, both on the sand and on the greene soile on the hills, as in the plaines, as well on every little shrubbe, as also climing towardes the tops of high Cedars, that I thinke in all the world the like abundance is not to be found: and my selfe having seene those parts of Europe that most abound, find such difference as were incredible to be written.

Three days later they saw a small boat with three people in it. One of the men in it got out and walked up and down the beach opposite the ships. Barlow, Amadas, Simon Ferdinando the Pilot and some others rowed ashore to meet him. Although neither side could understand a word the other said, they brought the man back on board, gave him a shirt and a hat, a taste of wine and meat, which 'he liked very well'. The next day the 'King's brother' arrived, with forty or fifty men, 'very handsome and goodly people, and in their behaviour as mannerly and civill as any of Europe'.

They stayed six weeks in America, arriving back in the West Country about the middle of September. The expedition brought back for Ralegh chamois and other skins, a necklace of pearls 'the bignes of good pease', and two Indians, both lusty fellows, called Manteo and Wanchese. The Indians were put on show in London. Leopold von Wedel, a Pomeranian visitor to England, wrote in his journal that a certain Master or Captain Rall (Ralegh) permitted him to see the Indians. They were like white Moors, and they usually wore a mantle of rudely tanned skins of wild animals, no shirts, and a pelt before their privy parts. However, they were dressed in brown taffeta when von Wedel saw them and he thought they 'made a most childish and silly figure'.

The Indians were very good publicity for the voyage, which Ralegh badly needed. He and his friends exerted themselves to promote the idea of colonizing the West, and to encourage Court and City and, most important of all, the Queen herself, to subscribe money for the venture. In July 1584 Richard Hakluyt, who was to be tireless in his propaganda for Ralegh's voyages, came back from Paris, where he was still chaplain to the English embassy. After discussions with Ralegh, Hakluyt wrote his treatise for the Queen on the prospects for English colonization, known as the *Discourse of Western Planting*. It was ready in October.

Meanwhile, Ralegh had been elected to Parliament as junior knight of the shire for Devonshire (Sir William Courtenay was the senior knight). It was the start of a long and distinguished parliamentary career. Ralegh sat in every Elizabethan parliament thereafter, except that of 1588, until the Queen's death in 1603. The general elections had been the first for more than twelve years, and there were many other new members in the House, including Francis Bacon, Robert Cecil and Sir Francis Drake.

The new Parliament assembled on 23rd November 1584, with the country in a state of

The arrival of the English in Virginia. A map of the coast of North Carolina showing Roanoke Island. Engraving from Theodore de Bry's *America*, Part I, 1590, of Thomas Hariot's *Brief and True Report of the New Found Land of Virginia*, 1588.

near-emergency, involving the Queen's personal safety. Any would-be murderer of Elizabeth had the blessing of the Pope, who had given his assurance that any English gentleman willing to undertake 'so glorious a task' would not be committing any sin. The new Parliament's first task was therefore to pass legislation to safeguard the Queen's person. The House adopted the Privy Council's Bond of Association which, in its final form, was a measure against Mary Queen of Scots who had been implicated in the Throckmorton Plot.

Ralegh had a private Bill of his own, to confirm his letters patent for the exploration of territories abroad. The Bill was passed to the Lords, with the provisos that Ralegh was not to press ships into his service, nor transport debtors or criminals to his colony, but in the Lords, it was quietly dropped. It seems that the Queen looked upon the additional provisos as impertinent infringements of her own Royal Prerogative. The Queen's letters patent were enough in themselves, and Ralegh needed no other authority. The Bill may have been intended to give a seal of government approval on Ralegh's plans. Like the Indians, it was excellent publicity.

It had been a most successful year for Ralegh. As Aubrey says, 'He was acquainted and accepted with all the heroes of our nation in his time.' He was on the way to becoming a rich man. He was a Member of Parliament; he had a house in town and a considerable household, clothes, and jewels. He was known as a patron who had the Queen's ear; artists, writers, poets, soldiers and inventors clamoured to see him, and waited for hours hoping to catch his eye. Those who watched him going about the Court day by day knew that he was probably planning something fresh and strange. His expedition to the Americas was the talk of the town. He had friends, interests, preoccupations, responsibilities, rewards. He had, above all, the Queen's regard. Thomas Morgan, Mary Queen of Scots' agent, was writing to his mistress about this time that 'Master Rawley is the Queen's dear minion, who daylye groweth in creditt.' Von Wedel the watchful Pomeranian saw the Queen dining at Greenwich in December 1584. He noticed that the Queen beckoned to young and old to come and talk to her. Everybody knelt to her, and she chatted with them in a friendly way. He noticed one courtier in particular: 'She said to a captain named Raleigh, pointing with her finger at his face, that there was a smut on it, and was going to wipe it off with her handkerchief; but before she could he wiped it off himself. She was said to love this gentleman now beyond all others; and this may be true, because two years ago he could scarcely keep one servant, and now with her bounty he can keep five hundred.'

On the Twelfth Day of that Christmas, 6th January 1585, Ralegh was knighted by the Queen. His seal of that time, dated 1584 (therefore struck between 6th January and the beginning of the Old Style new year on 25th March 1585), shows his coat of arms surmounted by a roebuck and the motto *Amore et Virtute*. The inscription reads *Propria Insstinia* [Insignia] *Walteri Ralegh Militis Domini & Gubernatoris Virginiae*, the arms of Walter Ralegh, knight, Lord and Governor of Virginia: the name the Queen herself had given to the new-found country.

Barlow's account of the first voyage was undoubtedly slanted to give a favourable impression, and in his efforts during the winter of 1584–5 to whip up financial support for a second voyage, Ralegh had the help of both Hakluyts. But neither Ralegh nor the Hakluyts were able to persuade the Queen to venture public money in the project (although Richard Hakluyt 'half persuaded' Sir Philip Sidney, who called him a 'very good trumpet'). Most of the finance for the voyage was raised by Ralegh himself, but Walsingham and others ventured some of their own money. The Queen may have contributed some money, and she certainly supported the expedition with payments in kind which amounted to an indirect subsidy. At Ralegh's request, she released Ralph Lane, the expert on fortifications, from his service in Ireland on very favourable terms for pay and allowances. She allowed Ralegh to draw more than £400 worth of gunpowder from the Tower, and to take up ships and seamen in Bristol and in the counties of Devon and Cornwall. She provided one of her own ships, the *Tyger*, though whether she rented, loaned or chartered the ship to Ralegh is not clear.

Ralegh probably saw himself as the *entrepreneur* and 'fixer' of the expedition, but, in any case, the Queen would not allow members of her intimate private circle to hazard themselves in such voyages. The expedition was to be commanded by Ralegh's cousin, Sir Richard

Sir Walter Ralegh's seal as Lord and Governor of Virginia, issued before 25 March 1585. 'Amore et virtute' was Ralegh's personal motto

Grenville. He was some ten years older than Ralegh, one of an old Devon family of land-owners and gentry, a Justice of the Peace, and a Member of Parliament. He had studied for a time at the Inner Temple and served as a soldier in Hungary and in Ireland. He had a background of violence; there was a mysterious episode in his youth when, at the age of twenty, he killed a Robert Bannister in a London street brawl. He was later pardoned by the Queen. Although Grenville had been associated with the Great South Seas Project with Sir Francis Drake and, as he was a West-Countryman, the sea and ships had always been part of his life, this would, in fact, very surprisingly, be his first voyage. According to Holinshed,

Grenville was 'a gentleman of very good estimation both for his parentage and sundry good virtues, who for the love he bare unto sir Walter Raleigh, together with a disposition that he had to attempt honourable actions worthy of honour, was willing to hazard himself in this voyage'.

The *Tyger*, and possibly some of the other ships, were fitted out in the Thames and sailed around to Plymouth where the rest of the expedition was being prepared. The voyage began on 9th April 1585, as Holinshed says, 'even in April, at the pleasant prime'. Sir Richard Grenville, admiral and general, was in the Queen's galleass *Tyger*, of about 160 tons. With him were the master and chief pilot of the fleet, Simon Fernandez; Ralph Lane, Grenville's lieutenant, and governor-designate of the new colony; the treasurer, Francis Brooke; and the vice-admiral, and admiral of Virginia designate, Philip Amadas. The other ships were Ralegh's own *Roebuck*, a 'flieboat' of 140 tons, commanded by John Clarke; the *Lion*, or *Red Lion*, of Chichester, 100 tons, commanded and possibly owned by George Raymond; the *Elizabeth*, 50 tons, commanded and probably owned by the expedition's high marshal Thomas Cavendish; Ralegh's 'small barke' *Dorothy*, 50 tons, probably commanded by Arthur Barlow; and two pinnaces, used as tenders for 'speedy services' and carried on board, one in the *Tyger* and the other most probably in the *Red Lion*. Other gentlemen of the expedition were Thomas Hariot, in charge of relations with the local natives, John White to make drawings and maps, and others whom Holinshed describes as 'diverse others, whereof some were captains and the others some assistants for counsel'. The total number of men on the expedition was about 600, of whom nearly 300 were seamen. The remainder were soldiers, factors, treasurers, brickmakers, apothecaries, carpenters and other tradesmen for the establishment of the new colony.

It was not a large expedition, but it was the largest Ralegh could organize and finance, and it must have taken up a major part of his capital. He was arranging for replenishment ships to follow later. Meanwhile, in that summer of 1585, relations with Spain deteriorated to the point of overt warfare. In May Philip II ordered all English ships in Spanish ports to be seized. Their cargoes were impounded, their crews imprisoned, their cannons sent to Cadiz. Sir Francis Drake was gathering a fleet to attack Spanish possessions but, largely because of the Queen's hesitations, he was delayed until September. In June, Ralegh was preparing reinforcements for Grenville and Lane when the news of the Spanish embargo arrived. He was instructed to send ships to Newfoundland to warn the English fishermen not to take their catches near a Spanish port, and to seize whatever Spaniards he could. At the end of the month the *Golden Royal*, of 110 tons, commanded by Bernard Drake, acting under Ralegh's orders, met George Raymond in the *Lion* from Grenville's expedition (possibly the *Dorothy*, too) off Newfoundland and together they captured seventeen Spanish fishing vessels. Ralegh's ships also took other prizes, including four Brazilmen and a French ship out from Guinea. Ralegh and his backers profited from this sortie (for which it is quite possible that Bernard Drake and Raymond had made prior arrangements to meet). One of the objects of the colony was, after all, to prey upon Spanish lines of communication.
While his ships were away, Ralegh continued to rise in the Queen's favour. He was a

persistent petitioner, for himself and for his friends and clients. 'When, Sir Walter,' the Queen asked, 'will you cease to be a beggar?' 'When your gracious Majesty ceases to be a benefactor,' he replied. That time was not yet. In promoting Ralegh, the Queen was not just gratifying one of her favourites. She was backing her own judgment of men, and giving new talent a chance to prove itself. She recognized that Ralegh had genuine administrative ability. He had a flair for bold, original thought. He could lead men, and he was very popular down in his own native West Country (except, possibly, in the city of Exeter). In July he succeeded the Earl of Bedford as Lord Warden of the Stannaries, with jurisdiction over the west of England tin-mining industry; in September he became Lord Lieutenant of Cornwall; and, in November, Vice-Admiral of Devon and Cornwall. By the end of the year, he was the most powerful man in the west, with high naval and military command of the most exposed and vulnerable part of the realm, at a time of growing national danger.

On 6th October the *Tyger* reached Falmouth, back from Virginia, but without Grenville, who arrived at Plymouth on the 18th, on board the prize ship *Santa Maria*. Grenville had fairly encouraging news of the progress of the new colony.

On leaving England in April, his squadron had been scattered by a storm in the Bay of Biscay. *Tyger* had made a moderately quick crossing. On 11th May the expedition arrived at a bay on the island of Puerto Rico, where the men rested, watered the ships and built a fort, because the Spaniards had a garrison on the island. Cavendish in the *Elizabeth* rejoined on the 19th, having been separated since the storm in Biscay.

For a few days, Grenville lurked in the Mona Passage, between Puerto Rico and Hispaniola, where he seized two Spanish frigates, one small and empty and abandoned by her crew at Grenville's approach, the other larger and loaded with cloth, and manned by Spaniards who were afterwards ransomed for 'good round summes'. Ralph Lane was sent in the smaller frigate to get salt from the mainland of Puerto Rico, where he seems to have thought himself unnecessarily in danger of Spanish attack. When he came back he had one of his several bitter quarrels with Grenville.

After a leisurely voyage north *Tyger* made a landfall on the mainland of Florida on 20 June and four days later reached a harbour, probably Beaufort, North Carolina.

On 21st July the fleet moved northwards to search for a better harbour and anchored on the 27th at Hatteras, or Port Ferdinando as they called it. On the 29th they were visited by Granganimeo, Amadas's friend of the year before. Other ships followed, when their cargoes had been discharged, until 8th or 9th September. Grenville sailed in the *Tyger* in late August, leaving Ralph Lane with 107 men to start the new colony.

Off Bermuda, Grenville overhauled a straggler from the Spanish treasure fleet, boarding her from a home-made boat made of 'boards of chests'. The crew surrendered, which was fortunate for Grenville, because his boat sank the moment he stepped out of it. The prize was the flagship of the Santo Domingo squadron, the 300-ton *Santa Maria* of San Vicente, loaded with sugar, ginger, hides, ivory tusks, gold, silver and pearls worth 120,000 ducats. Grenville and a prize crew of twenty men sailed her to England. They lost contact with the *Tyger* in a gale on 10th September, but reached Plymouth safely on 18th October.

Ralegh was in Plymouth to meet Grenville. At once, there was wrangling over the sharing out of the spoils from the prize. The sailors of the prize crew absconded with whatever they could take away. Grenville wrote to Walsingham to tell him that reports of the gold and silver and jewels on board were greatly exaggerated, but that everybody who had ventured his money would get it back, with some profit. Ralegh is said to have grudged the Queen the cabinet full of pearls she took for her share, but with the value of the prize cargo, of the ship herself, the two prizes taken in the West Indies, and what remained of their cargo, the goods traded in the West Indies and the novel specimens brought from Virginia, Ralegh must have covered the expenses of the voyage and most probably made a profit.

The expedition's principal backers, Ralegh and Walsingham, had now to consider the position. They had the prize ships, and their contents. Their credit in the City and at Court must have improved; even those who had been sceptical about a new colony would have been convinced by a tangible, visible treasure ship at Plymouth. They would have had a full, even though self-exonerating, account of the voyage from Grenville, who seems to have convinced himself, if not everybody else, that he had conducted affairs impeccably at all times. Clearly, Lane would need reinforcement. More ships, more men, more stores must be arranged for and sent out as soon as possible. Meanwhile, much would depend upon Ralph Lane himself.

Ralph Lane had been a soldier for more than twenty years. He had had command in Ireland where, like Ralegh, he had tended to argue with his superiors. He was a hard-working, conscientious man, a good organizer and a strict disciplinarian. He knew how to run a military establishment, paying attention to such details as routine, defence, health, and morale. If he had a fault it was that he lacked vision. Presented with a problem, he tended to seek the immediate, short-term, military solution. Although Lane was an able man Ralegh might have done better to have chosen as leader someone with a little of his own poet's imagination. New Virginia needed a man who could look beyond the palisade and the nearest river.

Lane's letters ranged from the ecstatic, when he is describing the new lands and their properties, to the bitterly accusing, when writing of Grenville's behaviour. The enmity between the two men became so great that the party split into two factions. Grenville's departure eased the situation, but Lane was always plagued by personality problems. Some of the expedition lost interest when they saw there was to be no quick reward of gold and silver. They longed to get home, and when they did, lost no chance of maligning the new settlement and its principal officers.

The main personalities of the party, after Lane, were Philip Amadas, the Admiral; Captain Edward Stafford, who proved to be Lane's right-hand man; and Thomas Hariot, the expert on Indian affairs. Hariot's 'mathematical instruments, sea compasses and perspective glasses' vastly impressed the Indians. The interest was reciprocated. Hariot studied the Indians closely, tried to convert them to Christianity, and generally acted as a tactful and sympathetic link between the colony and the Indian community. He also collected and examined the animals, plants and minerals of the new country.

Indian village of Pomeiooc, located between the present Lake Landing and Wyesocking Bay. Drawing by John White 1585, engraved by Theodore de Bry.

The clearest impression of the new settlement was given in the paintings of the artist and map-maker, John White. He made vivid and detailed drawings of what he saw in the Indian villages, of the Indians and their personalities, customs and way of life.

Lane's first act was to build a fort on Roanoke Island. It was tiny, enclosing only some seventy square feet, and shaped like a four-pointed star. Inside it was a two-storeyed store-house, guard-room and magazine. Outside the fort was a 'town' of houses for the settlers, near the Indian village on the northern tip of the island. Lane sent exploring parties north-wards towards the area of Chesapeake Bay, and southwards up the Pamlico River. He himself led two explorations, up the Chowan and Roanoke Rivers, in the spring of 1586. By that time relations with the Indians were growing strained. Granganimeo had died and his brother Wingina was increasingly hostile towards Lane's party – not without reason, for on occasions Lane had behaved with extreme harshness towards the Indians. With the possible exception of White and Hariot, Lane's party seemed to have regarded themselves as military occupiers rather than as settlers. After the twenty days' food, which was all that had survived from *Tyger*, had been eaten, the party was wholly dependent upon Indian goodwill. They planted no corn until the following spring. They never could capture the Indian trick of fishing in the rivers. They did a little hunting and collecting, but almost all their food was traded from the Indians. Lane's first euphoria towards Virginia and its prospect for settle-ment faded away. At last, Wingina attempted to ambush Lane's sortie up the Roanoke River. Lane was too cunning and too experienced a campaigner to be caught. Wingina himself was wounded in a skirmish, feigned death, and was killed by Edward Nugent, one of Lane's soldiers from Ireland, while trying to escape. By June 1586 Lane's party were isolated in a mainly hostile countryside. Their corn was not yet ripe. Many of them were looking longingly towards home.

Ralegh had begun to equip a relief ship for Lane as early as November 1585, but for some reason, possibly financial, she was delayed and did not sail until after Easter 1586. Grenville had also prepared reinforcements, an expedition of several ships and some hundreds of men, but one of his ships ran aground on the bar at Bideford when they sailed on 16th April and he, too, was delayed.

Thus the first arrival off Virginia in the summer of 1586 was Sir Francis Drake, with some of his fleet, fresh from their triumphs against the Spaniards at San Domingo, Cartagena and the Florida colony at Saint Augustine. The destruction of the Florida colony and the rendez-vous off Roanoke were most probably arranged beforehand by Ralegh and Drake. Drake anchored off Port Ferdinando on 11th June. He offered Lane the 70-ton ship *Francis* and her crew, and food and stores for 100 men for four months. Lane gratefully accepted, but while he was transferring his stores on board a storm blew up and raged for three days. When the weather cleared, *Francis* could just be seen, hull down, heading for England. Clearly her crew had chosen to return home with some of the spoils of Virginia rather than be pressed to serve in the colony under Lane.

Drake offered another ship, the much larger 170-ton *Bark Bonner*. Again, Lane accepted. But by this time his men had had enough. Their nerves were stretched. Their confidence was gone. The sight of *Francis* going for home, and the thought of the Indians at their backs, were too much for what remained of their morale. There was a breakdown in leadership and at the end Lane's men embarked in a state of near-panic, struggling to get into the boats, dropping or throwing maps, books, papers, botanical specimens, even pearls, into the water in their frantic haste to get away. Three men on an expedition up-country were simply abandoned to the Indians. Drake's fleet sailed on 18th or 19th June and the ex-colonists were landed at Portsmouth on 27th July 1586.

It was a pity that Lane was not more persevering, for help was only a few weeks away. Ralegh's relief-ship arrived after Lane had left, spent some time looking for the colony, and then sailed for England with all its stores and provisions still on board. About a fortnight later, possibly at the end of July when Lane was disembarking at Portsmouth, Grenville's ships arrived. He had enough men and stores with him to plant another colony. He chose not to do so. But he wished to keep England's stake in the new territory, and so he compromised by leaving a small and fatally weak party of fifteen men. They were never seen again.

The sight of Lane, back in England with little to show for his efforts, must have been a great disappointment to Ralegh. Most of Lane's men had been hired. They had never looked upon themselves as true colonists of a new land. They had worked for wages. Now they had been paid off, they could disperse, to spread their dissatisfaction with Virginia all over London and the south and west of England. It took a man with Ralegh's resilience of spirit to recover from such a depressing setback, but this he did at once, with plans for a third voyage.

The truth was that Lane's colony had not been a failure. He and his men had demonstrated that Europeans could live, albeit somewhat precariously, in the new land for almost a year. Certainly, there had been clashes of personalities, poor planning, mistaken attitudes towards the native Indians, and a fatal lack of resolute leadership in the end, but these were all lessons of experience and could be corrected. Ralegh had shown that there were possibilities in the West. Mental horizons in England had been enlarged by that much.

5. Fortune

IN APRIL 1585 Ralegh was at odds with Sir Christopher Hatton. The Court was at the Archbishop of Canterbury's palace at Croydon, and Ralegh had been given the room which Hatton thought should have been his (evidently Ralegh no longer had to share a room). Hatton, in complaint, sent the Queen through Sir Thomas Heneage a jewel fashioned like 'a true lover's knot'. The Queen's response, again relayed by Heneage, was quite astonishingly vehement and hostile to Ralegh. 'She had rather,' she said, 'see him hanged than equal him to you, or that the world should think him so.'

That reply would have been balm to Hatton's wounded feelings, but it was probably only one move in the elaborately coquettish game Elizabeth played with her favourites, never allowing one to remain too long or too consistently in her favours, never allowing one to be quite certain of his permanent standing, playing one off against another, repeating malicious gossip to one about another. She was the one sought-after woman in a circle of the most ambitious, quick-witted and quick-tempered men of her time, and she loved to make them jealous of each other. Ralegh himself went through several cycles of the Queen's apparent pleasure and displeasure with him, as she blew hot and cold. It was no wonder that his favourite poetic image for her was Diana, or Cynthia, the moon, cold and shining, splendid in the night sky, but waxing and waning by the month. Ralegh was never one of those who, like Hatton, gave the Queen expensive presents at New Year. There was always a part of him which remained aloof from the Court's frivolities. He had a strain of shrewd country sense under the courtier's role, which saw through the Court's vanities. One of his first poems was called 'A Farewell to false Love'. The earliest version was published in 1588 by William Byrd in his *Psalmes, Sonets and Songs*. It is an imaginatively worded invective against insincerity:

> Farewell false love, the oracle of lies,
> A mortal foe and enimie to rest:
> An envious boye, from whome all cares arise,
> A bastard vile, a beast with rage possest:
> A way of error, a temple ful of treason,
> In all effects, contrarie unto reason.

Ralegh may have had inklings that all his Court success would be only 'a substance like the shadow of the Sunne'. But in the meantime he lived in the broad sunshine, and was the observed of all observers. Aubrey was only half right when he said that Ralegh was 'the first that brought tobacco into England, and into fashion'. Drake and Hawkins both brought

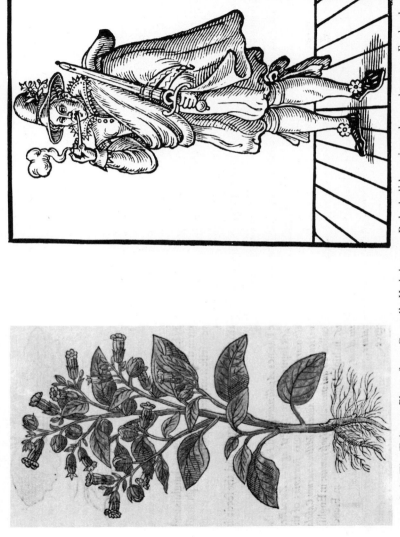

Left: The Tobacco Plant, from Gerard's *Herbal*, 1597. Ralegh did not introduce tobacco to England, but he certainly made smoking socially acceptable

Right: Title page of *The Roaring Girle or Moll Cut-Purse* by T. Middleton and T. Dekker, 1611 – by this time smoking was a common habit

tobacco to England before Ralegh's expeditions, but Ralegh certainly made smoking fashionable. He smoked at Court and even induced the Queen to try a puff although, according to Aubrey, he 'standing in a stand at Sir Robert Poyntz' parke at Acton, tooke a pipe of tobacco, which made the ladies quitt it till he had donne'. There were many stories of Ralegh and his smoking: that he was slowly poisoning the Queen by it, that his old man-servant in Ireland thought he was on fire and poured a jug of spiced ale over him to put out the flames; and that he once bet the Queen that he could weigh tobacco smoke; the Queen ridiculed the idea and struck the bet, whereupon Ralegh weighed his tobacco, smoked it, and then weighed the ash. The difference, he said, was the weight of the smoke. The Queen is supposed to have replied that she had heard of men who had turned gold into smoke but Ralegh was the first to have turned smoke into gold. The country followed the Court in the habit. In Aubrey's grandfather's time 'one pipe was handed from man to man round about the table. They had first silver pipes; the ordinary sort made use of a walnutshell and a straw.' In the space of one decade, pipe-smoking in public became a great fashion.

There was, of course, another side to Ralegh's public life. Those who saw him at Court might not have recognized the same man seated, for example, on a block of stone on a desolate hillside, giving judgment on matters of dispute in the tin-mining industry. As Lord Warden of the Stannaries he controlled the production of Cornish tin, which was an important strategic metal, used all over Europe. The Stannaries covered most of Cornwall and a part of Devon. For administrative purposes, they were almost kingdoms within the Kingdom, with their own courts and parliaments, and their own military musters and commanders. The Stannary Parliaments, one for Devon and one for Cornwall, met at infrequent intervals of about seven or eight years. The Devon parliament meeting-place was a circle of stones high on the side of Crockern Tor on Dartmoor.

The tin-miners were a rough, tough, poor community who worked in the damp, dangerous mines for an average yearly wage of about £3. They were a law unto themselves, with their own customs and idiosyncrasies. Their disputes were mainly on matters of boundaries and the courses of streams for washing the metal; of smuggled tin and impure tin. Every bar of tin was assayed and stamped by Ralegh's officers, and a fee paid to the Crown before it was exported abroad. Ralegh took his duties seriously. He appointed his elder brother Carew as Vice-Warden, to deal with routine matters in his own absence. He drew up regulations and standards for the mines, which lasted long after his lifetime. He stoutly defended the miners' interests against pressure from the Crown and other authorities. He made it clear that decisions on the miners' welfare and responsibilities were his, as Lord Warden, and his alone. For example, on 15th February 1592 he was writing from Durham House to his 'very loving friends the Justices of the Peace of the County of Devon', who had rashly suggested that the miners should contribute towards the cost of repairing a bridge at Okehampton. Ralegh disagreed and said that if the Justices persisted he would take the case to the Privy Council. Only then, if their Lordships judged that the miners should pay, would Ralegh cause the miners to yield. And even then, Ralegh added a pointed postscript: 'I will myself give order that the tinners shall contribute unto the bridge if upon examination I find cause to urge thereunto, *but not by any foreign authority*.'

It was the miners of the Stannaries who were in part responsible for a coolness between Ralegh and his old patron, Leicester. Leicester had already found out that Ralegh at Court, in Sir Henry Wotton's words, was 'an apprentice as knew well enough how to set up for himself.' The apprentice had now far outstripped his master. And yet, Ralegh's dealings with and manner towards Leicester in 1586 show that Ralegh's place at Court was secure but still, in a curious way, unexpectedly insecure. Ralegh could rely on the Queen. Yet he must still try to remain on good terms with the older generation of courtiers.

The Queen and Leicester had patched up their quarrel of 1582 and when, in 1585, the Queen decided to support the Low Countries (with the barest minimum of force) she appointed Leicester to command the English force. Since the murder of William of Orange, the Queen's policy towards the Low Countries had been decidedly ambiguous. She was supporting them in their struggle against Spain. At the same time, she herself was negotiating with Spain. Therefore she wished her aid to the Low Countries to remain unobtrusive and unofficial. She was allowed to garrison Flushing and other ports with English troops, but she of course did not intend her troops actually to fight the Spaniards, because she was still

Ralegh's seals: left, Warden of the Stannaries, Captain of the Queen's Guard, Governor of Jersey 1585. Centre, Governor of Colony of Virginia 1584 and, right, his private seal

delicately negotiating. Leicester, however, was a poor politician and an incompetent soldier. Insensitive to the currents flowing beneath the Queen's decisions, he wanted to bring the Spaniards to action, and he demanded reinforcements. In particular he asked for Cornish miners from Ralegh's Stannaries, to construct fortifications for his army and to dig under those of the enemy. There were, intentionally or not, delays, and the miners were not forthcoming. In the meantime, Leicester openly compromised the Queen's position by allowing himself to be sworn in as Governor-General of the Netherlands States in flat disobedience to the Queen's expressed wishes. The Queen was furious and demanded that Leicester eat his oath in public, or she would reduce him to 'the nothing' he came from.

People told Leicester that Ralegh was behind all his misfortunes. It was Ralegh who was fanning the Queen's wrath against him. It was Ralegh who was preventing not only the Cornish miners but also reinforcements of any sort from reaching him. It was Ralegh who spared no opportunity to denigrate him and belittle his military prowess. This was grossly unfair to Ralegh, who never withheld credit, even to Spaniards, where it was properly due. In fact, the poet Thomas Churchyard wrote in the introduction to his *Churchyard's Challenge*, published in 1593, how Ralegh organized a grand Shrovetide pageant in the Tiltyard, in which the gentlemen of the Guard and Ralegh himself re-enacted the Earl's achievements in Flanders.

Ralegh wrote to Leicester from the Court in March 1586. It was Ralegh at his most carefully conciliatory. 'My very good Lorde, You wrate unto me in your laste letters for pioners to be sent over; wher uppon I moved her Majestye, and found her very willing, in so mich as order was geven for a cummission; but since, the matter is stayd. I know not for what cause.' So, clearly, the delay is not Ralegh's fault. After giving good news of an appointment of one of Leicester's men, 'one Jukes', Ralegh approached the subject of his own feelings towards Leicester and his campaign. 'In ought else your Lordshipe shall find me most assured to my pouere to performe all offices of love, honor, and service towards you. But I have byn of late very pestilent reported in this place to be rather a drawer bake, then a fartherer of the action wher you govern.' Ralegh reaffirmed his hatred of the 'tirannus prosperey' of Spain, asked Leicester to deal directly with him 'in all matters of suspect dublenes' and to 'lett no poeticall scribe work your Lordshipe by any device to doubt that I am a hollo or a could sarvant to the action', and ended with a most encouraging postscript, 'The Queen is on very good terms with you, and, thank be to God, well pacified; and you are agayne her "Sweet Robyn".'

Ralegh asked if he could carry the Queen's dispatches to Leicester himself and make his point in person. The Queen refused. Instead, she made Walsingham write an appendix to the official dispatches, scotching rumours that Ralegh had been working against Leicester at Court and assuring Leicester, 'upon Her honour, that the gentleman hath done good offices for you; and that, in the time of Her displeasure, he dealt as earnestly for you as any other in this world that professeth the most goodwill for your Lordship. *This I write*,' Walsingham added, significantly, '*by Her Majesty's command.*'

The most memorable military exploit of Leicester's command was the siege of a small Dutch town called Zutphen in September 1586, during which Sir Philip Sidney, Governor of Flushing and the choicest flower of Elizabethan chivalry, received fatal wounds. There seem to have been two views about the cause of Sidney's death. Traditionally, he gave his last drop of desperately needed water to a wounded common soldier, whose need he considered was greater than his own and was himself wounded because he had lent his thigh-armour to another officer; on the other hand, he survived for nearly a month after being wounded, and (in a typically ribald story in Aubrey) he greatly increased the damage from his wounds by carnal knowledge of his very pretty young wife, Frances Walsingham. His body was embalmed and brought back to England for a public funeral in St Paul's Cathedral on 19th February 1587.

Ralegh attended the funeral and his elegy, written in Sidney's memory, first appeared in an anthology of poetry called *The Phoenix Nest* in 1593, although Sir John Harington mentioned it in the notes to his translation of *Orlando Furioso* in 1591. The verses are dutifully respectful. Sidney was, after all, a rival luminary of the Court and much better born than Ralegh. He had, by birth, advantages and rank which Ralegh had to struggle and scheme for. Nevertheless, the last four verses of Ralegh's elegy strike an authentic elegiac note which was to be recaptured in English war poetry centuries later:

England doth hold thy lims that bred the same,
Flaunders thy valure where it last was tried,
The Campe thy sorow where thy bodie died,
Thy friends, thy want; the world, thy vertues fame.

In 1569, Ralegh went up to Oriel College, Oxford, where he became 'the ornament of the juniors'. Detail from panel of life of Sir Henry Unton, artist unknown

Sir Walter Ralegh, looking unexpectedly baby-faced, but he was the Queen's 'dear minion' from the moment he came to Court

Nations thy wit, our mindes lay up thy love,
Letters thy learning, thy losse, yeeres long to come,
In worthy harts sorow hath made thy tombe,
Thy soule and spright enrich the heavens above.

Thy liberall hart imbalmd in gratefull teares.
Yoong sighes, sweete sighes, sage sighes, bewaile thy fall,
Envie hir sting, and spite hath left hir gall,
Malice hir selfe, a mourning garment weares.

That day their Haniball died, our Scipio fell,
Scipio, Cicero, and Petrarch of our time,
Whose vertues wounded by my woorthles rime,
Let Angels speake, and heavens thy praises tell.

('Their Haniball' is a reference to Count Hannibal Gonzago, who also died of wounds at Zutphen.)

The Queen had taken Ralegh's part and justified his conduct to Leicester, but that did not mean that the new favourite had entirely ousted the old. On the contrary, when Leicester returned from the Netherlands, he took up his old place as 'Sweet Robyn' and rumour had it that it was Ralegh who hurriedly left Court, with a sense of guilt, the day before Leicester returned.

Evidently the Queen had felt that she ought to intercede on Ralegh's behalf and, to a certain extent, defend him against those who were ready to slander him. Ralegh had plenty of detractors. He was heartily disliked on all sides because of his reputation for being proud. Yet there is no evidence of Ralegh's pride. There is no incident recorded of his behaving unduly arrogantly towards anyone; indeed all the signs point the other way – that in fact he often exerted himself to use his influence with the Queen on behalf of a wide range of clients, and by no means all of high rank, as in the case of Leicester's man Jukes. It could be that his very generosity contributed to people's dislike of him. Men hate to have to be grateful; they despised themselves for having to ask Ralegh a favour; they despised him if he failed on their behalf; and, perversely, despised him all the more if he succeeded. In general, Ralegh was insufferably successful, and always confident of his success. He had this con-foundedly superior attitude – what Aubrey called 'that awfulness and ascendancy in his aspect over other mortals'. Worse still, he did not seem to mind what other, lesser mortals thought of him. 'If any man accuseth me to my face,' he said, 'I will answer him with my mouth, by my tail is good enough to return an answer to such who traduceth me behind my back.' This maddened other courtiers, some of whom were already suspicious of a favourite who showed signs of wanting to mix in politics at the highest level. The Queen was entitled to fondle her favourite lovebirds in her bosom, or at least in her closet. That did nobody any harm. But this lovebird was beginning to look disconcertingly like a hawk. One courtier, Sir Anthony Bagot, said with feeling and probably with approximate truth that 'Sir Walter Ralegh is the best hated man of the world: in Court, city and country.' Not surprisingly,

TO THE RIGHT

WORTHIE AND HONOV-
RABLE, SIR VVALTER RALEGH,
KNIGHT, SENESCHAL OF THE DVCHIES OF
Cornewall and Exeter, and L. Warden of the ftannaries in Deuon
and Cornewall. T.B. wisheth true felicitie.

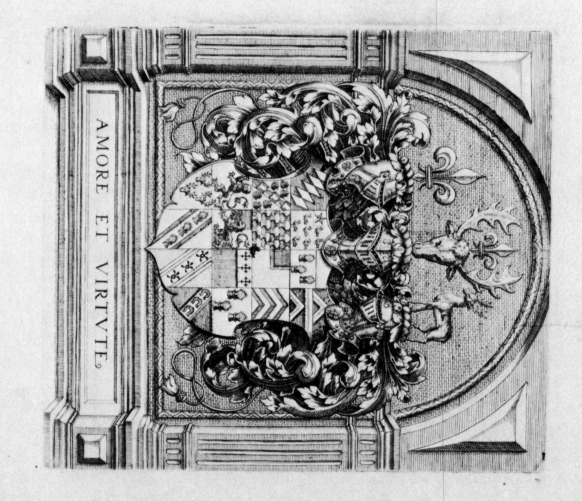

AMORE ET VIRTVTE.

IR, feeing that the parte of the Worlde, which is betwene the
FLORIDA and the Cap BRETON now enammed VIRGI-
NIA, to the honneur of yours moft fouueraine Layde and Queene ELIZABETH, hath ben defcouuerd by yours meanes. And
great chardges. And that your Collonye hath been theer eftab-
lished to your great honnor and prayfe, and noe leffer proffit vnto the common

Ralegh's business interests, his wine monopoly, his cloth export licence, and his jurisdiction over the Stannaries, also compounded his unpopularity.

Some of the most damaging criticism of Ralegh came from a fellow-poet, the same John Harington who translated *Orlando Furioso*. Harington was the Queen's godson, the inventor of the water-closet, and the author of many witty epigrams which were circulated in manuscript around the Court and eventually published. Over the years, Harington wrote some dozen epigrams attacking Ralegh, for whom he used the sobriquet 'Paulus'. The tone is consistently unflattering, jeering at Ralegh's grey hairs, mocking his ambition and his taste for tobacco, and attacking his atheism. Harington compares Ralegh to a pike, 'a greedy fish', refers to his 'scoffing fashion', his 'scorn and deep derision', his 'manner is to speake in mocke', and says that he would 'lose a friend to coin a jest'. In one of his wittiest epigrams, entitled 'Of honest Theft: To my good friend Master Samuel Daniel', Harington scores a bull's-eye. Ralegh had obviously accused Harington of too much plagiarizing from the classical poets. Harington had the perfect riposte:

Proud Paulus late my secrecies revealing,
Hath told I got some good conceits by stealing.
But where got he those double Pistolets,
With which good clothes, good fare, good land he gets;
Tush, those, he saith, came by a man of warre,
That brought a Prize of price, from countries farre.
Then, fellow Thiefe, let's shake together hands,
Sith both our wares are filcht from forren lands.
You'le spoile the Spaniards, by your writ of Mart:
And I the Romanes rob, by wit, and Art.

To Ralegh, privateering was not only good business but also almost a patriotic duty, faithfully performed by him and the rest of the West-Country gentry. As Vice-Admiral of Devon and Cornwall, Ralegh, with Sir John Gilbert and Lord Beauchamp, whom he appointed as his deputies, was in an excellent geographical position for commerce raiding. He was a freebooter at heart for the whole of his public life. The registers of the Acts of the Privy Council for Elizabeth's reign redound with complaints and counter-complaints, accusations and counter-accusations, charges and counter-charges, concerning Ralegh, his deputies, his sea captains, and captains and ship owners from the Netherlands, France, Spain and Portugal.

In June 1586 Ralegh sent three of his ships on privateering expeditions whose purpose was plain piracy. Off the Azores they took some prizes 'laden with sugars, Elephants teeth, waxe, hides, rice, brasill, and Cuser'. On the way home they met a fleet of twenty-four sail: 'two Caracks', of 1200 and 1000 tons, ten galleons and the rest small ships. They had a running fight with the 'two Caracks' for thirty-two hours before they had to give up and let them go, for lack of powder. They brought their prizes home to Southampton, 'where Sir Walter Raleigh being our owner, rewarded us with our shares'.

Ralegh had books of all kinds dedicated to him. This one is from Theodore de Bry's *America*, Part I, 1590

A much more important capture than the prize cargoes was Don Pedro Sarmiento de Gamboa, Governor of the Spanish colony in Patagonia, protecting the Straits of Magellan. He was met personally by Ralegh at Plymouth and later entertained in some style at Durham House. Ralegh seems to have found him congenial company. In the *History of the World* he calls Don Pedro 'a worthy Spanish gentleman' and relates a 'pretty jest' of his: they were both looking at a map of the Magellan Straits when Ralegh asked Don Pedro about a particular island. Don Pedro 'told me merrily, that it was to be called the Painter's Wife Island; saying that whilst the fellow drew that map, his wife sitting by desired him to put in one country for her'.

Apart from his pretty jests, Don Pedro could be useful to the State. He had talks with the Queen and Lord Burghley and agreed to act as negotiator for the Queen, in exchange for his freedom without ransom (thus leaving Ralegh financially the loser). It was agreed that if Philip lifted the embargo on English shipping, Elizabeth would do her best to stop English privateering against Spanish ships. On his way to Spain, Don Pedro was captured in France by Huguenots. Ralegh sent two of his men to procure his release.

Back in Madrid, Don Pedro had a tale to tell Philip which must have stretched his eyebrows and his credulity. Ralegh, he said, could be a most useful ally. He would look after His Majesty's interests, sell one of his warships to Spain for 5,000 crowns, perhaps sell another one as well; and he undertook to thwart English attempts to place the Portuguese Pretender Don Antonio on the throne of Portugal. Mendoza, the Spanish Ambassador, also seems to have been convinced of Ralegh's good intentions, reporting that Ralegh was trying to discourage fresh expeditions against Spain.

Ralegh was a renowned Hispanophobe, second only in the Spanish demonology to the fiery Drake himself. This suddenly friendly behaviour was highly suspicious. Though his servants might be deceived, Philip of Spain was not. 'They must guard themselves against the coming of the ships under this pretext,' he wrote to Mendoza, 'being a feint or trick upon us – which is far from improbable.'

So ended one of Ralegh's earliest dabblings in patriotic politics. He did not have the fine Greek hand of a Cecil for it. The negotiation had come to nothing. He had left himself with the faintest whisper against his reputation, which might possibly reappear at an embarrassing time in the future, that he had once been friendly and secret with the King of Spain. He could not even console himself with Don Pedro's ransom money.

On 14th August 1586 the midnight bells rang to celebrate the discovery of yet another plot against the Queen's life. The conspirators were a group of Catholics led by Anthony Babington, who planned to assassinate the Queen and raise the country for Mary Queen of Scots. Babington and his party were arrested, tried for treason, and condemned to death. It was the involvement of the Queen of Scots which gave Babington's otherwise undistinguished conspiracy its political importance. Mary Stuart was brought to trial and duly sentenced to death. After much hesitation, Elizabeth consented to her rival's execution; and the sentence was carried out in February 1587.

For Ralegh, the main consequence of the Babington Plot was increased financial pros-

Ships and shipbuilding were one of Ralegh's lifelong interests. Note the four conning towers on this galleon of c. 1588. Engraving by Visscher

perity. Babington had been a very rich young man, with an annual income of £10,000, a fantastic fortune in Elizabethan times. On his attainder his estate passed to the Crown, and in March 1587 an impressive list of properties was given to Ralegh (although he probably did not receive all the lands promised). They included manors, lands, tenements and closes in Lincolnshire, Derbyshire and Nottinghamshire, a house called Babington's Hall at Bredon in Lincolnshire, 'together with all goods, personals, and moveables' except for a certain 'curious clock' which was reserved for Her Majesty's personal use.

That summer of 1587 Ralegh stepped up to his point of highest favour with the Queen when he succeeded Sir Christopher Hatton as Captain of the Yeomen of the Guard, and became responsible for the Queen's personal safety wherever she went. The post was honorary, although the Captain was provided with his uniform. Ralegh was in close and constant attendance on the Queen, in the ante-chamber, at her door-post, or by her side. He rode with her, talked with her, laughed and joked with her, and wrote poems to her.

That mid-summer Ralegh's career, like the sun, stood at its solstice. From now on, the clouds began to gather. With Leicester, back from the Low Countries, came a very young man who had served so valiantly that his Commander-in-Chief knighted him on the battle-field. He was Robert Devereux, 2nd Earl of Essex.

6. The Armada

ESSEX had first been brought to Court at the age of ten when he had petulantly refused to kiss the Queen when asked. But that precocious, impertinent child was not recognizable in the splendid young knight whom Leicester introduced ten years later. Essex was just twenty years old, in the full prime of his early manhood, tall, good-looking, athletic, with a healthy complexion, reddish brown hair, and full pouting lips. 'He no sooner appeared in Court,' wrote Sir Robert Naunton, 'but he took with the Queen and Courtiers. There was in this young Lord, together with a most goodly person, a kind of urbanity or innate courtesie, which both won the Queen, and too much took upon the people, to gaze upon the adopted son of her favour.'

The Queen acted as though she were besotted with him. 'When she is abroad,' wrote Anthony Bagot in a letter to his father of May 1587, 'nobody near her but my lord of Essex; and, at night, my Lord is at cards, or one game or another, with her, till the birds sing in the morning.' Essex was the son of Lettice Knollys, whom Leicester married in 1569. One of his great-aunts was Anne Boleyn. Thus he was Leicester's stepson and a cousin of the Queen. He was the Queen's new darling at Court and, unlike Ralegh, he was highly popular in city and country. He was a scholar and a writer as well as a soldier. But he was also inordinately jealous of his own position, over-quick to take offence, immensely proud, intolerant of any restraints of common sense, good manners, or tactics, moody, argumentative, a 'great resenter'.

He particularly resented Sir Walter Ralegh, whom he recognized at once as his paramount rival for the Queen's favour. The dislike was mutual. Like Hatton and Leicester before him, Ralegh now felt the uncomfortable sensation of having his position at Court assailed by a much younger and better-equipped opponent. Ralegh's position was particularly weak because he had no faction, no political weight. Essex, on the other hand, was embarrassed by followers. Many of the older generation at Court supported him because of family connections or simply because he was Ralegh's rival, while the young flocked to him because he was the most glamorous, gifted, and obvious leader of their age-group.

However, Ralegh was a more formidable opponent than Essex expected. He had high position in Court and country; he was a man of many business affairs; a pioneer of Virginian exploration; he had had service in camp and command; he was a poet of repute, with many friends amongst the artists and intellectuals of the time. Ralegh had already achieved much that Essex himself longed to do and there was very much more to him than a well-turned leg and some well-turned poems. He was not to be brushed aside with ridicule or contempt – as Essex quickly found out.

That summer of 1587 the Court went on Progress as usual, and in July stayed at the Earl of Warwick's house, North Hall, in Hertfordshire, on the way to visit Lord Burghley at his great house Theobalds. It so happened that Essex's sister Lady Dorothy had given the Queen great offence, and had been banned the Court, for secretly marrying Sir Thomas Perrot (Ralegh's old opponent of 1583). Always jealous and suspicious of her ladies-in-waiting's love-lives, the Queen was never more furious than when she found out that they had married without her knowledge and permission. Although Lady Warwick must have been aware of the risk she was taking, she invited Lady Perrot to a party at North Hall; if she thought the Queen had mellowed towards Lady Perrot, she was mistaken. The Queen blazed with anger, and told Lady Perrot to keep to her room.

Essex could not brook such an insult to his sister. He was sure that Ralegh was behind it. Ralegh may have been, or he may not. But when Essex taxed the Queen over the matter, he had a surprisingly cool reception. He described the affair and its outcome in a letter dated 21st July 1587 to a friend and supporter, Edward Dyer. The letter reveals as much about Essex's character as about his feelings towards Ralegh. When Essex reproached Her Majesty for 'disgracing' his sister, 'being greatly troubled in myself',

her excuse was first, she knew not of my sister's coming; and besides, that the jealousy that the world would conceive that all her kindness to my sister was done for love of myself. Such bad excuses were a theme large enough both for answer of them and to tell her what the true causes were, why she would offer this disgrace both to me and to my sister, which was only to please that knave Ralegh, for whose sake I saw she would grieve me and my love, and disgrace me in the eye of the world. From thence, she came to speak of Ralegh; and it seemed she could not well endure anything to be spoken against him; and taking hold of my word 'disdain', she said there was 'no such cause why I should disdain him'. This speech did trouble me so much that, as near as I could, I did describe unto her what he had been, and what he was . . . I then did let her know, whether I had cause to disdain his competition of love, or whether I could have comfort to give myself over to the service of a mistress which was in awe of such a man. I spake, with grief and choler, as much against him as I could; and I think he, standing at the door, might very well hear the worst that I spoke of himself. In that end, I saw she was resolved to defend him, and to cross me. For myself, I told her, I had no job to be in any place, but was loth to be near about her, when I knew my affection so much thrown down, and such a wretch as Ralegh highly esteemed of her. To this she made no answer, but turned away to my Lady of Warwick. This strange alteration is by Ralegh's means; and the Queen, that hath tried all other ways, now will see whether she can, by these hard courses, drive me to be friends with Ralegh, which rather shall drive me to many other extremities.

There is a petulant note in the letter, as though written by a spoiled child, and Essex afterwards felt himself driven to a pettish escapade. He slipped away from the Court and rode to Sandwich where a ship of the Earl of Cumberland's was just about to sail for the Low

Countries. Evidently, to Essex, service in the field in Holland once again was preferable to the Court. But the Queen sent Robert Carey after him, to catch up with him as he was embarking, and bring him back.

Standing at his post as Captain of the Guard, outside the door of the Queen's chamber, Ralegh probably did hear all that Essex said in grief and choler about him, just as Essex certainly intended him to do. The Queen had once more stoutly taken Ralegh's part, and put the young puppy firmly in his place for the time. But there were aspects of the affair which gave Ralegh cause to ponder. Essex had the great advantage of birth. It was disquieting to see how the young man had been able to scold the Queen to her face in a way Ralegh would never have dared to do. Ralegh said nothing more, but may have fashioned his own witty answer, in a riddling, jingling rhyme of a poem perhaps written at this time, playing on Essex's words 'disdain' and 'what he has been and what he is':

If Synthia be a Queene, a princes, and supreame,
Keipe thes amonge the rest, or say it was a dreame;
For thos that like, expound, and those that louth, express,
Meanings accordinge as their minds, ar moved more or less;
For writinge what thow art, or shewinge what thow weare;
Adds to the one dysdayne, to th'other butt dyspaire;
Thy minde of neather needs, in both seinge it exceeds.

Also, that summer, Ralegh met the Lady Arabella Stuart, with whose name he was to be linked at the time of his trial. 'Arbell', then twelve years old, had a respectable claim to Elizabeth's throne, through her descent from Henry VIII's sister Margaret. Arbell was James VI of Scotland's first cousin, being the daughter of Charles Stuart, 5th Duke of Lennox, Darnley's elder brother. Elizabeth once introduced Arbell to the wife of the French ambassador (though probably in a mood of pure mischief) as 'she that will sometime be Lady Mistress here, even as I am'. Arabella had come to be presented at Elizabeth's Court. She dined 'in the Presence' and was rather afraid of her cousin, who must have seemed to her a very fierce and sharp-tongued old lady. Arbell said that she was relieved that the Queen 'examined her nothing touching her book'. The little girl had supper with Lord Burghley at Theobalds. Her uncle Sir Charles Cavendish and Sir Walter Ralegh were also present. Sir Charles wrote afterwards to Arbell's grandmother Elizabeth Hardwick, Countess of Shrewsbury ('Bess of Hardwick') that Lord Burghley had been pleased with Arbell. 'He spoke greatly in Lady Arbell's commendation, as that she had "the French and the Italian; played of instruments; danced; and writ very fair". Then he wished "she were fifteen years old" and with that rounded Sir Walter in the ear, who answered "it would be a very happy thing".'

The same letter, which is undated but was probably written that summer, includes an ominous comment on Ralegh.

Sir Walter Raleigh is in wonderful declination yet labours to underprop himself by my Lord Treasurer and his friends. I see he is courteously used by my Lord and friends, but I doubt the end, considering how he hath handled himself in his former pride, and surely now groweth so humble towards everyone, as considering his former insolency he committeth over-great baseness, and is thought he will never rise again.

Cavendish was undoubtedly overstating the position in saying that Ralegh 'will never rise again', but he was probably one of the many who were always watching and waiting for Ralegh's foot to slip. Possibly Ralegh was undergoing one of those periodic phases when he had to endure the dark side of the moon. He seems to have been aware, deep within himself, that Essex had thrown a shadow over the future. He may have recognized that summer as his zenith. The current of dark melancholy which was never far below the surface of his nature showed in another of his poems, possibly written about this time, based on the poem *Diana* by the French poet Phillippe Desportes:

Like to a Hermite poore in place obscure,
I meane to spend my daies of endles doubt,
To waile such woes as time cannot recure,
Where none but Love shall ever finde me out.

My foode shall be of care and sorow made,
My drink nought else but teares falne from mine eies,
And for my light in such obscured shade,
The flames shall serve, which from my hart arise.

A gowne of graie, my bodie shall attire,
My staffe of broken hope whereon Ile staie,
Of late repentance linckt with long desire,
The couch is fram'de whereon my limbs Ile lay.

And at my gate dispaire shall linger still,
To let in death when Love and Fortune will.

Something in this bittersweet piece greatly appealed to the Elizabethan mind. Set to music by Alfonso Ferrabosco, it became a very popular song.

Ralegh still had his eyes on Virginia, and that year dispatched yet another expedition. His earlier ventures had had military overtones, part of their purpose being to establish a base for privateering against Spain. The new expedition of 1587 was the first real attempt at colonization. For the first time the party included women and children. The colony would have its own self-administering government under a Governor, John White. On 7th January 1587 Ralegh incorporated John White and twelve others under a charter as 'Governor and Assistants of the citie of Ralegh in Virginia'. The new city was to be north of Roanoke, on Chesapeake Bay. Every volunteer was to get 500 acres of land in Virginia, and further land in proportion to the size of his investment. Later they would bring out their wives and families. The settlement, it was hoped, would become self-supporting and permanent. It is not known how many colonists there were originally intended to be. White himself in his account in Hakluyt says 150. That number eventually sailed.

The ships, the *Lion*, a flyboat, and a pinnace, were fitted out in the Thames before moving round to Portsmouth in late March or early April. After leaving Portsmouth, White called at Plymouth and finally sailed from there on 8th May, later in the year than the other expeditions. Simon Fernandez, one of White's twelve 'Assistants', was master of the *Lion*, Edward Spicer master of the flyboat. Edward Stafford commanded the pinnace.

White's account of the voyage constantly complains about Fernandez. Fernandez 'lewdly forsook our flyboate, leaving her distressed in the Bay of Portugal'. An island they visited was inhabited by savages, 'though Fernando had told us for certaine the contrary'. Going into a bay to collect salt, Fernandez inexplicably foiled the attempt: 'he suddenly began to sweare, and teare God in pieces, dissembling great danger, crying to him at the helme, beare up hard, beare up hard: so we went off, and were disappointed of our salt, by his meanes.'

They loitered from one island to another in the West Indies, with White hoping to pick up fruit, plants and livestock for the new colony, and Fernandez, hoping for prizes, frustrating all White's attempts to land or to trade with the Spaniards. As a result of their squabblings, the ships finally sailed for Virginia on 5th July with neither plants nor prizes.

They arrived off the mainland on 16th July, and anchored. Fernandez said they were at Croatoan Island. He was wrong. They were still south of Cape Fear. Sailing north, the ships were nearly wrecked in the night. They came within two cables' lengths of Cape Fear, and they would have been lost 'had not Captaine Stafford bene more carefull in looking out, then our Simon Ferdinando'. 'Such,' comments White, 'was the carelesnes, and ignorance of our Master.' At last they reached Hatarask, and anchored safely, on the 22nd.

White's written instructions from Ralegh were to land here, search for the fifteen men left by Grenville the year before, and then go on to Chesapeake Bay, where the colony was to be founded. White embarked in the pinnace with forty of his best men. He had no sooner put off from the *Lion* than he was hailed by a message from Fernandez. The forty men were to be left on Roanoke. Only White himself and two or three others were to be allowed to return on board the *Lion*, and then only to arrange for the landing of the rest of the colonists. According to Fernandez, 'the Summer was farre spent' (for privateering, he meant). The colonists had to stop here, at Roanoke.

Astonishingly, White agreed. The sailors evidently all said they would obey Fernandez, 'wherefore it booted not the Governor to contend with them'. It may have been that John White was too weak a character to disagree with Fernandez. Possibly he may even have preferred, himself, to stay at Roanoke, which he knew well, rather than go on to the unknown dangers of Chesapeake. But it does appear that White was too ineffectual a leader for a new colony.

There was no sign of any of the fifteen men. Ralph Lane's fort had been razed to the ground. The compound and the ground floors of the houses were overgrown with 'melons of divers sortes'. There were deer in the fort feeding on the melons.

On 25th July Edward Spicer arrived in the flyboat, to the great joy of everyone except

Fernandez who, according to White, 'grieved greatly at their safe coming'. In White's opinion, Fernandez deliberately deserted the flyboat in the Bay of Portugal, knowing that Spicer had never been to Virginia and might never find it by himself. White's unfavourable account of Fernandez' conduct and motives was probably coloured by his dislike of the man and his need to justify some of his own inadequacies. But if White's version is only partly correct, then Fernandez' behaviour is still hard to understand. He was, after all, a shareholder in the undertaking, and he was only sabotaging his own interests. Perhaps, in the end, Fernandez never had any faith in new colonies. To him they were only convenient opportunities for privateering. There were many in England who shared his opinion.

The Indians had apparently deserted the village near the fort, but they were still in the vicinity. On the 28th, a war party surprised and killed George Howe, one of White's 'Assistants', shooting him to death with arrows while he was catching crabs by himself on the shore. Two days later, Edward Stafford took Manteo and twenty men across to Croatoan Island, where Manteo had relatives, and established good relations with the Indians. They learned the fate of the fifteen men: two had been killed by the Indians and the other thirteen had escaped by boat to another island. It seemed that the same Indian tribe, from Dasemunkepeuc, had attacked Grenville's men and also murdered Howe. White decided on reprisals. On 9th August he and a party surrounded the village, but, after attacking, White discovered that there had been a misunderstanding. The Indians in the village were visitors, friendly natives from Croatoan, who had come to gather corn, beans and pumpkins from the site. The attack was hard to explain away convincingly but the Croatoans eventually accepted White's apologies. Four days later Manteo was christened and officially installed, as Ralegh's representative, as lord of Roanoke and Dasemunkepeuc.

On 18th August White's daughter Eleanor, the wife of Ananias Dare, gave birth to a daughter, the first English child to be born in America. The following Sunday she was christened Virginia.

By this date, as White says, 'our ships had unladen the goods and victuals of the planters, and began to take in wood, and fresh water, and to new calke and trimme them for England: the planters also prepared their letters and tokens to send backe into England'. By the 21st the Lion and the flyboat were almost ready to sail, but a storm blew up. Fernandez was forced to cut his anchor cables and put to sea with 'the most and best' of his sailors left on land. The ships were away for six days before they were able to beat back to Hattoras.

Meanwhile a storm had blown up on land. There were what White called 'some controversies' between himself and his Assistants. The colonists had built themselves new houses and cottages and had settled in with their belongings, but they were still short of many things, especially salt and livestock. They had also realized that the Roanoke site was a poor one for a permanent settlement. It was decided to send two Assistants back to England with Fernandez, to arrange for fresh supplies. But, oddly, nobody wanted to go. Christopher Cooper, one of the Assistants, first said he would go, and then changed his mind. At last, they made up their minds that White himself should go. Again astonishingly, White agreed. But first he insisted on safeguards for the belongings he would leave behind. The others reassured him. Then White demanded, and got, a written testimonial that he was not deserting them, but going at the request of them all. The document, dated 25th August, stated that 'wee all of one minde & consent, have most earnestly intreated, and uncessantly requested John White, Governor of the planters in Virginia, to passe into England, for the better and more assured help.' White may well have been the best man to go, but it still seems odd that he should, and that he did not have, or did not use, the authority to nominate two Assistants to go to England.

White sailed in the flyboat on 27th August. An accident on the capstan while they were weighing the anchor injured most of the flyboat's crew of fifteen, leaving her under-manned for the Atlantic passage. At the Azores Edward Spicer had only five fit men, and as Fernandez seemed to want to delay in search of prizes, the flyboat sailed on alone for England. With two of the crew dead and many sick, short of water and food, they reached Smerwick in Ireland on 16th October. White took another ship to England and reached Southampton on 8th November, three weeks after Fernandez, who had also had a difficult voyage, and had taken no prizes.

Once again, Ralegh had to listen to reports of only partial success, probably from Simon Fernandez, and certainly from John White whom he met on 20th November. White had left a settlement of eighty-five men, seventeen women, eleven children, and two Indians, Manteo and Towaye. They intended, he said, to 'remove 50 miles further up into the maine presently', probably meaning up to Chesapeake Bay in accordance with their original instructions. Meanwhile, they needed assistance, in the form of food and stores.

Ralegh at that time had many other preoccupations on his mind, particularly his part in preparing the defence of the kingdom against impending attack from Spain. But he did make some efforts, that winter, to relieve White's colony. By the time White returned home, a general stay of shipping in English ports had been imposed because of the danger from Spain, but in January 1588 Ralegh obtained the release of some small Dutch flyboats which had been impounded in south-western ports. In any case he seems to have regarded the relief of his Virginian colony as an exception to the general rule, for on 27th February he was writing from the Court to Sir John Gilbert that he had heard there was little regard taken of the general restraint, 'as though the restraynte were forgotten or not to be respected'. Ralegh assured Sir John that this was not the case, but meanwhile Sir Richard Grenville was carrying on with the preparation of some seven or eight privateering relief ships at Bideford. By the end of March they were almost ready, but the Privy Council had heard of them and had guessed Grenville's and Ralegh's intentions. On the 31st they ordered Grenville to 'forbeare to go his intended voyage'. Ten days later Grenville was ordered to send his ships to Plymouth for service in the Queen's Navy, and to make available for the Queen's service the provisions he had assembled. He was allowed to dispose of such small vessels as Drake did not need. He and Ralegh took this as a loop-hole, meaning that at least some small ships could be sent to Virginia. On 22nd April 1588 John White sailed from Bideford in the bark *Brave*, of thirty tons, commanded by Arthur Facy, with the *Roe*, a pinnace of twenty-five tons, in company.

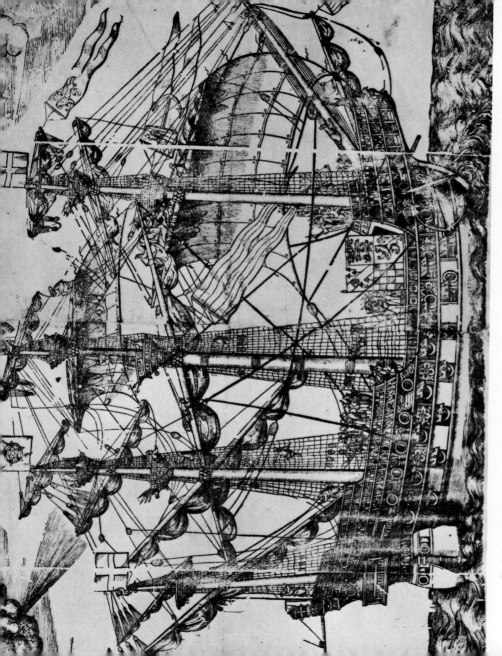

Bark *Ralegh*, built by Ralegh, renamed *Ark Royal*. The Queen never actually paid Ralegh for the ship – just knocked £5,000 off his debts when he was disgraced. Anonymous English woodcut, late 16th Century

Facy, like Fernandez, was much more interested in privateering than in colonizing. He chased and stopped every ship in sight. After some initial successes he met his match in a Frenchman from Rochelle who seized the *Brave*, killed most of her crew, took Facy prisoner and stripped the ship of all valuables and fittings. Facy and White were fortunate to be able to return home to Bideford, which they did on 22nd May. There was no further relief attempt that year.

The threat of invasion from Spain which hung over so much of Elizabeth's reign was once again looming. The execution of Mary Queen of Scots in February meant that Philip of Spain himself now had a direct claim on the throne of England. His intention to invade was well known; it was a constant ingredient in the political thoughts and actions of Englishmen of the time. In April 1587 Drake had 'singed the King of Spain's beard' at Cadiz and delayed the sailing of the Spanish Armada for almost a year. But the delay could only be

77

temporary and in November 1587 Ralegh, as Lieutenant General of Cornwall, was a member of a Council of War, with Lord Grey, Sir Thomas Knollys, Sir Thomas Leighton, Sir John Norris, Sir Richard Grenville, Sir Richard Bingham, Sir Roger Williams and Ralph Lane, which met to consider the defence of the realm. They recommended that Milford Haven, the Isle of Wight (one of the Armada's actual objectives), the Downs, Margate, the Thames and Portland should all be fortified against invasion. Giving Philip credit for more military acumen than he actually had, the Council decided that the Armada would not advance far up the Channel without first securing a major port as a base and refuge. Therefore they recommended that Plymouth should be fortified and garrisoned with 5,000 men of Devon and Cornwall. Portland was to be defended by 2,700 men of Dorset and Wiltshire. Ralegh was then petitioning Burghley for more cannon for Portland and Weymouth, and therefore it has been suggested that he was Mayor of Weymouth.

In December Ralegh was down in the West Country again, with Sir John Gilbert, Sir Richard Grenville and Lord Bath, who was Lord Lieutenant of Devon, raising 2,000 footmen and 200 horse for the defence of Cornwall and Devon. The city and county of Exeter, characteristically, objected to providing their quota of 200 footmen, on the ground that they already suffered great charges in the defence of their trade against Barbary and other pirates.

Ralegh's personal contribution to the defeat of the Spanish Armada is not known precisely. Certainly he provided the fleet flagship. His own ship, the *Ark Ralegh*, with improvements and fittings of his own design, was completed in June 1587 and sold to the Crown, when she was renamed the *Ark Royal*. Ralegh was never paid cash for her; £5,000 was written off his debts after his disgrace in 1592. She was Lord Howard of Effingham's flagship and he was very pleased with her: in February 1588 he was writing to Burghley from on board the *Ark*:

I protest before God, and as my soul shall answer for it, that I think there were never in any place in the world worthier ships than these are, for so many. And as few as we are, if the King of Spain's forces be not hundreds we will make good sport with them.

And I pray you tell her Majesty from me that her money was well given for the *Ark Ralegh*, for I think her the odd ship in the world for all conditions; and truly I think there can no great ship make me change and go out of her.

Ralegh's main contributions were the preparations of land defences in the west, and the sound advice he gave the Council. He appreciated the strategic advantages of sea-power, and the great mobility a fleet gave a commander. He comments upon this in his *History of the World*:

Our question is, of an army to be transported over sea, and to be landed again in an enemy's country, and the place left to the choice of the invader. Hereunto I say, that such an army cannot be resisted on the coast of England without a fleet to impeach it . . . There is no man ignorant that ships, without putting themselves out of breath, will easily outrun the soldiers that coast them . . . I know it to be true, that a fleet of ships may be seen at sunset, and after it, at the Lizard; yet by the next morning they

The Lord Admiral, Howard of Effingham, the fleet commander against the Spanish Armada. He was delighted with his flagship *Ark Royal* – 'the odd ship in the world for all conditions' Engraving by William Rogers

Carol. D. Howard. Comes
Nottingham Summ. Angl.

may recover Portland; whereas an army of foot shall not be able to march it in six days.

It is possible that Ralegh embarked in a ship of war and fought in the sea battles off Portland on 23rd July (Hakluyt records him as present, but Hakluyt also records Robert Cecil, who took no part). He does not mention such service anywhere in his own writings, and it seems most unlikely that he would omit to refer to such a day if he had been there. His ship the *Roebuck*, in company with the *Revenge*, captured Don Pedro de Valdes' galleon *Rosario* and took her back to Dartmouth, where the crew rustled some fourteen or fifteen coffers containing 'cloth of gold and other rich furniture'. Months later, the authorities were still making enquiries about these. Jacob Whiddon, commanding the *Roebuck*, also removed most of the *Rosario*'s large guns.

According to one Spanish source, Ralegh was sent by the Queen with personal messages to Lord Howard off Gravelines. The Queen wished Howard to grapple more closely, but the advice Ralegh actually gave the Lord Admiral was probably more on the lines of the comment in his *History*:

To clap ships together without consideration, belongs rather to a madman than to a man of war . . . In like sort had the lord Charles Howard, admiral of England, been lost in the year 1588, if he had not been better advised, than a great many malignant fools were that found fault with his demeanour. The Spaniards had an army aboard them, and he had none; they had more ships than he had, and of higher building and charging; so that, had he entangled himself with those great and powerful vessels, he had greatly endangered his kingdom of England.

By September the remnants of the shattered Armada were fleeing homewards down the west coast of Ireland. On 14th September Sir Richard Grenville was ordered to commandeer and assemble shipping along the north coasts of Cornwall and Devon. He and Ralegh were both at sea off Ireland that month, Ralegh in command of three Queen's ships, the *Foresight* of 160 men, the *Aid* of 120 men and the *Tyger* with 90 men, convoying troops to Ireland and guarding the western approaches to England.

By Christmas he was back at Court, back to the quibblings and manoeuvrings and petty jealousies. Essex was still working against him, and still as touchy as ever. When young Charles Blount, Lord Mountjoy's son, distinguished himself in the tiltyard, the Queen gave him a gold chess-piece – a queen – as a token. Blount wore it at Court the next day, tied to his sleeve with a ribbon. When Essex saw it, he scoffed, 'Now I see every fool must have a favour.' For that, Blount challenged him to a duel. They fought in Marylebone Park. Essex was slightly wounded in the thigh. The Queen heard of the duel, and although she may have been gratified to know that she was the cause of a quarrel between two men young enough to be her grandsons, on this occasion Essex's arrogant behaviour irritated her. 'God's death,' she said, 'it is fit that someone or other should take him down, and teach him better manners, otherwise there would be no rule with him.'

It was Ralegh who tried to take Essex down, and teach him better manners. Their

The launching of fire-ships by the English fleet in the Calais Roads, midnight, 28 July 1588. Unknown artist, 1588

quarrel in December 1588 was probably over something just as trivial as Blount's chessman. Ralegh was provoked into making some remark for which Essex challenged him. The Privy Council forbade the duel to take place, and the Queen was not allowed to know of the quarrel. She was still distressed by the death of Leicester early in that September, and the unruliness of Essex disturbed her even more. The Privy Council did their best to 'bury the incident in silence, that it might not be known to her Majesty, lest it might injure the Earl'. Ralegh's place was secure. It was Essex who could be injured by loose, scandalous talk.

But it was not long before the Queen once again showed how delicately she portioned out her favour amongst her courtiers. Early in the New Year of 1589 there was a row over the appointment of the rangership of the New Forest. The Queen refused Ralegh when he interceded for the Earl of Pembroke. Pembroke was deeply offended, and Ralegh lost face. The Queen gave the post to Blount, who had so recently fought Essex. The rebuff to both was nicely judged.

The Armada had been defeated, but the war against Spain still went on, certainly in Ralegh's mind. He felt that no chance should be missed of harassing Spain or anyone who assisted Spain. His sea captains had standing orders to attack Spanish shipping and the shipping of Spanish sympathizers. In February 1589 the *Roebuck* seized a Flemish ship, bound from the Lowlands to Cadiz. Her owners, one Albert Reynerson and his trading partners, brought a suit against Ralegh, who defended his own position by saying, 'Such people are Spaniards in disguise, seeking the good and profit of the common enemy, with the

81

loss and hindrance of such of Her Majesty's subjects as, to their great charge, do venture upon reprisals.' This was a somewhat ingenuous defence, suggesting that Ralegh believed that privateering was the pious duty of every citizen and that Ralegh only went to the considerable expense of doing it for the sake of Her Majesty.

In April there came a chance to strike a much bigger blow at Spain. It was planned to invade Portugal and place the Portuguese Pretender, Don Antonio, on the throne which Philip of Spain had occupied since 1580. It was to be a full-scale reprisal for the Armada, and a good opportunity to pay off some old scores. The Queen, Ralegh, and scores of others subscribed to the financing of the expedition, as though it were a business investment. Twenty thousand men embarked in some 130 ships, six of the Queen's and the rest private volunteer shipping. Sir Francis Drake was the naval commander and the very experienced old soldier Sir John Norris was general on land.

Essex had been forbidden to accompany the expedition but, to the Queen's fury, he disguised himself, sneaked away from the Court and embarked in the *Swiftsure*, with the connivance and help of her commander, and Norris's second-in-command, Sir Roger Williams. The ship sailed from Plymouth, nine days before the main body, and before the Queen could have Essex brought back. When the Queen discovered the escapade she swore she would make Drake and Norris pay the costs of the expedition, and she ordered them to hang Williams. They did no such thing. Sir Roger was a popular and very able soldier.

Spanish astrolabe, c. 1585, diameter 7", weight 5lbs

Nevertheless, Williams had taken a very real risk of losing his life through his rash support of Essex. Essex was Master of the Queen's Horse, a Court official, and he had deserted his post. Williams himself had taken one of the Queen's ships to sea without authority. The whole affair smelled of insubordination and wanton flouting of the Queen's name. The Queen must already have been wondering if she could ever tame someone of Essex's spirit.

Ralegh put up money and provided some of his ships for the expedition. He may also have sailed on it, without taking a prominent part. One ship was seized at Corunna, and others were burnt at Vigo. In the mouth of the Tagus, Drake captured or burnt some 200 ships. Thus the naval side of the expedition was fairly successful.

On land, the expedition was a failure. Sir John Norris landed his troops and undertook a long overland march to besiege Lisbon. Without siege artillery he could not take the city, and the Portuguese countryside did not rise in favour of Don Antonio, as Don Antonio had previously insisted it would. With more than half their number dying of disease, and the remainder drunk on the local wine, the soldiers straggled back to the ships. The expedition was supposed to have gone on to the Azores, but with their discouragement and sickness, and the favourable wind for England that happened to be blowing, they returned home, to face the Queen's critical tongue.

Ralegh did moderately well out of the venture. Prizes had been taken off the coast of Portugal, and Sir Roger Williams lent men to bring one of Ralegh's prizes home. Sir Roger afterwards claimed that this entitled him to the whole of that prize. But the Privy Council supported Ralegh, and the Queen, possibly to annoy Essex, gave Ralegh a gold chain for his good behaviour. Sir Roger told the Council that *he* deserved a gold chain as much as anybody. Ralegh made a profit of about £4,000, some of which he spent on resheathing the hulls of his ships *Revenge, Garland,* and *Crane.* But it was not all gain: on 21st July the Privy Council ordered Ralegh to repay to them the value of a 'bark of Olonne', loaded with barley, which his ships had seized off the coast of Portugal.

Ralegh could by now have sent another relief ship to the colony in Virginia. There was still some commercial interest in the venture. Thomas Hariot had finished his *Brief and True Report of the New Found Land of Virginia* in February 1588. It was a most persuasively argued and well-documented account of the good points of Virginia, of the fertility of the soil, the temperateness and healthiness of the climate, and the civility of the natives. Hariot dealt with the practical problems of living in such a land, and its prospects for trade and profit. On 17th March 1589, Ralegh made a tripartite agreement (still keeping one fifth of any gold or silver which might be found for himself) with William Sanderson, Thomas Smythe, and nineteen other business associates, and with John White and his Assistants. It seems to have been an attempt to connect White and his colonists with fresh sources of capital. But the impetus behind the colonizing expeditions temporarily died away. For some unknown reason, no relief ship was sent to Virginia that year, although White tried hard to arrange for one.

Although Ralegh seems to have escaped the blame for the débâcle of the Lisbon expedition, there is no doubt that he was under some kind of cloud at Court in 1589. The very fact

A briefe and true report
of the new found land of Virginia,
of the commodities and of the nature and manners of the naturall inhabitants. Discouered by
the English Colony there seated by Sir Richard
Greinuile Knight In the yeere 1585. Which Rema-
: ined Vnder the gouernement of twelue monethes,
At the speciall charge and direction of the Honourable SIR WALTER RALEIGH Knight lord Warden
of the stanneries Who therein hath beene fauoured
and authorised by her MAIESTIE
and her letters patents:

This fore booke is made in English
By Thomas Hariot seruant to the abouenamed
Sir WALTER, a member of the Colony, and there
imployed in discouering.

CVM GRATIA ET PRIVILEGIO CÆS. MATIS. SPECIALI.

FRANCOFORTI AD MOENVM
TYPIS IOANNIS WECHELI, SVMTIBVS VERO THEODORI
DE BRY ANNO CIƆ IƆ XC.
VENALES REPERIVNTVR IN OFFICINA SIGISMVNDI FEIRABENDII.

that he may have been allowed to go on the voyage suggests that the Queen's attachment to him may have been weakening. In August 1589, he left for Ireland. This, too, may be significant. No courtier ever left the Court for an extended period without a very good reason. Possibly, he may genuinely have asked and obtained the Queen's permission to go and see his Irish estates. But Court rumour had it otherwise. The whisper was that Essex had at last been successful in ousting his great rival from the Queen's affections. On 17th August one of Essex's faction, Sir Francis Allen, was writing to another, Anthony Bacon, brother of Francis, a great gossip, and later head of Essex's foreign intelligence service, 'My Lord of Essex hath chased Mr Ralegh from the Court, and hath confined him into Ireland.'

Ralegh was by no means defeated. As Naunton said, he was leaving the *Terra infirma* of the Court, but he would 'come in (as Rammes doe, by going backward) with the greater strength'. As he stood at the ship's rail and watched the shores of England receding, his 'Farewell to the Court', with its sad reference to his 'lost delights now clean from sight of land', suited his mood of the moment:

Like truthles dreames, so are my joyes expired,
And past returne, are all my dandled daies:
My love misled, and fancie quite retired,
Of all which past, the sorow onely staies.

My lost delights now cleane from sight of land,
Have left me all alone in unknowne waies:
My minde to woe, my life in fortunes hand,
Of all which past, the sorow onely staies.

As in a countrey strange without companion,
I onely waile the wrong of deaths delaies,
Whose sweet spring spent, whose sommer well nie don,
Of all which past, the sorow onely staies.

Whom care forewarnes, ere age and winter colde,
To haste me hence, to find my fortunes folde.

7. 'The Summer's Nightingale'

IN IRELAND the Desmond Rebellion had come to an end with the betrayal and murder of the Earl in November 1583. By that time Munster had been reduced to the state described by John Hooker in Holinshed: 'The curse of God was so great, and the land so barren, both of man and beast, that whosoever did travel from one end to the other of all Munster, even from Waterford to Smerwick, about six score miles, he should not meet man, woman, or child, saving in cities or towns, nor yet see any beast, save foxes, wolves, or other ravening beasts.'

Nearly six thousand acres of Cork, Kerry and Limerick, formerly belonging to Desmond and other rebels, were confiscated. The Crown's legal right to the land was sealed by Act of Parliament in 1585. The Crown therefore had a huge area of potentially valuable land, suitable for colonization. What was needed in Ireland was a large population of Protestant English, strong and numerous enough to crush further Irish rebellion, prosperous enough to contribute taxes to the Crown, and stable enough to prevent the land filling up with Irish again and becoming once more an ally of Spain. Another scheme, one of several Tudor plans for settling Ireland, was evolved (and Ralegh's advice may well have been taken on it). The plan of 1585 was to divide the land into portions, or 'seignories' of up to 12,000 acres of farming land, with waste-land, bog and mountain included. The seignories were then to be rented to powerful English 'undertakers' who undertook to repopulate their lands with new immigrants from England, transplanting a cross-section of English society into Ireland, and to have no Irish on the land. The Undertakers included Sir Christopher Hatton, Sir Edmund Fitton, the Earl of Ormond (ironically), Sir Richard Grenville, and Sir Walter Ralegh.

With no great estates behind him in England, Ralegh was always very interested in acquiring land in Ireland, even from his earliest days there as a soldier. The letters patent of 27th June 1586 showed him at the head of the list of Undertakers for Devonshire, Somerset and Dorset, followed by others such as Sir John Stowell and Sir John Clifton. Helped by the Queen, Ralegh pressed hard to get as much land in Ireland as quickly as possible. It was Ralegh at his most rapacious. There were no accurate maps of Munster and no precise data on how much land was involved in the scheme and where it lay. A new survey was required. When the Royal Commissioners for the survey reached Ireland in September 1586, the first estates they began to survey, obviously on instructions, were those to be allocated to Ralegh. They reported much of the land 'long overgrown with deep grass and in most places with heath brambles and furze'. Although the Undertakers were supposed to be limited to a seignory of 12,000 acres maximum, the Privy Council warrant of 27th February 1587

awarded Ralegh three whole seigniories of 12,000 acres, and a half (42,000 acres in all), in the counties of Cork, Waterford and Tipperary. It was a vast area, from ten to twelve miles long and five miles wide at its widest point, stretching inland from Youghal on both sides of the Blackwater River. The rent was fixed at £233 6s. 8d. yearly. The first years were rent-free, and half-rate was to be paid from 1591 to 1594. In fact, Ralegh never paid more than £66 6s. 8d. The Queen's favour to him was equivalent, as in some of his expeditions, to an indirect subsidy. The Undertakers were supposed to supply at their own cost all the men, stores and finance for their plantations. Ralegh maintained a troop of twenty horsemen under his own principal agent Andrew Colthurst, to protect his settlers' lives and property. They were doing Ralegh's business, but their wages were paid by the Queen. In March 1588 an order in Council was made authorizing the payment of £244 to Ralegh for the previous half-year's expenses. Ralegh's cavalry had been on the State pay-roll at least since May of the previous year. Ralegh was formally confirmed in the ownership of his Irish estates by an Irish patent dated 16th October 1587, although he did not get possession of all his property until early in 1589.

Ralegh was in Ireland in September 1588, after the defeat of the Armada. He and Sir Richard Grenville had convoyed reinforcements for the garrison, and they both stayed on in Ireland to look over their new estates. Ralegh was in Munster for about three months, arranging legal affairs and estate business with his agents Colthurst and Robert Mawle. He had two houses in Ireland, one at each end of his Plantation. One was the house of the warden of the College of Our Lady in Youghal, of which Ralegh had the patronage, and the other was Lismore Castle. In 1587 Ralegh bought, or thought he had bought, through a sub-lessee, the remainder of the lease of the manor and castle of Lismore from Meyler Mcgrath, Bishop of Lismore, for £13 6s. 8d. a year. But the lease of Lismore was to lead to one of those tedious lawsuits which constantly bedevilled Ralegh. He also acquired the Abbey of Molana, which he later rented to Thomas Hariot, and in 1591 leased the manor of Ardmore, across the river from Youghal, from the Bishop of Lismore.

Ralegh was one of the very few English Undertakers to make a serious attempt to populate his Irish land under the terms of the agreement. Some, like Sir John Stowell and Sir John Clifton, simply gave up in disgust almost at once over the chaotic state of Munster when they arrived. Others sold out to Catholics, or rented lands back to the native Irish who were the original owners (thus initiating what was to become a traditional form of exploitation by English landlords in Ireland). By May 1589 Ralegh had 144 men settled on his estates. At least 73 of them had their families with them, and they made up a community of some 300 to 400 souls. Most were from Devon, Somerset and Dorset, but there were in addition about fifty Irish or Anglo-Irish families. One settler was Michael Butler, who had been Ralegh's lieutenant in the old days in Munster.

Ralegh's Irish estates were as well-farmed and -pastured as he could make them, and they were better than those of almost every other English Undertaker. He had some of the bogs drained, and the roads metalled. He is said to have introduced to Ireland a strong-smelling yellow wallflower from the Azores, and the 'Affane cherry' from the Canary Islands, and he planted the potato, the vegetable Hariot described as the 'Openhauk', in his own garden at Youghal.

He also renewed his acquaintanceship with Edmund Spenser. They would certainly have met before, when they were both servants of the Lord Deputy Grey. They had been professional colleagues; now they became firm friends. Spenser had just succeeded Ludowick Bryskett as Clerk of the Council of Munster. He too had received an award of Irish lands after the suppression of the Desmond Rebellion. He had the manor and castle of Kilcolman in county Cork, about thirty miles from Lismore. His estate was 3,028 acres and he had six English families settled under him, to work the land.

Edmund Spenser was then thirty-seven years old, an almost exact contemporary of

Edmund Spenser, Ralegh's friend in Ireland, owed much to Ralegh's sponsorship at Court

Ralegh's, still a bachelor, and described by Aubrey as 'a little man, wore short hair, little band, and little cuffs' – the very picture of a minor provincial civil servant. Sir Philip Sidney had been his patron, and he had made some reputation as a poet with 'The Shepheardes Calendar', a little book of pastoral poems, published in 1579, which were to change the course of English poetry.

Life had rather passed Spenser by since Ralegh had last seen him. He had lived for a while in Dublin, where he had moved in a small circle of English culture, but now he was intellectually isolated, in his little castle on a little hill in the depths of the Irish countryside, longing for some intelligent company and conversation. He was then at work on his great allegorical poem *The Faerie Queene*, with which he hoped to make his international reputation as a poet of the first rank. It was to have twelve books, and he was just completing the first three. He needed the criticism and comments of a fellow-poet of Ralegh's stature.

Spenser described the visit of 'the Shepherd of the Ocean' (as Ralegh poetically called himself) in his later poem *Colin Clouts Come Home Again*. Ralegh himself was writing poetry. But Ralegh's:

> . . . song was all a lamentable lay,
> Of great unkindnesse, and of usage hard,
> Of Cynthia the Ladie of the sea
> Which from her presence faultlesse him debard.

This may be a reference to an earlier version of Ralegh's long poem *The Ocean to Scinthia*. It certainly suggests that Ralegh was temporarily out of favour with the Queen ('Cynthia the lady of the sea').

Spenser must have waited anxiously for Ralegh to finish reading and give his opinion on *The Faerie Queene*. Ralegh's help and sponsorship at Court could make a great difference to Spenser's future. He need not have worried. Ralegh was delighted with the poem and suggested that Spenser go back with him to London. They sailed for England some time in October 1589.

The first three books of *The Faerie Queene* were published in January 1590. Ralegh contributed two commendatory verses. The first, *A Vision upon this Conceipt of the Faery Queene*, is one of the most mysterious and majestic sonnets in the language:

> Methought I saw the grave, where Laura lay,
> Within that Temple, where the vestall flame
> Was wont to burne, and passing by that way,
> To see that buried dust of living fame,
> Whose tumbe faire love, and fairer vertue kept,
> All suddeinly I saw the Faery Queene:
> At whose approch the soule of Petrarke wept,
> And from thenceforth those graces were not seene.
> For they this Queene attended, in whose steed
> Oblivion laid him downe on Lauras herse:
> Hereat the hardest stones were seene to bleed,
> And grones of buried ghostes the hevens did perse.
> Where Homers spright did tremble all for griefe,
> And curst th'accesse of that celestiall theife.

Spenser sent *The Faerie Queene* to make its way with no less than eighteen sonnets, dedicated to everyone he thought might assist his reputation, including Hatton, Burghley, the Earl of Oxford, Essex, Walsingham, Sir John Norris, Lord Grey, the Countess of Pembroke, Lord High Admiral Howard, and all the 'gratious and beautifull Ladies in the Court'. He repaid Ralegh's compliment with a sonnet to 'the right noble and valorous knight, Sir Walter Ralegh, Lo. Wardein of the Stanneryes, and lieftenaunt of Cornewaile' praising his poem to Cynthia.

On 11th June 1594, back in Ireland, Spenser married Elizabeth Boyle, a relative of Sir Richard Boyle, afterwards Earl of Cork. He celebrated his wedding, which took place at the bride's home at Kilcoran near Youghal, with perhaps the greatest of his shorter poems, *Epithalamion*. The next three books of *The Faerie Queene* were published in 1596. They contain what have been supposed to be references to the scandal which took Ralegh to the Tower in 1592. The two men may have kept up their friendship by correspondence, but there is no record of it. Kilcolman was sacked and burned to the ground in October 1598, during the Tyrone Rebellion. Spenser and his family escaped to Cork. In December he came to London with dispatches from Sir John Norris, Lord President of Munster. He died suddenly on 12th January 1599, the last six books of *The Faerie Queene* still unwritten. He was buried in Westminster Abbey.

Spenser mock-deprecated his 'rusticke Muse' when comparing himself with Ralegh, calling himself 'a simple silly Elfe', and indeed he never received in his lifetime the critical esteem he knew he really deserved. But he owed much to Ralegh's encouragement and sponsorship. Had Ralegh done nothing else in his life, he would still have earned his country-men's gratitude for the help he gave Edmund Spenser.

But Ralegh's most pressing preoccupation, in Ireland as in England, was not poetry but litigation. Like many Elizabethan gentlemen, he was constantly bedevilled by law-suits. It seemed there was another, earlier lease of Lismore Castle, held by Sir William Stanley who had sub-let to John Egerton and two others before going to serve in the Nether-lands with Leicester and, eventually, to desert to the Spanish side. Lady Stanley appealed to the Privy Council for the return of Lismore to Egerton. Their Lordships referred the case to Sir John Perrot, Lord Deputy in Ireland, but nothing had been settled by the time Perrot was succeeded by Sir William Fitzwilliam.

Sir William Fitzwilliam was a grumpy old soldier who disliked gilded popinjays of court favourites on principle as much as Lord Burghley did. Either the thought of Ralegh, or an actual meeting with him, rubbed Sir William the wrong way. In the matter of Lismore, and for years afterwards, he was ready to take the part of any side opposing Ralegh.

On this occasion, it was Sir William who lost. Ralegh's cousin, Sir George Carew, was Master of Ordnance in Ireland, and he visited Ralegh at Lismore Castle in September 1589. Ralegh asked him to look after some business for him, to pay for extensions to buildings at Lismore until Ralegh could send money from England; and he must also have discussed his wrangles with Fitzwilliam. After his return to England, he wrote to Carew on 27th December 1589. It is a most revealing letter, showing Ralegh at his most assured, absolutely confident that with the Queen on his side everything could be arranged to his satisfaction. He assumes that Fitzwilliam is opposing him because he fancies that Ralegh is out of favour at Court; he is quite wrong, and will soon discover his error. Fitzwilliam may be a powerful man in Ireland, but in England it is Ralegh who has the influence, that 'nireness to her Majestye' which is all important:

For my retrait from the Court it was uppon good cause to take order for my prize. If in Irlande they thincke that I am not worth the respectinge they shall mich deceave them sealvs. I am in place to be believed not inferior to any man, to plesure or displesure the greatest; and my oppinion is so receved and beleved as I can anger the best of them. And, therefore, if the Deputy be not as reddy to steed mee as I have bynn to defend hyme – be it att is may.

When Sir William Fitzwilliams shalbe in Ingland, I take mysealfe farr his better by the honorable offices I hold, as also by that nireness to her Majestye which still I injoy, and never more so.

For the sute of Lesmore, I will shortly send over order from the Queen for a dismis of their cavelacions.

The letter is the clearest statement of a favourite's position. He can pleasure or displeasure the greatest, because his opinion is received and believed. Perhaps there is the faintest note of unease. He still enjoys that nearness to Her Majesty, but adds 'never more so', as though to reassure his cousin that his position is not slipping.

Ralegh was right about the Queen's intervention. In April 1590 she wrote to Fitzwilliam commanding him to stay the suit which had been commenced until she signified her further pleasure on the subject. Nothing more was heard of it. Whatever the legal rights and wrongs of the case, the Queen had arbitrarily settled it. Fitzwilliam was understandably angry. But he bided his time. His chance would come.

In 1590 Ralegh was back in favour while, by the turn of the wheel of fortune at Elizabeth's Court, it was Essex who was in disgrace. Early in 1590 he secretly married young Frances Walsingham, Sir Philip Sidney's widow, and daughter of Sir Francis, who died in April. The Queen only learned of the marriage in the autumn when Frances's pregnancy made it impossible to conceal it any longer. As always, the Queen was unreasonably outraged and shocked that one of her courtiers should desert her for another woman.

Oddly enough it was at this time that Ralegh and Essex joined forces to fight the cause of the Puritan John Udall. It was one of the rare occasions when the two men acted in concert. Ralegh's efforts to intercede with the Queen on Udall's behalf show the other side to his nature, his resistance to intolerance and bigotry. Perhaps he saw in Udall's predicament some forewarning of the forces of hatred and darkness which were one day to strike at himself.

John Udall was a leading Puritan scholar, and author of the first Hebrew dictionary to be published in English. In his treatises and sermons he strenuously advocated Church reform. At last, in 1590, he went too far when he wrote of the Bishops that they 'cared for nothing but the maintenance of their dignities, be it the damnation of their own souls, and infinite millions more'. Because the Bishops governed the Church on the Queen's behalf, this was held to be an attack on the Queen, tantamount to treason. Udall was convicted of authorship of the words, which was unjustly taken to be equivalent to a felony. He was sentenced to death.

Ralegh had been impressed by the defendant's bearing at his trial, and the way in which he answered his accusers. He sent word to Udall, and asked him to write down a statement of his beliefs, so that he could show it to the Queen. Udall did so, asking 'that yet it would

Boldor. The flying fishe.

Flying fish, drawing by John White, 1585

Loggerhead turtle, drawing by John White, 1585

please Her Majesty – that the land may not be charged with my blood – to change my punishment from death to banishment'. Although the Bishops were pressing for punishment, Ralegh's intercession had the execution stayed. Udall was to be banished instead to Guinea, where he was to be a chaplain, under the guardianship of the Company of Turkey Merchants. But when it was decided that the Company should be responsible for his custody, until the Queen gave him licence to return to England, the stubborn Udall objected. The matter was still under discussion when Udall fell ill and died in his cell in the Marshalsea.

Ralegh had done his best for Udall, the Puritan. He also tried to do his best, according to his own beliefs, for the Catholic priest Oliver Plasden, who had been condemned to be hanged, drawn and quartered for treason. Ralegh was present at the gallows on 10th December 1591, in his official capacity as Captain of the Guard. Plasden was already in the cart, with the rope around his neck, when Ralegh heard him praying for the Queen and for the realm, and asked him if he acknowledged the Queen as his lawful sovereign. Plasden replied that he did, sincerely. The account of their conversation is from the testimony of another priest, Father James Young. In any case, the infamous torturer Topcliffe was there

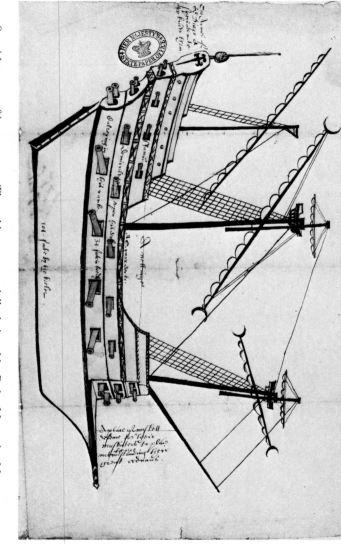

Spanish treasure frigate, c. 1590. These ships were specially designed by Pedro Menendez Marquez to carry treasure from the West Indies to Spain, along with some 150 men, soldiers and sailors. Her armament consists of culverins (18-pounders), demi-culverins (9-pounders) and falcons (3-pounders). Drawing sent home by an English spy

Sir John Hawkins in 1591 by Hieronymo Custodis. He reshaped English maritime strategy after the failure of the Lisbon expedition

ÆTATIS SVÆ LVIII
Anno Dñi 1591

to extract a fatal statement of faith from the young priest: 'I am a catholic priest, therefore I would never fight nor counsel others to fight against my religion, for that were to deny my faith.' Plasden looked up to the skies, and kissed the halter. 'O Christ, I will never deny thee for a thousand lives.'

At once, the crowd shouted that he was a traitor, the horses were whipped up and the cart drawn away. However, Ralegh allowed him to hang until he was dead, before the drawing and quartering was carried out.

Apart from his duties as Captain of the Guard, Ralegh had the cares of his offices in the West Country, and his estates and his household at Durham House to administer. He had his disputations with Hariot, his books, his pipes, and his conversation. They were busy days for him. As a later biographer David Lloyd wrote, 'Five hours he slept, four he read, two he discoursed; allowing the rest to his business and his necessities.'

There was also Virginia. John White was still agitating for relief to be sent out to his colony. In 1590 there was the threat of another Spanish naval attack, and another general ban on shipping movements was imposed in February. However, John White and William Sanderson suggested to Ralegh that he might try to have the ban lifted for ships going to relieve the Virginian colony. Virginia, once again, seems to have been regarded as a special case. Ralegh obtained the Queen's licence for three ships belonging to the privateering entrepreneur John Watts to sail. They were the *Hopewell*, of 140 tons, the *Little John*, and the *John Evangelist*. They could leave, provided they took White to Roanoke. One captain, Abraham Cocke in the *Hopewell*, took this literally, and would not embark any settlers or stores for the colony, only John White himself. (The ships were about to sail. There was no time to get in touch with Ralegh. John White had to agree.) However, Sanderson had fitted out another ship, the *Moonlight*, commanded by Edward Spicer, and she sailed with supplies for the colony later, catching up with the *Hopewell* off Cuba in July.

Cocke and his three ships sailed from Plymouth on 20th March 1590, and spent some months in the West Indies cruising and taking prizes, before anchoring off the old harbour of Port Ferdinando on 15th August. They saw what White called 'great smoke' rising from Roanoke which put him in hopes that some of the colony were still there. On 17th August White, Cocke and Spicer went in boats through the reef to Roanoke. Spicer's boat capsized, and he and six men were drowned. This so discouraged the rest of the sailors that Cocke and White had to work hard to persuade them to go on with the search for the colonists. That night a fire was seen, glowing through the tree-trunks on the island. They 'sounded with a trumpet a Call & afterwardes many familiar English tunes of Songs, and called to them friendly'. There was no reply. In the morning they landed at the place and found only grass and rotten trees burning. Going up a sandy bank, White saw the 'faire Romane letters' CRO carved on a tree. This was the secret token White had arranged with the colonists, that they should give some indication of where they had gone.

They came to the site of the houses built in 1587. They had been taken down, but the settlers had built a strong wooden fence, 'a high Palisado of great trees, with cortynes and flankers very Fort-like'. The bark had been removed from a post on the right-hand side and

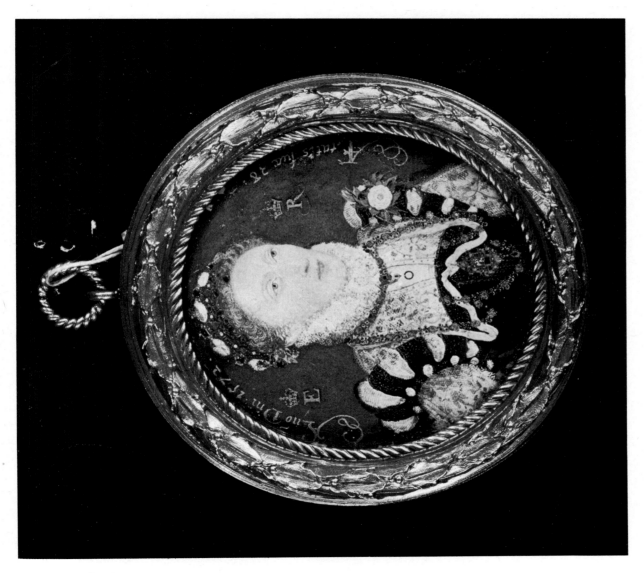

Elizabeth I, Ralegh's 'Cynthia, the Lady of the Sea'. Miniature by Nicholas Hilliard, 1572

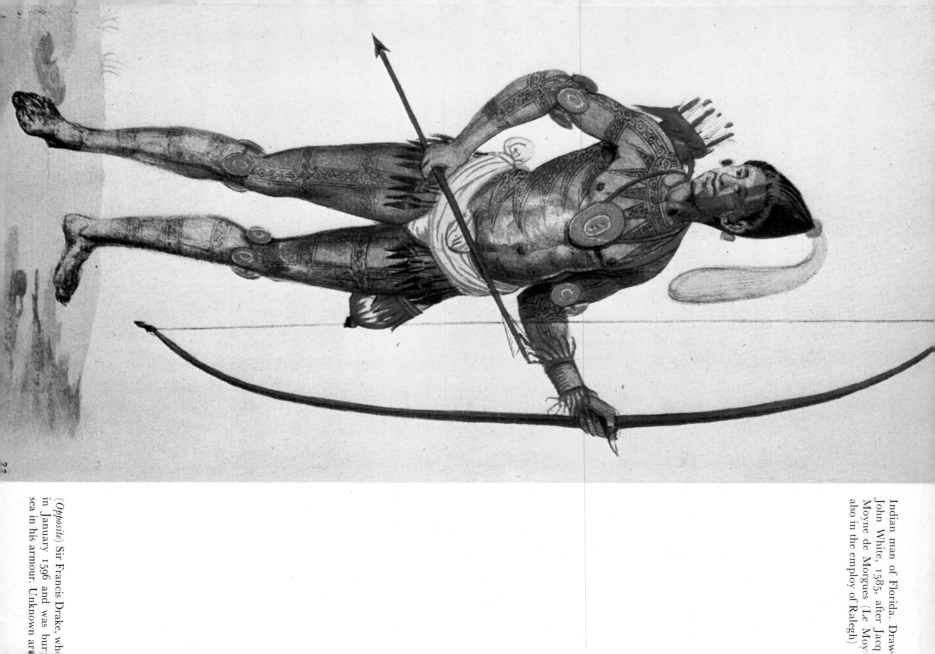

Indian man of Florida. Draw[n]
John White, 1585, after Jacq[ues]
Moyne de Morgues (Le Moy[ne]
also in the employ of Ralegh)

(*Opposite*) Sir Francis Drake, wh[o]
in January 1596 and was bur[ied]
sea in his armour. Unknown ar[tist]

carved on it 'in fayre Capitall letters' was CROATOAN. There was no carved cross, or any sign of distress. Inside, there were some bars of iron, and lead, four small cannon and some shot, all almost overgrown with grass and weeds. In a trench by a creek, dug by Philip Amadas two years before, they found five chests which had been broken into. Three of them were White's and he identified 'many of my things spoyled and broken, and my bookes torn from the covers, the frames of some of my pictures and Mappes rotten and spoyled with rayne, and my armour almost eaten through with rust'. It was dismal for White to have come so far after so long an interval, to find his own familiar belongings spoiled. None of the lost colonists was ever seen or heard of again.

Cocke had intended to go to search Croatoan, but the *Hopewell* lost all but one of her anchors in a storm and it was decided to sail for home. On 20th September they sighted and saluted the Queen's Fleet under Sir John Hawkins, then lying in wait off the Azores for the Spanish treasure *flota*. Finally, on 24th October, they 'came in safetie, God be thanked, to an anker at Plymouth'.

It was John White's last voyage. He moved to Ireland where he had a house at 'Newtowne in Kylmore'. The last record of him is a letter to Richard Hakluyt, from Newtowne, dated 4th February 1593, describing that last voyage. It is a philosophical letter, written by a man who seems to have come to terms with his disappointments. 'Yet seeing it is not my first crossed voyage, I remaine contented. And wanting my wishes, I leave off from prosecuting that whereunto I would to God my wealth were answerable to my will.'

It was left to Ralegh, as usual, to count up the costs of the expedition and to wrangle over shares and profits. The following year he joined John Watts's privateering syndicate. In October he was writing to Lord Burghley from Durham House complaining that the prizes they had seized did not amount to 'the increas of one for one, which is a small returne.' On the back of the letter are some figures in support of Ralegh's account. The value of the merchandise and bullion captured is estimated at £31,150. 'Wherout is to be deducted for the third of the mariners' part, £10,383; for my Lord his tenth, £3,015; for the Queen's customs, £1,600; in charges for bringing the goods, £1,200 = £16,198. Rests unto the owners and victuallers, to be divided amongst twelve, £14,952.'

Ralegh never forgot Virginia. In August 1602, he was writing to Cecil, 'I shall yet live to see it an Inglishe nation', and in 1603 he sent out yet another expedition under Bartholomew Gilbert; by the time it returned Ralegh himself was under attainder for high treason. Ralegh estimated that he spent some £40,000 of his own money on his voyages of exploration. It was a huge sum for his day, but it was not all lost, and not all of it was his. His colonies were only one of several of Ralegh's business enterprises, and he probably did not invest as much of his total resources in them as he implied. He, and the Queen, and every other investor, made the mistake of treating the new colonies solely as commercial undertakings, expecting them to show a quick financial profit. Nevertheless, Ralegh had shown the way, and in 1607 it was the English, not the Spanish, who set up the first permanent colony, on Chesapeake Bay.

8. *The* Revenge

FTER THE failure of the expedition of Drake and Norris to Lisbon, Drake retired
from active service, and the country's naval strategy was reshaped under Hawkins.
The policy of great offensive expeditions was dropped, temporarily; instead, the
ships of the Queen and of innumerable private volunteer gentlemen patrolled the seas
between the Azores and mainland Spain, looking out for the Spanish treasure *flota*, home-
coming from the Indies. A *flota* reached Spain early in 1590, but the continued activity of
Hawkins, Frobisher and the Earl of Cumberland off the Azores, and of John Watts off
Havana, frightened Philip into forbidding any further treasure fleets until the summer of
1592. By that time he knew, and the English knew, that a *flota* must sail, or the financial
underpinning of Spain's vast structure of conquest and alliance in Europe might collapse.

In January 1591 Ralegh was appointed Vice Admiral to Lord Thomas Howard, who was
to command a squadron of some twenty ships which were to ambush the Spanish treasure
fleet off the Azores that year. However, the Queen changed her mind and cancelled the
appointment. This may merely show that she had fully regained her old affection for
Ralegh and wished to keep him by her side, or there may have been some disagreement
between Ralegh and Howard.

Ralegh's place was taken, as before in 1585, by his cousin Sir Richard Grenville. But
Ralegh went on organizing and fitting out the expedition. He contributed his own ship the
Bark Ralegh, and victualled Grenville's flagship the *Revenge* of 450 tons. These, with five
other ships, were commanded by Howard in the *Defiance*, sailing from Plymouth in the
spring.

The force spent some four months off the Azores that summer. Though tied to the Queen's
side, Ralegh kept a watching brief for the expedition. In May he was sending a pinnace to
Howard to warn him of Spanish ships off the Scilly Islands.

At the end of August, Howard and Grenville were at Flores, one of the most westerly
islands of the Azores, with six Queen's ships, the *Bark Ralegh*, two or three pinnaces, and six
victuallers of London, lying at anchor. Many of their sailors were sick on shore, and most of
the ships were being cleaned and 'rummaged', having their old ballast removed and
replaced with new. English eyes looked to the west, where they hoped to sight the incoming
flota. But to the east, Don Alonzo de Bazan, the brother of the great Santa Cruz, was approaching the islands with a fleet of twenty warships, and a force of some 7,000. Spain had
recovered from the disaster of the Armada more quickly than the English suspected. She had
built new, faster and handier ships. She was, at last, employing the strategy of ocean convoy.
Don Alonzo's task was to escort the homeward *flota*, and if possible, to deal with Howard.

99

RICHARDVS GRENVILVS

Mil. aur.

Neptuni proles, qui magni Martis alumn
GRENVILVS patrias sanguine tinxit aquas

Howard, with five ships, sailed at once when the news of the Spanish fleet arrived. Grenville had ninety men sick and stayed to pick them up, 'disdaining' to leave them to the Spaniards. The delay lost him the wind and cost him his chance of escape. But he had had no intention of trying to escape. When advised by his sailing master to cut and run for it, he utterly refused. He would rather die than dishonour himself, his country, and her Majesty's ship. He would sail straight through the Spanish fleet and make them give way to him.

Even Ralegh thought this was rash. 'But the other course', he wrote tactfully, 'had been the better, and might right well have been answered in so great an impossibility of prevailing.' However, Sir Richard Grenville, 'out of the greatness of his mind, he could not be persuaded'.

The story of Sir Richard Grenville and the last fight of the *Revenge* at Flores in the Azores has become one of the most famous exploits in British naval history, and in Ralegh it found its proper chronicler. His 'A Report Of The Truth Of The fight about the Iles of Açores, this last Sommer' was published anonymously late in 1591. It was a best-seller. Hakluyt reprinted it, attributing its correct authorship, in 1599. The little pamphlet was Ralegh's first published work of prose, and it was a forerunner of things to come. It promised a new life for Ralegh, in his prose, after his Court death. The account is taken from first-hand, from two survivors of the *Revenge*'s own company, four more who were examined by Sir Francis Godolphin, and a Spanish captain who took part in the action and was later captured by the *Lion*. It is the very best kind of war reporting, taut, fast-moving, full of detail, and partisan:

The Spanish ships which attempted to board the *Revenge*, as they were wounded and beaten off, so always others came in their places, she having never less than two mighty Galleons by her sides, and aboard her: So that ere the morning, from three of the clocke the day before, there had fifteen several Armadas assailed her; and all so ill approved their entertainment, as they were by the break of day, far more willing to listen to a composition, than hastily to make any more assaults or entries. But as the day increased, so our men decreased: and as the light grew more and more, by so much grew our discomforts. For none appeared in sight but enemies, saving one small ship called the *Pilgrim*, commanded by Jacob Whiddon, who hovered all night to see the success: but in the morning bearing with the *Revenge*, was hunted like a hare amongst many ravenous hounds, but escaped.

All the powder of the *Revenge* to the last barrel was now spent, all her pikes broken, forty of her best men slain, and the most part of the rest hurt. In the beginning of the fight she had but one hundredth free from sickness, and fourscore and ten sick, laid in hold upon the Ballast. A small troop to man such a ship, and a weak garrison to resist so mighty an army. By those hundred all was sustained, the volleys, boardings, and enterings of fifteen ships of war, besides those which beat her at large. On the contrary, the Spanish were always supplied with soldiers brought from every squadron: all manner of Arms and powder at will. Unto ours there remained no comfort at all, no hope, no supply either of ships, men, or weapons; the Masts all beaten overboard, all her tackle cut asunder, her upper work altogether rased, and in effect evened she was with the water, but the very foundation or bottom of a ship, nothing being left

Richard Grenville from Holland's *Herωologia*, 1620

overhead either for flight or defence. Sir Richard finding himself in this distress, and unable any longer to make resistance, having endured in this fifteen hours fight, the assault of fifteen several Armadas all by turns aboard him, and by estimation eight hundred shot of great Artillery, besides many assaults and entries; and that himself and the ship must needs be possessed by the enemy, who were now cast in a ring round about him. The *Revenge* not able to move one way or other, but as she was moved with the waves and billow of the sea he commanded the Master gunner, whom he knew to be a most resolute man, to split and sink the ship; that thereby nothing might remain of glory or victory to the Spaniards: seeing in so many hours fight, and with so great a Navy they were not able to take her, having had fifteen hours time, above ten thousand men, and fifty and three sail of men of war to perform it withal: and persuaded the company, or as many as he could induce, to yield themselves to God, and to the mercy of none else; but as they had, like valiant resolute men, repulsed so many enemies, they should not now shorten the honour of their Nation, by prolonging their own lives for a few hours, or a few days.

Grenville was now badly wounded, and in a mad, fighting berserk fury. But to the *Revenge*'s master, enough was enough. Flatly disobeying Grenville's orders, he went across to Don Alonzo and arranged a truce. The lives of the crew were to be spared. They would be returned to England. Those who could would pay reasonable ransom. In the meantime they would not be imprisoned or pressed into the galleys. Grenville himself was carried across to the Spanish flagship, where he lived for another two or three days, an object of almost superstitious awe to the Spaniards, not the least because of his trick of crushing wineglasses with his teeth and then eating the fragments, while the blood ran out of his mouth.

Grenville died like a great gentleman, and with a dying speech which might be his own epitaph:

> Here die I Richard Grenville, with a joyful and quiet mind, for that I have ended my life as a true soldier ought to do, that fought for his country, Queen, religion and honour, whereby my soul most joyful departeth out of this body, and shall always leave behind it an everlasting fame of a valiant and true soldier that hath done his duty, as he was bound to do.

But even in his extremity, Grenville had words for those he thought had deserted him on the decks of the *Revenge*, when he went on, 'But the others of my company have done as traitors and dogs, for which they shall be reproached all their lives and leave a shameful name for ever.'

Grenville was talking about his own ship's company, but he could conceivably have been including Howard. Neither the Spanish nor the English commander came well out of the affair. In Spain, though there was general jubilation over the *Revenge* (the only English warship to be captured by the Spaniards during the whole war) there was also a feeling that Bazan should have made better use of his overwhelming superiority in numbers to destroy the whole of Howard's force. Howard was also criticized. He had, of course, been

Caca Fogo.

Caca Plata.

The *Golden Hind* capturing the Spanish treasure ship *Cacafuego* in the Pacific. From a drawing by
L. Hulsius, *c.* 1603

put in an impossible position. Had he followed Grenville's example, the Queen would have certainly lost six ships instead of one. And yet . . . he had sailed away, and left a subordinate to his fate. By October, everybody in London knew what had happened and on the 31st the decipherer and spy Thomas Phelippes was writing to another agent in Paris that 'Here they condemn the Lord Thomas infinitely for a coward and some say he is for the King of Spain. The quarrel and offer of combat between the Lord Admiral and Sir Walter Ralegh about the matter you are sure he hath heard of.'

Ralegh may have challenged Lord Howard. The Howards were not Ralegh's friends, then or ever. But in his 'Report of the Truth', Ralegh was extremely generous to Howard, and made it quite clear that he thought Howard's conduct was correct. Possibly, in trying to be magnanimous, Ralegh might have given even greater offence. Nothing would be calculated to annoy a proud family like the Howards more than someone like Ralegh putting in a good word for them.

The chief purpose of Ralegh's 'Report of the Truth' pamphlet was propaganda, against Spain. It was written in language violently and sarcastically anti-Spanish. The Spaniards had acted with great courtesy and honour towards Grenville himself, but their conduct otherwise had been despicable. They had broken their promise not to imprison the *Revenge*'s survivors but to send them home at once. The traitorous Irishman, Morrice Fitz-John of Desmond, had been allowed to try to persuade the English prisoners over to the cause of Spain. Ralegh painted a vivid picture of the fate of the Desmonds in Ireland, who had also given themselves to Spain. The Spaniards, wrote Ralegh, 'more greedily thirst after English blood, than after the lives of any other people of Europe'. Spanish greed was insatiable. If a country was of the reformed religion, they invaded it for religion's sake. If a country was Catholic, then they pretended the title to it. As if the Kings of Castile were the natural heirs of all the world! What had the Spaniards done in Sicily, in Naples, Milan, and in the Low Countries? They had not spared anyone for religion's sake there. If any English Catholic wanted an example, he need only look at what Spain had done to Portugal. In one island, Hispaniola, they had killed thirty hundred thousand of the natural people, 'a poor and harmless people created of God'. Spain, Ralegh wrote, wanted nothing less than to 'bewitch us from the obedience of our natural Prince, thereby hoping in time to bring us to slavery and subjection'.

It was a powerful diatribe, and it fitted the role in the Elizabethan public's eye which Ralegh was just beginning to assume. He himself was becoming the very symbol of resistance to Spain. Drake was in retirement. Leicester and Walsingham were dead. But Ralegh was still there, by the Queen's side, and in time people were coming to look to him for a lead against Spain. He seemed to embody the resistance of the Queen's people to slavery. He was the Queen's good right arm against the Holy See. Ironically, this was one role Ralegh never seems to have sought. He achieved his great reputation as a patriot unconsciously.

In the New Year of 1592 there were fresh rumours about Spanish intentions. It was said that Lord Howard's foray to the Azores had provoked Philip to retaliate, that he was preparing a new fleet of sixty ships, that another Armada was on the way. Once more, invasion scares swept the country. In England, a counter-stroke was planned, against the

Spanish treasure fleets off Panama. It was, as usual, a private-enterprise undertaking. Ralegh had the chief share of mounting it. On 28th February 1592 the Queen granted him a commission empowering him to levy 2,000 men, apply martial law and punishment of death, authorizing him to act by sea or land, 'on continents or islands', and permitting him to take up at sea all ships he found necessary. He could join in partnership with others and enjoy all plunder, after the payment of customs, if before distribution 'allowance be made to Us of all parts due to Us according to the tonnage of our own ships'.

The Queen later tried to evade this last condition, just as she tried to wriggle out of her commitment to pay a share of the mariners' wages. On 10th March Ralegh was writing to Cecil from Chatham, where he had gone to make preparations for the voyage, 'If it fall not out well, I can but lose all, and if nothinge be remayning, wherewith shall I pay the wages? Besides, her Majestie told mee herself that shee was contented to paye her part, and my Lord Admirall his, and I should but discharge for myne own shipps.' Ralegh was financially committed up to the hilt, having invested some £34,000, which he said was all he had, and which included about £11,000 he had borrowed. There is a rather shrill note of grievance in his writings about his own investment. 'I pray consider that I have layd all that I am worth, and must do, ere I depart on this voyage,' he wrote to Cecil. Months later, he was insisting to Lord Burghley that 'I protest, before the living God, both my three years' pension of the Custom-house – which was £6,000 – and all I have besides is in this journey.'

In the event, the Queen invested £1,800 and provided two ships, the *Garland* and the *Foresight*. Ralegh himself provided the *Roebuck*, commanded by the Vice-Admiral Sir John Borough, who signed himself 'Burgh', and Carew Ralegh provided the *Galleon Ralegh*, of 250 tons. The City of London ventured £6,000 and the Earl of Cumberland, the indefatigable adventurer, fitted out six ships of his own and had a total investment of £19,000. Ralegh himself, it seemed, was to command, in the *Garland*.

The expedition, of some fifteen or sixteen ships, was delayed for weeks by contrary winds. Eventually, according to the account in Hakluyt, the Queen herself became concerned about the delay 'and withall, her Majesty understanding how crossly all this sorted, began to call the proceeding of this preparation into question.' Ralegh was desperate to get away. At any moment the Queen might change her mind and forbid him to go.

At last, on 6th May, they were off. But only a day later Sir Martin Frobisher caught them up in the Lord Admiral's pinnace *Disdain*. He had instructions from the Queen for Ralegh to return to London.

It has been suggested that this was the moment when the Queen struck, having at last discovered her favourite's infidelity to her. But Ralegh was still at large and unmolested, carrying on his normal business affairs, for some weeks after his return to London. It is more likely that Ralegh never intended to complete the whole voyage himself. Frobisher's arrival seems to have been arranged beforehand. In that letter in March to Cecil, Ralegh wrote, 'And farther, I have promised her Majestie that, if I can perswade the Cumpanies to follow Sir Marten Furbresher, I will without fail returne; and bring them but into the sea but sume fifty or thriscore leagues, for which purpose my Lord Admirall hath lent me the

Sir Walter Ralegh in 1588 at the height of his fame and fortune, when he was 'the best hated man, in court, city and country'. Portrait attributed to the monogrammist 'H'

Disdayne.' Frobisher was a notorious martinet, unpopular with officers and ships' companies. Had it been known he was to command, it might well have been much more difficult to man the ships.

For all his reputation as a seaman and an adventurer, Ralegh disliked sea voyaging. It is possible that he was actually a poor sailor, who suffered acutely from sea-sickness. He travelled in some style, with his 'trunke' full of books, his fine cabin-bed with furniture of green silk and legs carved like dolphins, gilt with gold, his meals eaten off silver plate to the accompaniment of music. But Elizabethan sea travel was still, in a word, squalid, and after his return from Guiana he wrote, 'I am not so much in love with these long voyages.' Aubrey, too, has an odd little comment which may have some significance: 'I have heard old major Cosh say that Sir W. Raleigh did not care to go on the Thames in a wherry boat: he would rather go round about over London Bridge.'

On this occasion he may have been ready to return, but he interpreted the Queen's letters as giving him discretion to stay with the expedition, at least until they reached Cape Finisterre. There, the plan to attack Panama was dropped, because it was too late in the year. Ralegh split his fleet into two. Half, under Frobisher, stayed off the Spanish coast. The rest, under Borough, went to the Azores. They had captured a Spanish ship with an Englishman on board, Neville Davis, who had been a prisoner of Spain for twelve years. He said that there would be no treasure fleets that year. However, Ralegh gave directions that Frobisher would lie off the Spanish coast, 'thereby to amaze the Spanish fleet', while Borough waited for Spanish ships coming from Mexico or the West Indies. After surviving 'a tempest of strange and uncouth violence' on 11th May Ralegh went back to England, where a violent storm of another sort was already brewing.

9. Marriage and Disgrace

WHAT EXACTLY happened in that summer of 1592 when Sir Walter Ralegh was disgraced and dismissed the Court will probably never now be known. In January he was still high in favour. The Queen was, in fact, then arranging to transfer to him the lease of a property he coveted, Sherborne Castle in Dorset. He returned to England from his sea voyage on or about 16th May. On the 23rd Lord Burghley and the Lord Admiral were writing to tell him that the Queen approved his change of plan. In June he was still living at Durham House, carrying out his normal business affairs, as though nothing were amiss. But by the end of July or, at the very latest, August, he was in the Tower of London, his career as a Court favourite at an end. Elizabeth Throckmorton, the lady who was almost certainly the cause of his downfall, was also imprisoned in the Tower at the same time.

With so much in his favour, his swarthy good looks, his wit, his passionate poems, his extravagant clothes, his wealth and his flamboyant life-style, and his reputation as a swords-man and soldier and adventurer, Ralegh must have had a glamour which made him attractive to women. But he does not seem to have been at all a ladies' man. He was a courtier for more than ten years, the last five of them as Captain of the Guard, and he had the means of meeting every girl who came to Court. Yet there was never any gossip linking his name with any woman. In his 'Instructions to His Son', written many years later, he is decidedly cool towards the female sex. He advises his son not to be taken in by a pretty face and to take care that 'thou be beloved of thy wife, rather than thyself besotted on her'. He advises leaving most of an estate to the children, and only to the widow enough to live on, and only then for the period of her widowhood. 'Let her not enjoy her second love in the same bed wherein she loved thee, nor fly to future pleasures with those feathers which death hath pulled from thy wings.' These were the prudent, elder thoughts of a man who protested such profligate love for the Queen when he was young.

Ralegh seems not to have been much interested in women. In his *Apophthegms*, Francis Bacon repeats a catty little story that 'Sir Walter Ralegh was wont to say of the ladies of Queen Elizabeth's privy-chamber and bed-chamber: That they were like witches; they could do hurt, but they could do no good.' However, at least one of Her Majesty's ladies appealed to him, and she was not the one anybody would have expected. Elizabeth Throck-morton was not the girl likely to capture Sir Walter Ralegh. She was no heiress, and no great beauty. She was twenty-seven, well on the shelf by Elizabethan standards. Her portrait shows a fair-haired, blue-eyed, nice girl, with a pleasant face and figure. 'Homely' is the word that springs to mind. Yet it seems that, for love of her, Ralegh willingly jeopardized

his Court career. The two stuck by each other in the years to come. Their marriage was a resounding success.

Elizabeth's father was Sir Nicholas Throckmorton, of Coughton in Warwickshire, who had been a favourite of Edward VI, but who had become involved in Wyatt's Rebellion under Mary. He had defended himself and actually got himself acquitted of a charge of treason. Later, he was Queen Elizabeth's ambassador to the Court of France. Sir Nicholas's was a typical Throckmorton career. They were a large family, with relatives all over the country, and they had their ups and downs. Elizabeth was the only girl of seven children. She was particularly close to her second brother Arthur, who became a friend of Sir Walter's. Sir Nicholas died in 1571 when his daughter was six years old (she was baptized at Beddington, Surrey, on 16th April 1565, and she would almost certainly have been only a few days old when she was baptized). She was left £500 in her father's will for the period of her minority. In February 1572 her mother lent the money to the Earl of Huntingdon. It was never returned. Many years later, Ralegh's relatives were still trying to get it back.

Arthur Throckmorton kept a diary, in which he recorded that his sister was 'sworn of the Privy Chamber' on 8th November 1584. This was a very good chance for Elizabeth. For a fatherless, dowry-less young girl, a position at Court was about her only way of making a good marriage. On 1st January 1589 Elizabeth Throckmorton's name appears on a list of those who gave the Queen a New Year present. She gave 'two ruffs of lawn cut-work made' and received in return 'in gilt plate 15 oz. 3 qrs.'. She probably met Ralegh in his earliest years at Court, but of their courtship nothing is known, except two of his poems, which are believed to have been written in honour of 'Serena', which was supposed to have been Lady Ralegh's allegorical title. One of them is entitled 'To his Love when hee had obtained Her.' It is possibly the nearest Ralegh ever came to an explicitly sexual poem:

> Now Serena bee not coy;
> Since wee freely may enjoy
> Sweete imbraces: such delights,
> As will shorten tedious nightes.
> Thinke that beauty will not stay
> With you allwaies; but away;
> And that tyrannizing face
> That now holdes such perfect grace,
> Will both chaing'd and ruined bee;
> So fraile is all thinges aswee see,
> So subject unto conquering Time.
> Then gather Flowers in theire prime,
> Let them not fall and perish so;
> Nature her bountyes did bestow
> On us that wee might use them: And
> Tis coldnesse not to understand

Sir Nicholas Throckmorton, Ralegh's father-in-law, one of the very few Tudor men ever to be acquitted of a charge of treason. Artist unknown

What shee and Youth and Forme perswade
With Oppertunety, that's made
As we could wish itt. Lett's then meete
Often with amorous lippes, and greet
Each other till our wantonne Kisses
In number passe and dayes Ulisses
Consum'd in travaile, and the starrs
That looke upon our peaceful warrs
With envious lustere. If this store
Will not suffice, wee'le number o're
The same againe, untill wee finde,
No number left to call to minde
    And shew our plenty. They are poore
    That can count all they have and more.

It is a poem which in content and feeling looks back to Catullus and forward to the Metaphysical poets of the next century.

A delightfully coarse anecdote in Aubrey gives almost the only glimpse anywhere of Ralegh in any sexual activity. 'He loved a wench well: and one time getting up one of the mayds of honour against a tree in a wood ('twas his first lady) who seemed at first boarding to be something fearful of her Honour, and modest, she cryed Sweet Sir Walter, what do you me ask? Will you undoe me? Nay, sweet Sir Walter! Sweet Sir Walter! Sir Walter! At last, as the danger and the pleasure at the same time grew higher, she cried in the extacey Swisser Swatter! Swisser Swatter! She proved with child and I doubt not but this hero tooke care of them both, as also that the product was more then an ordinary mortall.'

In his anecdotal way, Aubrey was quite right. Sir Walter did get Elizabeth Throckmorton with child, although it is not clear whether in or out of wedlock. The lawsuit over her inheritance gives one clue about their date of marriage. One of the depositions states that 'on 20th day of February in the thirtieth year of the reign of Queen Elizabeth, or thereabouts, the aforesaid Elizabeth Throckmorton accepted as her man Walter Ralegh, knight.' This gives the wedding the incredible date of 20th February 1588, and means, if true, that Bess Throckmorton and Walter Ralegh, in the hot-house gossip atmosphere of the Court, concealed for four years their marriage, a pregnancy and confinement.

The year may be wrong, although the day and month may be correct. The documents quoted are dated some thirty years after the events they describe. A member of the Throckmorton or Ralegh families might remember the day and the month clearly but be mistaken about the exact year, after such a passage of time. The date of the marriage might be 20th February 1591. It does not seem part of Bess Throckmorton's character to permit intercourse before marriage, and by June of that year she was pregnant. On 19th November Arthur wrote of his sister's marriage in his diary and on the 30th, as a proper elder brother should, he had 'an interview' with Ralegh. It was by then perhaps too late to ask Sir Walter whether his intentions towards Bess were honourable.

The episode of Serena and the Blatant Beast in Book VI of *The Faerie Queene* has been taken to refer to Elizabeth Throckmorton and her 'Squire', Walter Ralegh. Serena and her squire have been badly hurt by that beast of scandal and ask a 'Hermite' for advice on what they should do.

> The best (sayd he) that I can you advize,
> Is to avoide the occasion of the ill :
> For when the cause, whence evill doth arize,
> Removed is, th'effect surceaseth still.
> Abstaine from pleasure, and restraine your will,
> Subdue desire, and bridle loose delight,
> Use scanted diet, and forbeare your fill,
> Shun secresie, and talke in open sight :
> So shall you soone repaire your present evill plight.

The advice was sound but by the year 1592 the murmurs of scandal were growing. On 24th February Arthur Throckmorton wrote urgently to Ralegh at Chatham, where he was gathering ships and men for his Panama expedition, and four days later Bess came to stay at her brother's house at Mile End, on the outskirts of London. It seems scarcely credible that a lady of the Privy Chamber, a woman well-known to the Queen and intimate with her, could travel about London in an advanced state of pregnancy without any inkling of her situation reaching the Queen's ears, but this seems to have been the case. The murmurs of scandal were growing louder, for in that letter to Cecil from Chatham on 10th March, Ralegh wrote that much-studied denial of his wife :

> I mean not to cume away, as they say I will, for feare of a marriage, and I know not what. If any such thing weare, I would have imparted it unto yoursealf before any man livinge; and, therefore, I pray believe it not, and I beseech you to suppress, what you can any such mallicious report. For I protest before God, ther is none, on the face of the yearth, that I would be fastned unto.

There seems little doubt that this letter was a flat lie, made up by Ralegh in a moment of desperation when he was afraid that scandal might cause his voyage to Panama to be cancelled.

Arthur wrote the sensational entry for 29th March 1592 in his diary 'My sister was delyvered of a boye betwene 2 and 3 in the afternowne. I wrytte to syr Walter Rayley, and sent Dycke the footmane to whom I gave hym 10s.' On 10th April he had another entry, just as sensational. 'Damerei Raelly was baptysed by Robert Earlle of Essexes (sic) and Arth. Throkemorton and Anna Throkemorton' [Arthur's wife].

Of all the mysteries in Ralegh's mysterious private life at this time, the part of Essex is the most baffling. Again, it seems scarcely credible that Ralegh should ask his chief rival and enemy at Court to stand godfather to his child – and just as incredible that Essex should agree. It is hardly possible that Essex would refrain from telling the Queen. Here was Sir Walter Ralegh, Knight, Captain of Her Majesty's Guard, Lord Warden of the Stannarys etc., with a secret marriage, or if he were not married, with a bastard child sired on one of Her Majesty's ladies of the Privy Chamber. Apart from any future advantage to be gained by Essex at Court from this situation, it made the most riveting personal gossip. There was a further point: if Essex actively took a part and then remained silent, he connived at deceiving the Queen.

It is more than probable that Essex did tell the Queen. She was now an old lady, and she brooded over her injury for a time, playing cat and mouse with the Raleghs, while she decided when and how to strike. Meanwhile, the Raleghs went on as though nothing had happened, thus adding insult to injury. On 27th April Damerei was put out to nurse with Throckmorton relatives at Enfield, while Bess calmly returned to Court. It seems amazing that she was able to give any convincing excuse for her absence. Bess Throckmorton had sworn to be faithful to the Queen. By returning to Court and saying nothing, she was now deliberately and directly deceiving the Queen. It was probably for this that she was never forgiven and never readmitted to Court.

On 6th May Ralegh sailed, 'set himself under sail at Falmouth towards the Indies' as Arthur wrote in the diary. His intrigue with Bess Throckmorton must by now have been an open secret in London. There seems to have been a slight but noticeable withdrawal of polite society from Ralegh's company, as though people did not want to be associated too closely with a man who was so soon to be disgraced. Many years later, Adrian Gilbert claimed in a Chancery Case what he had spent 'at Mile End and about London when the Lady Ralegh was first delivered of a child, and when most of Sir Walter's friends forsook him, being requested by the said Walter Ralegh to visit her'. This ostracism, if it ever amounted to so much, was short-lived. In later years Bess Throckmorton was always treated by everybody (except the reigning sovereign) with the greatest respect and consideration, as Sir Walter's wife.

Ralegh was back in England again on 16th May. On that day Arthur noted 'Browne came from Sir Walter hither.' Three days later, he 'paid the nurse 14 weeks wages come Monday next, 28s. ('Fourteen weeks' dates the engagement of the nurse at some time in the middle of February, just before Bess came to stay at Arthur's house.) The same day, 19th May, 'Browne and Sir George Carew came to have me seal the writings between Sir W. Ralegh and Eliz.' This was obviously the marriage settlement.

In May nurse and child were still being ferried about London with little attempt at concealment. On 21st May they were at Mile End. A week later they were at Durham House. By this time, the Queen *must* have known. On 31st May Ralegh was committed to the custody of Sir Robert Cecil. This was in no way imprisonment, but was more of a caution. It was oddly insensitive, and very foolish, of Ralegh that at no time does he appear to have gone to see the Queen, to explain himself, or to try to excuse himself. Perhaps he thought no explanations were necessary, or that they would avail him nothing. Neither he nor Bess Throckmorton ever seems to have taken the Queen's feelings into account.

Queen Elizabeth I, attributed to Marcus Gheeraerts the Younger – The Rainbow Portrait

SOLE

But *still* the blow did not fall. On 2nd June Ralegh was at Durham House, where Arthur Throckmorton visited him that day. The next day Bess Throckmorton was committed to the custody of the Vice-Chamberlain, Sir Thomas Heneage. Even now, Ralegh made no attempt to placate the Queen. His pride had made him stupid, or he may have believed, typically, that putting a bold face on it would carry him through. On the 8th he was writing to the Lord High Admiral from Durham House, defending the actions of his ships, including the *Roebuck*, against the accusations of certain merchants of Middleburgh. Ralegh's ships (from his Panama expedition) had engaged a fleet of thirteen Flemish ships off Cape Finis-terre on 13th May. Those that hove to and behaved respectfully he dismissed 'and suffered not the valew of a farthinge to be taken from any of them'. But the others had acted suspiciously and made it plain to Ralegh that their money 'belonged to thos of Anwerpe who dayly fraight shipps of Zelande for the trade of Spayne, to abuse Her Majestye'. It is not the letter of a shamefaced man, aware that he is about to be dismissed. On the contrary, it is Ralegh at his most confident, absolutely assured of his own rights and rightness, scornful of those who run away.

He was confined to Durham House, in the care of his cousin Sir George Carew, and now, at last, he seems to have had an inkling of what awaited him. Another relative, Arthur Gorges, went to call on him and later in a letter of 26th July described to Cecil what had happened. Ralegh had been standing at the window of his turret study, gazing and sighing at the bustle of boats and barges he could see down-river at Blackfriars Steps, when 'suddenly he brake out into a great distemper, and sware that his enemies had of purpose brought her Majesty thither, to break his gall sunder with Tantalus' torment'.

It was a preposterous suggestion, but Ralegh began to work himself up into a rage and 'as a man transported with passion, he sware to Sir George Carew that he would disguise himself and get into a pair of oars to ease his mind with but a sight of the Queen; or else he protested his heart would break'.

Sir George, of course, refused to let him do any such thing, whereupon they 'fell out to choleric outrageous words, with striving and struggling at the doors'. Sir George had his new periwig torn off his head.

Gorges had not taken this unseemly scuffling seriously, but now he saw that Ralegh's self-induced rage had become genuine. 'At last they had gotten out their daggers which when I saw I played the stickler between them, and so purchased such a rap on the knuckles that I wished both their pates broken. And so with much ado they stayed their brawl to see my bloodied fingers.' Gorges, also a poet, writes vividly of the scene and his Mercutio-like intervention. 'At the first, I was ready to break with laughing to see the two scramble and brawl like madmen, until I saw the iron walking, and then I did my best to appease the fury.'

'Good sir,' Arthur Gorges concluded, 'let nobody know thereof, for I fear Sir W. Ralegh will shortly grow to be Orlando Furioso if the bright Angelica persevere against him a little longer.' But Gorges perhaps spoiled his effect with an ingenuous little postscript: 'I could wish her Majesty knew.'

The Tower of London, where Ralegh was sent after his disgrace in 1592 – the first of his three visits there. Engraving by Wenceslaus Hollar

The Queen would have taken the point of the reference to Orlando Furioso, lately translated at her request by Sir John Harington, had Cecil ever shown the letter to her, which is debatable. But in any case it was now far too late for fine literary touches. It was common knowledge that Sir Walter Ralegh was bound for the Tower of London. On 30th July Sir Edward Stafford wrote to Anthony Bacon, another of the Essex faction, 'If you have anything to do with Sir Walter Ralegh, or any love to make to Mrs Throckmorton, at the Tower tomorrow you may speak with them; if the countermand comes not tonight, as some think will not be, and particularly he that hath charge to send them thither.' On 7th August 1592, Arthur Throckmorton recorded in his diary, 'Ma soeur s'en alla a la Tour, et Sir W. Raelly.'

The dates of Ralegh's imprisonment given by Stafford and Throckmorton are difficult to reconcile with other evidence. It is very probable that Ralegh was sent to the Tower much earlier than the end of July. In his letters to Cecil, marked 'from the Tower, July', he refers to events such as the Burke uprising in Ireland, which began on 2nd July. He is also concerned that Sir William Fitzwilliam, having heard of his downfall, is scheming against him. It would have taken some days for news of his disgrace to travel to Ireland, and for Ralegh to receive news back of Fitzwilliam's reactions. But perhaps the precise date on which his incarceration began is not so important. Of much more importance is the fact that Ralegh knew, Essex knew, everyone knew, that an era at Court had ended.

Ralegh's offence is nowhere defined. There were no formal charges, no hearings, and no evidence. His was a domestic Court misdemeanour, punished domestically. Nobody disputed the Queen's right to imprison her favourite without trial, and keep him in the Tower for as long as she liked; he was confined, literally, at the Queen's pleasure. A contemporary reference to Ralegh's offence is in Camden's *Annales* for the year 1595: 'Walter Ralegh, Captain of the Queen's Guards, for defiling the honour of a lady of the Queen (whom he afterwards led in marriage) dismissed from favour and kept in prison for many months, is now set free but banished from the Court.' In September of that year, writing to Heneage about Ralegh, Cecil said that he found 'him marvellously greedy to do anything to recover the conceit of his *brutish offence*'. This seems strong language. Ralegh had behaved no more brutishly than other courtiers. He himself in his letters writes of 'his disgraces' but in a letter to the Lord Admiral, probably written in August, he permits himself one sarcastic flash: 'it is more profitable to punishe *my great treasons*, then that I should ether strengthen the fleet, or do many other things that lye in the diches.'

It has been suggested that Ralegh's crime was somehow darker and deeper, perhaps even a treason against the State. That part of Camden's *Annales* referring to it was not published until 1627, long after Ralegh's execution; but Lady Ralegh survived him by many years and died, a very old lady, in 1647. She could have refuted Camden's account if she had thought it incorrect. The most likely solution is the simplest. Ralegh secretly married one of the Queen's ladies and afterwards tried to conceal it. For that, the Queen regularly imprisoned her favourites and banished their wives from Court.

Ralegh was confined in the Brick Tower, under the charge of Sir George Carew. His quarters were on the inland side of the fortress and had no view of the river and its passing traffic, but his imprisonment was not particularly rigorous. His friends could still visit him, more or less as they pleased. He had his own servants who lodged in rooms above his own. He carried on his business affairs, by deputy, messenger, and letter.

His letters to Cecil in July give some idea of Ralegh's state of mind and business preoccupations in the Tower. In Ireland Fitzwilliam had taken advantage of his adversary's disgrace and was putting pressure on Ralegh's tenants. He claimed that Ralegh had not paid his Undertaker's rent of four hundred pounds, and he seized five hundred 'milch kine' from the poor tenants in lieu. Ralegh protested – and quite truthfully – that the debt, of only fifty marks, had been paid, and that he was the only English Undertaker who had so far paid anything at all in rent. He warned that harassing the English settlers in Ireland would only weaken the Queen's position there and encourage Irish rebels. In another letter he asks for news and says that he forecast the Burke rebellion, but the Queen 'made a scorn' at his 'conceat'. 'But yow shall find it,' he goes on, prophetically, 'but a shoure of a farther tempest.' In this letter Ralegh shows that he is feeling sorry for himself. 'So I leve to trouble yow at this time, being become like a fish cast on dry land, gasping for breath, with lame leggs and lamer loongs.' This was the first reference to his ailments. The Thames damp was getting into his bones and his lungs. In the future, he suffered greatly from the ague.

Although he was banned from the Queen's physical presence, Ralegh was still officially Captain of the Guard and carried on his duties through deputies. It was under cover of these duties that he tried to appeal to the Queen's emotions and her memories of times past. The letter was, again, to Cecil, from the Tower, in July 1592:

> I pray be a mean to Her Majesty for the signing of the bills for the Gards' coats, which are to be made now for the Prograsse, and which the Cleark of the Cheeck hath importunde me to write for.
>
> My heart was never broken till this day, that I hear the Queen goes away so far of – whom I have followed so many years with so great love and desire, in so many journeys, and am now left behind her, in a dark prison all alone. While she was yet nire at hand, that I might hear of her once in two or three dayes, my sorrows were the less: but even now my heart is cast into the depth of all misery. I that was wont to behold her riding like Alexander, hunting like Diana, walking like Venus, the gentle wind blowing her fair hair about her pure cheeks, like a nymph; sometime siting in the shade like a Goddess; sometime singing like an angell; sometime playing like Orpheus. Behold the sorrow of this world! Once amiss, hath bereaved me of all. O Glory, that only shineth in misfortune, what is becum of thy assistance? All wounds have skares, but that of fantasie; all affections their relenting, but that of womankind. Who is the judge of friendship, but adversity? or when is grace witnessed, but in offences? There were no divinety, but by reason of compassion; for revenges are brutish and mortall. All those times past – the loves, the sythes, the sorrows, the desires, can they not way down one frail misfortune? Cannot one dropp of gall be hidden in so great heaps of sweetness? I may then conclude, *Spes et fortuna valete* [Farewell, hopes and fortune]. She is gone, in whom I trusted, and of me hath not one thought of mercy, nor any respect of that that was. Do with me now, therefore, what you list. I am more weary of life then they are desirous I should perish; which if it had been for her, as it is by her, I had been too happily born.

Ralegh signs himself 'Your's, not worthy any name or title'.

But even this appeal, eloquent almost to the point of being over-written, did not touch the Queen. Evidently, she did not agree that Ralegh's fault was just 'one frail misfortune' nor only one drop of gall hidden in heaps of sweetness. Or perhaps Cecil never showed the letter to the Queen, as Ralegh hoped he would.

In prison Ralegh's proud and volatile spirit soared up one day, sank down the next. He was cheerful and then gloomy, optimistic and then downcast, by turns. At times he was defiant, scorning everybody and defying them to do their worst. One of his finest poems is a superbly sustained piece of invective against the City, the Court and the world. It was no wonder he was the 'best hated man'. The poem gains in effect from its rhetorical repetitions until it pours over the reader, like some of Ralegh's prose, in a great irresistible wave. Called 'The Lie', the poem shows Ralegh *de contemptu mundi*, Ralegh *contra mundum*:

> Goe soule the bodies guest
>   upon a thankelesse arrant,
> Feare not to touch the best
>   the truth shall be thy warrant:
> Goe since I needs must die,
>   and give the world the lie.
>
> Say to the Court it glowes,
>   and shines like rotten wood,
> Say to the Church it showes
>   whats good, and doth no good.
> If Church and Court reply,
>   then give them both the lie.
>
> Tell Potentates they live
>   acting by others action,
> Not loved unlesse they give,
>   not strong but by affection.
> If potentates reply,
>   give Potentates the lie.
>
> Tell men of high condition,
>   that mannage the estate,
> Their purpose is ambition,
>   their practise onely hate:
> And if they once reply,
>   then give them all the lie.
>
> Tell them that brave it most,
>   they beg for more by spending,
> Who in their greatest cost
>   seek nothing but commending.
> And if they make replie,
>   then give them all the lie.
>
> Tell zeale it wants devotion
>   tell love it is but lust
> Tell time it meets but motion,
>   tell flesh it is but dust.
> And wish them not replie
>   for thou must give the lie.

Tell faith its fled the Citie,
    tell how the country erreth,
Tell manhood shakes off pittie,
    tell vertue least preferreth
And if they doe reply,
    spare not to give the lie.

So when thou hast as I
    commanded thee, done blabbing,
Although to give the lie,
    deserves no less than stabbing,
Stab at thee he that will,
    no stab thy soule can kill.

There were not many left unscathed by that, and the poem understandably aroused a good deal of contemporary resentment. Some were even provoked to composing replies to 'The Lie'. One of these began:

Go Eccho of the minde,
A careles troth protest;
Make answere that rude Rawly
No stomack can digest.

Ralegh might be kept in the Tower, but his ships were still sailing the seas, and his agents passing from country to country. He wrote to the Lord High Admiral about the affairs of the Navy, and mentioned 'a man of mine cumminge from the coast of Britayne'; there was also a captain of Ralegh's, John Floyer, and the controversy over the ship of Bayonne which he had taken as a prize. But as the days in the Tower lengthened into weeks, Ralegh slowly began to realize that his former place at Court was irretrievably lost. Pacing his room like one of the Tower lions the visitors came to see, he knew that, incredibly, life at Court and in the country was going on without him. Sometimes he despaired and said that he might as well be fed to the lions, and save everybody further trouble. At other times he was resigned, and told the Lord Admiral not to intercede for him with the Queen any more. It was doing more harm than good.

Physically, apart from the Thames dampness, Ralegh's captivity was not uncomfortable. His privation was in the mind. As he said, 'the torment of the mind cannot be greater.' Frustration is a powerful source of energy, and he expressed the melancholy which was always ready to overtake him in one of the most sombre poems ever written from inside a prison cell:

My boddy in the walls captived
Feels not the wounds of spightfull envy,
Butt my thralde mind, of liberty deprived,
Fast fettered in her antient memory,

Douth nought beholde butt sorrowes diinge face:
Such prison earst was so delightfull
As it desirde no other dwellinge place,
Butt tymes effects, and destinies dispightfull
Have changed both my keeper and my fare,
Loves fire, and bewties light I then had store,
Butt now close keipt, as captives wounted are,
That food, that heat, that light I finde no more,
    Dyspaire bolts up my dores, and I alone
    Speake to dead walls, butt thos heare not my mone.

Lady Ralegh was also in the Tower at this time, but it is not known whether she was allowed to visit her husband. One of her letters from the Tower to Heneage's son-in-law, Sir Moyle Finch, significantly signed E.R., not E.T., shows that she had been sick but was in good heart, still hoping for release. Lady Ralegh composed her words phonetically, just as they occurred to her, and the letter is a good example of her spectacularly idiosyncratic spelling:

Your kinness and me ladis conteneweth to the end and ever: wich must and douth bind me to aknookleg hit forever: for my sicke esstat I wryt to you the manner ther of befor: I contenew even so stell: yet have I such help as I may, but I will now tri your ladis medsen; I thanke you for your advis to wryt to Mr. vis-chambarlin: I will parform hit to moro in such sort as hee may shoo hit the q[ueen]: I can most willingly wryt to him wher I asur my selfe of helpe: sinc I have wrytten to me L Chambarlin wher I much hope for non: but so must I be reuled. I am dayly put in hope of my deliverey: but I protest I will not hope tell your fathar hether: I asur you treuly I never desiared nor never wolde desiar my lebbarti with out the good likeking ne advising of Sur W R: hit tis not this in prisonment if I bought hit with my life that shuld make me thinke hit long if hit shuld doo him harme to speke of my delivery: but Sur R. S(ecill?) was somwhat deseued in his Jugment in that and hit may be hee findeth his eror: I pray you tell your ladi I reserved heer kind lettar from Cubbam (Cobham): when wee mit wee will talke of hit: the towar standeth just in the way to Kent from Copthall: and who knooeth what will be com of me when I am out: the plage is gretly sesid and ever hath bin cliar heer a bout: and wee ar trew with in ourselfes I can asur you. Towar, ever assuredly yours in frinshep. E.R.

The letter shows some of Bess Throckmorton's qualities: her remembrances of her friends, her optimism, her submission to her husband's desires, and her wish not to do anything which might embarrass or discommode him. But Bess was never readmitted to the Queen's favour. Her offence, if anything, had been greater than Ralegh's. She had wiped the Queen's eye. She had stolen what the Queen had believed to be incontestably and permanently her own property. It was the sheer insolent unexpectedness of Bess Throckmorton's *coup* which took the breath away. She had never been outstanding amongst

The first page of Ralegh's long poem to the Queen – *The 11th* [or possibly the 21st] *and last booke of the Ocean to Scinthia*

Suffireth it to yow my ioyes interred,
in simpell wordes that I my woes cumplayne,
yow that then died when first my fancy erred.
ioyes vnder dust that never live agayne.
If to the liuinge weare my muse addressed,
or did my minde her own spirit still inhold.
weare not my liuinge passion so repressed,
as to the dead, the dead did thes vnfold.
sume sweeter wordes, sume more berninge verse
should wittness my mishapp in hygher kynd.
but my loues wounds, my fancy in the hearse,
the Idea but restinge, of a wasted minde.
the bloszumes fallen, the sapp gon from the tree.
the broken monuments of my great desires,
from thes so lost what may th'affections bee,
what heat in Cynders of extinguisht fiers?
Lost in the mudd of thos hygh flowinge streames
which through more fayrer feilds ther courses bend,
slayne with self thoughts, amasde in fearfull dreams,
woes without date, discunforts without end,
from fruitfull trees I gather withred leues
and glean the broken eares with misers hands
who sumetyme did in ioy the waighty sheues
I seeke faire flowres amidd the brinish sand.
all in the shade yeuen in the faire soon dayes
vnder thos healthless trees I syt alone
wher ioyfull byrds singe neather louely layes
nor phillomen recounts her direfull mone.
No feedinge flockes, no sheapherds cumpanye,
that might renew my dollorus consayte,
while happy then, while loue and fantasye
confinde my thoughts on ye faire flock to waite
no pleasinge streames fast to ye ocean wendinge
the messengers sumetymes of my great woes,
but all on yearth as from the colde stormes bendinge
shrinck from my thoughts in hygh heauens & below.
Oh, hopefull loue my obiect, and inuention,
Oh, trew desire the spurr of my consayte
Oh, worthiest spirit, my minds impulsion
Oh, eyes transpersant my affections bayte
Oh, princely forme, my fancies adamande
Deuine consayte, my paynes acceptance,
Oh all in one, oh heaven on yearth transparant.

the Queen's ladies. That such a plain-favoured little duckling should capture such a swan, the Queen's own black swan, passed all understanding – and all forgiveness.

In the Tower in 1592 Ralegh may quite possibly have worked on his long poem, the 'Ocean to Cynthia'. This is very unlikely to be the poem to Cynthia mentioned by Spenser three years earlier, but could well be a later instalment of it. This poem does not praise Cynthia, as Spenser's lines imply, but rather mourns her loss. It is a poem about the sensations of social and mental deprivation, as though the poet were grieving for the loss not only of the Queen but also of the life of the Court and the whole culture of which she was the centre.

The poem is unfinished, allusive and mysterious, often dealing in the connotations of words rather than their lexical meanings. A thread of expectancy runs throughout, arousing in the reader a feeling of tense anticipation, while he waits for the poet to broach his main theme, after due and respectful preliminaries. But the work never reaches so firm a resolution. The poem ends, and the reader is waiting for what he has already been told. The preparation was the consummation.

The poem begins with the death of love, and paints a picture of spiritual desolation, represented by dead fires, broken monuments, sapless trees and silent nightingales:

> Sufficeth it to yow my joyes interred,
> In simpell wordes that I my woes cumplayne,
> Yow that then died when first my fancy erred,
> Joyes under dust that never live agayne.
>
> If to the livinge weare my muse adressed,
> Or did my minde her own spirrit still inhold,
> Weare not my livinge passion so repressed,
> As to the dead, the dead did thes unfold.
>
> Sume sweeter wordes, sume more becumming vers,
> Should wittness my myshapp in hygher kynd,
> But my loves wounds, my fancy in the hearse,
> The Idea but restinge, of a wasted minde,
>
> The blossumes fallen, the sapp gon from the tree,
> The broken monuments of my great desires,
> From thes so lost what may th'affections bee,
> What heat in Cynders of extinguisht fires?
>
> Lost in the mudd of thos hygh flowinge streames
> Which through more fayrer feilds ther courses bend,
> Slayne with sealf thoughts, amasde in fearfull dreams,
> Woes without date, discumforts without end,
>
> From frutfall trees I gather withred leves
> And glean the broken eares with misers hands,

Who sumetyme did injoy the waighty sheves
I seeke faire floures amidd the brinish sand.

All in the shade yeven in the faire soon dayes
Under thos healthless trees I sytt alone,
Wher joyfull byrdds singe neather lovely layes
Nor Phillomen recounts her direfull mone.

Autobiographical references should not be pursued too closely, but eight lines (61–8) seem to describe the events leading up to Ralegh's imprisonment in the Tower:

To seeke new worlds, for golde, for prayse, for glory,
To try desire, to try love severed farr,
When I was gonn shee sent her memory
More stronge then weare ten thowsand shipps of warr,

To call mee back, to leve great honors thought,
To leve my frinds, my fortune, my attempte,
To leve the purpose I so longe had sought
And holde both cares, and cumforts in contempt.

One existing manuscript of the poem is in Ralegh's handwriting. It looks like a fair copy but is a working version, with corrections and additions. In places Ralegh has crossed out a word and written in another. He has left spaces in the text, and marked passages in the margin, as though he intended to revise them. One magnificent passage (69–103) has a space between lines 72 and 73, and a possible revision mark in the margin beside the incomplete three-line stanza of 101–3. The poet begins with a succession of paradoxes, 'heat in ice', and compares his remaining love with a body still warm after death, buds in winter and a mill-wheel still turning after the stream is diverted. So deprived, the poet turns to thoughts of strange lands and to the idea of writing a history of the world:

Such heat in Ize, such fier in frost remaynde,
Such trust in doubt, such cumfort in dispaire,
Mich like the gentell Lamm, though lately waynde,
Playes with the dug though finds no cumfort ther.

But as a boddy violently slayne
Retayneath warmth although the spirrit be gonn,
And by a poure in nature moves agayne
Till it be layd below the fatall stone;

Or as the yearth yeven in cold winter dayes
Left for a tyme by her life gevinge soonn,
Douth by the poure remayninge of his rayes
Produce sume green, though not as it hath dunn;   80

Or as a wheele forst by the fallinge streame,
Although the course be turnde sume other way
Douth for a tyme go rovnde vppon the beame
Till wantinge strength to move, it stands att stay;

So my forsaken hart, my withered mind,   85
Widdow of all the ioyes it once possest,
My hopes cleane out of sight, with forced wind
To kyngdomes strange, to lands farr off addrest.

Alone, forsaken, frindless onn the shore   89
With many wounds, with deaths cold pangs inebrased,
Writes in the dust as onn that could no more
Whom love, and tyme, and fortune had defaced,

Of things so great, so longe, so manefolde
With meanes so weake, the sowle yeven then departing
The weale, the wo, the passages of olde   95
And worlds of thoughts discribde by onn last sythinge:

As if when after Phebus is dessended
And leues a light mich like the past dayes dawninge,
And every toyle and labor wholy ended
Each living creature draweth to his restinge   100

Wee should beginn by such a partinge light
To write the story of all ages past
And end the same before th' aprochinge night.

Sometimes the bearing on his own life seems to be unmistakeable, as in the famous passage on the 'twelve years war', with its echoes of his 'Farewell to the Court' (120–7). The 'twelve years' can be computed from 1580 when Ralegh went to Ireland, up until the possible date of composition in 1592. But there are a number of possible solutions:

Twelve years intire I wasted in this warr,
Twelve yeares of my most happy younger dayes,
Butt I in them, and they now wasted ar,
Of all which past the sorrow only stayes.

So wrate I once, and my mishapp fortolde,
My minde still feelinge sorrowfull success
Yeven as before a storme the marbell colde
Douth by moyste teares tempestious tymes express.

Ralegh describes the Queen's terrible change from doting lover to vengeful sovereign in one exquisite coupling of animal and prison images, ending with what could be a reference to his 'error' with Miss Throckmorton which he somewhat ungenerously suggests was not due to love at all (327–39):

126

A Queen shee was to mee, no more Belphebe,
A Lion then, no more a milke white Dove;
A prisoner in her brest I could not bee,
Shee did untye the gentell chaynes of love.

Love was no more the love of hydinge
All trespase, and mischance, for her own glorye.
It had bynn such, it was still for th'ellect,
But I must bee th'exampell in loves storye,
This was of all forpast the sadd effect . . .

But thow my weery sowle and hevy thought
Made by her love a burden to my beinge,
Dust know my error never was forthought
Or ever could proceed from sence of Lovinge.

The poem moves to its majestic elegiac ending, with sudden flashes of light, as at 493–6:

Shee is gonn, Shee is lost! Shee is found, shee is ever faire!
Sorrow drawes weakly, wher love drawes not too.
Woes cries, sound nothinge, butt only in loves eare.
Do then by Diinge, what life cannot doo . . .

The last page of the manuscript begins with line 514, 'My steapps are backwarde, gasinge on my loss', and goes on to the end of the poem at line 522 'Her love hath end; my woe must ever last.' Under this is written 'The end of the bookes, of the Oceans love to Scinthia, and the beginninge of the 12 (22?) Boock, entreatinge of Sorrow'. There are twenty-one lines of this poem, which go down to the bottom of the page.

Over the page, only three words are written, 'For tender stalkes' – and nothing more. It is as though Ralegh were interrupted at his writing and never went back to this manuscript. It is pleasant to speculate that the interruption was a messenger from the Queen. Ralegh was urgently required on the Queen's business. The great Portuguese carrack *Madre de Dios* was at Dartmouth and was being pillaged by everyone who could get to the scene. Ralegh was the only man who could make sure that the Queen got her share of the booty. Where poetry and pleading had failed, money had succeeded. Ralegh was released from the Tower.

10. 'Fortune's Fold'

RALEGH'S SHIPS had captured the richest single prize ever brought into an English port. The *Madre de Dios*'s cargo was so valuable that its repercussions lasted for years, affecting the market prices for some commodities in England, causing men to quarrel and kill each other, and inspiring others to send ships to sea in hopes of another such prize.

After Ralegh left them, Borough and Frobisher captured a great Biscayan ship, the *Santa Clara*, which they sent home, with her cargo of 'all sorts of small yron-worke, as horse-shoes, nailes, plough-shares, yron barres, spikes, boults, locks, gimbols & such like' worth some six or seven thousand pounds. Then the ships separated. Frobisher in the Queen's ship *Garland* with the *Alcedo* (Captain and Rear-Admiral George Gifford), *Susan Bonaventure*, *Margaret and John*, *Dainty* and others patrolled the Spanish coast off Cape St Vincent. Sir John Borough in the *Roebuck*, with the Queen's ship *Foresight* (Vice-Admiral Robert Crosse) and the remaining ships went to the Azores.

Borough reached Flores on 26th July, where he found two London ships, the *Dragon* and the *Prudence*. Their captains, Christopher Newport and Hugh Merritt, agreed to join him. Some of the Earl of Cumberland's ships also joined him, including Captain Norton in the *Tyger*. One great carrack, the *Santa Cruz* from the East Indies, was chased into the Azores by Cumberland's ships. She was partly unloaded and then set on fire by her crew. The English landed, and took prisoners, from whom they learned that four more carracks were expected from the Indies. Borough had by this time been joined by Thompson in the *Dainty* who had had a disagreement with Frobisher and conveniently 'lost' him.

Borough's and Norton's ships spread out in a line west of Flores to intercept. On 3rd August they were rewarded by the sight of the great carrack *Madre de Dios*, all by herself, running gently towards them before a south-westerly wind, some twelve or fourteen leagues to the west of Flores. The first to engage was the *Dainty*, followed by the *Foresight*, the *Roebuck*, and the *Tyger*. The battle lasted from about eleven that morning until the early hours of the next morning, the *Madre de Dios*'s captain, Fernando de Mendosa (who had been Medina-Sidonia's flag captain in 1588), and his Portuguese crew defending themselves and their ship with (for merchantmen) unexpected vigour. But at last the crew surrendered, the sails were cut down, and the pillaging began. It was every man for himself and there were wild scenes between-decks as the sailors scrambled for jewels, rich cloths and booty. The ship was several times set on fire because of 'the disorder of men with candles in their rifling'.

Frobisher had had far less luck. He took one Brazil prize laden with sugar and sent the *Galleon Ralegh* home with her. He heard of Borough's success from Crosse in the English

Indians dancing around a circle of posts – drawing by John White, 1585. According to Hariot, this represents a dance at night held 'at a Certayne tyme of the yere', with the attendance of visitors from neighbouring towns

Channel and took the news of the rich prize into Plymouth. At once merchants, shopkeepers, jewellers, gold- and silver-smiths began to hurry to every port on the south coast.

The *Madre de Dios* arrived in Dartmouth on 7th September, accompanied only by Borough in the *Roebuck*. The rest of the privateers had dispersed to various ports, to dispose of their plunder while the going was good. Thompson in the *Dainty* went to Harwich, where there were no preparations by the Queen's officers, and sold £1,200 of plunder without any difficulty. Crosse, according to Frobisher, had £10,000 worth, and when he arrived at Portsmouth the scene on the quayside soon 'resembled Bartholomew Fair'. Sailors sold for trifling sums valuable articles they had risked their lives to get. The same articles were resold the same day for four or five times the original price. The Queen's officers found it dangerous to interfere. 'Customers, surveyors, searchers, or who else dareth not once to check these doings lest they receive a stab.'

Everybody knew somebody else who had plunder from the carrack. One man was said to have 320 diamonds, another 150, some had 'packets' of diamonds and 'half a peck of pearls', rubies, gold chains, strings of pearls, and crusados by the thousand. Almost all the jewellery on board was stolen. The ship's bill of lading was 'lost' and never found, despite the rigorous searches and questionings carried out by the Queen's officers.

The widespread plundering from the *Madre de Dios* made the Queen and her ministers anxious for the Crown's share of the cargo. But there seemed to be nobody who could control the half-mutinous sailors of the West Country – nobody, that is, except one man. 'Sir Walter Ralegh', Sir John Hawkins wrote to Lord Burghley on 11th September, 'is the especial man.' With the most exquisitely delicate phrasing, Hawkins hinted at the desirability of Ralegh's release. 'Therefore if it might please your Lordship to be a means to her Majesty, that, for the time, he might be in some other place near London, it might very much set forward her Majesty's service, and might benefit her portion . . .'

Burghley took the hint, and wasted no time. Ralegh was released from the Tower on 15th September and set off for the West Country. He was still a State prisoner, with Mr Blount as his appointed keeper.

Sir Robert Cecil was already on his way down to the west. The looting was so blatant he could smell it. He arrived in Exeter on the 19th and wrote to his father the same day.

> I have passed by Exeter. Whomsoever I met by the way within seven miles, that either had anything in cloak-bag or in mail which did but smell of the prizes, either at Dartmouth or Plymouth (for I assure your Lordship I could smell them almost, such hath been the spoils of amber and musk amongst them), I did, though he had little about him, return him with me to the town of Exeter; where I also stayed any that should carry news to Dartmouth or Plymouth, at the gates of the town.

The West-Country men resented this officious little spoilsport from London, with his sniffings and fussings and complainings. Cecil had to deal hardly with them. 'I compelled them also, to tell me where any trunks or mails were. And, by this inquisition, finding the people stubborn till I had committed two innkeepers to prison – which example would have won the Queen £20,000 a week past – I have light upon a Londoner's in whose house we have found a bag of seed pearls.'

Eventually, by what he called his 'rough dealing', Cecil 'left an impression with the Mayor and the rest'. He ordered every bag of mail coming from the west to be searched. Yet he feared that the birds had flown; the jewels, pearls and amber had already gone. But he was sure he had saved enough for the Queen to make his journey worthwhile. 'My Lord,' he exclaimed, 'there never was such spoil!' After complaining that he had never met 'fouler ways, desperater ways nor more obstinate people', Cecil concluded, 'Her Majesty's captive comes after me, but I have outrid him, and will be at Dartmouth before him.'

Two days later, Cecil witnessed the arrival at Dartmouth of 'Her Majesty's captive'. Ralegh had a reception from the men of the west rather different from Cecil's own. Cecil wrote to describe the scene to Sir Thomas Heneage in tones of mixed surprise, chagrin and reluctant admiration. 'I assure you, Sir, his poor servants, to the number of a hundred and forty goodly men, and all the mariners, came to him with such shouts and joy, as I never saw a man more troubled to quiet them in my life.' However, Cecil fancied he could see the scars of his imprisonment still on Ralegh. 'But his heart is broken; for he is very extreme pensive longer than he is busied, in which he can toil terribly.'

Ralegh somewhat disconcerted Cecil by saying, 'No: I am still the Queen of England's poor captive' whenever anybody came up and congratulated him upon his new freedom. This was bad for the Queen's name and, Cecil thought, bad for Ralegh's reputation, in that 'it doth diminish his credit' at the very time when Ralegh needed all his credit and powers of command to take charge of the situation. Sir John Gilbert greeted his half-brother with tears in his eyes. He had been so angry at Ralegh's imprisonment that he had pointedly stayed away from Dartmouth and had not gone on board the *Madre de Dios*.

The *Madre de Dios* was the biggest ship ever seen in England. For her times, she was a truly colossal leviathan, of 1,600 tons burden, with seven decks and nearly 800 souls on board (including 400 negroes, who had been landed in the Azores). She measured 165 feet in length from her 'beakhead' to the lantern on her stern. Her maximum beam was 46 foot and 10 inches. When she left Cochin she had drawn 31 foot of water, but drew 'not above 26' when she reached Dartmouth. The difference was caused partly by the stores consumed during the passage, but also by what the Hakluyt account obliquely calls 'divers meanes', meaning the removal of plunder, mouthwateringly described as 'spices, drugges, silks, calicos, quilts, carpets and colours &c'.

Cecil, Ralegh, and William Killigrew were appointed joint commissioners at Dartmouth, with Sir Francis Drake and others. They paid the sailors their wages, and something more besides. They tried to trace missing goods and decide on their ownership. They even examined Sir John Borough's chests. They were 'no common chests', but Sir John thought himself hard done by and he was allowed to keep the china, taffetas, quilts, damasks, gilt boxes, and a bunch of seed pearls.

Ralegh was concerned to protect his own investment. He had been writing from the Tower to Burghley about the value of the *Madre de Dios*, and on 16th September and again

Robert Cecil, 1st Earl of Salisbury, the Queen's Principal Secretary. He was Ralegh's friend for years (or so Ralegh thought) but he was directly responsible for Ralegh's eventual ruin. Portrait by John de Critz the Elder, 1602

SERO, SED SERIO

the next day, when he was on his way to Dartmouth, he was working out his sums and calculating that everybody was coming out of the affair better than he, who had been the chief investor and instigator of it all. He calculated that the Queen was entitled to £20,000 for her investment, assuming an (optimistic) value of the ship at £200,000. But Ralegh offered her finally £80,000. 'If God have sent it for my ransom,' he wrote, 'I hope her Majesty of her abundant goodness will accept it.' Ralegh was quite right. *Madre de Dios* had indeed ransomed him out of the Tower. Over a period of time he began to suspect that his release from his 'unsavoury dungeon' as he called it, was just about all the profit he was going to make out of his prize. As early as 17th September he was planning reprisals against some of those who, he thought, had robbed him. He wanted the City of London to inquire which goldsmiths and jewellers had gone down to the West Country. 'If I meet any of them coming up,' he wrote, 'if it be upon the wildest heath in all the way, I mean to strip them as naked as ever they were born. For it is infinite that Her Majesty hath been robbed, and that of the most rare things.'

But it was his own losses, rather than the Queen's, that rankled most. He even accused Cecil (somewhat naively writing to Lord Burghley, complaining to the father about the son), saying 'I protest before the living God, I speak of truth, without all affection or partiality, for (God is my judge) he hath more rifled my ship than all the rest.'

The wrangling over the partition of the spoils went on for years. Two years later Borough was killed in a duel after a quarrel about booty from the *Madre de Dios*. In December, Ralegh wrote indignantly to Burghley about his share. He and his fellow adventurers were only to get £36,000, which was a mere £2,000 profit over their investment. But the Earl of Cumberland also got £36,000, a profit of over £17,000. The City of London had only ventured £6,000 but they had doubled their money to £12,000. '*I* tooke all the care and paines,' Ralegh protested. '*They* only sate still.' They adventured for themselves. '*I* adventured for the *Queen*,' Ralegh insisted.

His point seems to have been taken in official circles, for Sir John Fortescue, the Chancellor of the Exchequer, wrote to Burghley, that 'it were utterly to overthrow all service, if due regard were not had of my Lord of Cumberland and Sir Walter Ralegh, with the rest of the Adventurers, who would never be induced to further adventure, if they were not princely considered of.'

Fortescue said that he found Her Majesty 'very princely disposed'. But that did not apply to Ralegh. The Queen did not wish to offend the City of London, nor a great northern landowner like Cumberland. But Ralegh was her creation. All his money had come from her in the first place. He had forfeited any claim on her good nature and she did not mind how she treated him now.

At least Ralegh had his freedom. On 13th December 1592 he was writing to Lord Burghley about the claim of one Filippo Corsini in the Admiralty Court. The letter was, significantly, signed from 'Dirrham House'. Lady Ralegh was also freed the same month. Nothing more is known of the baby Damerei.

The Raleghs spent much of the year 1593 at Sherborne in Dorset. The town lay on the

Sir Walter Ralegh's study at Sherborne Castle

road from London to the West Country. Ralegh had ridden through it many times. He particularly noticed Sherborne Castle. As Sir John Harington later wrote, 'this castle being right in the way, he cast such an eye upon it as Ahab did upon Naboth's vineyard'. Once, according to Harington, while Ralegh was talking about the castle, 'the commodiousness of the place, and of the great strength of the seat, and how easily it might be got from the bishoprick', his horse stumbled and Ralegh fell on his face on the ground. He took this as a very bad omen, but Adrian Gilbert who was with him said that he should 'interpret it as a conqueror, that his fall presaged the quiet possession of it'.

Ralegh coveted the castle and, as he later wrote to Cecil, he asked the Queen for it, and gave her a jewel worth £250 'to make the Bishop'. The Bishop was Salisbury, owner of the castle and estate of Sherborne. John Piers, the then Bishop, had leased the properties to the Queen in 1577. When Piers became Archbishop of York in 1589, the See of Salisbury remained vacant until Dr John Coldwell became Bishop in December 1591. Coldwell was no match for the combined pressure of Queen and favourite. On 14th January 1592, within a month of his consecration, he transferred the lease to the Queen for a term of ninety-nine years, for an annual rent of £200 16s. 1d. The Queen at once made over the lease to Ralegh. Coldwell was said to have been manipulated by the 'wily intrigues of Sir Walter'. He later regretted his pliancy and exerted himself until his death in trying unsuccessfully to get the castle and estates back.

The castle was a Norman fortification, with four great three-storeyed towers, built by Roger de Caen in the twelfth century. It was 'very strong and full of vaults', with a moat and drawbridges, but by Ralegh's day it was in a state of decay. At first, Ralegh began to repair and modify the old castle but he seems soon to have given up, probably by the end of 1593, and set about building a new home on the other side of the river Yeo to the southward.

The new home was not a castle but a more graceful type of building, like a lodge. Designed by Simon Basyl, it was made of red Tudor brick, with mullioned glass windows, and four small hexangular towers set one at each corner of a central tower structure. The house stood near the crossing of the London road and the main road from Bath to Portland, and it looked southwards over a most pleasant fertile valley of rolling champaign country with fields and trees. The Raleghs were delighted with it. Sir Walter called it, in his letters and his poetry, his 'fortune's fold'. Harington, writing in the reign of James I, gives an indication of what Ralegh did with Sherborne (although he appears to have disapproved of the expense), 'with less money than he has bestowed since in Sherborne (in building, and buying out leases, and in drawing the river through rocks into his garden) he might very justly, and without offence to either church or state, have compassed a much better purchase.' However, Ralegh made it into a beautiful home, as Aubrey testified. 'Sir W.R. begged it as a bôn from queen Elizabeth: where he built a delicate lodge in the park, of brick, not big, but very convenient for the bignes, a place to retire from the Court in summer time, and to contemplate etc. In short and indeed 'tis a most sweet and pleasant place and site as any in the West, perhaps none like it.'

Here, at Sherborne, the Raleghs made their home. Here their second son Wat was born

Sherborne Castle, which Ralegh called his 'fortune's fold'. Aubrey called it 'a most sweet and pleasant place and site as any in the West, perhaps none like it'

in October 1593. He was baptized on All Saints Day at the little parish church of Lillington near Sherborne. Here, they laid out the grounds and planted trees, and Lady Ralegh grew pinks in her garden. Here, Sir Walter bred and raced horses, and trained falcons. Falconry was one of his passions all his life. He once offered to pay the reversion of a leasehold manor in Ireland for the price of one goshawk. In Munster, one of his most prized assets was his entitlement to half the produce of an eyrie of hawks 'in the wood of Mogelly'. In August 1593 he was writing from Gillingham Forest, of which he was Joint Ranger with his brother Carew, to Cecil, who was also a falconer: 'The Indian falcon is sike of the buckworme; and therefore, if yow wilbe so bountefull to geve another falcon, I will provide yow a roning geldinge.' In 1617, on his last voyage, he had a trial of hawks at Cloyne in Ireland.

Inside Ralegh the adventurer, courtier and entrepᵉneur, there lurked Ralegh the home-loving family man. He yearned to settle, and put down firm family roots. At Sherborne, he seemed to have achieved his desire. He had his house, a family seat to pass down to future generations, and by the end of 1593 he had a family, too. But he was never entirely easy about his hold on Sherborne. There was, after all, the curse of an early Bishop, St Osmond of Seez, upon anybody who despoiled or diminished it, without making restitution. Ralegh had his share of superstitiousness, and he was always half-afraid (with very good reason, as it transpired) that somebody or something would conspire to take Sherborne away from his family. He was continually engaged in lawsuits and manoeuvrings over leases, to safeguard and reinforce his legal position as lease-holder of Sherborne.

Only the lease of Sherborne manor had been vested in Ralegh. He also wanted the leases of the accompanying manors of Long Burton, Holnest and Yetminster. He later achieved Yetminster, but the other two were held by a neighbour, John Fitzjames of Leweston.

Fitzjames was well thought of in London and, with the aid of Bishop Coldwell and the clergy of Salisbury, now Ralegh's deadly enemies, he gave Ralegh a deal of local trouble in Sherborne. After quarrelling with the Dean and Chapter, Ralegh eventually transferred his reversion and term of years on the two manors to Fitzjames in an indenture of 10th April 1594 'in consideracion of a good some of money to him payde by the said John Fitz-james'. But in the following August, Ralegh was complaining to Cecil that the priests of Salisbury had signed and sealed the 'fee-farms' more to benefit Fitzjames, who had given them a 'good fine', than himself. 'This Fitzjames,' Ralegh wrote, 'is a smooth knave as any leveth, and a false.' Ralegh's legal shufflings are perhaps too complicated to follow in detail, but his bribes and counter-bribes left him, he protested, 'not only farthinge the better, butt the assurance of my estate only; which I purchase att a most terribell rate'. However, for someone of Ralegh's insecurity, no rate was too terrible to assure his estate. The irony of his case was that, for all his precautions, all was lost through someone else's slip of the pen.

The Queen, on Ralegh's behalf, also tried to drag the manor and estate of Banwell from Thomas Godwin, Bishop of Bath and Wells. Aged and wracked with gout as he was, Bishop Godwin had just married (most unsuitably, in the Queen's opinion) a rich City widow. Godwin stoutly held on to Banwell, but did part with a ninety-nine-year lease of Wilscombe.

In August 1592, when Ralegh was still in the Tower, he appointed John Meere of Castleton, as his 'man, to take, cut, carry away or cause to be cut down all such manner of trees growing in my manor of Sherborne'. Meere was also given authority to keep the keys of the castle, and to act as overseer of woods and game. He became, in effect, Ralegh's bailiff and steward at Sherborne.

He turned out to be a most unfortunate choice. Ralegh may have met Meere first as a young man at the Inns of Court, or he may even never have met him before at all, but only heard of him, because of his local knowledge; 'he had all the ancient records of Sherborne, his father having been the Bishop's officer.' Meere was a Sherborne man, with long-standing family connections in the district. He was in prison for debt when Ralegh appointed him; he had been in prison before, on suspicion of committing a felony, and for clipping the coinage. He was reputed to have slandered most of the gentry in the county, and to be a little mad and something of a sorcerer. He had been involved in some trouble with Lord Henry Howard of Bindon, a Dorset neighbour of Ralegh's. This quarrel, and Meere's connection with Essex (his wife was a relative of the Earl), were one day to spread from Dorset to London and to be a disadvantage to Ralegh in a time of political trouble. In 1596 Ralegh appears to have made up his mind to get rid of Meere. He appointed Adrian Gilbert as keeper of the castle. But he found, as he had with Richard Browne over the farm of wines, that it was much easier to appoint Meere than to discharge him.

Ralegh was also engaged in wrangling on another front. His old adversary Sir William Fitzwilliam was still taking advantage of Ralegh's fall from favour, and had brought a new accusation. In 1589 Ralegh had used his influence with the Queen to get a royal licence to export commodities from Munster, whether or not there was legal restraint on those exports. He had gone into partnership with Henry Pyne, Edward Dodge, and a Dutchman, Veronio Martens, to export wood to the Canary Islands for making pipe-staves and hogshead-staves. (Trade with these islands continued in spite of the war with Spain.) Some of the wood from Ralegh's estates was also used for warship building. In 1592 Fitzwilliam put a stop on the trade. It was claimed that Ralegh and his partners were supplying ship-wood to Spain, and were acting as couriers for information between Catholics on the Continent and in England. Ralegh was also accused of denuding the woods in Ireland of valuable trees. He defended himself and Pyne vigorously, and Pyne was acquitted of all charges. By January 1594, the trade in pipe-staves was resumed. Later the same year, Ralegh sent over fifty of his Cornish miners to start a trade in iron-smelting. It was an imaginative idea, but it was opposed by the Irish who lived on the proposed sites. Later in the sixteenth century, iron-smelting was established in Munster, and the industry may have had its roots in Ralegh's venture of 1594.

Fifteen ninety-three was an especially bad year for plague in London. The streets were spread with herb rosemary, bells tolled, and abandoned dogs howled all night. The theatres were closed, and the normal processions through London for the opening of Parliament were cancelled. The Queen went down river by barge to open Parliament on 19th February.

Her late favourite was a member of that Parliament. Their eyes must have met in the debating chamber and one wonders what their expressions were. Ralegh had not been able to get a nomination for knight of the shire in Devon, Cornwall or Dorset in the elections held in the winter of 1592. Possibly the county gentry still resented the Queen's favourite, and, now that he had fallen, they surreptitiously prevented his nomination. He had been elected as a parliamentary burgess for the petty Cornish borough of St Michael. However, all Members had an equal voice, whatever their seats, and throughout his parliamentary career Ralegh's voice was always raised (albeit not strongly: the House complained they could not hear him) on the side of tolerance and moderation, free speech, and the freedom of the individual within the law.

This Parliament's most important considerations were to vote money for the subsidy to continue the war against Spain, and to pass more severe measures against religious extremists. On the first, Ralegh inevitably voted in favour of the subsidy. In a speech on 28th February he said he was for the increased tax 'not only, as he protested, to please the Queen, to whom he was infinitely bound above his desert, but for the necessity of what he saw and knew'. As usual, Ralegh was in good form when he spoke against Spain. He advocated open war. Spain, he said, 'possessed all the rich parts of the world'. The King of Spain had 'beleaguered us' by his bribes and subornings. Spain had bought the aid of Denmark and Norway, was strong in the French parliamentary towns and in the Low Countries, had corrupted the nobility of Scotland, and assisted Irish Catholic rebels. In Ireland, he said, speaking from personal experience, 'the people are so addicted to Papistry that they are ready to join with any foreign forces' against us. 'I think there are not six gentlemen of that country of our religion.' He saw the present situation as more dangerous than in Armada year. Then the Spaniard who came from Spain had to pass dangerous seas and had no refuge if he failed. Now, he had great store of shipping in Brittany and a landing-place in Scotland. 'Let us,' Ralegh concluded, and one can imagine the House listening to his passionate voice, 'send a royal army to supplant him in Brittany, and to possess ourselves there; and send also a strong navy to sea, and lie with it upon the Cape, and such places as his ships bring his riches to, that they may set upon all that come. This we are able to do; and we shall undoubtedly have fortunate success, if we undertake it.'

There was some debate on how the subsidy should be levied. Ralegh offered the House the views of a man of the world. The number of beggars about the country, about whom the House had been concerned because they suggested that the country was poverty-stricken, arose from two major causes: maimed soldiers returning from the wars but not going to their home towns; and clothiers who took the spinning wool into their own hands and thus drove the spinners into unemployment and beggary. Sir Henry Knivet proposed a form of 'wealth tax'. Ralegh opposed this, saying that many men's wealth was their credit. They were thought to be richer than they were. With a wealth assessment they would be creditless beggars. Time was short, Ralegh said. Since this Parliament began, over £44,000 had been seized from West-Country men at sea. There was a fleet of colliers at Newcastle unable to put to sea for fear of Spanish capture. 'This is certain: the longer we defer aid, the less able we shall be to yield aid; and in the end, the greater aid will be required of us.' Ralegh's speeches, like his prose, had a cumulative effect. He built up his sentences, buttressed his argument with more and more examples, furnished his theme with ever more wide-ranging

Sir Walter Ralegh and his son Wat, then aged 8. Artist unknown, 1602

illustrations, until the force of his reasoning broke over the listener like a wave.

During the passage of the Bill, there was a procedural dispute between the House and the Lords, which ended in bitter deadlock. It was Sir Walter Ralegh, the man always accused of arrogance, who smoothed over the situation. He proposed that the two houses confer in very general terms over the subsidy and the Bill. After asking him to say it again, because they had not heard him properly, the House gladly took up his suggestion.

In another debate, on 23rd March, Ralegh turned his attack on the allies of Spain, the Dutch. He spoke in favour of a bill to prevent the Dutch and Germans from retailing their foreign wares in this country. 'We have no Dutchmen here,' he said, 'but such as came from those provinces where the Gospel is preached, and here they live disliking our Church.' Again, his speech had a certain characteristic ring to it. 'The Dutchman by his policy hath gotten trading with all the world into his hands, yea, he is now entering into the trade of Scarborough fishing, and the fishing of the Newfound-lands, which is the stay of the West Countries. They are the people that maintain the King of Spain in his greatness.' If anything, Ralegh had more contempt for Spain's satellites than for Spain herself. His references to the West Country showed that he was fully aware of the political capital to be made by mixing a little local and regional grievance into a speech on foreign affairs. 'And so to conclude, in the whole cause I see no matter of honour, no matter of charity, no profit in relieving them [the Dutch].'

Apart from voting money, Parliament re-approached the question of safeguarding the national security against the activities of religious nonconformists. A new Act was framed to strengthen the existing (and fiercely penal) Act passed against Catholics in 1581. Archbishop Whitgift, the Queen's 'little black husband', who had been a moving spirit behind the earlier legislation, was also strongly in favour of the new Act. In its progress through the debates in the House, the more moderate spirits saw that the Bill would not only affect Catholics but extreme Protestants such as Brownists, Barrowists and Separatists. Ralegh was one of those who realized the hidden dangers in this sort of legislation. When the Bill had its second reading on 4th April he made the vital political and moral point that the House could punish a fact, but not an idea. He counted the Brownists, in his conscience, worthy to be rooted out of 'any Commonwealth'. But, he said, 'what danger may grow to ourselves if this law pass, it were fit to be considered. For it is to be feared that men not guilty will be included in it; and that law is hard that taketh life, or sendeth into banishment, where men's *intentions* shall be judged by a jury, and they shall be judges what another means. But that law that is against a fact, that is but just, and punish the fact as severely as you will.'

As a practical man of affairs, Ralegh went on to show some of the practical difficulties of administration, finance and transport, if the bill were strictly enforced and the Brownists were banished for their opinions. 'If two or three thousand Brownists meet at the sea-side, at whose charge shall they be transported? Or whither will you send them? I am sorry for it: I am afraid there is near twenty thousand of them in England. And when they be gone, who shall maintain their wives and children?'

It was an admirable speech which went some way to open the eyes of the House to the sheer practical difficulties of bigotry. Ralegh had made a major contribution to the feeling of moderation which had begun to spring up in the House, and he was one of a 'great committee' which sat most of the following day and which drew most of the Act's fiercer teeth. Whitgift and his party had been defeated. But they took a quick and sinister revenge. The leading Brownist, Henry Barrow, was already in prison and under sentence of death for publishing seditious books and pamphlets. He had in fact been twice reprieved, and was expected to escape with his life. But on 6th April, only a day after the committee had sat, Barrow was executed at Tyburn.

Parliament was dissolved on 10th April. Ralegh went to Bath to take the waters, but they did him no good, for in May he was writing to Cecil from Sherborne that 'I am the worse for the Bath, and not the better.'

He may have been cheered up by a book of Elizabethan poetry which was published that year and contained some of his own work. Ralegh may have had the amateur's scorn for professional publication – and he himself made no attempt whatsoever to make sure that his poems survived him – but he would have been a very unusual poet if he did not enjoy seeing his own verses in print. The book was called *The Phoenix Nest*, an anthology of the 'refined workes of Noble men, woorthy Knights, gallant Gentlemen, Masters of Arts, and brave Schollers. Full of varietie, excellent invention, and singular delight. Never before this time published. Set foorth by R.S. of the Inner Temple Gentleman'. The identity of the editor, R.S,, is not known but he seems to have compiled the work of a group of friends, many of whom were at Oxford together. Less than half the poems are initialled, but such poets as Sir Edward Dyer, Robert Greene, Sir William Herbert, Thomas Lodge and Nicholas Breton are represented. *The Phoenix Nest* contains the largest contemporary collection of Ralegh's poems ever published – seventeen poems: his elegy to Sir Philip Sidney, and sixteen other poems which have been definitely identified as his or which can be convincingly argued to be by him. They include some of his most famous poems, such as 'Like to a Hermite poore in place obscure' and 'Like truthless dreams, so are my joyes expired' and 'The Excuse':

CALLING to minde mine eie long went about,
T' entice my hart to seeke to leaue my brest,
All in a rage I thought to pull it out,
By whose deuice I liu'd in such vnrest,
    What could it say to purchase so my grace?
    Forsooth that it had seene my Mistres face.

Another time I likewise call to minde,
My hart was he that all my woe had wrought,
For he my brest the fort of Loue resignde,
When of such warrs my fancie neuer thought,
    What could it say, when I would him haue slaine?
    But he was yours, and had forgone me cleane.

At length when I perceiu'd both eie and hart,
Excusde themselues, as guiltles of mine ill,
I found my selfe was cause of all my smart,
And tolde my selfe, my selfe now slay I will:
    But when I found my selfe to you was true,
    I lou'd my selfe, bicause my selfe lou'd you.

11. 'Damned Atheist'

FOR YEARS, Ralegh suffered under accusations of being an 'atheist'. It was a charge that stuck to him remorselessly. 'He was scandalised with atheisme,' wrote Aubrey, 'but he was a bold man, and would venture at discourse which was unpleasant to the churchmen. I remember [the] first lord Scudamour sayd "'twas basely sayd of Sir W.R. to talke of the anagramme of Dog".'

By the definitions of his day, Ralegh was an atheist. The word was a general insult, often a convenient epithet for blackening an adversary's reputation. When the creditors of George Gascoigne, the soldier-poet for whom Ralegh wrote commendatory verses years before, were looking for charges to accuse him of, one was of being an atheist. 'Atheist' was capable of a range of meanings, from one who genuinely rejected the existence of any god, through various graduations of deists, sceptics, unitarians, and non-conformist thinkers, to one who was merely of doubtful reputation or who held unorthodox views. Ralegh had an enquiring, sceptical mind. He did not tolerate fools. He had an irritating conviction that he was in the right. He was known to be friendly with mathematicians, astrologers, and men of unusual scientific accomplishments. Most important of all, he was unpopular in the country. It was inevitable that sooner or later Ralegh would be accused of being an atheist.

Gascoigne was not the only early link between Ralegh and the taint of atheism. In 1580, one of the many charges brought by Charles Arundel against the Earl of Oxford was 'Blasphemy against scripture and Christ in presence of a number as my Lord Winsor, Mr Russell and Ralegh'. On this occasion, Ralegh was only an onlooker, but the connection between him and atheism was there. Even Lady Ralegh, if Ben Jonson's account of his conversations with William Drummond are accurate, seems to have believed that her husband, as a young man, 'inclined' to atheism. Ralegh had sent Ben Jonson to France in 1613 as governor to his son Wat who was a lively young spark 'being knavishly inclined, among other pastimes (as the setting of the favour of damosels on a codpiece)'. Young Ralegh got his governor drunk, placed him on a cart and dragged him through the streets, pointing out to passers-by that his governor stretched out was 'a more lively image of the crucifix than any they had'. 'At which sport' Jonson concludes, 'young Ralegh's mother delighted much (saying his father young was so inclined).' However, 'the father *abhorred* it', Jonson ends significantly.

The first really well-publicized charge of atheism against Ralegh was made in the early 1590s, after the Queen had approved a penal edict against Jesuits on 18th October 1591, which provoked an immediate and violent response from the Catholic press on the Continent. Of several Catholic replies, the best written, most closely argued, and most subtly misleading,

John Dee, astrologer and astronomer, another friend of Ralegh's
and another accused of atheism

143

was known as the *Responsio*, written in Latin by the Jesuit Father, Robert Parsons, under the pseudonym of Andreas Philopater. The *Responsio* was only one of several Catholic tracts which mentioned Ralegh by name or by implication, but it was the most widely-read, being printed in several editions and in four languages.

The *Responsio*'s main target was Lord Burghley, but Ralegh was an irresistible secondary objective. He was noted for his anti-Spanish and anti-Catholic sentiments. He was the living symbol of Elizabethan and Protestant England. He was known to have helped Puritans, such as John Udall, in the past. One passage of the *Responsio* referring directly to Ralegh disparages his military prowess, accuses him of running a school of atheism and of practising black magic:

> Certainly if the school of atheism of Walter Ralegh flourishes any longer – which he is wellknown to have in his house, with a certain necromantic-astrologer as teacher, so that no small number of noble youths may mock at the old law or Moses and the new law of Christ, laughing at their bright jokes and witticisms amongst themselves – if, as I say, this school should take root and grow strong, and Ralegh himself was chosen for the Council, and thus have influence on state affairs (which everybody, not without good reason, expects, since he now holds first place in the Queen's affection after Leicester and Hatton, and they see him almost from the ranks in Ireland made a powerful and prestigious man, thanks only to the Queen, he having no ability) what (as I say) else must be expected but at some time or other an edict drawn up by that Epicure and Magus, Ralegh's teacher, and published in the Queen's name, in which every single divine being, every soul's immortality, and the expectation of another life, are clearly, briefly, and without argument denied, and all would be accused of *lèse majesté*, as though they were disturbers of the state, who against that kind of doctrine, so sweet and easy in the voluptuous sins of the flesh, raised any scruples or moved any opposition.

It was not at all unlikely, in 1591 or early 1592, that Ralegh might become a Privy Councillor. But Parsons was also incorporating older material; he refers to Leicester as though he were still living.

The *Responsio* was abbreviated in English and published as *An Advertisement*. The passage above was condensed into one neat and damning paragraph: 'Of Sir Walter Raleigh's School of Atheism by the way, and of the conjuror that is M[aster] thereof and of the diligence used to get young gentlemen to this school, where both Moses and our Saviour, the Old and New Testaments are jested at, and the scholars are taught amongst other things to spell God backwards.'

The 'conjuror' and the 'certain necromantic-astrologer' was most probably Thomas Hariot, although John Dee thought that it was himself who was libelled. Ralegh had known Dr John Dee, geographer, astrologer, astronomer, mathematician and sometimes scientific adviser to the Queen, since his earliest days at Court. In April 1583 Dee noted in his diary that the Queen, riding from Richmond to Greenwich, had stopped by him at Ralegh's

Frontispiece design for a book, by John Dee, *Generall and Rare Memorials Pertayning to the Perfect Art of Navigation, c.* 1577

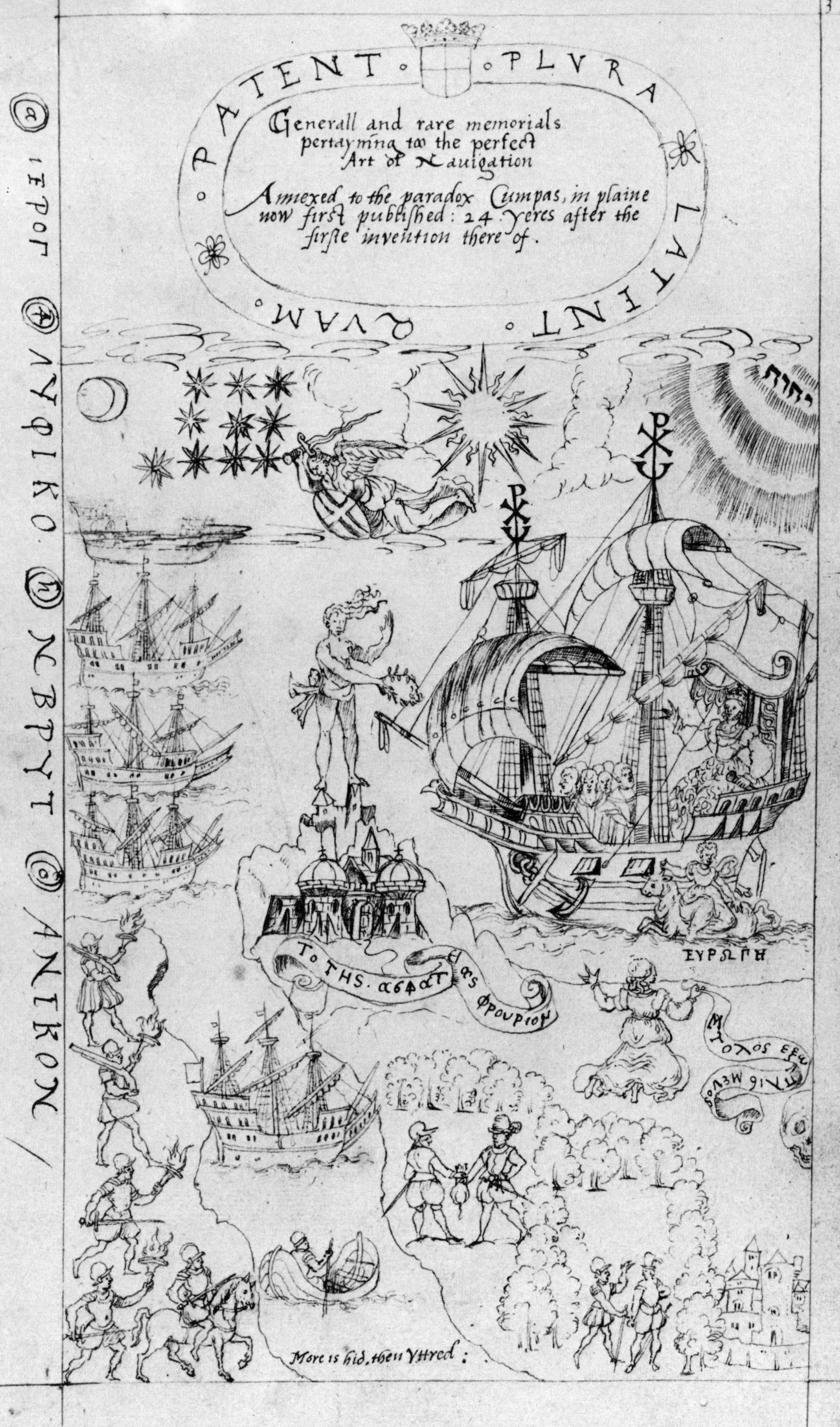
PATENT · PLVRA LATENT · QVAM ·
Generall and rare memorials pertayning to the perfect Art of Nauigation
Annexed to the paradox Cumpas, in plaine now first published: 24 Yeres after the first invention there of.
ΙΕΡΟΓΛΥΦΙΚΟΝ ΒΡΥΤΑΝΙΚΟΝ
יהוה
ΕΥΡΩΠΗ
ΤΟ ΤΗΣ ΑΣΦΑΛΕΙΑΣ ΦΡΟΥΡΙΟΝ
More is hid, then vttred :

ANNO DÑI ÆTATIS SVÆ 21
1585
QD ME NVTRIT
DESTRVIT

Christopher Marlowe, dramatist, poet and spy, who was reported to have 'read the atheist lectures'
to Ralegh and others

reminder and had given him her right hand to kiss, saying somewhat cryptically *Quod
defertur non aufertur*, What is deferred is not put off for ever. Dee had the reputation of being
able to converse with the dead, through a medium. In 1583 his priceless library at Mortlake
was burned by a superstitious mob. Friendship with such a man would certainly increase the
suspicion of atheism against Ralegh.

The slanders grew much stronger in the early summer when, on 12th May, the dramatist
Thomas Kyd, author of *The Spanish Tragedy*, was arrested on suspicion of having written
certain libellous attacks on foreigners (many of them Huguenots from France) then living

in London. Amongst Kyd's belongings were found documents which were held to be heretical. Kyd's testimony under torture implicated another and greater dramatist, Christopher Marlowe. Marlowe, who himself had a murky background as an agent for the government, was arrested on 20th May, ordered to appear before the Privy Council, and to report himself in person daily. He had, evidently, a kind of limited bail.

Accusations of atheism were on much stronger ground in Marlowe's case. In his play of *Dr Faustus* an actor recited before a scandalized and fascinated audience the actual Latin words of an incantation to raise Mephistophilis from Hell. The whole play brought vividly before its watchers' eyes the very close connection between science, magic and religion in the Renaissance. There is a link between Ralegh and Marlowe, but a tenuous one – Ralegh's answer to Marlowe's poem *The Passionate Shepherd to his Love*. Ralegh could have written his poem without ever meeting Marlowe. But, arguably, the intimate relationship of the two poems, in wording and subject matter, does suggest that the two poets knew each other.

Another, and potentially more dangerous, link between the two men was revealed in the interrogation of a certain Richard Baines who testified that Marlowe had once said that 'Moses was but a juggler and that one Heriots being Sir W. Ralegh's man can do more than he.' Even more damaging was his statement that a spy called Richard Cholmeley had told him that Marlowe had converted him to atheism. 'Marlowe is able to show more sound reasons for atheism than any divine in England is able to give to prove divinity.' Cholmeley said that Marlowe told him 'that he hath read the atheist lecture to Sir Walter Raleigh and others'. Marlowe himself was killed in a tavern quarrel at Deptford, in circumstances which have never been fully made clear, and before any case could be brought against him.

The Court gossip about Ralegh and his atheism was picked up by Sir John Harington, who mocked it in one of his epigrams, *In Paulum Athaium*:

> Proud Paulus, led by Sadduces infection,
> Doth not beleeve the bodies resurrection,
> But holds them all in scorne and deepe derision,
> That talke of Saints or Angels apparition:
> And faith, they are but fables all, and fancies
> Of Lunaticks, or folkes possest with frensies.
> I have, saith he, travell'd both neere and farre,
> By land, by sea, in time of peace and warre,
> Yet never met I spirit, or ghost, or Elfe,
> Or ought (as is the phrase) worse then my selfe.
> Well, Paulus, this I now beleeve indeed,
> That who in all, or part, denyes his Creed;
>> Went he to sea, land, hell, I would agree,
>> A fiend worse then himselfe, he could not see.

Years later, when Ralegh was on trial and in peril of his life for his involvement in the Main Plot against James I, Harington wrote a letter in quite a different vein to Dr Still, the Bishop of Bath and Wells. Harington had been present at Sherborne when such matters as theology had been discussed. He told the Bishop he was sure that Ralegh had no 'evil design in point of faith or religion. As he hath oft discoursed to me with much learning, wisdom and freedom, I knew he doth somewhat differ in opinion from some others, but I think also his heart is well fixed in every honest thing as far as I can look into him'. This was written when Ralegh stood in the shadow of the gallows, when the occasion for witty epigrams was past and it was time for the truth.

Whether or not Sir Walter Ralegh was a member of various 'clubs', 'societies' and 'schools' is very largely a question of conjecture. The belief that he was a member of a 'Mermaid Club', a group of poets, playwrights and wits who gathered at the Mermaid Tavern to exchange witticisms and read each other's verses, is a very old one. In his note on Sir Francis Stuart, Aubrey says that 'he was a learned Gentleman, and one of the Club at the Mermayd, in Fryday Street, with Sir Walter Ralegh, etc, of that Sodalitie: Heroes and Witts of that time.' Possibly Marlowe, Shakespeare, Jonson and others may have foregathered in the Mermaid, and possibly Ralegh may occasionally have joined them (hence the birth of the legend) but it is hardly likely that he was a regular attender or in any sense a member of the 'club'. The picture of Sir Walter Ralegh sitting in a tavern, hobbing and nobbing with all and sundry, exchanging toasts and guffaws with riff-raff, does not fit the image of him as the Queen's courtier (and, incidentally, as Her Majesty's Captain of the Guard). The gatherings that Francis Beaumont (born in 1584) refers to in his Letter to Ben Jonson ('What things have we seen, Done at the Mermaid!') took place in James I's reign, when Ralegh was in the Tower.

Ralegh may have been a member, perhaps even one of the founders, of the Society of Antiquaries, which was formed sometime in the early 1580s. This society had a serious scientific purpose, and formally applied to the Queen to become an incorporated Royal historical society, with the national responsibility for collecting, cataloguing and preserving historical records and matters of historical interest. If Ralegh was not a member, he certainly knew men who were, such as William Camden, of the *Annales*, Richard Hakluyt, of the *Voyages*, Lancelot Andrewes, one of the translators of the Authorized Version of the Bible, and John Stow, author of *The Survey of London*. Ralegh's friends also included the antiquaries John Hooker, Richard Carew and Sir Robert Cotton, Ralegh's next-door neighbour at Durham House. He was a patron of Matthew Roydon, a minor poet, and a friend of a major poet, George Chapman. He was also a patron of Thomas Hariot, and of two other mathematicians, Walter Warner and Robert Hughes. In the Tower, Hariot, Warner and Hughes were to be called the 'Magi' of Henry Percy, Earl of Northumberland (and himself Ralegh's friend of many years). A wide selection of works was dedicated to Ralegh, their authors obviously repaying his interest in them: John Case's *Praise of Music*, Thomas Churchyard's *Spark of Friendship*, Martin Bassaniere's translation of Rene Laudonniere's *History of Florida*, Theodore de Bry's large folio edition of Hariot's *True Report*, published in Frankfurt in four languages in 1590, and many others.

In all the rumours and accusations of Ralegh's atheism, the name of Thomas Hariot

MEVM PECCATVM. SI BONVM.

Anno

SI MALVM.

DEI DONVM.

Francisco Delaram.

Thomas Hariot, mathematician and 'necromancer'. It was his
long friendship with Hariot that did most to give Ralegh his
reputation of 'atheism'

occurs again and again. Hariot was born in Oxford ('tumbled out of his mother's womb into the lap of the Oxonian muses', as Anthony á Wood expressed it) in 1560. He went to grammar school in Oxford and was 'either a batler or commoner' of St Mary's Hall, taking his degree as Bachelor of Arts on 12th February 1580. His ability as a mathematician was brought to the attention of Ralegh, who befriended him in the same year. They remained friends for life. Hariot had the quintessential Renaissance intellect, interested in and curious about everything, wherever it chanced to look. His *Brief and True Report* shows his interest in botany, agriculture, anthropology and ethnography; it was also one of the first attempts at a statistical survey of population. Besides his navigational tables and calculations, Hariot wrote works on geometry, algebra and his theory of equations. He carried out observations in meteorology, mechanics, hydrostatics, and optics. He could explain how a rainbow was formed. He was using a telescope as early as Galileo, making sketch-maps of the moon's surface, observing sun spots, and predicting the paths of meteors. He translated part of the Gospel according to St Matthew into French. Ralegh introduced him to the Earl of Northumberland who gave him an annual pension of £300 for life. Hariot was a regular visitor to Ralegh and Northumberland in the Tower. In 1607, Northumberland gave him a residence in the grounds of Syon House, the great house at Brentford on the outskirts of London. Hariot was a Deist rather than an atheist. Many clerics admired his intellect but he gave great offence with his views on the Creation as described in Genesis. His comment *Ex nihilo nihil fit* – Nothing comes of nothing – was widely repeated and aroused scandalized opposition. But, as Aubrey says, 'a *nihilum* killed him at last.' He had a cancer on his nose ('a little red speck – exceeding small – which grew bigger and bigger') of which he died on 2nd July 1621.

After Ralegh's disgrace he and friends such as Hariot became vulnerable to attacks from the envious and the ignorant, and from the opposition at Court. Thomas Nashe, one of the so-called 'University wits', attacked atheists in his pamphlet 'Pierce Pennilesse his Supplication to the Devil', published in 1592. There was at least one possible reference to Thomas Hariot: 'I hear say there be Mathematicians abroad, that will prove men before Adam, and they are harboured in high places, who will maintain it to the death, that there are no devils.'

At about this time, Ralegh and his friends may have been under attack from another quarter – the London stage. Again, the suppositions are mostly conjectural, but the accumulation of scholarly deductions, taken together, begins to be convincing. During the outbreaks of plague in December 1593 and the beginning of 1594 when the theatres were closed, William Shakespeare wrote a discreetly erotic poem, *Venus and Adonis*, which he dedicated to his patron Henry Wriothesley, Earl of Southampton, one of Essex's faction. A little later, Shakespeare began work upon a comedy, *Love's Labour's Lost*, which poked fun at the academic pretensions of a group of courtiers who vowed to deny themselves the pleasures of women for three years but who succumbed to temptation at the first opportunity. In the play, the pedantic character Holofernes has been supposed to have resemblances to Thomas Hariot, while Don Adriano de Armado is Sir Walter Ralegh himself.

Various resemblances between Ralegh's life and the play's action have been pointed out. The 'love's labour' that was lost may have been Ralegh's poem 'The Ocean to Scinthia', which failed to regain him the Queen's favour (assuming, that is, the Queen ever saw it). Armado professes to love the Princess of France (Queen Elizabeth) and the country maid Jacquenetta (Bess Throckmorton); his pronunciation of 'Sirrah' as 'Chirrah' may be a reference to Ralegh's broad Devonshire accent. There has even been supposed to be a direct comment upon Ralegh and his 'school' of atheist friends. When one of his courtiers says that his love is like ebony and that 'No face is fair that is not full so black', the King Ferdinand of Navarre exclaims

> O paradox! Black is the badge of hell,
> The hue of dungeons and the school of night;
> And beauty's crest becomes the heavens well.

The word 'school' in the text might be a misreading of 'schoot' or 'suit'. The 'suit of night' would be a reasonable, if not particularly striking, metaphor for the colour of black. But 'school' could just as well be the correct reading, and it has been suggested that the 'School of Night' was the name given to Sir Walter Ralegh and friends such as George Chapman, Matthew Roydon, Christopher Marlowe, and Thomas Hariot who met to debate and instruct themselves in atheistic and necromantic studies.

In 1594 George Chapman published his poem 'The Shadow of Night', which Shakespeare may have seen in manuscript before publication; the poem advocated the contemplative studious life over the worldly pleasure-seeking life. Chapman dedicated the work to Matthew Roydon and in his dedicatory letter praised 'most ingenious Darbie' (the Earl of Derby, who died in 1594), 'deepe searching Northumberland' (Ralegh's friend), and 'skill-imbracing heire of Hunsdon' (Sir George Grey, later Baron Hunsdon, Lord Chamberlain, and Shakespeare's patron). Chapman also wrote dedicatory verses to Hariot with his poem 'Achilles Shield' and spoke warmly of his learning in the preface to his translation of Homer's *Iliad*. Chapman calls Hariot 'Mayster of all essentiall and true knowledge'. Chapman was possibly the poet whose 'proud full sail of his great verse' Shakespeare was referring to in his 86th Sonnet. Line 7 refers to 'he, nor his compeers by night'. Chapman's poem addresses night in enthusiastic terms. 'Imperiall Night', 'deare Night', 'most contentful Night', 'deare Night, o goddesse of most worth', 'sacred Night', and contains the couplet:

> No pen can any thing eternall wright,
> That is not steept in humour of the night.

Clearly, Ralegh, Chapman, Roydon and Hariot knew each other, and clearly Chapman's poetry dwells upon the subject of night, but the existence of a 'School of Night' has not been firmly established.

Love's Labour's Lost was almost certainly performed privately, perhaps at the Earl of Southampton's house at Christmas 1593, before an exclusive aristocratic audience who would take all the personal allusions, understand the private jokes, and appreciate any intended attacks or innuendos directed against other courtiers. Possibly, the audience was the Earl of Essex and his friends, who included Southampton. Possibly, Shakespeare intended his play to ridicule Ralegh, Essex's greatest rival, and his friends at Court, for the enjoyment of Essex and *his* friends at Court.

The Essex–Ralegh feud may also have been carried on in Shakespeare's next long poem, *The Rape of Lucrece*, published in 1594. Shakespeare himself may have intended nothing by it, but Elizabethan readers were accustomed to look for second meanings, and some of Essex's supporters may well have seen 'Ralegh the Proud' in Tarquin the Proud.

Ralegh and his side may have been driven to reply, in the form of a curious long poem called *Willobie His Avisa*, also published in 1594. Willobie may or may not be a real person, but in the poem he tries for the hand of Avisa, described on the poem's frontispiece as 'a modest Maid, and a chast and constant wife'. From the text of the poem it has been deduced that Avisa was the witty, beautiful (and faithful) wife of the innkeeper of the George Inn at Sherborne. Avisa's virtue is assailed by several suitors, some nobly born, such as the Earl of Southampton, and one of them a certain 'W.S.' who may be William Shakespeare. But Avisa remains triumphantly chaste. It can be argued that *Willobie His Avisa* was written by one of Ralegh's friends, such as Matthew Roydon, who intended to ridicule Essex and his friends, including Shakespeare and his patron, Southampton. But the relevance to Essex and Ralegh of *Willobie His Avisa*, *The Rape of Lucrece*, or *Love's Labour's Lost* is a matter of opinion.

By the beginning of 1594 the reputations of Ralegh and his friends of having atheistic or at least unorthodox opinions had spread wide enough and caused enough comment for the Commissioners in Causes Ecclesiastical to hold an enquiry into them. This could have been dangerous for Ralegh. He was discredited at Court, but he was not without power or status still. If the label of atheist could be pinned on him, it would be a major political success for Essex and his party.

The members of the enquiry were Thomas Lord Howard of Bindon, Sir Ralph Horsey, a deputy Lieutenant for Dorset, John Williams of Herringston, Francis Hawley from Corfe Castle, Francis James, Chancellor of the diocese of Bristol, and others. They met and began to take evidence at Cerne Abbas in Dorset, on 21st March 1594. There was a strong local Dorset flavour in the enquiry, but its results could have national repercussions.

The most important witness was the Reverend Ralph Ironside, minister of Winterborne Abbas. He and a friend, Parson Whittle of Fordington, had attended a dinner-party the previous summer at Wolveton House, near Dorchester, the home of Sir George Trenchard, Sheriff of Dorset. The other diners were Sir George himself, Sir Ralph Horsey, John Fitz-james of Leweston, Sir Walter Ralegh, his brother Carew, and some others.

Towards the end of the meal some 'loose speeches' by Carew Ralegh caused Sir Ralph Horsey to reprove him gently, saying *Colloquia prava corrumpunt bones mores* ('Wild speech corrupts good behaviour').

Mischievously, Carew Ralegh asked the cleric what danger he ran by making such speeches. Ironside said that the wages of sin is death. Carew retorted that everybody had

Sir Walter Ralegh, as a courtier (by his exotic dress) and as explorer (the globe and compasses). It is just possible this painting may be of his elder brother Carew

SIR WALTER
RAWLEIGH

SIR WALTER RALEIGH

to die, whether they were righteous or a sinner. Ironside 'inferred further' that as that life which is the gift of God is life eternal, so that death which is properly the wages of sin is death eternal, both of the body and the soul.

'*Soul?*' said Carew, 'what *is* the soul?' Ironside, who must have felt himself getting into deep water, said that they would all do better to concentrate on saving their souls rather than finding out what their souls were.

This was not good enough for Sir Walter Ralegh, who asked Ironside to answer his brother's question. Sir Walter said he had himself been a scholar at Oxford and a Bachelor of Arts and he had many times discussed this question with divines and all manner of people and had never had a satisfactory answer. They told him the soul was *primus motor*, the 'first mover' in a man. Ralegh had replied that the soul was the *fons et principuum*, the fountain, beginning and cause of motion in man. But the first *mover* was the brain, or the heart.

Ironside was probably willing to let this conversation lapse, but he was again urged to give his opinion, and so he quoted Aristotle's definition of the soul. This, however, was 'misliked of Sir Walter as obscure and intricate'. With an effort at tact, Ironside then said it could not be obscure to Sir Walter, being a learned man, though it probably would seem obscure to the rest of those present. 'Plainly,' said Ironside, 'the reasonable soul is a spiritual and immortal substance breathed into man by God, whereby he lives and moves and understands, and so is distinguished from other creatures.'

Ironside was begging the question, and Ralegh was quick to seize on it. 'Yes,' he said, 'but what *is* that spiritual and immortal substance breathed into man by God?'

'The soul,' replied Ironside, beginning to argue in a circle.

'Nay then,' said Ralegh, evidently disappointed, 'you answer not like a scholar.'

Ironside protested that it *was* scholar-like and tried to prove that it was sometimes necessary to argue in a circle. 'For example, if one asks, what is a man? You will say that he is a creature reasonable and mortal. But if you ask again, what is a creature reasonable and mortal, you must of force come backwards and answer, it is a man. And so on.'

'But we have principles in our mathematics,' said Ralegh, 'such as *totum est minus quamlibet sua parte*. The whole is less, as you like, than its parts. Ask me of it, and I can show it in a table in the window in a man, the whole being bigger than the parts of it.'

One can almost see Ironside growing hotter under the collar. He said that Sir Walter had, first, shown *quod est,* not *quid est,* that it was, but not *what* it was, and second, that such factual explanations were in any case inappropriate. Material things could be discussed in a material way. Similarly the soul being spiritual could only be defined or discerned in a spiritual way.

This was obviously a familiar controversy for Ralegh and his friends. 'Marry,' he said, 'these two be like, for neither could I learn hitherto what God is.'

Mr Fitzjames now made his only recorded contribution to the discussion, saying that Aristotle would define God as *Ens Entium*, the Thing of Things.

Ironside welcomed the support. 'That God was *ens entium,* a thing of things, having been of Himself, and giving being to all creatures, it was most certain, and confirmed by God Himself unto Moses.'

Once again Ironside was begging the question, and once again Ralegh pounced. 'Yes, but what *is* this *ens entium*?'

'God,' said Ironside, simply.

At this point Ralegh gave it up and 'wished that grace may be said'. That, he said, would be better than this disputation. Ironside did not stay the night. 'Thus supper ended and grace said, I departed to Dorchester with my fellow minister.'

The account of the dinner-party was given under oath, and it is probably as accurate as any eye-witness recollection can be. It shows Ralegh gently fencing with an adversary intellectually inferior to him. There was a streak of perverseness in his nature. There is the suspicion that he argued against Ironside partly for the sake of it; had Ironside taken a different stance in the argument, Ralegh would have argued just as vigorously against that. Sir George Trenchard and Sir Ralph Horsey are not mentioned by Ironside. They may have taken no part in the debate. More probably they did, but their share was suppressed; they were both very powerful men in Dorset. Horsey actually served on the enquiry.

Someone must have taken an accurate account of the supper-party conversation to London, for the Commissioners had the air of men who knew what they were looking for. The witnesses were asked to reply to nine questions on atheism, such as, Whom do you know, or have heard to be suspected of atheism or apostasy? And in what manner do you know or have heard the same? And what other notice can you give thereof? Or, whom do you know, or have heard, that have argued or spoken against or as doubting, the being of any God? Or what or where God is? Or to swear by God, adding if there be a god or suchlike? And so on.

Some bizarre items of local gossip emerged both in the questions and in the answers. Two questions were directly aimed, as everyone knew, at Ralegh's lieutenant in command of Portland Castle, Thomas Allen. 'Whom do you know or have heard hath blasphemously cursed God, saying one time (as it rained while he was hawking) if there be a God, a pox on that God which sendeth such weather to mar our sport?' and 'Whom do you know or have heard to have said that when he was dead his soul should be hanged on the top of a pole and run God, run devil, and fetch it that would have it?' These were both stories told about Allen locally.

Apart from Ironside, the rest of the witnesses, almost all of them local parsons, had nothing much that was incriminating to say. Some had merely heard that Ralegh was supposed to have atheistic views. Hariot's name cropped up again. Much of the evidence was a mixture of unsupported assertion and pure hearsay. Thomas Norman, minister of Melcombe Regis, said that a Mr Jones had told him that Allen of Portland Castle would make a fool of any minister such as Norman himself. Mr Jones's *son* had said that Allen used two leaves of the Bible to dry his tobacco on. Norman, too, had heard of Hariot. Nicholas Jeffreys, parson of Weekes Regis, also said that Allen was a great blasphemer; he had heard of Hariot, that he had been summoned before the Lords of the Council for denying the resurrection of the body. But Jeffreys' main complaint was a three-year-old one. At Blandford, Sir Walter Ralegh and Carew had taken his horse for a post-horse, and when he protested that he must ride home because he had a sermon to preach on Sunday, the next day, Carew Ralegh told him he could go home where he liked, his horse would preach a sermon before him.

Another deponent, William Arnold, vicar of Blandford, gave evidence of one statement by Carew Ralegh which certainly was atheistic by the definitions of the time. It was atheism to make any admission of the existence of any pagan god such as Pan. Arnold said he could remember hearing Carew Ralegh say at Gillingham 'there was a god in nature.' But Carew Ralegh was never called to give evidence himself at the enquiry. Similarly, John Dench, churchwarden of Weekes Regis, told the story of Allen and his soul being put on the top of a pole. But Allen was not called.

Sometimes, the enquiry did follow up supplementary witnesses. Francis Scarlett, the puritan minister of Sherborne, was the Raleghs' own parish priest; they attended his services at Sherborne Abbey. Scarlett gave evidence that one Oliver, Thomas Allen's servant, had once scandalized two Sherborne ladies returning from church; he had complained of the preacher's praise of Moses and said that Moses had fifty-two whores. At this the ladies' ears 'did glow'. Scarlett also said that Robert Hyde, a shoemaker, had told him that 'a company about this town' of Sherborne believed that Hell was nothing but 'poverty and penury in this world, and Heaven was nothing more than to be rich and enjoy pleasures'. The enquiry later interviewed the two ladies whose ears glowed, and Robert Hyde. But they made no attempt to find who were the 'company' of people in Sherborne who held these undoubtedly heretical views.

Nor did they ever interview the most important witness of all, Sir Walter Ralegh. Nothing more was heard of the enquiry. There were no consequences for Ralegh. If it had been a political manouevre, then it had no effect, except possibly to remain in the popular memory as one more sign that Ralegh was intellectually suspect, and his friends also. It could well be that by this time Ralegh had achieved a stature of his own, quite apart from the Queen's favour. He was not to be attacked other than by carefully laid accusation and influentially prepared evidence. Atheism was not the charge, nor were the Ecclesiastical Commissioners the instrument, to bring him down.

Less than a month later, Ralegh was riding with Sir Ralph Horsey and Sir George Trenchard to 'take the examination' of a recusant priest who had been captured at Lady Stourton's house, Chideock Castle, near Lyme Regis. 'Sir Georg and Sir Raufe have used great dillegence in the fynding of this notable knave', he wrote to Cecil from Sherborne on 14th April. In a postscript, he said 'Hee calls hyme sealf John Mooney, but hee is an Irishman and a notabell stout villayne; and I thinke can say miche.'

The 'notabell stout villayne' John Mooney, Moone, or O'Mahoney, was actually the Blessed John Cornelius SJ, an ascetic and visionary, and one of the best-known Catholic priests in Dorset. He had lived at Chideock for years, as the Sheriff George Morton well knew. Cornelius's betrayal and arrest were brought about by treachery. He was taken to Wolfeton

156

House, where he would not say grace at a protestant table. He was examined in theological debate by four clergymen (one of them Ralph Ironside). Trenchard and Horsey were both present, with Ralegh who (the Catholics later said) was so interested in the priest's opinions that he and Cornelius debated theology together all night.

Cornelius was tried and convicted of high treason, and he was executed at Dorchester on 4th July 1594, thus achieving the martyrdom he wanted. He tried to address the crowd from the ladder of the gallows but Ralegh prevented him, being concerned at the possibility of violence in the crowd. John Cornelius was a popular and revered figure and indeed the authorities had been unable to find anybody willing to carry out the sentence of drawing and quartering him alive, as the law demanded, nor would anybody provide a cauldron in which to boil his members. So he hung until he was dead, and his head was nailed to the gallows.

Amongst his public preoccupations of that year, Ralegh had a private grief. His mother died in the spring. She was buried beside her husband in St Mary Major, Exeter. Her will is dated 18th April 1594. She left some unpaid bills, and some small bequests to servants, and a message to her family:

> Dear sons, by my last will and testament I most earnestly entreat you that after my death you will see such debts to be satisfied as shall be demanded after my departure, and to have their due in such things as I have bestowed upon them to the uttermost farthing, to the end I may end my days towards God with a pure heart and faithful conscience. And so I bid you farewell.

Katherine Ralegh must have followed her younger son's progress at Court. He had gone a long way since he left East Budleigh. But she probably sometimes wished that he was a little more humble, and had not offended so many people.

12. Eldorado

ALTHOUGH RALEGH was banned the Court, his enemies constantly feared his return. In January 1594 the rumour was that he was coming back and was to be made a Privy Councillor. Nicholas Faunt, who had been Walsingham's private secretary and was one of Essex's party, wrote to Anthony Bacon, 'And it is now feared of all honest men that he shall presently come to Court; yet it is well withstood. God grant him some further resistance!'

Faunt need not have worried. The furthest resistance to Ralegh was from the Queen herself, and Ralegh knew it. He needed to make some spectacular gesture to win back his place at Court. He decided he would make an expedition to the golden empire of Guiana. One of the earliest clues to his intentions is in a letter of 8th February written at Sherborne by Lady Ralegh, to Cecil. She thanks him for the gift of a book of tablets and with a charming echo of the new Prayer Book ('if all hartes weare opene and all desiars knowne') refers somewhat cryptically to the Queen's (or perhaps Lady Cecil's) 'great curiosetye of decipher-ing'. She continues, in her unique spelling,

> Now, Sur, for the rest I hope for my sake you will rather draw sur watar towardes the est then heulp hyme forward toward the soonsett, if ani respecke to me or love to him be not forgotten. But everi monthe hath his flower and everi season his content-ment, and you greate counselares ar so full of new councels, as you ar steddi in nothing; but wee poore soules that hath bought sorrow at a high price desiar, and can be plesed with, the same misfortun wee hold, fering alltarracions will but multiply misseri, of wich we have allredi felte sufficiant. I knoo only your par-swadcions ar of efecke with him, and hild as orrekeles tied to them by Love; therfore I humbelle besiech you rathar stay him then furdar him. By the wich you shall bind me for ever.

Poor Lady Ralegh's eloquent appeal was of no avail. Cecil did not help Ralegh with the 'east', even if he could have done, and he could not have dissuaded him from the 'sunset' even if he would; in fact, Cecil probably subscribed to the venture.

The *Madre de Dios* had lifted Ralegh out of the Tower. Guiana, he hoped, would take him back to the Queen's side. It was the perfect quest. Lying westwards beyond the sunset, Guiana was a fabulous realm where dwelt a king called Eldorado, the Golden One, who anointed his body with oil and rolled in gold dust, so that he became literally a man of gold. There was a city of gold, called Manoa, and a garden of gold in which every tree and flower in Guiana had its replica in gold. There were mountains of crystal, and rivers of pearls, and hillsides of gold; plates, statues and billets of gold, carpeting the ground. With such a prospect before him, hopes of treasure and conquest and empire and restoration to Court rolled around in Ralegh's mind.

The Spaniards had been trying to find Eldorado for nearly seventy years. They believed that there was another Inca civilization, to rival that of Peru, somewhere in the interior where the Incas had fled from Francisco Pisarro. One of the strangest, but most circumstantial, accounts of Eldorado was given on his deathbed by a Spaniard called Martinez who had been a member of Diego Ortas's expedition. For negligence, Martinez had been condemned to be set adrift in a canoe, without food or water. He was picked up by natives and taken, blindfolded, to the city of the golden emperor. He said that he had entered that city at noon, when his face was uncovered, and that they had travelled through the city all the rest of that day and all the next, from sunrise to sunset, before they reached the Palace of the Inca. It was Martinez who first called the city Eldorado 'for the abundance of gold which he saw in the city, the images of gold in their temples, the plates, armours and shields of gold which they use in the warres'.

The latest attempts to find Guiana had been made by Don Antonio de Berreo, the son-in-law of Don Gonzales Ximenes de Casada who had first annexed the great territory of New Granada for Spain. Berreo was an old soldier who first went out to New Granada in 1580, when he was already sixty, to administer some lands left to his wife. He had mounted three unsuccessful expeditions into the interior. He does not seem ever to have gone on one of them himself, but he later told Ralegh that he had spent 300,000 ducats and travelled 1,500 miles before entering Guiana. He thought he had located Manoa in the highland hills by the river Caroni, a tributary flowing into the Orinoco from the south.

Ralegh had read all the published narratives of journeys into New Granada and Guiana. In 1594 he had more recent news, when George Popham captured some letters in a Spanish ship at sea. In one letter it was said that, on 23rd April 1593, Dominga de Vera had gone up the Orinoco and claimed the land for Berreo. Berreo had sent Vera back to Spain for reinforcements and now had his headquarters at San Josef on the island of Trinidad, of which he was Governor. Ralegh sent Jacob Whiddon on a voyage of reconnaissance of the Orinoco river and its entrances. Whiddon brought back a native who could be trained as an interpreter, and the news that the native lords or 'caciques' were unfriendly to Berreo because of his cruelty. Eight of Whiddon's own men had been ambushed and killed through Berreo's treachery.

Ralegh spent much of the year 1594 preparing his Guiana expedition, and meeting the usual difficulties. In August he was at sea in the Channel, under the Lord Admiral Howard, waiting to repel a possible Spanish invasion fleet. In a letter to Cecil he expresses his doubts about the wisdom of their situation 'att the Forelande'. They were in the wrong place, unless the enemy was so obliging as to attack the mouth of the Thames. If the wind blew strong anywhere from south to south-west, which it was sure to do, the fleet would be in danger, shifting anchorages, by night, off the Goodwin Sands. He still meant 'for goinge westwarde'. But as the days passed, in these unwieldy ships in which he could never get to sleep at night, he was afraid he would be there until Christmas.

In September, he was still at the coast, and still as depressed and downhearted as ever. He had just had mail from Sherborne. The plague was 'very hote' in the town. 'My Bess is on one way sent; hir sonne, another way; and I am in great troble therwithe.' At sea later the same month, Ralegh seemed to be in the depths of despair. 'This unfortunate yeare,' he wrote, 'is such as thos that weare reddy and att sea too moneths before us ar beaten bake agayne and distressed. This longe staye hath made mee a poore man, the yeare farr spent, and what shalbe cum of us God knowes. The boddy is wasted with toyle; the purse with charge; and all things worne. Only the mind is indifferent to good fortune or adversety.' He was not so indifferent as he pretended, for on 26th December he was writing to Cecil from Sherborne that 'this wynde breaks my hart. That should cary mee hence now stayes mee heere, and holds 7 shipps in the river of Temes. As soone as God send them hither, I will not lose one houre of tyme.' He also feared competition. From Alresford he wrote a postscript asking for a 'restraynt of shippinge bound out to the warrs' and fearing that if a Captain Eaton's ships 'attempt the chefest places of my enterprize, I shalbe undun'. He signed himself 'with a hart half broken'. Although Ralegh was never one to suffer in silence and always tended to magnify his woes, the tone of his letters hardly suggests the intrepid and optimistic explorer.

In December 1594 Ralegh received his patent from the Queen which was addressed, significantly, not to her 'trusty' and 'wellbeloved', but coolly to 'her servant'. Ralegh was commissioned to discover and conquer lands unpossessed by any Christian prince, and was also authorized to 'offend and enfeeble' the King of Spain. His patent was all Ralegh received from the Queen. There was no other acknowledgement, no reconciliation, no ships, no money.

However, there was a moderately good response from others. The Lord Admiral Howard ventured his own ship, *The Lion's Whelp*, commanded by Captain George Gifford. Captains Amyas Preston and George Somers were expected to join. George Popham and Sir Robert Dudley arranged to meet Ralegh when he reached Trinidad. Captain Crosse and Captain Caulfield each commanded a bark, Ralegh's old friend Laurence Keymis a small galley. There were 100 officers, soldiers and gentlemen volunteers. Amongst them were Sir Humphrey Gilbert's son John, John Grenville, son of Sir Richard, and another of Ralegh's cousins, young Butshead Gorges. The younger generation of the Devon county families were carrying on the tradition and going to sea with their kinsmen, just like their fathers and uncles before them.

Ralegh had a refresher course in navigation from Hariot, whom he left in charge of his affairs. One legal matter, the task of staying the litigation of a Widow Smith against him, he entrusted to Cecil. Widow Smith 'hath a son that waytes on the Keper, and her doughter maried Mr Wilkes, so as it wilbe the harder to clere'. In spite of this family influence, Ralegh had no fears that the Smiths would win. However, he was strangely uneasy. The 'interest is in my soonn, yet the discreditt wilbe great if I be driven to shew that conveance.' Above all, Ralegh did not want Bess to hear of it, for she would then know that 'shee can

'La Virgenia Pars', map of North America, Florida to Chesapeake Bay, drawn by John White, *c.* 1585. Shows whales, dolphins, and flying fish, and six three-masted ships. On the mainland, within the inscription 'La Virgenia Pars' are the arms and crest of Ralegh. Indian villages on the mainland and islands are indicated by red dots

The manner of their fishing.

Cannow

The capture of Don Antonio de Berreo, Governor of Trinidad, by Sir Walter Ralegh. From Theodore de Bry's *America*, Part VIII, 1599, 'Occidentalis Indiae Pars Octava'

have no intrest in my livinge, and so exclayme'. Possibly here Ralegh was once again carrying out his own principle of making his offspring's financial future secure before that of his wife.

Ralegh went down to Devon at the end of January 1595, with Lady Ralegh, Hariot, Sanderson, who still acted for him in business affairs, and Keymis. After a disagreement with Sanderson, he embarked at Plymouth at midnight on 5th February, and the next day, Thursday, the expedition sailed. Ralegh was on his way, in what he called the winter of his life, to discover 'a better Indies' for Her Majesty.

They arrived in the Canaries on the 17th, having lost touch with *The Lion's Whelp* and Keymis's 'small gallego' on the way. Ralegh waited for seven or eight days but nobody

'The Manner of their fishing'. Drawing by John White, 1585, of the Indians in Virginia

arrived. Preston and Somers, who had been expected, never did join and did not meet Ralegh until 13th July, off Cuba when he was coming home. Ralegh went on to Trinidad, with Crosse in company, and anchored off the Serpent's Mouth on 22nd March. He was disappointed not to see Dudley and Popham. They had arrived ten days earlier and left again.

At home, Lady Ralegh was having news of Sir Walter. In March she learned that he had come across six Portuguese ships laden with fish. His crews took some fish, some water and some wine from each, and let them go. One of them was afterwards captured and taken as a prize to Plymouth, where her captain reported that Ralegh had seemed 'merry and in good health', and he had sailed off in a south-south-west direction. On 10th May Captain Martin White wrote to Lady Ralegh to say that 'My Lord took (at the Canaries) a Spaniard laden with fire-arms. He also took a Fleming laden with wine, and took out of her twenty butts of wine.'

Lady Ralegh was writing on 20th March a sweet letter to Cecil, once again asking for his help.

> Sur Wattar's remembrans of me to you at his last departur shall ad and incres, if itt weer possibell, mor love and dew respect to him. I am in hope, er hit be longe, to heer of him, thought not of long time to see him. In which tim I shall fly to you in all my cumbars, as to the shurest staf I trust to in Sur Wattar's absens.

Lady Ralegh took the chance to put in another word about that £500 marriage portion lent to the Earl of Huntingdon. 'I must intret your faforabell word to me Lord Keppar that hee will suffar me to folow the cours of law to me Lord of Huntington. I desiar noo fafor ther in, but only sufferans. I rathar chuus this time to folow hit in Sur Wattar's absens, that my selfe may bear the unkinnes, and not hee; the moni being long time past dew to me.' Ralegh's name and fame were in safe and tender hands while he was away.

In Trinidad, Ralegh had his barge hoisted out and he sailed close inshore, landing at every cove to map the coast and to examine the countryside. He noted the 'divers little brookes' of fresh water, and one salt-water river, where the trees had oysters hanging from their branches. He noted, too, the Trinidad pitch and afterwards tried trimming his own ships with it. Always alert to commercial possibilities, he found 'it to be most excellent good, and melteth not with the Sunne as the pitch of Norway, and therefore for shippes trading the South parts very profitable'.

Ralegh's barge rejoined the ships at Port of Spain, where there was a small Spanish garrison, who 'offered sign of peace (more for doubt of their own strength)'. Two Indians came out in a canoe. Whiddon had met one of them the year before. They told Ralegh the Spanish strength, how far it was to San Josef, and spoke of Don Antonio de Berreo. He had forbidden any Indian to trade with Ralegh on pain of hanging and quartering. He later executed two men for that reason.

Some Spanish soldiers came on board the ships. They had not tasted wine for years. Ralegh's hospitality (the butts taken from the Flemings) loosened tongues. 'A few draughts made them merrie in which mood they vaunted of Guiana and of the riches thereof.' (Ralegh himself strongly disapproved of drunkenness. He called the Guianans' great drunkenness 'a vice', and in his Instructions to his son he warned that wine 'transformeth a man into a beast, decayeth health, poisoneth the breath, destroyeth natural heat, deformeth the face and rotteth the teeth'.)

Ralegh decided to stay at Port of Spain for a time, so that he could take revenge for Berreo's treachery on Whiddon's men the year before, and because, as he said, 'by discourse with the Spaniards I dayly learned more and more of Guiana, of the rivers and passages, and of the enterprise of Berreo.' He himself was careful to give the Spaniards the impression that he was calling at Trinidad only on his way to relieve his colony in Virginia. (He later claimed that he would indeed have visited it 'if extremitie of weather had not forst me from the said coast'.)

One evening, at 'a time of most advantage', Ralegh and his men set upon the Spanish garrison and put them all to the sword. This was done to revenge Whiddon's men, and also because to enter Guiana in small boats, going 400 or 500 miles from the ships, leaving behind a Spanish garrison who were interested in doing the same thing and who were daily expecting reinforcements from Spain would, as Ralegh said, 'have savoured very much of the asse'. He then sent Captain Caulfield with sixty men and followed himself with another forty to Berreo's new city of San Joseph which they stormed at daybreak, and then burned down. They took Berreo himself and a companion as prisoners. They found five *casiques* who had been tortured by Berreo, chained together, one of them almost dead of hunger. They found that the stories of Berreo's treating the natives like slaves, dropping burning bacon on their naked bodies, and other torments, were quite true.

That day Captain George Gifford in *The Lion's Whelp* and Keymis in his gallego both arrived with divers gentlemen and others who were a great comfort and supply to Ralegh's little army.

Before he left, Ralegh gathered together all the *casiques* who were enemies of Spain and addressed them through an interpreter, saying that he was the servant of a Queen who was the great Casique of the North, and a virgin, and had more Casiques under her than there were trees in Trinidad. He showed them the Queen's picture, which apparently the casiques admired and honoured almost to the point of idolatry. 'Her Majesty,' wrote Ralegh, was 'in that part of the world very famous and admirable.' She was called Ezrabeta Cassipuna Aquerewana, which means Elizabeth the great princess or greatest commander.

Ralegh sailed for the coast of Guiana, with Berreo on board his ship, more as a guest than a prisoner. Ralegh was always able to make the distinction between Spain and a Spaniard. While hating and despising Spain, opposing and thwarting her at every chance, he was at the same time capable of befriending and honouring an individual Spaniard, judging the man on his own merits and using him, in his own words, according to his estate and worth. Don Antonio de Berreo, he found, was a well-descended gentleman, who had served his King in Milan, Naples, the Low Countries and elsewhere. He was very valiant and liberal, a gentleman of great assuredness, and of a great heart. Berreo was also a cunning old campaigner and intellectually Ralegh's equal at least. As their acquaintance deepened into something very like real friendship, Ralegh became more of a disciple than a captor. He concealed his true purpose, keeping up the pretence that he was on his way to Virginia. Thus he learned a great deal about the country from Berreo, who was probably the world's greatest authority on Guiana at that time. If Ralegh had needed any further spur to explore the country, Berreo's fierce enthusiasm for Guiana provided it.

The first important fact which Ralegh learned was that Manoa lay 600, not 400, miles from the sea. He hid this news from his men because if they had known 'they would never have been brought to attempt the same.' When Berreo at last heard Ralegh's real objective, he 'was stricken into a great melancholy and sadnesse'. Then he did his utmost to dissuade Ralegh. He said that Ralegh would not be able to go up any of the rivers in his barks or pinnaces because they were so low, sandy and full of flats. Even Berreo's party, though they were in canoes drawing only a foot, had grounded every day.

'None of the country will come and speak with you,' he told Ralegh. 'They will all fly away from you and if you try and follow them to their villages they will burn them down. It is a very long way. Winter is at hand. Once the rivers begin to rise it will be impossible to stem the currents. In those small boats it will not be possible to carry enough victuals for even half the expedition.'

Worst of all, and this Ralegh found most discouraging, the kings and lords of the Guiana borders had decreed that nobody should trade with any Christians for gold, because that would lead to their own overthrow. For love of gold, they said, the Christians meant to conquer and dispossess them.

Experience was to show that Berreo was right on almost every point. But Ralegh had made up his mind to try it, come what might. He sent *The Lion's Whelp* and Caulfield's bark to reconnoitre the mouth of the Capuri river, to the eastward, where Whiddon and John Douglas, master of Ralegh's own ship, had previously surveyed and buoyed a passage. But they were unable to sail their ships across the sand-bars. At the same time he sent King, master of *The Lion's Whelp*, away in one of his ship's boats to try the mouth of another branch of the river. Here again, the water was too shallow, and King had to withdraw because his Indian guide assured him that the natives on the banks were cannibals and shot poisoned arrows.

There was nothing for it but to embark the whole expedition in small boats. 'Fearing the worst,' Ralegh had his carpenters cut down Keymis's gallego so that it drew only five feet, and fitted it with banks of oars for rowing. Ralegh himself went in the gallego, with Captain Thynne, John Grenville, John Gilbert, Whiddon, Keymis, and nearly sixty more. Captain Caulfield had ten men in his wherry including Butshead Gorges. Captain Gifford had ten men in *The Lion's Whelp* wherry, and there were another ten in the ship's boat. Ralegh's own barge also had ten men, to make a total expedition strength of a hundred men. They carried victuals for a month.

The boats had to cross rough water, with cross-winds and currents, as wide a channel as 'betweene Dover and Calais', before entering the mouth of a river, one of four discovered by John Douglas. It was to be a hard existence for the men in the boats, as Ralegh described it: they were

> al driven to lie in the raine and weather, in the open aire, in the burning Sunne, and upon the hard bords, and to dresse our meat, and to cary all manner of furniture in them, wherewith they were so pestered and unsavory, that what with victuals being most fish, with wette clothes of so many men thrust together, and the heat of the Sunne, I will undertake there was never any prison in England, that could bee found more unsavorie and lothsome.

For Ralegh it was a great change from silks and satins, with a pearl in his ear and a plume in his hat. He was well aware of the incongruity. 'Especially to my selfe,' he wrote, 'who had for many yeeres before bene dieted and cared for in a sort farre more differing'. Ralegh was in his forties, and soft from years of easy living.

They had as a guide an Indian who came from the south of the Orinoco. He was called

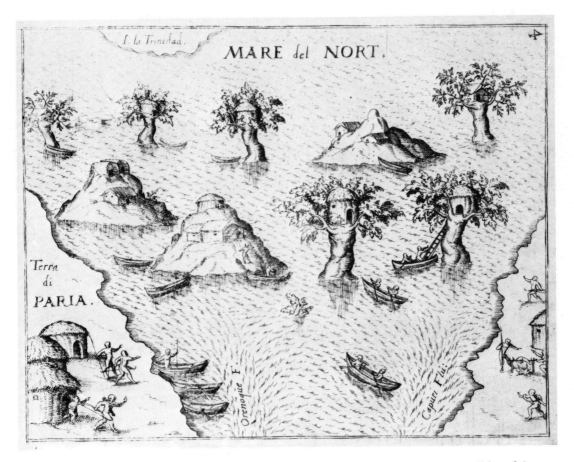

Tree houses that Ralegh reported seeing in Guiana. From L. Hulsius 1599, a German edition of the discovery of Guiana

Ferdinando (perhaps an ironic christening in memory of Simon the Portugal who went to Virginia). Ferdinando had not seen the Orinoco river for twelve years and he proved unreliable. The expedition was very nearly lost in a great maze of rivers which crossed and recrossed. They were all large and they all looked alike. The boats were carried in circles around islands, and every stretch of the river was bordered with high trees so that nobody could check their position. On 22nd May they entered an unknown river which they called the 'River of the Red Cross' because they were the first Christians to sail on it. Here they sighted three Indians in a canoe, and quickly overtook them.

When more Indians, watching from the river bank, saw that Ralegh's party meant no harm to the men in the canoe, they were prepared to trade for such goods as they had. Ralegh took his barge to the mouth of the little creek which led up to the Indian village. Ferdinando went ashore 'to fetch fruits, and to drinke of their artificiall wines'. He was at once seized by the village chieftain, who accused him of bringing strangers into the district to rob and despoil his people. Ferdinando escaped and the Indians hunted him through the woods like 'Deere-dogges'. He was lucky to reach the river's edge, and he swam out to the barge, half dead with fear. Fortunately, Ralegh had a very old Indian from the village as a hostage, and he became the expedition's pilot. In a few days' time Ferdinando 'knew nothing at all, or which way to turne'. The old man himself was often in doubt. However, without this old man, Ralegh doubted whether they could ever have found their way to Guiana, or back to their ships.

For three days they went on up the river with the flood tide, anchoring during the ebb. On the third day the galley ran aground and stuck so fast that even Ralegh thought the expedition was going to end there and then, leaving 'fourscore and ten of our men to have inhabited like rooks upon trees' (like the Indians of those parts who built their houses in the trees). But the next day they took out the galley's ballast and with much tugging and hauling to and fro got her off.

On the fourth day they came to the great river Amana where they soon lost the effect of the tide and had to row against a current which became stronger the further they went. Although they all took turns to row and gave each other spells every hour, the heat and the violent exercise wearied them, and they began to despair. Ralegh had to rally them and encourage them to persevere with a mixture of enticements and threats. He kept telling them there was only one more day to go, and then they would have everything they wanted. If they turned back, he said, they were sure to starve on the way. Most powerful argument of all, 'the world would also laugh us to scorne.'

At the same time, Ralegh kept an observant eye on the passing scenery and its wild life. He saw enough different sorts of trees, flowers and fruits to 'make tenne volume of herbals'. There were birds of all colours, 'some carnation, some crimson, orenge-tawny, purple, watchet [pale blue]'. The crews caught fish, and shot birds with their fowling pieces, and ate fruit from the trees as they passed.

The old Indian now told Ralegh that if he anchored the galley in the main river and took the small boats up a tributary to starboard, he would find a town where he could get bread, hens, fish and wine. Ralegh was very glad to hear this speech and embarked with a small party in the boats. Because they were told the town was so near, they took no food with them. After rowing for three hours, they were surprised not to see the town. The old Indian said it was a little further. After three more hours' rowing, when the sun was setting, they began to suspect treachery, especially when the old man confessed that there were Spaniards along that river. By now night had fallen and when they asked the old man how much further, he said 'four reaches more'. They rowed four reaches, and four more, and another four, and there was still no sign of the town. They were now forty miles from the galley and 'our poore water-men, even heart-broken, and tired, were ready to give up the ghost.'

At last, they decided to hang the old pilot, and if they had known the way back again by night 'hee would surely have gone'. It was as dark as pitch, and the river had narrowed until the trees met overhead. They had to hack through the branches with their swords. Still, the old Indian insisted it was just a little further. At one o'clock in the morning, they saw a light and heard dogs barking. The old Indian was vindicated.

The lord of the village was away on an expedition, but in his house they found plenty of food and drink. They stayed the night, and in the morning set off for the galley, with bread, fish and hens. Going down river again, in broad daylight, with a full stomach, Ralegh saw the river quite differently:

> On both sides of this river, we passed the most beautifull countrey that ever mine eyes beheld: and whereas all that we had seene before was nothing but woods, prickles, bushes, and thornes, here we beheld plaines of twenty miles in length, the grasse short and greene, and in divers parts groves of trees by themselves, as if they had beene by all the arte and labour in the world so made of purpose: and still as we rowed, the deere came downe feeding by the waters side, as if they had been used to a keepers call.

Even in that Eden there was a serpent, indeed thousands of them. The river swarmed with lagartos (alligators), and it was actually called locally the river of Lagartos. One of the party, a Negro, 'a very proper yoong fellow', went for a swim at the mouth of the river, and was 'taken and devoured' by an alligator.

They rejoined the men in the galley, who were beginning to think they were all dead, and went on up river. The next day Captain Gifford sighted and pursued four canoes, capturing two loaded with excellent bread which, in Ralegh's view, was almost as good as gold. It was a tremendous boost to morale and all his men cried out, 'Let us go on, we care not how farre!' The other two canoes were run ashore by their crews, three of whom were Spaniards, who escaped into the bush. Ralegh landed to look for them and while he was creeping through the bushes he found a hidden Indian basket. It was a refiner's basket, containing quick-silver, salt-petre and 'divers things for the trial of metals', with some dust of the ore he had refined. This was even more encouraging, and Ralegh landed more men, offering a reward of five hundred pounds to any soldier who captured one of the Spaniards. The Spaniards escaped, but Ralegh had managed to capture the Indians from the canoes. He kept the 'chiefest of them', who had been christened Martin by the Spaniards. After he had been reassured that Ralegh was not going to eat him (as the Spaniards had said he would) Martin became the expedition's guide, and the old man and Ferdinando were sent down river in another canoe.

The conduct of Ralegh's men was a source of wonder to the Indians. Ralegh could not prevent all petty pilfering by the 'meaner sorte' in his party, but whenever it happened he carried out an investigation through his interpreter, restored the property, or paid compensation, and publicly punished the offender. There was no trouble over native women. None of Ralegh's party ever slept with a native woman, unlike the Spaniards who 'tooke from them both their wives and daughters dayly, and used them for the satisfying of their owne lusts'.

On the fifteenth day of their journey, after the galley had once more run hard aground and with great effort had been kedged off, they were all very cheered to see the mountains of Guiana away to the south. That evening they anchored at 'the parting of three goodly Rivers'. One was the Amana, down which they had come from the north, and the other two were both the great Orinoco, flowing from the west towards the sea in the east. That night they dined on turtles' eggs, of which there were thousands on the sandy beach of an island. 'Our men,' wrote Ralegh, 'were now well filled and highly contented both with the fare, and neereness of the land of Guiana which appeared in sight.'

In the morning the local chieftain Toparacima came down to the river-side with some thirty or forty of his followers carrying presents of fruit, wine, bread and fish. Ralegh gave them some of his 'good Spanish wine' of which he had a few bottles left and 'which above all things they love'. Afterwards they went a mile and a half inland to Toparacima's town of Arowocai, where some of Ralegh's captains 'karoused' on Toparacima's wine until they were 'reasonable pleasant'.

There were two *casiques* there, each lying in a cotton hammock, attended by two women who ladled wine into cups, which the *casiques* drank three at a time. Ralegh was much impressed by the wife of one of the *casiques*. In all his life he had seldom seen a better favoured woman. 'She was of good stature, with black eyes, fat of body, of an excellent countenance, her hair almost as long as herself, tied up again in pretty knots, and it seemed she stood not in awe of her husband, as the rest, for she spoke and discoursed and drank among the gentlemen and captains, and was very pleasant, knowing her own comeliness, and taking great pride therein.' He adds, intriguingly, 'I have seene a Lady in England so like to her, as but for the difference of colour, I would have sworn might have been the same.'

Toparacima lent them an experienced pilot, and the next day they sailed up the Orinoco with a good easterly wind behind them. Here the river, Ralegh judged, was thirty miles broad and it had islands in it which he estimated were twice the size of the Isle of Wight. The river banks were high and stony, and the rocks were a 'blew metalline colour, like unto the best steele-ore', which Ralegh was sure it was. There were mountains of this same blue stone.

The following day, the land opened up to the north, to champaign country of rolling

Engraving of Indian women from L. Hulsius 1599, a German edition of the discovery of Guiana

grassland. The river flowed between banks which were now a 'very perfect red'. The plain stretched for hundreds of miles, the pilot told Ralegh, and on it lived four principal Indian nations. One of them was a race of men black as negroes, smooth-haired, 'a very valiant or rather desperate people' called the Aroras. They used poisoned arrows and the Spaniards had never by bribe or by torture been able to learn the secret of the antidote. But the Indians told it to Ralegh, and also the properties of other roots and juices which cooled fevers and healed internal haemorrhages.

On their fifth day on the Orinoco, they arrived at the port of Morequito. Messengers were sent to Topiawari, the king of Aromaia; he had succeeded as king after his nephew Morequito had been killed by Berreo. Topiawari was a hundred and ten years old but he walked fourteen miles to see Ralegh. With him came many of his people, including women and children, bringing venison, pork, hens, chickens, fowl, fish, excellent fruit and roots, pineapples, 'the princes of fruites, that grown under the Sunne', bread and wine, and a species of parakeet, 'no bigger than wrennes' (possibly humming-birds). They also gave Ralegh an armadillo, a beast which was 'all barred over with small plates' and had a 'white horn growing in his hinder parts, as bigge as a great hunting horne, which they used to winde instead of a trumpet'. (The 'horn' was actually the animal's scaly tail).

Ralegh had a little tent put up for the old King to rest in, while he talked to him through an interpreter. He told the King that he had come to defend him and his people from the Spaniards and deliver them from tyranny. Topiawari had personal experience of Spanish methods. After the murder of his nephew, he himself had been put on a chain for seventeen days and led from place to place like a dog, until he paid his ransom of a hundred gold plates. By contrast, Ralegh spoke at length of Her Majesty's greatness, her justice and charity to all oppressed nations, her beauties and her virtues.

Topiawari was a valuable source of first-hand information about the country. Ralegh asked him about the people who lived beyond the mountains (which, Ralegh thought, was the probable direction of Manoa). Topiawari said, with a great sigh, that they were a very strong and numerous people, who had killed his eldest son in battle. They wore large coats, and hats of a crimson colour (the same colour as the wood of the pole of the tent they were sitting in). Their houses had many rooms, and their borders were defended by three thousand men.

Ralegh asked Topiawari to stay the night, but the king said that he had far to go, he was old and weak, and in his own words, he was every day called for by death. (Ralegh was always quick to pick up a striking phrase). The old King walked back to his town, making a round trip for the day of twenty-eight miles.

The next day the expedition sailed westward up the Orinoco to its meeting with the 'famous River' Caroli. They could hear the roar of the river from far off. When they tried to row up it, they found that an eight-oared barge could not go further than a stone's throw in an hour, though the river was as wide as the Thames at Woolwich at this point. They landed parties, and some of them walked to see that 'wonderful breach of waters', which was a series of water-falls. They could hear the thunder of the falls as they walked. From the top of a hill Ralegh saw

> the river how it ranne in three parts, above twentie miles off, and there appeared some tenne or twelve overfals in sight, every one as high over the other as a Church-tower, which fell with that fury, that the rebound of the water made it seeme, as if it had bene all covered over with a great shower of rain; and in some places wee tooke it at the first sight for a smoke that had risen over some great towne.

Ralegh was now ready to go back to the boats, being as he said 'a very ill footeman', but the others persuaded him, little by little, to go on. The sight was well worth the trouble.

> I never saw a more beautifull countrey, nor more lively prospects, hils so raised here and there over the valleys, the river winding into divers branches, the plaines adjoyning without bush or stubble, all faire greene grasse, the ground of hard sand easie to march on, either for horse or foote, the deere crossing in every path, the birdes towards the evening singing on every tree with a thousand severall tunes, cranes and herons of white, crimson, and carnation pearching in the rivers side, the aire fresh

with a gentle Easterly winde, and every stone that we stouped to take up, promised either golde or silver by his complexion.

Some of the party picked up stones which were lying around; others dug them out with their daggers. The rocks were 'minerall Sparre', as hard as flint. Jacob Whiddon and the surgeon Nicholas Millechap had some which may have been sapphires but most of the stones were just coloured stones, no more, and were used to discredit Ralegh's exploits when he got home.

It was while he was among the Indians of the Orinoco that Ralegh heard the story which eventually did more than anything else to discredit him as a man of truth and a serious scientific observer. It was the famous legend of the 'nation of people, whose heads appear not above their shoulders. They are called Ewaipanoma. They are reported to have their eyes in their shoulders, and their mouths in the middle of their breasts, and that a long traine of haire groweth backward between their shoulders.'

Ralegh himself thought this may well have been a fable, but he had hearsay evidence

The Ewaipanema, 'men whose heads do grow beneath their shoulders'. From L. Hulsius 1599, a German edition of the discovery of Guiana

from all sides. 'Every child in the provinces of Arromaia and Canuri affirmed the truth.' Topiawari's son, whom Ralegh brought back to England, testified that the Ewaipanoma were the most mighty men of the land, and used bows, arrows and clubs three times as big as any of the Guianans. They had slain many hundreds of his father's people. Ralegh did not hear about the Ewaipanoma until he had left the district. He wrote that if he had heard one word about them while he was there he might have brought one of them with him to put the matter beyond doubt. He made his own position quite clear. 'For mine own part I saw them not, but I am resolved that so many people did not all combine, or forethinke to make the report.' (Where Ralegh is speaking from his own experience and his account can be checked against other sources, he normally proves a most reliable and conscientious witness.)

True or untrue, Ralegh's story had a powerful effect upon the Elizabethan imagination. Shakespeare refers to the Ewaipanoma in *Othello*:

> And of the Cannibals that each other eat,
> The Anthropophagi, and men whose heads
> Do grow beneath their shoulders. This to hear
> Would Desdemona seriously incline.

and again in *The Tempest*, when Gonzalo asks:

> When we were boys
> Who would believe that there were mountaineers
> Dew-lapp'd like bulls, whose throats had hanging at 'em
> Wallets of flesh? or that there were such men
> Whose heads stood in their breasts?

Ralegh also made enquiries about the Amazons, and these too became ammunition for his detractors. But he intended a serious scientific investigation, and he repeated the results for what they were worth, that the Amazons did not cut off their right breasts, but they did gather once a year, in April, to feast, dance, drink, and copulate. If they conceived and bore a son, he was returned to his father. A daughter was kept with the Amazons. They were cruel and bloodthirsty, and they valued gold plates and spleen stones.

The party had now been a month away from the ships. The weather had turned foul. The Orinoco was raging and overflowing 'very fearfully'. The rains came down in terrible showers and gusts in great abundance. Water that was shallow enough to wade in in the morning was shoulder-deep by the evening. Ralegh's men had begun to complain about their clothes; 'no man had place to bewstowe any other apparell then that which he ware on his backe, and that was throughly washt on his body for the most part tenne times in one day.' So they turned back and went downstream to Morequito, where Ralegh met Topiawari again.

They talked about the rich town of Macureguarai, up the Caroni, where the gold plates came from. The people there had repelled a force of three hundred Spanish soldiers, smothering them by setting fire to the pampas grass in their path. Ralegh asked the King

Map of Guiana by Sir Walter Ralegh. The fabled Lake and City of Manoa is shown in the centre of the map with El Dorado slightly left. The map is reproduced upside down, the northern coast of Guiana and the Atlantic Ocean being now at the bottom.

whether he thought Ralegh's party was strong enough to storm the town. Topiawari said he thought they were. He and his borderers would come with them, provided Ralegh could leave fifty soldiers to guard Morequito, and provided the rivers were still fordable. Ralegh said he did not have fifty such soldiers, 'he had not above fiftie good men in all there, the rest were labourers and rowers.' Captain Caulfield, John Grenville, John Gilbert and some of the other young men wanted to try. Ralegh produced excellent practical reasons why they should not. He had not enough men, not enough powder, shot, spades, pickaxes, or anything else. Ralegh was probably right, although a Pisarro or a Cortes might still have gone on in spite of the difficulties. But Ralegh was not the stuff of a *conquistadore*. He said he would leave it for the present, and try to come back next year.

Topiawari gave Ralegh his only son to take back with him to England. Ralegh left behind Francis Sparrow, one of Gifford's men, who wanted to stay and write an account of the country. He was later captured by the Spaniards, taken to Spain, and eventually made his way back to England in 1602. A boy called Hugh Goodwin was also left behind, to learn the language. Ralegh met him again in 1617. These exchanges were not hostages so much as pledges of good faith.

When they left, another *casique* called Putjima came with them and offered to show them a gold-mine on his land. They went ashore to see it, but once again Ralegh was no great walker and when he realized that their destination was another half-day's march more he told Keymis to go on and look at the mine, and rendezvous with Ralegh further downstream.

By this time, 'their hearts were cold to behold the great rage and increase' of the Orinoco river. The weather was very foul, with terrible thunder and showers. The only good thing was that they made a hundred miles a day downstream in the current. They could not return by the Amana, as they had come, because the 'great brize and current of the sea were so forcible.' They took another branch, the Capuri, and so reached the sea, where there was a storm raging over the sandbars. The longer they waited, the worse it looked, 'so being all very sober, and melancholy, one faintly chearing another to shewe courage' they steered for Trinidad and found the ships at anchor, 'then which there was never to us a more joyfull sight'.

It was time, as Ralegh wrote, 'to leave Guiana to the Sunne, whom they worshippe, and steare away towardes the North'. But before doing so, he steered west to attack three Spanish settlements along the coast, at Cumana, St Mary's and Rio de la Hacha. He did not visit Virginia, but turned for home, reaching Plymouth at the end of August, having been in company with Preston and Somers for a few days off Cuba before losing them on 20th July.

Lady Ralegh was overjoyed to hear of Sir Walter's safe return and wrote ecstatically to Cecil:

Sur hit tes trew I thonke the leveng God Sur Walter is safly londed at Plumworthe with as gret honnor as ever man can, but with littell riches. I have not yet hard from him selfe. Kepe thies I beseech you to your selfe yet: only to me lord ammerall.

In haste this Sunday. Your pour frind E. Raleg. Mani of his mene slane; himselfe will now. Pardon my rewed wryteng with the goodnes of the newes.

Lady Ralegh's postscript repeated a general rumour: that Ralegh had lost some of his best and bravest men, such as Gifford, Whiddon, Caulfield, Grenville, Vincent and Thynne. In fact, the only casualty was the Negro killed by alligators, although Ralegh does refer to Jacob Whiddon in his account of the very first meeting with the Spaniards in Trinidad, when Whiddon was sent to speak with them. Ralegh goes on, of Whiddon, 'whom afterward to my great griefe I left buried in the said yland after my returne from Guiana, being a man most honest and valiant'. This reads like an epitaph.

The health of the expedition was very good, considering they had travelled through malarial coastal marshes and river-banks, had spent weeks in open boats subjected to the rigours of sun, rain and wind, with no proper diet, but eating whatever food they could get. However, the climate inland was, as Ralegh himself said, 'so healthfull, as of an hundred persons & more (which lay without shift most sluttishly, and were every day almost melted with heate in rowing and marching, and suddenly wet againe with great showers)' and yet they did not lose one person through disease.

Ralegh's leadership had been excellent. He had held together several boat-loads of ambitious, quarrelsome and gold-hungry adventurers through the perils and uncertainties of an unknown land and through the worst that the weather, disappointment, over-crowding, irregular food and hard physical exercise could do. He had kept morale high, and had brought them safely back home.

Ralegh's friends were delighted to see him and longed to hear of his adventures. Sir Hugh Beeston, for instance, had heard the comfortable news of Sir Walter's return and said that he 'sat on thorns' until he could see Ralegh's face. But there was also a powerful counter-reaction of amused disbelief. Some said that Ralegh had never been on the expedition himself at all, but had hidden in Cornwall the whole time. They said that the marcasite he had brought back had not come from Guiana but from the Barbary Coast. He should have returned with great store of plunder and ships full of gold. All he had were these wildly hilarious tales of Amazons who fornicated annually, and men with no heads and men who lived perched up in trees. He had *tales* of gold, but no gold; stories of unimaginable wealth, but no wealth. More damning still, an Alderman of London and an official of the Mint had assayed some of the ore Ralegh had brought back and had pronounced it almost worthless.

It was largely to answer these slanders, and to prove, as he said to Cecil, that 'it is no dreame which I have reported of Guiana' that Ralegh wrote his great travel classic 'The Discoverie of the Large, Rich and Bewtiful Empire of Guiana'. It was published in 1596, dedicated to Cecil and the Lord High Admiral, and became a best-seller, running to several editions. Grimly, Ralegh set about his accusers.

I am not so much in love with these long voyages, as to devise, therby to cozen myselfe, to lie hard, to fare worse, to be subjected to perils, to diseases, to ill savors, to be parched & withered, and withall to sustaine the care and laboure of such an enterprize, except the same had more comfort, then the fetching of Marcasite in Guiana, or buying of gold oare in Barbary.

As for the suspect ore, it was true, Ralegh admitted it, that while they were in Trinidad members of his party had picked up stones which he had assured them at the time were marcasite and of no value. But they had brought some home all the same and sent them for assay, thus tending to devalue the ore Ralegh himself had brought, which certainly did bear gold. Similarly, some of the rocks were picked up from ground beside the falls of Caroni by those 'who kept al that glistered' and would not be persuaded that they were just pretty stones.

The truth was that the expedition had not been equipped for a serious geological survey. Ralegh evidently expected to find gold already mined and worked into the form of billets, plates, statues, utensils or other artefacts. Otherwise, the members of his party merely scrabbled about with their daggers, axe-heads, even their finger-nails. Even after they had found the refiner's basket, the expedition made no real attempt to carry out a mineralogical survey. Ralegh defends this decision in a passage full of specious reasonings, about attracting attention, and very hard stones, and being 400 miles from his ships, ending with a statement of pure hypocrisy: 'I *could* have returned a good quantitie of gold ready cast, if I had not shot at another marke, then present profit!'

He was no better equipped for geographical survey. His expedition's finest scientific instrument was himself, with his sharp eye and his fluent pen. Certainly Hariot was working on a large map of the area, from information given to him by Ralegh. But this was intended as more of an advertisement. In fact, the whole expedition from start to finish was a brilliant advertisement.

The advertisement failed to attract its intended buyer, although Ralegh's friends did their best. On 27th September 1595, Rowland Whyte was telling Sir Robert Sidney that Sir Walter Ralegh's friends were impressing upon the Queen how well he had done. George Chapman wrote a celebratory poem, *De Guiana, Carmen Epicum*, in which he urged the Queen:

> Then most admired Soveraigne, let your breath
> Goe foorth upon the waters, and create
> A golden worlde in this our yron age,
> And be the prosperous forewind to a Fleet.

He refers in the warmest and most sympathetic terms to Ralegh himself and his patriotic unselfishness:

> O how most like
> Art thou (heroike Author of this Act)
> To this wrong'd soule of Nature: that sustainst
> Paine, charge and perill for thy countreys good,
> And she much like a bodie numb'd with surfets,
> Feeles not thy gentle applications
> For the health, use, and honour of her powers.

Chapman was even brave enough to venture a forecast of how the Queen would receive Ralegh's discovery of Guiana:

> Me thinkes I see our Liege rise from her throne,
> Her eares and thoughtes in steepe amaze erected,
> At the most rare endevour of her power.
> And now she blesseth with her woonted Graces
> Th'industrious Knight, the soule of this exploit,
> Dismissing him to convoy of his starres.

He was quite wrong. The Queen did not bless the industrious knight. She ignored him altogether, and showed no visible interest whatsoever in his discovery. Essex and his faction may have persuaded her that Ralegh's exploits were only second-hand travellers' tales. Perhaps she believed that investment in Guiana was properly left to private enterprise. Or perhaps she guessed that the whole undertaking had been designed as a glittering lure for her and, perversely, decided not to accept it.

Ralegh did not give up. He sent Keymis in the *Darling* back to Guiana in January 1596 and Leonard Berry in the *Watte* the following December. Both men reported optimistically about prospects, and Ralegh himself always sang Guiana's praises in the most eloquent language:

> Guiana is a countrey that hath yet her maydenhead, never sackt, turned, nor wrought,
> the face of the earth hath not bene torne, nor the vertue and salt of the soyle spent by
> manurance, the graves have not bene opened for golde, the mines not broken with
> sledges, nor their Images puld downe out of their temples . . .

But it was no use. Ralegh had failed to win the Queen. No matter what other success or riches Guiana might or might not have brought him, he had still failed. As he wrote himself in the 'Ocean to Cynthia': 'When she did ill, what empires could have pleased?'

13. The Knight of Cadiz

AFTER the defeat of the Spanish Armada off Gravelines in 1588, Spain had for a time lain prostrate as a naval power. If the Queen had so chosen, Spain could have been utterly crushed and left powerless at sea for the next generation. But, with her own particular kind of hesitation and equivocal foreign policy, the Queen refrained. Spain was allowed to recover to some extent, and the war rumbled on into the 1590s.

Ralegh's hatred of Spain remained one of the central strands in the core of his nature. He held to this animosity as other men might to religion or to a good woman. At times, he seems almost neurotically obsessed. He was, in a way, trapped by his past; had he ever secretly mellowed towards Spain, his reputation as a Spaniard-baiter would still have driven him on. Everything about Spain conspired to arouse his jealousy and disgust. He had imperial longings: Spain had empires. He yearned for and needed gold: Spain shipped tons of it from her possessions. He respected justice, and order, and free thought: Spain's persecution and torturings and bigotry deeply offended him. Ralegh was always studying Spanish affairs, always trying to read the Spanish mind, always drawing conclusions from Spanish moves in dependent states. 'The Kinge of Spayne seeketh not Irlande for Irlande,' he wrote to Cecil in May 1593, 'but havinge raysed up troops of beggers in our backs, shall be able to inforce us to cast our eyes over our shoulders, while thos before us strike us on the braynes.' The war against Spain, in Ralegh's view, was always the most important offensive. It was Spain who struck at England's heart. 'We are so busyed and dandled in these French wars, which are endless, as we forgett the defens next the hart.'

The wars in France did indeed seem endless, and a year later Ralegh was trying to involve himself in them. In June 1594 he wrote to the Lord High Admiral, offering his services and hoping that his past 'offences' would not prevent him serving under Howard.

> If your Lordship will vouchsaife her Majesty for me to attend you privatly in her service, I hope I shall stand your Lordship in the place of a poore marriner or soldier. I have no other desire but to serve her Majestye. And seinge I deserve nor place, nor honour, nor rewarde, I hope it wilbe easely graunted – if I be not condemned to the grave; no libertye nor hope left that ether tyme or the geving of my life may recover, or be a sacrifice for, my offences.

Ralegh was referring (in humble terms, for him) to the latest events in France. The Spaniards had begun to fortify Crozon (or 'old Croydun', as Ralegh wrote it in his letters) which commanded the harbour of Brest. In May they brought up siege guns to bombard the town of Brest. Sir John Norris wrote to the Queen that 'there never happened a more dangerous enterprise for the state of your Majesty's country than this of the Spaniard to possess Brittany.' In July an expedition was planned to capture Crozon, under Norris and Frobisher. They sailed in August with eight ships and 4,000 men. It is possible that when Ralegh wrote to Cecil in August 1594, from 'the Forelande', and complained of sleepless nights, he was on board a ship escorting or guarding the seaward flank of Norris's force. The assault on Crozon began in September but the fort was not captured until November. Sir Martin Frobisher was killed – one more of the old generation of adventurers to die.

Frobisher was soon followed by Hawkins and Drake. They sailed in August 1595 from Plymouth on a raiding expedition to the West Indies. They had six of the Queen's ships, and eleven others, and 2,500 men under Sir Thomas Baskerville. The Spaniards having introduced the convoy system (which had led to Grenville's death), the treasure *flota* could now only be attacked with a reasonable chance of success at its assembly ports in the Caribbean. In spite of the magic of the names Hawkins and Drake, the expedition had an old-fashioned air about it. The commanders belonged to an age that was past, and certainly they laboured under all the old disadvantages: the Queen's hesitations and changes of mind, niggardly financing, and joint commanders who were always uneasy in each other's company. The result was failure. The attack on Las Palmas failed. Hawkins himself fell sick and died at Puerto Rico. After an abortive landing at Panama, Drake caught dysentery and died on 28th January 1596. He was buried at sea, wearing his armour. With him, over the ship's side, went an Elizabethan era. (The Queen at once made arrangements to recover Drake's debts to her from his estate.)

However, a new era was beginning and a new generation was planning the offensive against Spain, led by the Earl of Essex, who was becoming the foremost military personality of his day in England. Although Ralegh was still not welcome at Court, he was an experienced military commander. He could be of use to the Queen and to Essex. In November 1595, after his return from Guiana, he was advising the Privy Council on the defences of Devon, recommending that if reinforcements were needed, they should be supplied from Dorset and not from Cornwall, which was isolated and vulnerable and would need all its men to protect itself. He also warned that he had intelligence of a Spanish fleet of sixty ships. A few days later he was telling Cecil of his fears for Drake and Hawkins. News of the disasters to the expedition would not arrive for some weeks, but Ralegh wrote prophetically 'for, as sure as God lives, if the Spanishe fleet arive while the soldiers ar over lande, bothe the shipps att ancor and thos at Panama wilbe both lost.'

In the New Year of 1596 an old idea for an attack on Spain was revived – a raid on the fort and town of Cadiz. The new plan seems to have arisen as a result of consultations and contacts between the Lord High Admiral, the Earl of Essex, Sir Francis Vere, who commanded the English army in the Netherlands, and a Spaniard called Antonio Perez, who had once been Philip of Spain's secretary. Troops were actually withdrawn from the Netherlands to take part in the attack, whereupon the Cardinal Archduke Albert, the Duke of Parma's successor as commander of the Spanish army in the Low Countries, launched an attack upon Calais in April 1596.

'Calais' was still, as in Mary's reign, an emotive word in English ears. Essex pleaded to be allowed to go across and relieve the beleaguered city. The Spanish guns, he said, could be heard at Greenwich. The Queen, as usual, hesitated, and asked King Henry of France whether her troops would be allowed to enter Calais. In the meantime, on 14th April, Calais fell to Spain.

After such a blow to English pride, it became more than ever necessary to deliver some counter-attack. Reluctantly, the Queen agreed to the plan to assault Cadiz from the sea. 'Cadiz' had as emotive a sound in Spanish ears as Calais had in English. The news of the deaths of Drake and Hawkins had arrived in England. In Ireland, a new revolt had broken out, led by Tyrone and fostered by Spain, just as Ralegh had warned. It was high time some retaliation was inflicted upon Spain.

As usual, Ralegh was involved in the expedition up to the hilt and expended all his energies in preparing for it. He spent most of April and May in London and in towns along the Thames, assembling ships, transports and men. The difficulties of manning, victualling, and contrary weather were enormous, and delayed Ralegh so much that they laid him open to criticism of dragging his feet. 'I pray you,' said Howard to Cecil, on 16th April, 'hasten away Sir Walter Ralegh.' Essex echoed the words a few days later.

Ralegh was doing his best. On 3rd May he wrote to Cecil from Blackwall, 'I am not able to live, to row up and down every tyde from Gravsend to London.' He was, he said, 'more greved then ever I was, in anything of this world, for this cross weather'. He also, he said, delivered the names of those men who refused to serve Her Majesty to Pope, the Marshal of the Admiralty. In a flurry of letter-writing the same day, Ralegh wrote to Cecil to recommend Hugh Broughton for the bishopric of Lismore and Waterford; to recommend his 'ancient servaunt' Charles Cartie for a grant of lands in Ireland; and to ask if Cecil would take further action in the long-running litigation against the Widow Smith.

The following day, at Northfleet, Ralegh was still complaining about desertions. Pope, he said, could inform Burroughs, the Controller of the Admiralty, for Pope had pressed all the ships. Pope could also inform Cecil of how little Her Majesty's authority was respected. 'For as fast as wee press men on day the cum away another, and say the will not serve.' Essex, Ralegh and the rest of the Court's brilliants might be on fire to strike at Spain, but the ordinary man in the street was heartily sick of the war. Ralegh was thoroughly depressed. 'The winde is so strong as it is impossible to turne downe, or to warpe downe, or to tooe downe.' The messenger had found Ralegh in a country village a mile from Gravesend, hunting after runaway mariners, 'and dragging in the mire from ale-howse to ale-howse'. He could not even find paper to write this letter on, but had to borrow a piece from the messenger. 'Sir,' he assured Cecil, 'by the leving God, ther is nor King, nor Queen, nor generall, nor any elce, can take more care than I do to be gonn.'

Meanwhile, at Plymouth, the Earl of Essex was frantic with impatience to be away. At first, he had been extremely polite to Ralegh. On 3rd May he wrote, kindly, 'Your pains and travail in bringing all things to that forwardness they are in doth sufficiently assure me of your discontentment to be now stayed by the wind.' (This rather suggests that somebody

Sir Walter Ralegh, the Queen's 'dear Walter' and Spenser's 'Sommer's Nightingale'. Portrait attributed to Federico Zuccaro (c. 1540–1609)

had been assuring Essex that Ralegh was *not* discontented to be stayed by the wind.) Essex said he would not entreat Ralegh to make haste although, he added meaningfully their stay at Plymouth was very costly. Essex wished and prayed for a good wind for Ralegh. When he did come, Essex would make him see that he desired to do Ralegh as much honour and give him as great a contentment as he could. 'For this is the action and the time in which you and I shall be both taught to know and love one another'. Essex would show him 'the fairest troops for their number that ever were looked upon'.

That was a very handsome letter, but only a few days later, on 12th May, Essex was writing to Cecil in quite a different vein. 'Sir Walter Ralegh, with the rest of our fleet, is not yet come, and yet he hath had (if the winds be the same there that they are here) all the wished winds he could desire.' The malicious had begun to whisper that Ralegh's delay was intentional. Anthony Bacon wrote to his brother that Ralegh's 'slackness and stay by the way is not thought to be upon sloth, but upon pregnant design'. There seems no reason to attribute any sinister motive to Ralegh's delay. It is likely that it was caused, as he said, by bad weather and reluctant seamen. By the date of Essex's tetchy letter, Ralegh was well on his way. He was at Queenborough, near Sheerness, on the 6th, at Dover on the 13th, when he left instructions for the recovery of anchors and cables slipped in a storm, and on the 21st he joined the fleet at Plymouth.

The fleet was one of the largest and most magnificent England had ever assembled. The joint commanders-in-chief, by sea and by land, were the Lord Admiral Howard and the Earl of Essex. Lord Thomas Howard was vice-admiral, Sir Walter Ralegh rear-admiral. Ralegh was also an advisory member of a council of war of five, consisting of himself and Lord Thomas Howard to represent the navy; Sir Francis Vere, Marshal of the army, and Sir Conyers Clifford, sergeant-major, representing the land forces; and Sir George Carew,

The Queen had made it clear that all plunder was to be brought home and turned over to the Crown to defray the costs of the expedition. She objected to 'the likelihood of the spoil of such riches, by the private soldiers, without preserving such wealth, towards the great charges of this voyage'. She sent Sir Anthony Ashley to look after her interests. The Lord Admiral and Essex both reassured her that they would take steps to 'stay such spoilings' (and they were sharply reminded of their promise by the Queen on their return). However, the prospect of exciting military adventure and the possibility of loot attracted to the expedition many of the young bloods in England, as well as some of the most experienced military and naval men. Amongst the commanders were Sir William Monson, Sir Alexander Clifford, Sir Christopher Blount and Sir Amyas Preston. Also present were Ralegh's young brother-in-law Arthur Throckmorton; William Hervey, who may have been the Mr. W.H., the 'onlie begetter' of Shakespeare's sonnets; the poet John Donne; and many more young men and 'green-headed youths' from most of the leading families in England.

With such a mettlesome company, all cooped up together in Plymouth, Essex had difficulty in keeping order. He called it a purgatory 'to govern this unwieldy body and to keep these sharp humours from distempering the whole body'. He himself quarrelled with

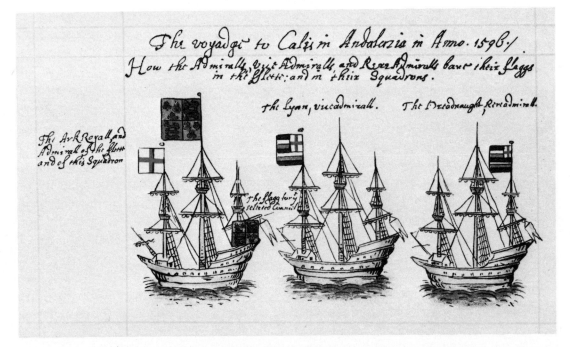

The Cadiz Expedition 1596. Left, Howard's flag ship *Ark Royal*, with *Lyon* and *Dreadnought*. Drawings from a facsimile manuscript of Sir William Slingsby's *Relation of the Voyage to Cadiz 1596*. Slingsby was an officer who sailed in Ralegh's squadron and was on the staff of Sir George Carew

Howard, and Howard went so far as to cut out Essex's signature on a joint letter signed by them both, because he did not wish another's signature as high as his own. Everybody was squabbling about precedence. Ralegh quarrelled bitterly at the dinner-table with Vere and Sir Conyers Clifford in the presence of all the Generals and the Dutch admirals. Ralegh and Vere agreed that Ralegh should have precedence at sea, Vere on land. Throckmorton took Ralegh's part so hotly that he was dismissed and cashiered, though he was later reinstated and sailed on the expedition. Ralegh behaved with the utmost politeness towards Essex; indeed he was so correct he may have overdone it. On 30th May, Sir Anthony Standen, who had once been one of Walsingham's spies, wrote to Anthony Bacon that 'Sir Walter Ralegh's carriage to my Lord of Essex is with the cunningest respect and deepest humility that ever I saw or have trowed.'

At last, on 1st June 1596, the great fleet sailed from Plymouth, and anchored in Cawsand Bay. The wind shifted to the north-east, ideal for the coast of Spain, and on the 3rd they were off.

Essex had between six and eight thousand soldiers, two thousand of them veterans from the Low Countries. They, and about 1,500 sailors, were embarked in a fleet of over ninety ships: seventeen Queen's ships, a dozen London men-of-war, and more than sixty victuallers and transports. The Dutch contributed twenty-four ships, under Admiral Jan van Duyvenvoord, of which eighteen were men-of-war. The fighting fleet was disposed in four squadrons, commanded by the Lord Admiral, in *Ark Royal*; Essex, in *Repulse*; Lord Thomas Howard, in *Merhonour*; and Sir Walter Ralegh, in *Warspite*. Ralegh's sailing-master was Roger Hankyn.

Some of the London men-of-war were sent out ahead of the main fleet to intercept Spanish 'carvels of advice'. A few ships were taken up and one or two captains, such as Sir William Monson, congratulated themselves that the fleet was consequently undetected. In fact, they had already been sighted and reported. In any case, an expedition of such a size could hardly have been mounted without any word of it reaching the King of Spain. The only doubt could be about its destination. In the event, Philip had a good deal of information about the fleet, but he had no proper force with which to oppose it. It was believed to be on its way to Lisbon, and caused a panic in that city for some time. But when Lisbon was left unmolested, the only possible target was Cadiz. Yet such was Spanish inefficiency that Cadiz received no proper warning of attack.

On 18th June Ralegh's squadron was detached from the main fleet to stand inshore and prevent ships escaping from Cadiz to San Lucar, which was the next port to the north, on the Guadalquivir river.

While Ralegh was away, the expedition began to suffer the usual Elizabethan dis-advantages of a divided command. It was decided on the 18th that the 'former resolve' (which was probably a direct assault upon the Spanish fleet inside Cadiz) should be abandoned. Instead, Essex would attack the town, while the Lord Admiral Howard either attacked the Spanish fleet or simply guarded it to prevent it taking part. The next day the plan was changed yet again: Essex was to carry out an assault upon the town at Santa Catalina, while Howard anchored and gave him cover. When Essex had established himself ashore, Howard would carry out a second landing on the isthmus to the east of the town. Ralegh (when he returned) was to anchor at the harbour mouth and prevent the enemy coming out. But he was not to interfere, or take any action except in self-defence. This plan (probably Howard's) was agreed upon.

The fleet arrived off Cadiz before dawn on 20th June, earlier, as Monson said, 'than the masters made reckoning of'. The Lord High Admiral flew his colours of 'bluddy' crimson; Essex's flagship wore his colours of orange-tawny. Lord Thomas Howard was flying the blue; Sir Walter Ralegh was rear-admiral of the white. The hundreds of gentlemen volunteers packed in the waists were dressed in silver and gold lace. The 'green-headed youths' were covered with feathers, gold and silver lace. When dawn broke and the early sunlight shone on the colours of the banners and glinted on the armour and weapons, the ships looked, as a Spanish eye-witness ashore said, 'the most beautiful fleet that ever was seen'.

The fleet had anchored between one and two miles to the south-west, and to seaward, of the Fort of San Sebastian. High tide at Cadiz that morning was at 5.27 a.m., and a strong ebb-tide would be flowing very soon afterwards. If the boats were to be put ashore, it were best it were done quickly. The boats were hoisted out, and embarkation began at once. But there were difficulties. A heavy swell was running from the south. A couple of boats capsized at the stern of *Repulse;* men were thrown into the water, and some in armour were drowned. It was much further to the shore than had been expected and the embarkation was taking much longer than anticipated. Suddenly, the assault on Cadiz began to look much more dangerous and difficult.

In that early half-light, with things going wrong, and men looking to him for a decision, Essex could not make up his mind. It would have been far wiser to have cancelled the operation there and then. But Essex no doubt thought that would smack of cowardice, and he let the embarkation go on.

Ralegh came up at 7 o'clock and saw what was happening. Clearly, the landing as planned simply was not feasible. He boarded *Repulse* and, according to his own account of events that day, 'in the presence of all the Colonels protested against the resolution, giving him (Essex) reasons, and making apparent demonstrations, that he thereby ran the way of our general ruin'. Essex said that the plan was the Lord Admiral's, who was in supreme charge at sea, and nothing could be changed without his consent. 'All the Commanders and Gentlemen present besought me,' said Ralegh, 'to dissuade the attempt.' They could all see the danger and were afraid that they might not even get ashore, with the present sea running, let alone take Cadiz.

At Essex's request, Ralegh agreed to go across to *Ark Royal* and ask the Lord Admiral to agree to a change of plan, that the fleet should now go into Cadiz harbour first and attack the Spanish ships inside. The Lord Admiral 'was content to enter the port'. Returning, Ralegh called out to Essex from the boat '*Intramus*', 'We're going in!' whereupon the Earl of Essex tossed his hat into the sea for joy and gave orders to weigh anchor.

All these changes of plan caused delays. By the time the decision had been taken and all the boats had been rounded up and the soldiers re-embarked in the ships, it was too late to undertake the attack that day. Many people, described by Ralegh as 'seemingly desperately valiant', thought the delay was Ralegh's fault, although, as he says, the fleet commanders had not agreed in what manner to fight, nor appointed who should lead, and who should second, by boarding or otherwise. However, Howard and Essex were pleased to listen to Ralegh and 'many times to be advised by so *mean* an understanding'. The fleet weighed anchor and moved to another anchorage, in the very mouth of the harbour. The attack was to go in the following morning.

At about ten o'clock that night Ralegh wrote a letter to the Lord Admiral suggesting that the Queen's ships go up harbour and batter the great Spanish galleons. Each galleon should have two 'great flyboats' allocated to board it. This was agreed at a conference held in *Ark Royal* in the early hours of the morning. The Lord Admiral and Essex would bring up the main body of the fleet, while Ralegh, to his great joy, was given the command of the van. The ships appointed to 'second' him were *Mary Rose* (Carew), *Lion* (Southwell), *Rainbow* (Vere), *Swiftsure* (Crosse), *Dreadnaught* (Sir Conyers and Alexander Clifford), *Nonpareil* (Dudley), twelve ships of London, with certain flyboats. Lord Thomas Howard, piqued by the honour done to Ralegh, left his flagship *Merhonour* to Dudley and embarked in the *Nonpareil*, so that he could share in the first attack. Ralegh might have given him precedence, but was determined he would not, 'holding mine own Reputation dearest'.

According to an account by Sir William Monson, one of Essex's men and no friend of Sir Walter's, Ralegh first anchored *Warspite* in a position where he could never have done any damage to the Spaniards, excusing himself to Essex on the ground that there was not enough depth of water. This, said Monson, was 'thought strange, that the Spaniards which drew much more water, and had no more advantage than he of tide, could pass where his ship could not'. Furthermore, Vere in *Rainbow* managed to go up further, to starboard of Ralegh. Ralegh weighed anchor and went closer before anchoring for the second time. If this curious comment was intended as a slur on Ralegh's honour, it was removed once and for all by the events of that day.

Ralegh was up and weighing anchor at the 'first peep of day' and bore away for the Spanish ships. These had been strung out in a straggling line in the lee of Fort St Philip but when they saw the English fleet under way, they retreated further up the harbour to a point where the channel narrowed, under the guns of Fort Puntal. The Spanish force consisted of four great royal galleons of Spain, the *St Philip, St Matthew, St Thomas* and *St Andrew*; two great galleons of Lisbon; three frigates of war accustomed to transport the Treasure; two Argosies very strong in Artillery; and the Admiral, Vice-Admiral and Rear-Admiral of Neueva Espagna, with forty other great ships bound for Mexico. There were also seventeen oared galleys, which left their position later and were interlaced 'three by three' amongst the other ships. The Spanish ships were now in their strongest possible defensive position. The great galleons were anchored with their broadsides to seaward, and the three frigates beside them, on the Matagorda side. There, they waited for the English advance.

This was very slow. The tide was ebbing, and there was very little wind. *Warspite* was 'saluted', as she advanced, by the guns of Fort St Philip, by the 'Ordnance on the Curtain', and lastly by the galleys 'in good order'. Ralegh scornfully answered them all with a blast of the trumpet, 'disdaining to shoot one piece at any one or all of those *esteemed dreadful monsters*'. The ships following *Warspite* beat a hot fire upon the Spanish galleys (still, at that time, under Fort St Philip) forcing them to retreat. As they came past *Warspite* on their way to the Puntas narrows, Ralegh 'bestowed a Benediction amongst them'.

But the galleys were just 'wasps'. Ralegh's main targets were the *St Philip* and the *St Andrew*, which had both boarded *Revenge*. Ralegh 'resolved to be revenged for the *Revenge*, or to second her with mine own life'. As Ralegh brought *Warspite* to anchor beside the two great galleons and began to batter them, there was an almost comical jostling for position behind him, as the rest of the Elizabethan gentlemen strove to be first, in the place of greatest honour. Lord Thomas Howard in the *Nonpareil* and Southwell in the *Lion* anchored on one side of *Warspite*, *Mary Rose* and *Dreadnaught* on the other. Sir Francis Vere, the Marshal, was on the Fort Puntal side. At about ten o'clock my Lord General Essex himself grew impatient of staying away from the battle and, hearing 'so great Thunder of Ordnance', drove *Repulse* up through the fleet until he had headed all the ships on *Warspite*'s port side, and anchored next to her. After her came Captain Crosse in the *Swiftsure*. But, Ralegh insisted, 'Always I must, without Glory, say for myself, that I held single in the head of all.'

The Cadiz Expedition 1596. Left, Ralegh's flagship at Cadiz, the *Warspite*, with *Swiftsure* and *Quittance*. Drawings from a facsimile manuscript of Sir William Slingsby's *Relation of the Voyage to Cadiz 1596*

Warspite had now been in action against the two great galleons for nearly three hours, and so heavy were their broadsides that she was in danger of sinking. Ralegh went across to *Repulse* in his skiff and asked Essex to bring up the promised flyboats for boarding, for *Warspite* could not endure this battering for much longer. 'I declared, that if the Fly-boats came not, I would board with the Queen's ship, for it was the same loss to burn or sink, for I must endure the one.' Here, Ralegh pays the most elegantly worded of compliments to Essex. 'The Earl, finding that it was not in his power to command fear, told me, that whatso-ever I did, he would second me in person upon his honour.' It was in such moments of heat and danger that Ralegh and Essex came closest together.

The channel was now choked with English ships. The six flyboats could not get up, having fouled other ships. The Lord Admiral himself could not take *Ark Royal* through the press of shipping, and transferred to the *Nonpareil* with Lord Thomas. Ralegh had only been away in *Repulse* for a quarter of an hour but already the situation had changed. Vere in the *Rainbow* had now headed *Warspite*, and Lord Thomas had headed him. From first place, Ralegh had dropped to third. He now slipped *Warspite*'s anchor and thrust up ahead of them both. Essex followed him and placed *Repulse* in front of all except Lord Thomas on the port-hand side of *Warspite*. Vere secretly secured a rope to *Warspite*'s stern, while Ralegh's attention was engaged elsewhere. But when Ralegh was told of it, he had the rope cut, and Vere fell back 'into his place, whom I guarded, all but his very Prow, from the sight of the enemy'. Now, Ralegh placed *Warspite* broadside on in the channel, 'so as I was sure none should outstart me again for that day'.

He then made the crucial move in the battle. Realizing that there was no hope of the flyboats, and that Essex and Lord Thomas Howard would support him in whatever he did, he made as if to board the *St Philip*, although the wind blowing down channel actually prevented him at first from getting alongside her. This seemed to have a crushing effect on the Spaniards' morale. From a disciplined fighting force they seemed in a few minutes to degenerate into a panic-stricken rabble, with every man fighting to save himself.

> I laid out a Warp [wrote Ralegh] by the side of the Philip to shake hands with her (for with the Wind we could not get aboard) Which when she and the rest perceived, finding also that the *Repulse* (seeing mine) began to do the like, and the Rear Admiral my Lord Thomas, they all let slip, and ran aground, tumbling into the Sea heaps of Soldiers, so thick as if Coals had been poured out of a Sack in many Ports at once, some drowned, and some sticking in the Mud. The Philip and the St Thomas burnt themselves. The St Matthew and the St Andrew were recovered with our Boats ere they could get out to fire them. The spectacle was very lamentable on their side; for many drowned themselves; many, half burnt, leapt into the water, very many hanging by the Ropes ends by the Ships' side under the water even to the lips; many swimming with grievous wounds stricken under water, and put out of their pain; and withal so huge a fire, and such tearing of Ordnance, in the great Philip and the rest, when the fire came to 'em, as if any man had a desire to see Hell itself, it was there most lively figured.

Ralegh notes that the English spared the survivors after the victory, 'but the Flemings who did little to nothing in the Fight, used merciless slaughter, till they were by myself, and afterward by my Lord Admiral beaten off.' In fact, because of the restricted channel, very few ships took an active part: *Warspite, Nonpareil, Lion, Mary Rose, Rainbow, Dreadnaught, Repulse* and *Swiftsure*, only eight of the Queen's ships and these, as Ralegh says, 'were all that did ought against six goodly Galleons, two Argosies, three Frigates, seventeen Galleys, and the Fort of Puntal, backed by the Admiral of Nueva Espagna, and others; in all fifty-five or fifty-seven'.

The army now landed on the narrow isthmus which connected Cadiz to the mainland. Three regiments under Sir Conyers Clifford, Sir Christopher Blount and Sir Thomas Gerard were detached to the south to take the Ponte Suaso, preventing escape to the mainland, and also preventing reinforcements (of which there were none in any case) being brought up to Cadiz. The rest of the army led by Essex and Vere went north to storm the walls and take Cadiz.

Ralegh watched them from the deck of *Warspite*. He himself was crippled by a wound in the leg received towards the end of the engagement. It was 'a grievous blow, interlaced and deformed with splinters'. Later he had himself carried ashore on the shoulders of his men and went into Cadiz, where there were already wild scenes of looting and burning. But he soon had to come back. 'I was not able to abide above an hour in the Town for the torment I suffered, and for the fear I had to be shouldered in the Press, and among the tumultuous disordered Soldiers, that being then given to Spoil and Rapine had no effect.' It was the best chance of Ralegh's life for some Spanish booty, and he had done so much to make it possible. Yet ironically, he was not able to take advantage of his success.

Ralegh returned because he was not fit 'for ought but ease at that time', but chiefly to take charge of the situation at the ships. That night 'there was no Admiral left to order the Fleet, and (indeed) few or no people in the Navy, all running headlong to the sack'. Because of the excitement of taking and sacking Cadiz, and the previous coolness and lack of proper consultation between Essex and Lord Admiral Howard, no plans had been made to capture the great fleet of merchant ships which lay that night helpless and ready to surrender in the bay of Port Royal. This was a very serious operational omission for which both Essex and Howard later tried to excuse themselves. Of the two, Howard had the command at sea and was most to blame. Ralegh, too, could have acted with more firmness. In the morning he sent Sir John Gilbert and Arthur Throckmorton to ask my Lord General Essex for instructions. He would have done better to have gone ahead and acted on his own initiative. With 'the Town new taken, and the confusion great, it was almost impossible for them to order many things at once, so as I could not receive any answer to my desire'. Thus Ralegh received no orders about the disposal of the fleet.

In the town, the merchants of Cadiz and Seville were already bargaining with Essex, offering him a ransom of two million ducats for the ships (which Ralegh thought were possibly worth as much as twelve million). But nothing had been decided when the Duke of Medina-Sidonia, the Governor of the province and the man responsible for the defence of Cadiz, took his long-delayed revenge for the defeat of the Armada. In one stupendous gesture of immolation, he ordered the whole fleet to be burned, where it lay in the roads, regardless of price or ransom. Every ship was burned except the two great galleons captured by the English during the fight. Twelve galleys under Portocarrero also escaped by breaking down the arches of the Suaso bridge, fighting off Blount and Gerard's men, and going down the San Pedro Channel to reach the safety of Rota.

The English stayed in Cadiz for a fortnight. Essex dubbed the hilarious number of sixty-six new knights. Much of the town was burned down on 3rd and 4th July, and when the English sailed away on the 5th, they had inflicted a blow upon Spanish prestige almost equivalent to the defeat of the Armada. Although the Spaniards had been warned by a previous raid on Cadiz (by Drake), they had still left it without proper defences, and they had paid the penalty for their incompetence. A foreign army had landed and stayed on the soil of metropolitan Spain, looting, capturing, rioting, burning, doing as it pleased, for as long as it pleased.

The English commanders had not known quite what to do with Cadiz when they had it, and when they had left it, they did not quite know what to do next. Essex wanted to garrison the town permanently, but he was persuaded against it by Howard. At sea, various new objectives were canvassed, Lagos, Seville, Corunna and Ferrol amongst them. Essex then suggested lying in wait for the incoming treasure *flota*, either at the Azores, or off Lisbon. The *flota* was actually on its way, and arrived at San Lucar in September. Essex was opposed by Howard and Ralegh, who both recommended a return home. Howard was always liable to oppose Essex, for the sake of it, and he may also have been imagining the Queen's fury if he did not deliver her favourite back to her safe and sound. Howard may have felt that

Overleaf: Baptista Boazio's map (1596), engraved by Thomas Cockson, of the Cadiz Expedition. The English Fleet headed by Ralegh in *Warspite* is in action against the Spaniards moored in the Puntas narrows, while the army under Essex is seen landing on the Isthmus

In this Description gentle Reader
you maie behould in Alphabeticall
sort explained vnto you the true forme
manner and Scituation of the towe of
CADIZ with her strenghts and Fortifications alse part of her Iland Geometricallie
and in her distances set forth with such
accidents or services as happened betwene
her Ma:ties Royall fleet and the Kinge
of Spaines both by Sea and Land per-
ormed by her Ma:ties most Valiant and
Honnorable Genneralls the EARLE
OF ESSEX and the LORDE
HIGHE ADMIRALL OF
ENGLAND It war taken the
21st of June
1596

II

HH

HONO

CC

PB
X
Z
Y
W

A

GG

TT

FF

MM
AA

W

M.

MAP OF THE TOWN OF CALES,
OMMANDMENT OF THE LORDS GENERALS.

BAPTISTA BOAZIO
MADE THIS DESCRIPTION
1596

Essex had taken enough personal risks already.

Ralegh's reasons for wanting to return home are not known. There was an outbreak of sickness amongst *Warspite*'s crew, which might have been sufficient reason. It was certainly not so that he could enjoy his plunder. Ralegh's eventual share of the Cadiz spoils was valued at only £1,769. Otherwise, as he said himself, all he got was 'a Lame leg, and a deformed. For the rest, either I spake too late, or it was otherwise resolved. I have not wanted good words, and exceeding kind and regardful usance; but I have possession of naught but poverty and pain. If God had spared me that blow, I had possessed myself of some House.' So much for the hero of Cadiz.

In the event, Essex carried out a landing at Faro on 13th July. The chief prize was the library of Jerome Osorio, bishop of the Algarves, which Essex later presented to the newly-formed Bodleian Library at Oxford. Corunna and Ferrol were also visited, but there was nothing to be seen at either.

Various stragglers from the Cadiz expedition, merchantmen and others, had been arriving in England throughout July. Sir Anthony Ashley brought dispatches at the end of the month. The first of the main commanders to reach home was Ralegh, who arrived at Plymouth with 'a great and dangerous infection on board' on 6th August. He was followed at two-day intervals by the Lord Admiral Howard and then by Essex.

They had to face a Queen seething with rage and frustration, who had heard nothing but rumours, most of them suggesting that she might be put to more expense. While maintaining an outward show of welcoming the home-coming heroes the Queen was inwardly furious that they had disobeyed her orders and attacked Cadiz direct, that they had missed the treasure *flota*, and that they had allowed so much plunder to escape into the hands of the common soldiery.

Sir Walter Ralegh. Miniature by an unknown artist

14. The Islands Voyage

RALEGH HAD done very well at Cadiz (Sir George Carew said that what 'he did in the sea-service could not be bettered'), and not even the most prejudiced supporter of Essex could deny it. Standen, who had written of Ralegh's 'cunningest respect' towards Essex, wrote to Lord Burghley from Cadiz that Ralegh 'did (in my judgment) no man better, and his artillery most effect. I never knew the gentleman till this time' [although he had written slightingly of him!]; 'and I am sorry for it, for there are in him excellent things beside his valour. And the observation he hath in this voyage used with my Lord of Essex hath made me love him.'

Ralegh made little of his own injuries. He had, he told Cecil, received a blow, but now (7th July, on the way home) it was well amended. Only a 'little eyesore' would remain. He obviously was not quite so fit as he pretended, for when he arrived in England he said that besides the great and dangerous infection on board, he was not well in health himself. His main praises went to Essex. Essex had behaved himself both valiantly and advisedly in the highest degree, without pride and without cruelty. He had got great honour and much love of all.

Cecil must have read this handsome tribute to his rival with mixed feelings. For Essex now certainly was Cecil's rival. While Essex had been away at Cadiz, there had been an important political change at home. Cecil had been appointed the Queen's Principal Secretary of State. The political battle-lines were being drawn up. The two adversaries could not have been more different: Essex was like a unicorn, solitary, splendid, fated. Cecil was a fox, with the odd goose-feather still sticking to his narrow chops. Between them, and apart from them, stood the enigmatic figure of Ralegh. Nobody knew what Ralegh would do in a political crisis. He was unpredictable: like the ocean, he had both shallows and depths.

In his letter to Cecil written on the way home, Ralegh also wrote, 'I hope her most excellent Majestye will take my labors and indeavors in good parte. Other ritches then the hope thereof I have none.' But these hopes were disappointed for the time being. In any case, the Queen was still displeased over the disposal of the booty from Cadiz. It was no recommendation to her that Ralegh had played a prominent part in that adventure. The position of Essex at Court was now particularly difficult. The Queen jealously kept him close to her side, but refused his petitions, and ignored his nominees for offices. She was almost obsessively fond of him, and pettishly angry with him. However, Essex was still Ralegh's best hope for a return to the Queen's presence. His friendship was worth cultivating, for that reason alone. For his part, Essex realized that he needed Ralegh's military experience.

Robert Devereux, 2nd Earl of Essex, Ralegh's chief rival at Court. Portrait attributed to Marcus Gheeraerts the Younger, painted after Essex's return from the Cadiz Expedition in 1596

Ralegh's relations with Cecil were more complicated and more intimate. Ralegh looked upon Cecil, not only as a help at Court, but also as a genuine friend of his family. The Raleghs and the Cecils were very close – or at least the Raleghs thought so. When Lady Cecil died in January 1597, Ralegh wrote Cecil a most tender letter of condolence. He advised a stoical acceptance of sorrow which he himself would be required to show when his time came.

> There is no man sorry for death it sealf, butt only for the tyme of death; every one knowing that it is a bonnd never forfeted to God . . . I beleve it, that sorrows are dangerus cumpanions, converting badd into yevill and yevill in worse, and do no other service then multeply harms. They ar the treasures of weak harts and of the foolishe. The minde that entertayneth them is as the yearth and dust wheron sorrows and adversetes of the world do, as the beasts of the field, tread, trample and defile. The minde of man is that part of God which is in us, which, by how mich it is subject to passion, by so mich it is farther from Hyme that gave it us. Sorrows draw not the dead to life, butt the livinge to death.

The signs of a growing friendship between the triumvirate of Ralegh, Cecil and Essex did not, of course, go unnoticed at Court. One good observer, the courtier Rowland Whyte, recorded its progress in a series of letters to his patron Sir Robert Sidney, who was at that time Governor of Flushing. In March 1597 Whyte wrote that '24' (his code for Ralegh) 'had been very often private with 1000 [Essex] and is the mediator of a peace between him and 200 [Cecil] who likewise had been very private with him. Ralegh acknowledges how much good may grow of it.'

Ralegh may have realized, or he may not, that just as he was trying to use Essex and to some extent Cecil, so he himself was being used for private ends by them. If he was being used, there were compensations. By 3rd April Whyte could see that Ralegh was 'now again coming ordinarily to the Privy Chamber and doth continue his resorting to 1000'. By 19th May, 24 was even nearer his final goal. He was 'daily in Court, and a hope is had he shall be admitted to the execution of his office as Captain of the Guard, before he goes to sea. His friends you know, are of greatest authority and power.'

But what of Essex? Rowland Whyte foresaw no trouble there. 'Essex gives it no opposition, his mind being full of conquering and overcoming the enemy.'

With Essex distracted, the reconciliation between Queen and former favourite was not long off, although Essex could not bear actually to witness the scene. Rowland Whyte had the news on 2nd June:

> Yesterday my Lord of Essex rid to Chatham. In his absence Sir Walter Ralegh was brought by 200 to the Queen, who used him very graciously, and gave him full authority to execute his place as Captain of the Guard, which immediately he under-took, and swore many men into the places void. In the evening he rid abroad with the Queen, and had private conferences with her; and now he comes boldly to the Privy Chamber, as he was wont. This was done with the Earl's liking and furtherance.

So, after a banishment of some five years, Walter Ralegh was back in the Queen's good graces again – although things were not quite the same as before. Lady Ralegh was never readmitted to Court.

Ever since the taking of Cadiz, there had been rumours of Spanish counter-attacks. Philip longed for revenge. In October 1596 he succeeded in assembling another Armada to invade England, but it was defeated by very bad weather. At that time Ralegh prepared an appreciation of the situation in answer to a list of questions from Essex on the likelihood of a Spanish invasion and its possible outcome. Ralegh did not think the Spaniards would come before the spring of 1597, and they would not be so ill-advised as to try to take a port in southern England without first gaining command of the Channel. (In fact, King Philip was not nearly so able a strategian as Ralegh; this Armada, and the one of 1597, had precisely such objectives.) If the Spaniards made a landing, Ralegh guessed that it would be somewhere along the Thames, in an attempt to take London. Ralegh did not place much faith in plans to defend natural obstacles such as rivers, passes, or bridges, and he quoted several examples, including one from his own experience during the French wars, where such plans had gone awry. Ralegh suggested a form of 'scorched earth' policy, removing victuals and driving off stock in front of the invader. As for tactics in battle, he was content to leave those to the day and the man. *De hoc in campis consultabimus*: 'We shall decide that in the field.'

It was an admirable summary, but it was probably a trifle too defensive in tone for Essex, who was once more haunted by dreams of martial glory. He felt himself thwarted (albeit very delicately) at Court and turned again to war in the hope of gaining some success. In March 1597 he became Master of Ordnance, one of the very offices he had been specifically warned against in a famous letter of advice from Francis Bacon on 4th October 1596. Bacon cautioned Essex against military feats and advised him to try for some such office as Lord Privy Seal, which held third place amongst the great offices of the Crown and (a most significant phrase) 'hath a kind of superintendence over the Secretary'. Above all, Essex must *win the Queen*. It was excellent advice, but Essex did not take it. He was still the darling of the country. The fame of Cadiz still rang in his ears. In a sense, Essex had already embarked on the course which took him to the scaffold.

Essex overcame the Queen's misgivings and obtained her consent for yet another offensive stroke against Spain. After the usual hesitations and changes of plan, a scheme emerged with a dual purpose: Essex was to attack and destroy the Spanish fleet at Ferrol, and to ambush the *flota*. In the event, in a compromise typical of the Queen, Essex was given enough force to accomplish the second aim, and to have an excellent chance of performing the first, but no chance of doing both.

Ralegh had the responsibility for the victualling of the land forces. He contracted to provision six thousand men for three months, at ninepence a head. He complained that he would be out of pocket but, according to Rowland Whyte, 'few are of that opinion.' Whyte had heard that Ralegh's victualling was 'very well done, and that he hath let the Earl of Essex have much for his private provision. They are grown exceeding great, and often goes the Earl to Sir Robert Cecil's house, very private, where they all meet.' In July, Whyte put the situation in a nutshell: 'None but Cecil and Ralegh enjoy the Earl of Essex; they carry him away as they list.'

In the early days of July, Essex and Ralegh rode together to London, and were entertained by Cecil. On 6th July, from Weymouth, Ralegh wrote Cecil one of his more mysterious letters. After asking for supplies to be sent urgently, or the expedition would be at risk, and time and the sheer number of men to be fed would prevent them reaching 'the place of our greatest hope,' Ralegh went on

> I acquaynted the Lord Generall (Essex) with your letter to mee, and your kynd acceptance of your entertaynmente; hee was also wonderfull merry att your consait of 'Richard the Second'. I hope it shall never alter, and whereof I shall be most gladd of, as the trew way to all our good, quiett, and advancement, and most of all for Her sake whose affaires shall thereby fynd better progression.

Cecil, Ralegh and Essex might have visited the theatre together and seen a performance of what may have been Shakespeare's *Richard the Second*. The play's politically sensitive Deposition Scene in which King Richard lost his throne may be what Cecil had referred to in his 'conceit of Richard II'. But there is nothing disloyal in Ralegh's letter, and nothing else to suggest what caused the Earl of Essex such merriment.

The preparations for the expedition were much like those of a year before. There were complaints from the officers about the quality of the pressed seamen. The seamen themselves were discontented and inexperienced. Some of the soldiers were going on their second expedition, having been drafted direct to the Low Countries or to Ireland after Cadiz, with no chance to visit their homes. There were frantic last-minute rearrangements, and the inevitable disagreements between the commanders. At Weymouth, Ralegh quarrelled again with Vere. The quarrel was patched up by Essex, who persuaded both men to shake hands. This they did, as Vere said, 'the more willingly because there had nothing passed between us that might blemish reputation'. In his *History of the World*, Ralegh wrote approvingly of Vere, describing him as one of the Queen's captains (Sir John Norris was another) who 'have done as great honour to our nation as ever any did' but who were never adequately rewarded by the Queen for their services.

Ralegh went down to Plymouth, wrote out his will on 8th July, and had it witnessed on Sunday the 10th, the day the expedition sailed. The objectives were: the fleet at Ferrol; the *flota*; and, lastly, a landing and establishment of a garrison at Terceira in the Azores and other islands. The venture was known as the Island or Islands Voyage.

There were three squadrons of English and one of Dutch. Essex as Lord General led the first in *Merhonour*, with five Queen's ships and six armed merchantmen. Lord Thomas Howard was Vice-Admiral in *Repulse*, with seven of the Queen's ships and the armed merchantman *Sun*. Ralegh was Rear-Admiral, flying his flag in *Warspite*, with Sir Arthur Gorges as his flag captain. In his squadron were Sir George Carew in one of the great galleons from Cadiz – the *St Matthew*, Sir John Gilbert in the *Antelope*, Sir William Hervey

Essex at the time of Cadiz and the Island's Voyage (1597).
From an engraving by Thomas Cockson

HONI SOIT QVI MAL Y PENSE

BASIS   CONSTANTI
VIRTVTVM

CADIZ

A: 1596

eras, Trecera,
orge,

Pico,

lish Fleet,

tues honor, Wisdomes ualure, Graces seruaunt, Mercies loue,
elested   Truths   beloued Heauens affected Doe a proue Foch

in the *Bonaventure*, Marcellus Throckmorton in the other great galleon *St Andrew*, two armed merchantmen, the *Guiana* owned by Ralegh himself, and the *Consent*, ten transports, and twenty of what Ralegh described as 'voluntary barks of the west country that came out with me'. The Dutch had provided a squadron of ten ships, again under Duyvenvoord. The lure of loot on the Cadiz scale was strong, and the fleet for the Islands Voyage, with all its attendant 'voluntary barks' was put at between 120 and 170 ships. Once more there was a great number of gentleman volunteers, perhaps as many as five hundred, and once again they included the poet John Donne, in *Merhonour*.

On the first day at sea it blew a gale from the north-east and that night Ralegh and most of his squadron became separated from the main fleet. Ralegh later said he had to 'abate sail' because he had to stand by the *St Andrew* and the *St Matthew*, both sluggish and ungainly sailers compared with the Queen's ships. On Tuesday morning the wind backed suddenly and blew from the south and west. In his poem 'The Storme' John Donne described how quickly the wind changed and increased. 'Sooner then you read this line, did the gale.' The poet's eye noted the terrible conditions on board the *Merhonour* at the height of the storm.

> Some coffin'd in their cabbins lye, 'equally
> Griev'd that they are not dead, and yet must dye;
> And as sin-burd'ned soules from graves will creepe,
> At the last day, some forth their cabbins peepe:

In his account, Essex said that the *Merhonour*'s seams opened, her decks and upper works gave way, 'and her very timbers and main beams, with her labouring did tear like lathes'.

In *Warspite* Ralegh was having just as uncomfortable a time. He told the Privy Council later that his ship 'hath shaken all her beams, knees, and stanchens well ny asunder; in so mich as on Saterday night last we made accompt to have yielded our sealvs up to God. For wee had no way to worke, ether by triinge, hollinge, or drivinge, that promised better hope; our men beinge wasted with labor and watchings, and our shipp so open every wher, all her bulk-head rent, and her verye cook-rome of brike shaken down into powder.'

After some days' hard battering, most of the fleet returned shamefacedly to England, the ships water-logged, the sails torn, and the crews half-dead with sea-sickness. Ralegh arrived at Plymouth on 18th July, Essex a day later at Falmouth. Lord Thomas Howard was either a better sailor than the other two or experienced better weather, for he stayed at sea, cruising at one time within sight of Corunna, until 31st July; he described the great storm simply as 'a stiff gale'.

The whole expedition was now in jeopardy. As Rowland Whyte said, the storm had killed the hearts of many voluntary gentlemen (in one case, literally: Sir Richard Ruddale died of sea-sickness). The Queen, Burghley and Cecil had serious doubts as to whether anything useful could be accomplished against Spain. Realizing this, Ralegh trod very carefully in his report to the Privy Council. He said he did not know what would become of the expedition now, or how the damage could be repaired, so late in the year. He left it to their Lordships to decide. He himself dared not advise them. 'It weare to great a presumpsion;

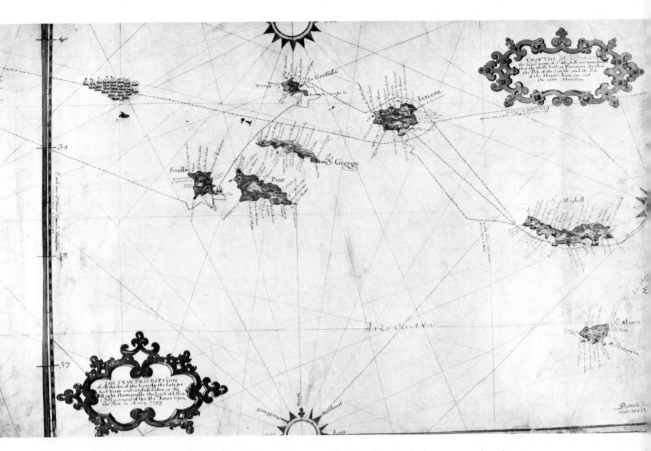

Baptista Boazio's chart of the Islands Voyage of 1597. The tracks wandering across the chart are symbolic of Essex's uncertain leadership

the persons and natures of the affaires being as the are.'

With all his preoccupations, with people clamouring at him to supply them with new sails and masts, or asking for fresh supplies of bread to replace the loaves soaked in sea-water, and with so many of his crews sick and likely to infect the rest, Ralegh still remembered the predicament of Essex. He asked Cecil to work some comfort from Her Majesty to my Lord General, 'who, I know, is dismayed by these mischances, eeven to death'. Essex, Ralegh said, had done all that a man possibly could. God himself had turned the heavens with that fury against them all, 'a matter beyound the powre, or valure, or will, of man, to resiste'.

Cecil's reaction was to make some distinctly odd remarks about Ralegh to Essex. He talked of 'good Mr Ralegh, who wonders at his own diligence (because diligence and he are not familiars)'; of 'your Rear Admiral', 'making haste but once a year'; and of the next storm at sea that Essex endured not being appeased 'by praying until Jonah be thrown into the sea, which will be the captain of the *Warspite*'. These elliptically insulting references to Ralegh may have been intended playfully. But a man like Cecil was seldom playful without good reason. For Essex himself, Cecil had only words of honey. 'The Queen is now so disposed to have us all love you, as she and I do talk every night, like angels, of you.'

The Queen might be talking of Essex like an angel, but the other talk from Court was that the expedition was about to be cancelled. The Queen was now very doubtful that anything could be achieved. Many gentlemen had already left the expedition, some, as Sir Arthur Gorges pointedly said, 'without saying goodbye to the Lord General'. In any case, the ships were wind-bound for weeks at Plymouth. The days were passing. July turned to August and the summer was drawing on. It certainly was growing late for offensive enter-prises at sea. Ralegh suggested a sortie to the West Indies. On 1st August he and Essex rode up to London to discuss the future. Another expedition, on a smaller scale, was suggested. All but 1,000 of the soldiers were to be landed. Ralegh was to command fire-ships which were to be sent into Ferrol.

The Queen showed herself as tight-fisted as ever. She authorized the sum of £2,000 to be paid to Essex to repair the fleet, but gave no money to pay the discharged soldiers. Essex had to find the money himself. At such an anxious time, when he had so many cares, in the fleet and at Court, Essex seemed to turn to the company of Ralegh. He stayed in *Warspite* as his guest on 26th July. Ralegh said that he 'would have taken it unkindly if my Lord had taken up any other lodging until the *Lion* comes'. Essex might fare worse, but he would sleep the sounder, because Ralegh was 'an excellent watchman at sea'. Ralegh might be Essex's rival, but Essex recognized that he was generous, and not an intriguer. Sir Arthur Gorges had the opportunity to see the two men together and he noted that, although Essex had many doubts and jealousies 'buzzed into his ears' against Ralegh, on active service and at 'times of his chiefest recreations' he preferred Ralegh's counsel and company to that of many others who thought themselves more in Essex's favour.

On 13th August the Queen at last approved the modified plans for the fire-ship raid at Ferrol, and for the disbandment of the troops except Vere's 1,000 from the Low Countries.

After a false start on 14th August, when some ships got out of Plymouth before the wind changed again, the main fleet at last sailed on the 17th. The weather at sea was almost as bad as it had been in July. On the 23rd the fleet reached the coast of Spain and was close inshore off Cape Ortegal, beating about for two days in very rough seas, while the Spaniards lit warning beacons ashore. Here, the *St Matthew* lost her foremast overboard and had to bear away across the Bay of Biscay. She eventually reached La Rochelle, where her size made the French gape at her in wonder. Sir George Carew tried to follow the fleet overland and then gave it up. He returned to England where he later became captain of the *Adventure*. On the 27th, *Repulse* (now Essex's flagship in place of the *Merhonour*) sprang a very serious leak. She had to lie to, to bring the damaged part of the hull out of the water, while the leak was plugged. On the same day *Warspite*'s main yard broke into two halves. They had to be lashed together in a jury rig. As a result, *Warspite* could only run before the wind. Unable to manoeuvre with the rest of the fleet, Ralegh once again became separated from Essex. When Essex reached the first fleet rendezvous off Cape Finisterre on the 28th, *Warspite* and about twenty other ships were missing.

Charitably, Essex was prepared to believe that Ralegh had met with some mishap, and that the rest of his squadron had merely followed his stern-light through the night and thus become separated. But Essex always suspected Ralegh more the further he got from him, and there were plenty of people ready to whisper that Ralegh was up to some trick of his own. The first suspicions of Ralegh's loyalty were sown in Essex's mind.

The wind had set in from the east, and it stayed there, making an attack on Ferrol even more difficult. Ralegh was missing. The Spaniards ashore were now thoroughly alarmed. The harbour entrance of Ferrol was particularly difficult for navigation, and the attacking ships would be faced with a narrow two-mile passage before they reached the enemy. The wind was still blowing steadily in their faces. On the 28th Essex cancelled the attack and, though the Spanish fleet in Ferrol was weak and disorganized at that time, he was probably wise to do so. Though he did not intend to attack Ferrol, he stayed off the coast near it for the next two days.

Meanwhile Ralegh (who said he had not gone to bed for ten days) had driven south to the second fleet rendezvous off Cape Rocas, near Lisbon. There he had news from a pinnace that the Spanish fleet had sailed for the Azores, to meet and to escort the incoming *flota*. He sent on this information to Essex who received it on 30th August. He abandoned his watch on Ferrol the next day and sailed for the Azores. He ordered Ralegh to follow him, and Ralegh did so.

Ralegh's source of information, a privateer captain from Southampton, was unreliable. When Essex reached Terceira he found that the Spanish fleet, the Adelantado as it was called, was not there, and not expected there. Furthermore, that year's *flota* was also not expected to be routed through the Azores (if it ever sailed at all).

Essex could not be blamed for acting on unreliable but plausible information. But he could perhaps be criticized for not now returning to the coast of Spain, where he could watch for the incoming *flota* (if it ever arrived). But this did not appeal to him. Instead, he and his council decided on a radical change of plan. When Ralegh arrived at Flores on 15th September, he found that Essex had already decided to take the islands of the Azores. Essex himself and Ralegh, when he arrived, were to capture Fayal; Lord Thomas Howard and Sir Francis Vere, Graciosa to the north of Fayal; Mountjoy and Blount, St Michael to the east; and the Dutch, the island of Pico, nearest to Fayal.

Essex received Ralegh with at least an outward show of friendliness, saying that he had never believed Ralegh would leave him, although people had been trying to convince him that he had done so. Ralegh was given time to take in stores and fresh water, but at midnight on 16th September he suddenly received orders from Essex to sail at once for Fayal, and assist the Lord General to attack the island. Essex had already sailed some six or eight hours before. When Ralegh reached Fayal the next day, he was mystified to see no sign of Essex. Essex had had some hours' start on Ralegh, and was supposed to have been sailing direct for Fayal. Yet he had not arrived. Ralegh was now in an embarrassing position, unsure whether or not to act in his chief's absence. His relationship with Essex was delicately poised at the best of times, and he was anxious not to give offence. He decided to wait.

Two Portuguese had swum off to the *Warspite*, and Ralegh learned from them that the Spaniards in the nearest town of Horta were beginning to remove their property. Ralegh's sailors, with the prospect of losing plunder, began to grow restive. But some supporters of Essex in Ralegh's squadron still insisted that they should wait for the Earl.

On 20th September there was still no sign of Essex, and Ralegh took advantage of a shift of wind to move to a better anchorage four miles off Horta. He could see a Spanish flag flying from the fort. This provocation, and the need to replenish his ships with fresh water, goaded him to act.

He might still have delayed a little longer, but the Spaniards began to fire on the boats he had sent inshore for water. He also fancied he could hear murmurs behind his back that he might be unwilling to take action. There were already enough people eager to point out the difficulties of a landing and, of course, the need to wait for Essex. Ralegh decided to make a landing and, so as to confound any doubters, to make it at the most strongly-defended point. He embarked 160 of his sailors and 100 soldiers from the ships into boats. So that the commanders of some of the Low Countries troops and others 'not of mine own squadron' (meaning, presumably, those of Essex's faction) could not afterwards say that he had needed their help, Ralegh took with him 'none but men assured'. Their officers included Arthur Gorges, Marcellus Throckmorton, Henry Thynne, Charles Morgan, Laurence Keymis, Berry, and William Hervey – all familiar names of men who had followed Ralegh in so many adventures.

Horta was garrisoned by about 500 Spanish troops, and defended by two forts, one in the town itself, and the other on a hill guarding the approaches to the town. The coast was rocky, with steep cliffs, and there were trenches and earth-works, manned by Spanish soldiers, on the beach. The nearer the boats came to it, the less the sailors liked the look of it. The fire from shore was so heavy that the boats' crews hesitated and would probably have turned back. Some of the landing party were just as dismayed. Gorges said later that he saw some of them 'stagger and stand blank, that before made great shows, and would gladly be taken for valiant leaders'.

Ralegh noted the faces of the waverers and rebuked them openly, with 'disgraceful words, seeing their baseness'. He could also see that the rowers had stopped pulling. He shouted to them to row full in upon the rocks, and he called upon all those who were not afraid to follow him. So saying, he himself leaped ashore, armed only with a stick. The Spanish troops on the beach left their trenches and withdrew towards the town.

Having established himself ashore, and made his point, Ralegh sent back to the ships for two hundred more soldiers, most of them from the Low Countries. Then, with no other armour but his collar – the more pragmatic Gorges said this 'was a bravery in a commander not to be commended' – Ralegh led the way towards the fort on the hill. He and the forty gentlemen with him went 'with soft march, full in face of the fort', down a little hill and into some trenches and barricades at the foot of the fort escarpment, while the fort defenders 'shrewdly pelted' them with great ordnance and musketry. The main body of Ralegh's little army had started off in good order but they began to break ranks under fire, straggled, and finally ran for cover. It was undignified but justifiable behaviour, but Ralegh and the rest of the gentlemen cried out on them for this shameful disorder. Gorges excused the soldiers' behaviour on the grounds that they were only garrisons of the 'cautionary' towns (held by the Queen as security for the money she had lent the Netherlands States), and had had no experience of active service in the field.

Ralegh and his party were still under heavy fire from the fort's cannon. He asked for a volunteer to reconnoitre a way past the fort. When nobody offered, he indignantly said he would go himself, although it was hardly the business of a commander to act as scout. He called for his helmet and breast-plate.

When they saw that Ralegh was serious, Berry, Sir Arthur Gorges and a handful of others said they would go with him. Ralegh thanked Gorges for his offer, but said he did not need to go if he did not want to. Gorges insisted and so he, Ralegh and about eight or ten others worked their way up the hill, through trenches and old walls of the fort, to find out the strengths and the weak points of the defences.

It was dangerous work. Two of the party had their heads removed from their shoulders by cannon-balls. Gorges suffered a flesh wound in his left leg, the bullet burning his silk stocking and buskin, as if they had been singed with a hot iron. Ralegh was himself shot through the breeches and doublet-sleeves in two or three places. At last, he advised Gorges to take off the large red scarf he was wearing, because it made too obvious a mark for the Spaniards to shoot at. Gorges retorted that Ralegh's own large white scarf was just as good a target, and he would take off his scarf when Ralegh took off his. This piece of bravado evidently cost Gorges something. He said later that although he was determined not to do the Spaniards so much honour by taking off his scarf, he 'could have wished it had not been on me'.

So, their two scarves flying like bright banners, Ralegh and Gorges, with the survivors of the party, completed their reconnaissance and returned to the main body sheltering under the fort. They advanced upon the town, and discovered that it and the fort had been abandoned. Ralegh decided to assault the fort on the hill the next day.

But the next day Essex and Howard arrived. They had changed their plans without telling Ralegh, going off on a wild-goose chase after a carrack. Now, they were surprised and somewhat chagrined to find that their Rear-Admiral had already been in action, and apparently with some success.

Sir Christopher Blount, Sir Gilly Meyrick and Sir Anthony Shirley and others of Essex's party had stayed in the ships and had taken no part in the attacks ashore. They had, in fact, done nothing except carp and criticize. Now, they hurried over to Essex's flagship to accuse Ralegh of disobeying fleet orders by carrying out a landing on his own authority. They said he should be court-martialled for his offences. Essex ordered all the officers who had played any part in Ralegh's sortie to be relieved of their appointments, and he summoned Ralegh himself to repair on board *Repulse* at once.

Unsuspecting, Ralegh had himself rowed over to the flagship in his barge. No doubt the Lord General wanted to commend him for his initiative. He had no inkling of trouble until he was on board *Repulse* and found 'all men's countenances estranged against him'. In the admiral's great cabin, Essex gave Ralegh a 'faint welcome', and immediately accused him of disobeying orders. One of Essex's officers, Sir Francis Vere, actually described Ralegh's action as 'a crime'. There was talk of court-martials, even of capital punishment.

At last it began to dawn upon Ralegh that, far from being warmly commended, he was facing a very serious accusation. But, as he quickly realized, the charge had no foundation. As he explained, he had done nothing wrong. Certainly, there was an article that no *captain* should land without direction from the Lord General or some other principal commander, on pain of death. But Ralegh was not a captain. He was a principal commander, third in seniority in the whole fleet after the Lord General and the Lord Thomas. As Rear-Admiral, Ralegh was a commander who could, if it ever became necessary, take over command of the expedition. He was not subject to court martial. Besides, Ralegh argued, he had been ordered to sail to Fayal and capture it!

His position was unassailable in martial law, although it took him half an hour to make out his case. Always susceptible to the last argument he had heard, Essex was impressed by Ralegh's reasoning, and even accompanied him back on shore. He was about to accept Ralegh's invitation to dine, but he was persuaded not to by Blount.

There was, of course, a slight flaw in Ralegh's case. He had undoubtedly dallied an unusually long time off an enemy coast, waiting for Essex to arrive before landing; this suggests that, in his heart of hearts, he really did know that Essex expected him to wait. Perhaps this occurred to Ralegh. When Essex had gone back to *Repulse*, Ralegh had time to think over what had happened, and it occurred to him that Essex's hangers-on might still convince him that he ought to take a stern line against his Rear-Admiral. Ralegh made up his mind that if the Earl tried to seize him, he would take *Warspite* into action against him.

At this point, Lord Thomas Howard stepped in as peacemaker. He persuaded Essex that he ought to accept Ralegh's apology. He then went to Ralegh and persuaded him that he ought to make an apology. At first, Ralegh could see nothing to apologize for, and he was very chary of stepping on board *Repulse* again. Lord Thomas Howard assured him that if Essex offered him any personal violence, he, Lord Thomas, would come to his aid. Thus Ralegh went back to *Repulse*, was reprimanded by Essex and his council, and duly apologized – for an offence he did not believe he had committed. He asked that his officers be reinstated, and this was granted.

It is possible that Essex accepted Ralegh's apology and took no further action because he was afraid of public opinion at home. One of his own men, Sir William Monson, certainly thought this was one reason. He said that Ralegh's act of landing at Fayal was 'held such an affront and indignity to my Lord, and urged with that vehemence by those that loved not Sir Walter that I believe he had smarted for it if my Lord had not been a man of mild and flexible nature and perhaps might fear it would not be well taken in England'. Essex took a petty revenge by omitting to mention the capture of Fayal in his report of proceedings, but, as Monson had suspected, public opinion was against him. In November Whyte was

John Donne, the poet, *c.* 1595, present at Cadiz and was on board Essex's flagship on the Islands Voyage.

writing that her Majesty was not pleased with Essex's service at sea in the Azores. The Earl's 'proceedings towards Sir Walter Ralegh in calling his actions to question before a Council of War is misliked here'.

Belatedly, Essex remembered the hill fort which Ralegh was to have attacked. But when the fort was assaulted it was found to be abandoned. There were two bodies inside, one English and one Dutch, both with their throats cut. For this, the English burned the town of Horta in revenge. The troops re-embarked on 24th September, in an atmosphere of bitter recrimination. Essex's men complained because Ralegh had left the fort intact and had allowed the Spaniards (and their possible ransom moneys) to escape. On their side, Ralegh's men were quite justified in saying, as Gorges did, that Essex would have done better to have attacked the fort at once instead of wasting time 'disciplining and correcting our own pretended faults for landing'.

Ralegh's exploit at Fayal was the one success of the Islands Voyage. The rest was a story of bad luck, bad management, and, ultimately, bad weather. As a commander, Essex never seemed to have a clear idea of what he was about. From Fayal he sailed north-eastwards to Graciosa, where he was joined by the Dutch, who had behaved with despicable cruelty at Pico. Essex's intention had been to get supplies and water for Graciosa and then to extend his whole fleet, in three squadrons under himself, Lord Thomas and Ralegh, in a great line to the west of Terceira, in wait for the incoming treasure *flota*. But Thomas Grove, the master of the *Repulse*, ('a dull, unlucky fellow', according to Gorges) persuaded Essex that the anchorage at St Michael was safer. Acting on this unlucky advice, Essex sailed on the night of the 26th for St Michael, inexplicably taking the longer route to the east of Terceira.

Four of his fleet, including Sir William Monson in the *Rainbow*, were left to the west of Terceira because of a misunderstanding. That night these four ships encountered the incoming treasure *flota*, a great and rich fleet of forty-three ships, including six galleons laden with silver, with a total value estimated at ten million *pesos*. Desperately, Monson tried to hinder the *flota* and make them give battle, but they only gave him 'some shots and ill language' and sailed on, 'craftily'. Monson lit flares, blew trumpets, and fired his guns, to attract the attention of Essex's ships, but they were well out of sight or sound. Had Essex sailed west-about round Terceira, instead of east, he must have met the *flota*. As it was, he missed them by a matter of a few hours and a few miles, and the whole treasure-fleet reached the safety of the fortified harbour of Angra, in the south of Terceira.

Essex received the news on the 30th, and nearly went out of his mind with rage and disappointment. He had already been at St Michael for a day, futilely cannonading Ponta Delgado. It took him two or three days to beat back to Terceira. A party of senior captains and masters in a pinnace reconnoitred Angra harbour and its approaches. They reported that it would be too dangerous to take the fleet in. In council, there was talk of seizing the harbour with an overland expedition. Lord Howard and Ralegh seem to have called the military's bluff on this. They offered 3,000 sailors to strengthen the landing party – whereupon, Gorges noticed, the soldiers became markedly less keen on the project.

Essex might possibly have been able to land enough men to storm Angra, but only by

Frontispiece of *The Light of Navigation* (1612), a Dutch Waggoner which illustrates instruction in the art of navigation, and the use of various instruments – compass, running-glass, charts, astrolabes, and cross-staff

depleting his ships' crews to a dangerous degree. It was then late in a particularly stormy year, and his sailing-masters advised him that one gale could blow his ships away, leaving his expeditionary force stranded. The ships might never be able to get back to Terceira that year. Essex was forced to the bitter decision that he must leave Angra. Ralegh was one of those who concurred in that. He remembered Angra in his *History of the World*: 'Yet this is true that where a fort is so set, as that of Angra in Terceira, that there is no passage along beside it, or that the ships are driven to turn upon a bowline towards it, wanting all help of wind and tide there, and in such places, it is of great use and fearful; otherwise not.'

Essex was back off St Michael on 4th October. That night he and Ralegh explored the coast in a pinnace, looking for a possible landing place. The next day Essex landed between two and three thousand men, with the intention of taking Ponta Delgado. Ralegh remained on board, bombarding the Spanish troops who were in trenches on the beach. His bombardment was so ineffective, according to the Spanish, that it did not kill or even wound a single man and eventually the soldiers were running to pick up Ralegh's cannon-balls where they lay on the sand so that they could sell them to the Governor.

Essex had taken three prizes between Terceira and St Michael, which helped to defray the cost of the voyage. Ralegh took a Brazilman which, when sold in England, paid for the wages of *Warspite*'s crew. But he and the whole fleet suffered yet another disappointment when a valuable prize escaped them on 6th October. She was a great carrack of about 1500 tons, sailing unsuspectingly towards St Michael, her captain being confident that all the ships he could see in the bay were Spanish. The English waited for her, making no move. To everybody's consternation, a rash Dutchman sprang the trap prematurely by suddenly weighing anchor in sight of the quarry. Alarmed, the carrack's crew drove her ashore under the castle of Ponta Delgado and set her on fire. Ralegh went in his barge through the surf to try to put the fire out, but he was too late. The carrack burned down to her keel. She burned for two days, covering the harbour with her spice-scented smoke.

The soldiers re-embarked on 10th October, having not taken Ponta Delgado, and indeed not having done anything. It was one more failure, and Essex could now do no more than turn for home. All discipline vanished, another storm blew up, and, as Sir Francis Vere said, 'the fleet kept no order at all, but every ship made the best haste they could.' *Warspite* sprang a bad leak, and was very short of fresh water, so that 'we were fain to begin to set our great stills on work', as Gorges said (suggesting that Ralegh had on board *Warspite* some apparatus for distilling fresh water from salt water).

Ralegh tried to follow *Repulse*, in spite of misgivings about the flagship's navigation. He preferred to trust his own master, Broadbent, 'a careful man and a right good mariner' rather than Grove in *Repulse*, who was using the sailing-directions of the explorer John Davis (which Ralegh seemed to think were unreliable for the English Channel).

Some of Essex's ships were driven as far as Ireland. Ralegh made for St Ives, in Cornwall, where he was astonished to find Spanish pinnaces and transports in the bay, sheltering from the weather.

Unknown to the English, yet another Spanish Armada was at sea, and was being battered by the same gale as themselves. The new invasion fleet was commanded by Don Martin de Padilla, the Adelantado of October the year before. He had a fleet of some 140 ships, with about 4,000 sailors and over 8,000 troops. He had sailed from Corunna on 8th October, intending to seize Falmouth and garrison the town, and then lie in wait off the Scillies for Essex. Having defeated Essex, Don Martin intended to take Plymouth, and any other town he could.

The plan was impractical, because Spain did not have command of the sea, nor could she win it, at that time, in one fleet action. But in any event Don Martin's Armada, like its predecessors, was destroyed by bad weather. (The continual intervention of the elements in Spanish invasion attempts convinced everyone in England that the hand of God was working against Spain.) Some of Don Martin's ships were blown across to Irish ports, some up the Bristol Channel, some to Brittany, but most straggled back to Spain.

News of the threatening invasion did not reach England until about 26th October (the same day that Essex arrived at Plymouth), by which time most of Don Martin's ships were on their way back to Spain. The invasion scare was brief, and by the end of October some of the Queen's ships were being paid off.

The Islands Voyage had been a failure. The Queen herself told Essex so. As commander-in-chief he must bear the responsibility. He had not achieved any success in the islands of the Azores. He had not captured the *flota*. He had not brought the Adelantado to action. The only man who seemed to have emerged from the affair with any credit was Ralegh. He had his Brazil prize (although the Dutch were grumbling about that) and he had the honour of his exploit at Fayal. It must have seemed to Essex that his rival had scored off him once again. It was not going to be difficult for Ralegh's enemies to rekindle Essex's suspicions about him.

15. The Fall of Essex

THERE IS a portrait of Sir Walter Ralegh dated 1598, when he was forty-four years old. In this picture Ralegh's splendour has clearly begun to age and fade. The broad forehead, the long proud nose and the full lips are the same, but time has begun to take its revenge in the eyes, which are warier, and in the expression of watchful resignation. He is still magnificently dressed, in high lace ruff, black and silver tunic and breeches with their intricate design worked in silver and enhanced by single hanging pearls, the silver-grey silk hose and silk shirt fastened with jewelled buttons set with small square rubies and emeralds. He has a sash of fine, almost transparent, material tied round his left arm, possibly to distinguish him as a commander at Cadiz (a chart of Cadiz harbour, with ships approaching the Puntal narrows, hangs above his right shoulder.) But his hair is thinning and going grey, and receding from his temples. His beard, too, is thinner, not so smartly or sharply trimmed, and has grizzled grey hairs. His waist-line is thicker, and his legs are planted rather stiffly apart, and, though his left hand grasps a gold sword-hilt, his right leans on a wooden cane. This is a man still splendid, still powerful, still strangely fascinating to look at, but one whom time and cares have begun to weary.

In the last years of the sixteenth century there was a new mood of discontent in England. People were exasperated by the seemingly endless wars against Spain, by a succession of cold stormy summers, and by soaring prices. But for Ralegh the last years of Elizabeth's reign were a halcyon period, a time of renewed busy prosperity and pleasure in his public life which was broken only once, during the crisis over Essex's rebellion. Restored to Court, Ralegh did not attempt to presume on his position nor did he try to recreate the intimacy of the past. There were no more poems, but he and the Queen had known each other for nearly twenty years and their relationship was one of mutual respect based on old acquaintance. Like the Queen herself, Ralegh was a survivor from great days which were passing. He continued to give the Queen his whole allegiance at a time when others, who were perhaps better politicians, were already looking to the future, to the succession, and beginning to trim their sails to a new wind from the north – from Scotland.

The will Ralegh drew up before he sailed on the Islands Voyage gives a good idea of his financial position and his standard of living in the late 1590s. The will was witnessed by John Meere, Adrian Gilbert, William Strode of Newnham, who was Ralegh's deputy-lieutenant in Cornwall, and Christopher Harris of Redford, Ralegh's deputy as Vice-Admiral of Devon. The will begins

> In the Name of god the Father the sonne & the holye ghoste Three persons and one god The eighth Daye of Julye Anno Domini 1597 I walter Raleghe of Colliton

Raleghe in the Countye of Devon knighte Captaine of her Maiesties garde and Lord Warden of the Stanneryes in the Countyes of Devon and Cornewall acknowledginge that all fleshe ys grasse and that the Daye of our birthe ys the first steppe to Death though the hower be uncertaine when the spiritt shall retorne to the lord that gave it doe orden ye Declare & make this my laste will and Testament in manner and effecte followinge.

In brief, Ralegh's estate was to pass to his son Wat, then four years old. Failing him, then to the next male heirs; failing them, the female heirs. The heir was to be the executor. If there were no children, then the estate passed to Lady Ralegh, after which it would go to a person or persons whom Ralegh would nominate or appoint.

The estate consisted of Ralegh's 42,000 acres in Cork and Waterford; the manor of Sherborne, with Newland, Castletown, Wootton, Whitefield, Yetminster, and Caundle Bishop; the patent for the sale of wine and the licensing of vintners which the Queen had granted Ralegh in 1583; woods in Hazelbury-Plucknett in Somerset; 'the lease of Spilmane her Maiesties Juillers house neare Durhame House London'; Ralegh's plate, furniture, books and jewels; Lady Ralegh's marriage portion which had been lent to the Earl of Huntingdon in 1572; five hundred pounds owing by the Earl of Derby, which was to be used for settling the estate's debts; and the proceeds of the sale of Ralegh's three-quarter share of the *Roebuck*, with her anchors, tackle and furniture, and 'all my Artylerye and greate ordinance therein'.

The trustees to administer the estate during the minority of the heirs were Sir Arthur Throckmorton, Alexander Brett, Sir George Carew, and Thomas Hariot. The trustees themselves had legacies. Hariot was left £200 from the sale of the *Roebuck*, £100 a year from the wine patent, all Ralegh's books and the furniture in his room and his bedroom at Durham House, together with such 'blacke suites of apparell' as there were at Durham House. Throckmorton had 'my beste horse and my beste saddle with the furniture'; Brett 'my longe Blacke velvett cloake now in my Wardrobe at Durham House'. Ralegh left his best rapier and dagger to Sir Arthur Gorges, and £100 to Lawrence Keymis from the sale of the *Roebuck*.

The will gives interesting details of some of the Raleghs' household furniture. The bequests include a suite of porcelain set in silver and gilt (left to Cecil); two great flagons of silver gilt, two great silver gilt pots of the same suite, a silver basin and ewer, a bedstead of mother of pearl and a 'Chyna' bed of silk embroidered with silk and China gold with a gilt bedstead and furniture, and eight pieces of 'richest Hanginges' with Ralegh's coat of arms worked on them.

Ralegh's most startling bequest was five hundred marks (£331 13s. 4d.) to 'my Reputed Daughter begotten on the bodye of Alice Goold now in Ireland'. There is other evidence that Ralegh had an illegitimate daughter. In a letter to Lady Ralegh written in the Tower in July 1603 he referred to his poor daughter, to whom he had given nothing. He asked Lady Ralegh to be charitable to her, and to teach her son to love her for his sake. Ralegh was Governor of Jersey from 1601–3 and an entry in the journal of the Revd. Elie Brevint, of

Sark, records that Ralegh gave his illegitimate daughter in marriage to his ward and page Daniel Dumaresq, Seigneur of Saumarez. The daughter (unnamed) died of the plague 'at London or Kingston' (probably Kingston-upon-Thames, eleven miles outside London). A manuscript book of 1605 in Jersey notes that Dumaresq made Ralegh's daughter 'no Jointure' and disowned the marriage at her death. Dumaresq then married again.

Alice Goold was probably Irish. There were many Goolds, Goulds, or Golds in Devon in Ralegh's time, but there were also many Irish Goulds in Cork, and the will specifically mentions Ireland. It is more likely that young Ralegh would sow his wild oats away from home, and a daughter sired when he was a soldier in Ireland would be of marriageable age when he became Governor of Jersey.

Ralegh had been elected senior knight for Dorset in the autumn of 1597, but when Parliament assembled, on 24th October, he was still in Plymouth attending to the defences of the West Country and making arrangements for the disposal of the prizes from the Islands Voyage. The physical strain of the life he had been leading was beginning to tell on him. He and Lady Ralegh went to Bath, so that he could take the waters. The Privy Council sent him their good wishes for a quick recovery, and the Speaker of the House gave Adrian Gilbert special permission, on 21st November, to go down to Sherborne and visit him, taking the good wishes of the House also.

Ralegh had recovered by Christmas time, for on 20th December he was one of a committee appointed to consider a Bill against persons pretending to be soldiers or sailors. Ralegh spoke on this Bill and on a similar one sent down by the Lords. After a conference with the Lords on these Bills, Ralegh reported to an angry House that the Lords had remained seated and kept their hats on in committee, while he and his fellows from the Commons had had to stand and take off their hats. The Lords eventually justified themselves in a somewhat roundabout way, saying that when the Commons brought Bills to the Lords, they would meet the members in due form, but when the Commons arrived for an answer from the Lords they would be received as in the manner given. This was accepted with no more debate. Ralegh also spoke on Bills relating to the upkeep of the Navy, the recruitment of men for the services, and the discharge of the Queen's debts. The Parliament was dissolved on 9th February 1598.

John Meere of Sherborne was one of the witnesses of Ralegh's will, and was left £20 in it; he was charged to be as faithful and diligent a servant to Lady Ralegh as he had been to Ralegh himself. But these good relations were already in jeopardy by the time of the signing of the will in 1597. Two years earlier, Ralegh had made Adrian Gilbert Constable of Sherborne Castle, a vague office whose duties and status *vis-à-vis* Meere were never properly defined. The two men disliked each other. Adrian Gilbert was not a man of prepossessing character; Aubrey called him 'a man of great parts but the greatest buffoon in England, who cared not what he said to man or woman of what quality whatsoever'. Meere simply called him a gorbellied rascal. At some time Ralegh decided to dispense with Meere's services as bailiff, but he found that Meere was not easily dismissed. The case came to a head in 1601 when Meere brought a Star Chamber case against Ralegh. He claimed

An older and somewhat sadder Essex just before he left for his disastrous expedition to Ireland. Artist unknown

that Ralegh had appointed him bailiff for fifty years, should he live so long. Ralegh appointed another bailiff, Robert Dolberry, but Meere refused to stand down, and the Sheriff of Dorset, John Stocker, supported him by continuing to send him writs, addressed to him as bailiff. Ralegh's supporters resorted to force. They obstructed Meere in the course of his duties, and kept him and his wife awake by singing ribald songs outside their house at night. Meere retaliated by arresting Dolberry. Ralegh's supporters freed Dolberry, and put Meere in the stocks in Sherborne, while the townsfolk pelted him. Ralegh himself locked the stocks and kept the key. Meere was there for six hours. Meere also claimed the ownership of a house, near the old castle of Sherborne, worth a thousand marks. Ralegh confined Meere to the gatehouse of the castle, and accused him of counterfeiting his signature on behalf of the Earl of Essex. 'He writes my hand so perfectly,' Ralegh told Cecil, 'as I cannot any way decerne the difference.' However, on 3rd October 1601, John Meere wrote to Cecil (possibly under duress) a letter astonishingly admitting his errors, and acknowledging that his violent speeches against Ralegh were 'spoken furiouslye and foolishlie'.

Ralegh does not seem to have had much justification for his treatment of Meere, and his case for the defence in the Star Chamber was weak. Even so, it is unlikely that Meere would have been able to resist Ralegh for so long and so successfully without powerful assistance. The involvement of Essex and Cecil shows that the affair was by no means a storm in a provincial teacup. Meere's wife was a kinswoman of Lady Essex. The Meeres's part against Ralegh was taken by the Howards, Ralegh's enemies. In August 1601 Ralegh was complaining to Lord Cobham that John Meere's elder brother Henry had been to Court to lay charges against him, and had been assisted by Lord Thomas Howard. Almost a year later, Ralegh was again complaining to Cobham that another Howard, this time Viscount Howard of Bindon, Ralegh's neighbour in Dorset, had 'exalted' Meere's suits against him while he was out of the country, in Jersey.

Ralegh seemed quite unable to avoid offending the Howards, even when he was trying to act as peacemaker. The Queen employed Ralegh to end a dispute in December 1597 between Cecil, Essex and Lord Charles Howard. The Queen had made Howard Earl of Nottingham and, as Lord High Admiral, he had precedence over the other earls, including Essex. Essex felt that he had been slighted, and retired from Court and Council in a sulk, saying that he was unwell and had headaches. Ralegh suggested that Essex might be mollified by being made Earl Marshal. But when this was done, it was Howard who then retired from Court pleading illness, resenting the fact that Essex had stepped ahead of him again. Both sides joined to blame Ralegh.

That month, however, all was well between Essex, Cecil and Ralegh, at least on the surface. Whyte said that 'all the world wondered to see the great familiarity' between them. Cecil had a reason for promoting friendliness. He was just about to leave the Court to go to France and negotiate with Henry IV, to try to prevent him concluding a separate peace-treaty with Spain. Cecil wanted no upsets at Court, or any threats to his own position, while he was away. The others responded with entertainments, and expressions of mutual goodwill. Ralegh offered Essex a share of his prizes, while Cecil obtained for him a grant of £7,000 from the sale of cochineal belonging to the Crown. For his part, Essex reassured Cecil that nothing disagreeable should happen to his interests in his absence. For Ralegh, Essex promised his help in having him appointed as a Privy Councillor.

But this promise was of no avail. Ralegh had reached his ceiling at Court and in the country. He hoped to be made a peer, but was disappointed. He hoped to be made Vice-Chamberlain and again was disappointed. He never became a Privy Councillor, though he had high hopes in August 1598, after the death of Lord Burghley. But always Cecil seemed to be there, to intervene, to suggest unacceptable conditions, and generally to frustrate Ralegh's hopes. In the political times that he could see ahead, Cecil did not want Walter Ralegh in the Privy Council.

The Queen could have made Ralegh a Privy Councillor, in spite of Cecil's manoeuvrings. But though she recognized that he had administrative ability, and though she listened to his advice on many matters, the Queen seemed to realize that Ralegh was not, at heart, a good committee man. There were inconsistencies in his nature. He was a courtier, yet secretly he despised the Court. He could give a penetrating summary of a political situation, and behave thoughtlessly in his private affairs. He had a cool head for strategy, but a hot temper for rebuffs. He was too ready to show contempt for those he thought his intellectual inferiors, always liable to 'give them all the lie'.

As a sop to Ralegh's ambition, the Queen made him Governor of Jersey on 26th August 1600, after the death of Sir Anthony Paulet. Ralegh was Governor until the accession of James I and, though he had to recompense his unsuccessful rival for the post, Lord Henry Seymour, and had to pay an annual fee to the Crown, he took his duties in the island seriously. He visited it in October 1600 and again in the summer of 1602. He reconstructed the island's defences, instituted a public register of land, relieved the men of the Mont Orgueil district of the obligation to compulsory military service, and fostered the island's trading and fishing connections with Newfoundland. He also acted as judge on the island, and as advocate for island affairs at Court. Had he been Governor longer, he would have carried out important educational reforms. He liked Jersey, saying that he had never seen a more pleasant island, and Jersey liked him, entertaining him 'royally with joy', as Lady Ralegh said.

But the Governorship of Jersey was only a consolation prize. It removed Ralegh from Court, while giving him no more power there. In March 1598 Ralegh had a chance of a much more important post; that of Lord Deputy of Ireland. It was rumoured that the choice lay between him, Sir Robert Sidney and Sir William Russell. But on 18th March Whyte reported to Sidney that Russell absolutely refused to go and Ralegh 'doth little lyke it'. In the event, a fourth was chosen, whom nobody could have forecast.

It is very unlikely that Ralegh would, or could, have refused the Lord Deputyship if he had been seriously offered it. It was an important position of great responsibility and power under the Crown, in a field of political affairs which Ralegh knew something about. For years he had been urging his own policies, invariably tougher ones, for Ireland. Had he been able to carry out his own draconian measures, the history of Ireland, and the careers of himself and the Earl of Essex, would have been greatly different.

The policies of Elizabeth's governments in Ireland had been a tale of half-measures. They were not harsh enough at one extreme, or imaginative enough at the other, to succeed. Rebellion always lay just under the surface, and in 1598 a fresh and successful revolt in Ulster was led by Hugh O'Neill, Earl of Tyrone. His forces were not the ragged, half-starved kerns of Ralegh's days in Ireland, but a well-armed and well-trained army who inflicted a severe defeat upon an English force on the Blackwater river in August. Encouraged by O'Neill's success and assisted by his guerillas, the insurrection spread to Leinster and Connaught and finally to Munster, where there was a general rising in October. The English settlements and houses were burned, English men and women were killed, or forced to flee to Dublin and Cork for refuge. Some of these newly dispossessed settlers were Ralegh's tenants. Ralegh had always looked upon the native Irish as no better than vermin. Nothing was too harsh for Ireland. At the time of the Munster rising, Ralegh wrote to Cecil advocating political assassination as a policy. 'It can be no disgrace,' he said, 'if it weare knowen thet the killinge of a rebel weare practised; for you see that the lives of anoynted Princes are daylye sought, and we have always in Ireland geven head money for the killinge of rebels, who ar evermore proclaymed at a price. So was the Earle of Desmonde, and so have all rebels been practised agaynst.' Ralegh evidently had an assassin ready, 'that knave', who had been recommended to him. Cecil's name was to be kept out of it, but the postscript suggests that Ralegh himself was openly involved – 'He hathe nothinge under my hand butt a passport.' It seemed that Ralegh had personally signed the assassin's papers or passport.

The crisis in Ireland was discussed in London in July, and the question of a new Lord Deputy was the cause of an extraordinary scene between Essex and the Queen. Cecil, the Lord Admiral, and Thomas Windebank, Clerk of the Signet, were also present. The Queen suggested that the appointment be given to Essex's uncle, Sir William Knollys. Essex disagreed, and proposed his friend (and Ralegh's cousin) Sir George Carew. The Queen argued for her choice. Essex countered with arguments for his. The conversation grew heated. At last Essex lost his temper and turned his back on the Queen. Outraged by this rudeness, the Queen boxed Essex's ears. Instantly, Essex clapped his hand to his sword-hilt and swore that he would not have tolerated such an insult even from Henry VIII. Fortunately, the Lord Admiral was able to restrain him. Essex turned on his heel and rushed out of the Council Chamber, leaving the rest looking at each other in an appalled silence.

The Court waited for retribution to fall upon Essex. But the Queen did nothing. Essex retired to his house at Wanstead, to brood over the injustices done him, and to nurse his anger against Walter Ralegh. Although Essex was absent from Court, Ralegh was still aware of his personality – unstable, hostile, ready to seize upon suspicions and plan revenge.

As usual, Ralegh himself had other preoccupations. In September 1598 the future Charles IX of Sweden was urging him to send another expedition to colonize Guiana. Charles offered to lend twelve of his own ships. A month later there was a strong rumour in London that Ralegh was about to go to Guiana with his nephew Sir John Gilbert. But nothing came of it. John Gilbert was a man very like his uncle. It is amusing to read Ralegh's admonitions to

English army on the march in Ireland. The Lord Deputy is escorted by a guard of cavalry, preceded by trumpeters and standard bearers. From John Derricke's *Image of Irelande*, 1581

his nephew, reproaching him for his ambition, presumption, ingratitude and acquisitiveness – a case of an older pot calling a younger kettle black.

Essex was constantly seeking ways of belittling Ralegh, of undermining his position at Court, just as he imagined Ralegh was doing to him. One such attempt to insult Ralegh publicly was probably the celebrated 'feather triumph' in the tiltyard, which may have taken place as part of the celebrations of the Queen's accession day on 17th November 1598 (although another source, John Chamberlain writing to Carleton, says that that particular day 'passed without any extraordinary matter more than running and singing'). In a seventeenth-century account by Sir Henry Wotton, Essex had 'a glorious feather-triumph, when he caused two thousand orange-tawny feathers, in despite of Sir Walter Ralegh, to be worn in the Tiltyard, even before her Majesty's own face (all which would have found regret in the stomachs of most Princes).' It is difficult to see how this insulted Ralegh in particular, but in any case Essex did not perform well in the tournament and, as Wotton's account suggests, the Queen was displeased.

By this time an astonishing story had begun to circulate, that Essex was to be the new Lord Deputy in Ireland (Chamberlain had the news on 8th November). It seemed hardly credible to Essex's friends that he would voluntarily remove himself from the Court, so that he could pursue the remote possibility of military success in Ireland, a land which had already laid waste so many men's hopes. But it was true enough. Essex had gone through some form of reconciliation with the Queen. There was another discussion about the Lord Deputyship. Essex had allowed his hot temper to get the better of him and, while hardly knowing what he was saying, insisted in the strongest terms that he be allowed to take on the appointment of Lord Deputy. The Queen agreed. Cecil made no objection. And so, on 27th March 1599, Essex rode through London at the head of his army. He was cheered in every street and from every roof-top. The crowds ran beside him crying, 'God bless your Lordship.' Some followed him until that evening, only, as John Stow said, 'to behold him'. Shakespeare compared his Irish expedition to King Henry V's campaign in France, and the Chorus in Act V of *Henry V* welcomes the prospect of as happy a return to London:

> As by a lower, but by loving likelihood,
> Were now the General of our gracious Empress,
> As in good time he may, from Ireland coming,
> Bringing rebellion broached on his sword;
> How many would the peaceful City quit,
> To welcome him?

Had Ralegh really wished to destroy Essex, he could have done no better than send him to Ireland. Essex was not the military genius he believed himself to be. Ireland found him out. His army of 16,000 infantry and 1,300 cavalry was the largest expeditionary force Elizabeth had ever sent to Ireland, and it should have been enough to crush Tyrone. But Essex succumbed to the strange, enervating influence of Ireland. His ability to make a decision seemed to be sapped. He seemed quite unable to separate diversions from essentials. Arriving in Dublin in April, he marched south to engage subsidiary enemies instead of the main adversary in the north. He besieged unimportant castles. He frittered his strength away in strategically futile engagements, and was actually defeated twice. He dubbed scores of knights. He wrote passionate protesting letters to the Queen who replied, bitingly, that he was costing her a thousand pounds a day to go on Progress. He blamed his favourite scapegoat. In June, he wrote to the Queen

> Is it not lamented of your Majesty's faithfullest subjects, both there and here, that a Cobham and a Ralegh – I will forbear others, for their places' sakes – should have such credit and favour with your Majesty when they wish the ill success of your Majesty's most important action, the decay of your greatest strength, and the destruction of your faithfullest servants?

The insinuation against Ralegh's loyalty was an absurd and baseless slander. Ralegh was still a major landowner in Ireland. His tenants were being molested and murdered, and

Tyrones false Submission afterwards rebelling.

Conscientia mille testes.

Hugh O'Neill, Earl of Tyrone, Essex's wily opponent in Ireland. Engraving from Carlton, *A Thankful Rememberence*, 1627

their property damaged. If for no other reason than his own interest, Ralegh would wish Essex success in Ireland.

By July, Essex's force had been reduced by disease, desertion and defeat to only 4,000 men, no longer enough to defeat Tyrone. Essex began to fear for his reputation at home. He began to make the wildest accusations, and to announce the wildest military plans to restore his own position. These had an effect at home. The fleet was mobilized on 9th August. Ralegh went down to the coast as Vice-Admiral under Lord Thomas Howard. It was said that the Adelantado was at sea again. But some said secretly that the real enemy was the Earl of Essex, who intended to land at the head of his army and seize the throne. (At his trial two years later, Sir Christopher Blount confessed that Essex had indeed contemplated landing at Milford Haven and marching on London.)

At last, in September, Essex was reduced to the ignominious course of having to ask Tyrone for a parley (in direct contravention of the Queen's orders). The two men met at a river ford at Annaclint. Tyrone agreed to a truce, renewable every six weeks. In his position, he would have agreed to anything to gain time. For him the truce was a resounding military and political success. For Essex, it was a shameful end to a disastrous campaign. He decided to make one last attempt to retrieve his personal standing with the Queen. He would go and see her personally. She could hardly resist him. On 24th September he abandoned his command and left Ireland (again, in direct disobedience of the Queen's orders).

From the time he reached the Court on 28th September and burst in on the Queen early in the morning, Essex's tragic course began to run out with seeming inevitability. The Queen was at first glad to see him, but her mood changed later. Essex was given into the custody of the Lord Keeper, and confined to York House for almost a year. He was formally admonished by the Privy Council in June 1600, but not allowed to go to his own home until August, and was still banned from the Court.

The Queen handled Essex in the worst possible way. She should either have reinstated him fully, or have dismissed him finally from any prospect of employment in Court or country. Instead, she left him suspended in an uneasy half-world, where he alternated between hope and despair. As a Court favourite he was only half-dismissed; as a political force he was only half-scotched. In this state, aggravated by the Queen's refusal to renew the monopoly of sweet wines which gave him most of his income, Essex became the source of a dissidence which eventually began to border on treason.

Ralegh could see the danger, and as Captain of the Guard he was especially concerned with the safety of the Queen's person. But he could never understand that the best way to deal with Essex was simply to let him rush on to his own ruin. In a letter which is undated, but was possibly written in the summer of 1600, when Essex was about to be brought before the Council, Ralegh attempts to give Cecil advice.

> I am not wize enough to geve yow advise [this was certainly true] butt if yow take it for a good councell to relent toward this tirant, yow will repent it when it shalbe too late. His mallice is fixt, and will not evaporate by any your mild courses. For he will ascribe the alteration to her Majesties pusillanimitye and not to your good nature; knowing that yow worke but uppon her humor, and not out of any love towards hyme. The less yow make hyme, the less he shalbe able to harme yow and your's. And if her Majesties favor faile hyme, hee will agayne decline to a common parson.

Ralegh himself knew about declining to a common person, once Her Majesty's favour failed. He went on to reassure Cecil that he need fear no family feuds as a result of taking action against Essex, and he gave some examples.

> For after-revenges, feare them not; for your own father that was estemed to be the contriver of Norfolk's ruin, yet his son followeth your father's son, and loveth him. Humors of men succeed not; butt grow by occasions and accidents of tyme and poure. Summersett made no revendge on the Duke of Northumberland's heares. I could name yow a thowsand of thos.

In his postscript, Ralegh urged, 'Lett the Q. hold Bothwell while she hath hyme. Hee will ever be the canker of her estate and sauftye. Princes ar lost by securetye; and preserved by prevention. I have seen the last of her good dayes, and all ours, after his libertye.'

Cecil ignored Ralegh's advice. The time was not ready. Essex had not yet done anything directly treasonable.

However, Essex soon obliged his enemies. Throughout the winter of 1600–1 he was the focus of all the discontents of the realm. The rooms and courtyard of Essex House were always thronged with new faces. Disaffected Puritans, Catholics, and all who had any grievance against Queen Elizabeth and her ministers gathered together in the hope of redress, possibly even of revolution. Revolution was not impossible. In his tormented state of frustrated ambition and wounded pride, Essex was capable of doing anything and saying anything, so that even his own supporters, such as Sir John Harington, took fright, because Essex's 'speeches of the Queen becometh no man who hath *mens sana in corpore sano.*'

Essex tried to persuade Charles Blount, Lord Mountjoy, his successor as Lord Deputy in Ireland, to send his troops to England to aid Essex's designs. But Mountjoy was alarmed by the risks and, in any case, he was genuinely interested in his new duties; an unexpected success in Ireland, Mountjoy was the man who finally crushed Tyrone. Essex meanwhile began a secret correspondence with James VI of Scotland. He warned James of a plot to put the Spanish Infanta on the English throne instead of himself. Amongst those implicated, Essex said, were Sir Walter Ralegh and Cecil. Ralegh was particularly useful to the conspirators. With his power and influence in the West Country, and his position as Governor of Jersey, Ralegh could offer the invading Spaniards all the assistance they would require. These details were, as Cecil later described them, 'hyperbolical inventions'. But they served to arouse James's suspicions of Ralegh.

James was sufficiently impressed by Essex's revelations to send an envoy, the Earl of Mar, to London. But before the Earl of Mar arrived, Essex's revolt had already come to a head. The conspirators, except Essex, had gathered at the Earl of Southampton's house to discuss plans on 3rd February 1601. Four days later, Saturday the 7th, Sir Gilly Meyrick went across to Southwark to ask the players at the Globe Theatre to put on the play of *Richard the Second*. The players were unwilling. The play was old. There was no money in performing it. Meyrick offered them forty shillings. The players accepted. Thus Essex was able, as was said at his trial, to 'feast his eyes' on the deposition of a sovereign.

Cecil and the Council knew of the movements of Essex and his followers and guessed at their intention. Ralegh was ordered to double the guard in Whitehall. That morning a message had been sent to Essex House, asking the Earl to present himself before the Council. Essex refused. He said he was ill. But here he was, that same evening, with his friends at the theatre. Clearly, the events of the next day would be decisive. It would be either Essex or Cecil. The Queen herself would not be touched. Essex had always said so.

That day, Sunday, 8th February, began with a strange incident on the Thames. Ralegh had sent for Sir Ferdinando Gorges, Governor of Plymouth Fort, to come by boat and see him at Durham House. Gorges was Ralegh's kinsman, but was also a friend and follower of Essex. Essex allowed Gorges to see Ralegh but told him to meet in mid-river and to have two witnesses present. Sir Christopher Blount said that Gorges ought to kill Ralegh, but Gorges rejected the suggestion.

Ralegh rowed himself out alone. He advised Gorges to go back to Plymouth, and warned him that if he did not he might find himself in prison. Gorges replied with a warning of his own: Ralegh should get back to the Court as quickly as he could. Essex had a strong force at Essex House and Ralegh was likely to have a bloody day of it.

While they were speaking, somebody, possibly Blount, fired four shots at Ralegh from the bank, but all missed. Gorges saw armed men climbing into a boat at the steps of Essex House and beginning to row towards them. He pushed Ralegh's boat off, and told him to hurry to the other bank. Gorges returned to Essex House; Ralegh went to the Court. This incident was recounted in some detail at Essex's trial, presumably to establish that Essex and his followers meant harm to Ralegh – hardly an original line of evidence. But Essex's real enemy was not Ralegh, but Cecil, and the anecdote may have been designed to cloud over that fact.

Meanwhile, at Essex House there were scenes of utter confusion. Men had been pouring into the courtyard since daybreak and by ten o'clock there were three hundred gathered, Essex in their midst. At the height of the uproar, the Lord Keeper, the Lord Chief Justice Popham, Sir William Knollys and the Earl of Worcester arrived to inquire in the Queen's name the reason for this riotous assembly. But rational conversation was impossible. Essex's followers seized the four men and shut them up in Essex House. On that day, they were lucky not to come to serious harm. Essex's followers implored him to act. 'Away, my Lord!' they cried. 'They abuse you! They betray you! They undo you! My Lord, you lose time!'

The mob rushed out into the street, and Essex led the way towards the City of London, calling out as he walked that there was a plot against his life, that there was a plot to put the Spanish Infanta on the throne.

But the cry had gone up that Essex was a traitor. At that word, all possible support for him was frozen. Nobody moved to his side. His shouts echoed down the silent streets. He reached St Paul's, walking at the head of a silent, dwindling body. The sweat ran down his forehead. His face was twisted with horror at the realization of what was happening to him. This was the end. He was a dead man.

The Sheriff allowed Essex into his house for refreshment, but slipped out himself by another way. When Essex came to leave the City he found the Lud Gate barred with chains and soldiers. There was a scuffle. One man was killed; Blount was wounded. Essex reached his house to find that his four hostages had been released. The house was surrounded by troops, who were soon reinforced by artillery. Lord Admiral Howard threatened to blow Essex House up. So, that evening, Essex surrendered, and was taken to the Tower of London. His was not a rebellion, nor a revolt. It was not even a properly managed riot. It was a sad, sorry, bungled mess which ruined Essex, and made Cecil the first man in the land.

Cecil's victory was completed at the trials for high treason, at which the confessions of the accused were extraordinarily detailed and abject. Amongst other retractions, Blount said that nobody had ever really believed that Cobham or Ralegh meant any harm to the

Charles Blount, Lord Mountjoy, who succeeded in Ireland where Essex and many others had failed. Engraving by Thomas Cockson

HONI · SOIT · QVI · MAL · Y · PENSE

HONI SOIT QVI MAL Y PENSE

VIGILANTER GVBERNASTI

IRELANDE

Ilands Saltes
Waterford
Wexford
Arcklo
Wicklow
Barnemore
St Patricke Iland
Irelandt eye
Dublin
Dodagh
Doudalck
Carlingford
Kingesfoard
Trone
Fayreforland
Raghline

St GEORGES CHANNELL

D. Reuemone Angl.

ANGLESEY

Ile of Man

Holihead

triumph's Thou therein first did'st breathe.   Ireland presents Thee with a laurell wreathe.

NOBLE MONT-IOYE ioyes to giue thee name.   All Theis loue Thee & all the Worlde Thy Fame.

Earl of Essex. This had merely been 'a word cast out to colour other matters', and was not the reason for the Earl of Essex's actions. (Essex had let it be known that the reason for his sortie from Essex House was his discovery that Cobham and Ralegh had musketeers placed along the river bank to ambush him.)

Blount, Meyrick, Sir Charles Danvers and Essex's secretary Henry Cuffe were all executed. The Earl of Southampton was spared, and sentenced to imprisonment instead, because of his youth, and because it was reckoned he had erred only through his affection for Essex.

The trial of the Earl of Essex began on 19th February. One of the chief prosecutors was Francis Bacon. This was a bitter personal betrayal for Essex, who had often been Bacon's friend and benefactor. Essex himself behaved with a striking mixture of arrogance and flippancy. 'What boots it to swear the fox?' he called scornfully, when Ralegh was sworn as a witness. He accused Cecil, who darted unexpectedly out from behind a curtain to refute the charges.

Essex was found guilty, and sentenced to be hanged, drawn and quartered. The verdict was a foregone conclusion, as it was in all State treason trials, but it was confidently expected that a reprieve would come from the Queen. It did not do so, for Essex had offended the Queen personally, as well as politically. Ralegh believed that in the end Essex died for something he said, not for anything he had done. In his *Prerogative of Parliaments* Ralegh wrote that 'Undutiful words of a subject do often take deeper root than the memory of ill deeds do. Yea, the late earl of Essex told queen Elizabeth, that her conditions were as crooked as her carcass; but it cost him his head, which his insurrection had not cost him but for that speech.' Ralegh may well have been right.

Ralegh was present at the executions, in his capacity as Captain of the Guard. He was reconciled to Blount on the scaffold. He prevented the Sheriff from interrupting Blount's prayers, and when Blount heard he was there, he asked his forgiveness, which Ralegh very readily gave.

He had no such chance at the Earl of Essex's execution on 25th February (Essex's sentence had been changed to beheading, with respect to his rank). Again, he was there in the court-yard of the Tower as an official of the Crown, and he listened to the Earl's long and often emotional speech of confession, in which he repeated his written statements that he bore Ralegh and Cobham no malice, and acknowledged that they were both true servants of the state. He waited at the foot of the scaffold, in case Essex saw him and wished to speak to him. But there were angry murmurs from some of Essex's friends and out of respect for the condemned man Ralegh moved away to the White Tower and watched from the armoury window. Afterwards there were those ready to say that he had gloated over Essex, and had disdainfully puffed out tobacco smoke while he watched the dreadful proceedings and had said of Essex's death that 'the great boy died like a calf and a craven.' Ralegh had a right and a duty to be present, as Captain of the Guard, and when he later heard that the Earl had indeed asked for him and had wished to make his peace with him, he regretted literally to his dying day that he had not been able to be reconciled with the Earl of Essex.

Ironically, it was Ralegh who was most blamed for Essex's death. Essex was mourned

Sir Richard Grenville of the *Revenge*, Ralegh's cousin, who died of wounds at Flores in the Azores. Artist unknown, after a portrait of 1571

An° · DÑI · 1571 ·
ÆTATIS · SVÆ
· 29 ·

Sir Richard Granville, killed
in a sea-fight near the Azores.

throughout the country. 'Sweet England's pride is gone,' they said. 'Our Jewell is gone from us, the valiant knight of chivalry,' they sang. People conceded that justice had been done, but nevertheless 'The most and best of all sorts wept.' Those who saw Ralegh said that he went home to Durham House after the execution with a sad and gloomy face. There were ominous signs for the future for him in Essex's fate. But still people made up scornful little rhymes about him, and about Cecil:

> Little Cecil tripping up and down,
> He rules both Court and Crown.
> He swore he saved the Town.
> Is it not likely?
> Ralegh doth time bestride,
> He sits twixt wind and tide,
> Yet uphill he cannot ride,
> For all his bloody pride.
> He seeks taxes in the tin,
> He polls the poor to the skin,
> Yet he vows 'tis no sin,
> Lord for thy pity!

The popular view was that this proud man Ralegh was still prosperous, still in the Queen's favour, while he had most foully and diabolically engineered their idol's downfall:

> Essex for vengeance cries
> His blood upon thee lies,
> Mounting above the skies,
>   Damnable fiend of hell,
>   Mischievous Matchivel!

This was most unjust. The man who had profited most was not Ralegh but Cecil. Of his two main rivals, one now lay in a traitor's grave, and the other was more widely hated in the country than ever. If anyone deserved the name of Machiavelli, it was Cecil.

Elizabeth Throckmorton, Lady Ralegh, as a young woman. She was no beauty but her marriage to Walter Ralegh was long and successful. Artist unknown

16. End of the Reign

THE DEATH of the Earl of Essex was like the snuffing out of one of the last and brightest lights of the Elizabethan age. The century had changed, and the mood of the times with it, to something sadder and more sombre. The Queen was in her late sixties and neither the most indulgent eye nor the most skilful cosmetics could any longer conceal that she was, and she looked, an old woman. The shadows were growing around her Court. The Queen still laughed as she had done with Leicester, swore as she had at Walsingham, danced as she had with Hatton and her enchanting Essex, but all much more rarely than of old. Those days were done, and of all that brilliant company of the past Ralegh was now the only true survivor.

Ralegh had two years left to him of public life after the death of Essex, and he employed them and enjoyed them, as always, to the full. It was as though he too were giving out one last flare of brilliant light before the end. His own letters and the Court gossip of the time give some idea of the range of his interests and activities, and of the restless and energetic life he led. He was in London, at Durham House, and in the House of Commons. He was down in Sherborne, looking after his castle and estate. He was at Bath, taking the waters; in the West Country on provincial business, and in Jersey as Governor; on the Channel Coast serving with the Fleet, and he was on Progress with the Court. In July 1600 he went to Ostend with Lord Cobham, to visit the camp of Prince Maurice of Nassau, who was trying to relieve the city from the siege of the Archduke Albert; Cecil said they had no business there, having 'stolen over, having obtained leave with importunity to see this one action', but other accounts said that they had messages 'which did no harm' and they were entertained with much honour and extraordinary respect. Ralegh acted as a kind of official censor, reading a translation of Jerome dei Franchi Conestaggio's history of the conquest of Portugal and the wars in Africa; he made some corrections in it, and told Cecil that the book would now pass. He was still recommending officers as captains of companies for service in Ireland. He interceded for the son of his cousin Henry Carew, who was in prison. While impatiently waiting in hope of employment in Jersey, he was writing to Cobham to complain that he might be better off keeping sheep. He was hoping to meet Cobham at Bath. He was concerned at the damage done by a fire on the ground floor of Durham House (which was caused, according to Lady Ralegh, by the negligence of their co-tenant Lady Darcy). He negotiated new rates for the tin industry in Cornwall but let slip the information that he had arranged for twenty shillings in the thousand less than he had been authorized to give; whereupon the tinners at once petitioned for the balance, and Ralegh took their side. He took the tinners' part again in a conflict over certain 'clash mylls' erected by a Mr Crymes to work the tin on Roborough Down, just outside Plymouth. Crymes had also diverted watercourses to the tinners' disadvantage. Ralegh insisted that the tinners' business be heard, according to tradition, in the Stannaries Courts, and not in the Star Chamber. He praised the expertise in fortifications of a Mr Paul Juey in Jersey, and complained about the incomprehensibility (the 'unmeasurabell reckninge') of the accounts kept by his predecessor Sir Anthony Paulet. He passed on to Cecil the local Sherborne gossip of a great ship of Lisbon said to be worth seventeen million, and of two thousand Spanish soldiers being assembled for Flanders or Ireland. He told Cobham about a Spanish fleet off St Malo, and made his own forecasts about its probable movements and destinations. He complained of the decay of English sea power, protesting about a ship of the South Sea, a Dutchman, 'with a lantern of clean golde in her stern' which had arrived at Amsterdam, 'infinit riche', without anybody laying a finger on her. He wrote a paper for the Queen on the dangers of a Spanish faction in Scotland. And he was still sending out colonizing expeditions to Virginia. In 1602 (after, he said, two earlier unsuccessful attempts), he sent Samuel Mace with two ships, one of them a pinnace, to Cape Hatheras; Mace returned with, amongst other things, a kind of sarsaparilla which was a contemporary treatment for syphilis. In May 1603 Ralegh sent off his last expedition, under Bartholomew Gilbert; Gilbert was killed by Chesapeake Indians and his expedition came home, discouraged, in September. Ralegh himself was then in the Tower, but once again he had aroused interest in Virginia.

In his final years at Court, Ralegh was always particularly in demand when there were foreign visitors. He was possibly the most widely-read, widely travelled, and had the widest acquaintance, of all Elizabeth's courtiers. He also had a knack for being on the spot when anything was happening. In March 1601 he was employed, by the Queen's order, to show a Spanish envoy around London during negotiations for a possible truce with Spain. Later that summer, he was with the Queen on Progress at Dover, where she had gone in the hope of meeting Henry IV of France, who was then at Calais. Henry sent instead his great minister the Duc de Sully. Sully recounts in his memoirs how he was 'arrested' jokingly by the Queen's Captain of the Guard, who embraced him warmly and took him at once into the Queen's presence. The familiar terms of Sully's account suggests that he and Ralegh may well have met and become friends much earlier.

On 5th September that year another of Henry IV's ambassadors, the Duc de Biron, came to England to inform the Queen of his master's marriage to Marie de Medici. Biron arrived in London with a great retinue, expecting to be received with due ceremony. But things had gone awry. The Lords who were supposed to meet him were not there. The only person available was Ralegh who, as he later told Cecil, was surprised to see 'so great a person so neglected'. Ralegh took charge of the situation. Assisted by Sir Arthur Savage and Sir Arthur Gorges, who both spoke good French, Ralegh showed Biron the sights: the monuments at Westminster and, the following Monday, the Bear Garden, which he said they had great pleasure to see. Ralegh, in his own words, sent to and fro and laboured like a mole to fashion things. The Queen was then at Basing House. Ralegh arranged for the arrival of Biron and his suite at The Vyne, Lord Sandys' red-brick mansion four miles north of Basingstoke, which had been specially furnished for the visitors. The gentry of Hampshire had lent, amongst other furnishings, some 140 beds for the Frenchmen to sleep in.

Ralegh saw that the French wore 'all black and no kind of bravery at all' and, evidently so as not to embarrass them with his own fine clothes, he rode specially back to London through the night to get himself a 'playne black taffeta sute, and a playne black saddell'. However, the Duke de Biron's visit went so well and the Queen was so pleased with Ralegh's exertions that she knighted his elder brother Carew.

Ralegh continued to be uneasy about his hold on Sherborne. Bishop Coldwell had died in October 1596, and again there was another long delay before the Queen appointed a successor to the see. Henry Cotton was consecrated in November 1598 and it seems to have been part of the conditions under which he received the appointment that he should do what was required of him *vis-à-vis* Ralegh and Sherborne. A tripartite indenture was drawn up, on 20th August 1599, between the Queen; Cotton, and the Dean and Chapter of Salisbury; and Ralegh and John Fitzjames. The Bishop and the Dean and Chapter granted the manor and castle of Sherborne, with the Hundreds of Sherborne and Yetminster, and the Manors of Burton and Holnest, in fee for ever, to the Queen. The grant was conditional on the Queen enfeoffing Ralegh with the Sherborne and Yetminster estates, and John Fitzjames with Burton and Holnest. Ralegh was to pay the Bishop an annual rent of £260; Fitzjames was to pay £60. But Ralegh was still not satisfied. Four years later, in 1602, he accepted a challenge from Sir Amyas Preston. The duel was never fought – Ralegh made it clear in his writings in several places that he strongly disapproved of duelling – but as a result he put his affairs in order, in case of an accident. He arranged another indenture, through Sir John Doddridge who was later a Justice of the King's Bench. This was sealed and delivered in the presence of six witnesses on 12th April 1603, and it conveyed all Ralegh's Sherborne estates in favour of his eldest son Wat, and the heirs male of his body lawfully begotten. Ralegh now hoped, in vain, that this would safeguard Sherborne for his heirs once and for all.

As Ralegh was attempting to tighten his grip on Sherborne, he was relinquishing his estates in Ireland. He seems to have grown tired of his Irish ventures even before the fresh troubles of the late 1590s. An an absentee landlord, he was involved in endless disputes and legal suits. He suspected Henry Pyne, his business associate in Ireland, was swindling him as successfully as he thought John Meere was doing in Sherborne. The Munster rising of October 1598 completed Ralegh's disillusionment. He had already, on 27th May 1598, conveyed his Irish estates to a friend Thomas Southwell (although that transaction did not seem to affect Ralegh's own title to the properties), but the rebellion was the last straw. His tenants were driven out, and their houses burned. The new English settlements were in ruins, and the native Irish swarmed back to the lands they had always reckoned were still theirs. The only man who seemed to profit from the unrest was Pyne. He made money from victualling the English garrison at Youghal, and he himself commanded an English garrison at Mogeely Castle. He strengthened his control over the pipe-stave manufacturing business to such an extent that by 1601 Ralegh and the other partners were petitioning the Privy Council on the grounds that Pyne had been cheating them.

228

Queen Elizabeth I opening a new Parliament. Ralegh was a member of every Elizabethan House of Commons from 1584 to 1603, except that of 1588. Engraving from Robert Glover's *Nobilitas Politica Vel Civilis*, 1608

Procerum   Cãcellarius   Thesaurarius   primogeniti

R Scotiæ

Cancellarij sedes

Prolocutor

In November 1601 Mountjoy defeated and captured the Spanish who had landed at Kinsale, and on Christmas Eve he routed Tyrone in open battle; Tyrone was left little option but to surrender, which he did in March 1603. By 1602 Sir George Carew had crushed the revolt in Munster. But Ralegh had had enough. He was anxious to sell, and Carew found him a buyer in the secretary to the Munster presidency, young Robert Boyle, afterwards Earl of Cork. Ralegh sold Boyle his Irish estates on 7th December 1602, for a lump sum of £1,500, keeping only the castle of Inchiquin Ralegh, where the incredible old lady Katherine, dowager Countess of Desmond, who had reputedly been born in 1464, was tenant for life. (She died in 1604, and Ralegh refers to her, with some awe, in his *History of the World*.) Boyle appears to have got a bargain, but Carew said that the Munster seignories were costing Ralegh £200 a year when he sold them. Boyle could only raise £500, and the balance was still outstanding when Ralegh was attaindered. King James then claimed the lands, but Boyle eventually had his title confirmed by paying James the remaining £1,000 in 1604.

In September 1601 Ralegh was too ill of some (unnamed) sickness even to go to Bath for his usual treatment, but he was fit enough to take his seat as senior knight for the county of Cornwall in the next House of Commons, which met on 27th October and sat until 19th December. It was the tenth Parliament of Queen Elizabeth's reign, and it was the last both for the Queen and for Ralegh.

This Parliament was a restless and rebellious one. Members were always being called to order for shouting, hawking and coughing their disapproval of speakers. One of the main items of parliamentary business was the customary subsidy of money to the Crown. Although members knew that a large Spanish force had landed at Kinsale that same month and was still undefeated, and although Cecil insisted that the Queen needed £300,000 by Easter, the House was in a touchy mood and the members hemmed and laughed and hooted when one speaker said that the Crown could confiscate all private property if the Queen so wished. Cecil reproved the House, and told members they were behaving more like a grammar school than a parliament.

When the committee met to debate the subsidy, nobody would take the lead. They all 'sat silent a good while', expecting some guidance from the members of the Privy Council present. It was, almost inevitably, Ralegh who broke the awkward silence. He said that the last Parliament had granted three subsidies, for fear that the Spaniards were coming. Now, the Spaniards *had* come, and the Queen herself was selling her own jewels and land to raise money, 'sparing even out of her own purse and apparel for our sakes'. One member, Sir Edward Hoby, had been unable to find a seat, and he took out his sulkiness on Ralegh, shouting at him to speak up so that they could all hear him, and telling him to stand up when he spoke (Ralegh was sitting, as was customary in committee). Ralegh looked at his interrupter 'with a countenance full of disdain'.

The next speaker suggested a tax levied on all lands valued at or under £3. There was some discussion, in which Ralegh took part, warmly supporting the principle that all men should pay alike. The committee debated the level at which the assessment should be fixed, without coming to any conclusion. Cecil said he was glad that the three-pound men would also contribute. 'Neither pots nor pans,' he said, 'nor dish nor spoon, should be spared when danger is at our elbow.' This was too much for Ralegh. Selling kitchen ware to pay subsidies seemed to him a poor way of going about it. Rising to answer 'the gentleman on my left hand', he told Cecil, 'Well may *you* call it policy, but I am sure it argues poverty in the State.'

Ralegh was in good form. His next victim was Francis Bacon who said smugly that it was commendable to tax the poor as well as the rich. 'It was *dulcis tractus pari jugo* – 'it was pleasant to draw in equal yoke.' 'Call you this *par jugum?*' Ralegh retorted, 'when a poor man pays as much as the rich? Peradventure his estate is no better, or little better than he is assessed at, while our estates are £30 or £40 in the Queen's books – not the hundredth part of our wealth. It is neither *dulcis* nor *par.*' This was the authentic voice of the parliamentarians of the next century. It silenced Bacon. In due course, Parliament granted the whole subsidy.

But the main target of that House of Commons was the Crown's practice of granting monopolies to private individuals, who were then able to hold up their fellow-men to ransom for that particular commodity. Politically, the matter was highly sensitive, since it affected the Crown's prerogative. The question was the crucial one: where should the line be drawn between the powers of the Sovereign and of Parliament? Feelings ran high on the subject in debate. A list of monopolies was read out, which included playing-cards, whereupon it was noticed that Sir Walter Ralegh actually blushed (unaccountably, since the monopoly was Sir Edward Darcy's). The list was so long that a sarcastic voice wondered openly why *bread* was not included on it.

When the monopoly on tin was mentioned, Ralegh did more than blush. He made 'a sharp speech' in his own defence.

> I am urged to speak in two respects. The one because I find myself touched in particular; the other, in that I take some imputation of slander offered unto her Majesty, I mean by the gentleman that first mentioned tin: for that being one of the principal commodities of this kingdom, and being in Cornwall, it hath ever, so long as there were any, belonged to the Dukes of Cornwall, and they had special patents of privilege. It pleased her Majesty freely to bestow upon me that privilege; and that patent being word for word the very same the Duke's is, and because by reason of mine office of Lord Warden of the Stannaries I can sufficiently inform this House of the state thereof, I will make bold to deliver it unto you.

Ralegh gave some interesting details of the tin industry under his direction.

> When the tin is taken out of the mine, and melted and refined, then is every piece containing one hundred weight sealed with the Duke's seal. Now I will tell you, that before the granting of my patent, whether tin were but of seventeen shillings and so upward to fifty shillings a hundred, yet the poor workman never had above two shillings the week, finding themselves. But since my patent whosoever will work may;

and buy tin at what price soever, they have four shillings a week truly paid. There is no poor that will work there but may, and have that wages.

Ralegh then went on to stun the House with his peroration. 'Notwithstanding, if all others may be repealed, I will give my consent as freely to the cancelling of this as any member of this House.' After that, 'a great silence' fell upon the House. Sir Francis Hastings, who eventually got up to speak, implicitly rebuked Ralegh by asking for tolerance and free speech for *all*. He wondered whether everybody's recollection of the facts was the same as the last speaker's. Sir Francis congratulated the House for having given Ralegh a fair hearing. However, no other holder of a monopoly spoke, nor offered to give up his privileges.

The situation was calmed by the Queen herself. Seeing that she must give some ground, she came specially to the House to make her last and one of her greatest speeches, which was afterwards, indeed, called the Queen's Golden Speech. In it, she promised to abolish some monopolies and said that monopoly holders would have to defend their privileges at common law, like everybody else. The speech was received rapturously by the House.

Ralegh was always able to bring the House down to earth with some practical observations. On a Bill to enforce church attendance he spoke against so much power being put in the hands of the church-wardens. As he had done before on the deportation of Brownists, he reminded the House of the practical difficulties of their intended legislation. He imagined the legal processes of the country being swamped by crowds of church-wardens. 'Say, then, there be 120 parishes in a shire: there must now come extraordinarily 240 churchwardens. And say but two in a parish offend in a quarter of a year: that makes 480 persons, with the offenders, to appear. What great multitudes this will bring together; what quarrelling and danger may happen, besides giving authority to a mean churchwarden!' Possibly because of Ralegh's speech, the Bill was lost by one vote. Afterwards a member claimed that he had wanted to vote for the Bill but somebody had pulled him back and kept him in his seat. But Ralegh was too old a parliamentary hand to be impressed by that. 'Why, if it please you,' he said, 'it is a small matter to pull one by the sleeve, for so have I done myself oftentimes.'

This remark caused a great stir in the House and there were suggestions that Ralegh should apologize. However, Ralegh was by now an experienced campaigner, and in this parliament of 1601 he gave what was possibly his finest performance. He spoke always on the side of men having the freedom to do what they liked with their own property, under the law. Speaking for the repeal of a law compelling a farmer to till one third of his land, he said, 'I think the best course is to set at liberty, and leave every man free, which is the desire of a true Englishman'; and for the repeal of another law compelling men to grow hemp (for cordage), he said 'For my part, I do not like this constraining of men to manure or use their grounds at our wills; but rather, let every men use his ground to that which it is most fit for, and therein use his own discretion.' This was a new, refreshing and inspiring opinion to be voiced in the heavily paternalistic society of the Tudors, and again it pointed the way for the parliamentarians of the coming century.

To the end, Ralegh retained his scorn for Spain. Objecting to the export of iron ordnance from England, he said that many of the guns found their way to Spanish ships. 'I am sure,' he said, 'heretofore one ship of her Majesty's was able to beat twenty [another account gives a hundred!] Spaniards. But now, by reason of our own ordnance, we are hardly matched one to one.' To that House of Commons, as they looked across at the survivor of the Armada actions and the victor of Cadiz, Ralegh must have seemed like a face and voice from an heroic past. He was exaggerating, but it is appropriate that the last picture of Ralegh in Parliament is of him warning the House against complacency towards England's enemies.

The Parliament had been a qualified success for Cecil. He had made some excellent speeches. The Queen had the subsidy she needed. But as Her Majesty's Principal Secretary Cecil had been an oddly hesitant leader. Perhaps there was some secret sense of insecurity in that small, hunch-backed figure. He may have felt that he still stood in the shadow of his father, who had supported Queen and State like a giant oak-tree for more than forty years. He had cut a poor figure compared to Ralegh, who had wiped his eye on more than one occasion in debate. Ralegh, if he thought about these exchanges at all, put them down to the normal cut-and-thrust of parliamentary debate; they were no more than that. Ralegh had no doubt that Cecil was his firm and constant family friend. In his letters he called himself Cecil's poorest but truest friend and servant. Lady Ralegh, too, sent her best wishes and an occasional gift of gloves. 'Bess,' said Ralegh, 'returns yow her best wishes, notwithstanding all quarrels.' After Cecil had been to stay at Sherborne, Ralegh said in a postscript, 'My wife says that yow came hither in an unseasonabell tyme, and had no leasure to looke abrode; and that every day this place amends, and London, to her, groes worse and worss.' The picture conjured up by Ralegh's letters is a comfortable secure relationship between people who had known each other for a very long time.

The Raleghs had Cecil's motherless young son Will to stay at Sherborne. Ralegh wrote to tell Cecil that his son had been troubled with a little looseness in the bowels but was much better. His weak stomach was 'altogether amended', and he was eating well and digesting rightly. He was also being better kept to his studies at Sherborne than anywhere else. Will Cecil was as fond of Ralegh. 'Sir Walter, we must all exclaim and cry out because you will not come down. Your being absent, we are like soldiers that when their Captain absent they know not what to do.' Ralegh could have been excused for being confident that if there ever were any political danger, it could not be from Cecil.

Another frequent visitor to Sherborne at this time was Cecil's brother-in-law, Henry Brooke, Lord Cobham. He was, at first sight, an unlikely friend for Ralegh. He was very talkative and loved idle gossip; he took offence easily, and gave it as easily; he was vain, and indiscreet, and in the end, when his character was put to the test, he proved to be a moral coward. He was rich, with an annual income of £7,000; he could spend £150 a time on books, and he had travelled widely. He was a charming but lightweight personality, and it is hard to see what Ralegh saw in him, or why Ralegh gave him his confidence for so long, although Ralegh was notoriously slow to recognize danger in those he thought his friends. Cobham's relationship to Cecil may have given him some added value in Ralegh's estimation.

Lady Ralegh also liked Cobham. Again and again, Ralegh's letters to Cobham refer to his wife's affection for him. She would despair ever to see Cobham at Sherborne again, if he did not come. If he did not come on Saturday, her oysters would be spoilt and her partridges stale. (Interestingly, that letter was dated August; the Elizabethans did not wait until there was an R in the month before eating oysters, nor until September for the partridge season.)

The only snag in the friendship was the new wife Cobham married in 1602. She was a Howard, Frances, Countess Dowager of Kildare, and daughter of the Lord Admiral. She had been Lady Ralegh's enemy for years, and was always criticizing her and working against her, both with her father, and with the Queen. The Howards were never friends of Ralegh's, and it was most unfortunate that a man he did call his friend should marry one of that family.

Cecil's brushes with Ralegh in the House may have been the surface indications of his deeper purpose, for by the time of that Parliament, late in 1601, Cecil was already engaged in political manoeuvrings of the utmost delicacy concerning the great political question of the day: the succession. The Queen herself was understandably sensitive on the subject and forbade any public discussion. Cecil's preparations for the future, therefore, had to be made with the greatest care and secrecy.

In theory, there were about a dozen claimants, including Edward Seymour, Lord Beauchamp, the representative of the Grey family; the Earl of Huntingdon, who was descended from the Duke of Clarence (drowned in a butt of malmsey); and the Infanta Isabella Clara Eugenia, through her father King Philip II of Spain. But in fact there was only one serious claimant. The people of England seemed to have decided it at their own firesides. With Elizabeth, the line of Henry VIII came to an end. Therefore the succession must go back to the line of Henry VII. The Lady Arabella Stuart had a claim through Margaret, Henry VII's daughter. But so also had King James VI of Scotland, and his father was an elder son. James therefore was the rightful heir and the great majority (including, ironically, Ralegh) recognized his claim.

But there were difficulties in the way. For example, James was an alien and under the law could not own a cottage nor a single acre of land in England; it would seem strange to offer such a man the throne. Then there were difficulties caused by James' own personality, and the personalities of some of the leading figures of Elizabeth's Court. Cecil set himself to smooth all the roughnesses out of the path and to replace the House of Tudor with the House of Stuart with the minimum of fuss and disorder.

He could not carry out his task without incurring some casualties, and the chief one, in the end, was Walter Ralegh. Ralegh was unpredictable, as indiscreet (in Cecil's opinion) as Cobham; at any moment he might do or say something to upset Cecil's carefully laid designs. Ralegh was still the Queen's man, through and through. He was perilously loyal, and dangerously obsolete. Gently but inexorably, Cecil began to disassociate himself from Ralegh, to leave Ralegh isolated and friendless. He used his influence to prevent Ralegh becoming Earl of Pembroke, and when the question of Ralegh entering the Privy Council arose again, he made it a condition that Ralegh should relinquish his post as Captain of the Guard. Ralegh could not bring himself to accept what he believed would have been a

Henry Brooke, 11th Baron Cobham, 1564–1619, Ralegh's friend and eventually his betrayer. Artist unknown, c. 1600

desertion of his Queen. Above all, Cecil made Ralegh feared and hated by James VI.

After Essex's death, James had held Cecil and Ralegh equally in suspicion, believing them both responsible for Essex's fall, and for planning to put the Infanta on the throne. But Cecil arranged a secret meeting with James's envoy, the Earl of Mar, when he was in London and, through him, pledged James his support. James, however, was not to press his claim to the succession publicly, nor in any way to advertise his negotiations with Cecil. This was so as to pay proper respect to the feelings of the Queen, and also, of course, to safeguard Cecil. James was to leave matters to Cecil, and simply do nothing, while Cecil arranged everything. James managed to play his part, although he did occasionally cause Cecil moments of alarm by careless talk which was immediately picked up by George Nicholson, the English agent in Scotland. Cecil himself had his awkward moments, one in particular when he was out riding with the Queen. The mail from Scotland arrived containing, as Cecil well knew, letters it were better the Queen did not see. Cecil capitalized upon the Queen's known distaste for bad smells, and said the letters needed airing because they had been in a smelly wallet. He was thus able to remove the compromising items before the Queen saw them.

Meanwhile, the campaign against Ralegh went on, with Cecil continuing to play a double role. Cecil seems in some unfathomable way to have been hurt by Ralegh's friendship with Cobham. The little man was unduly resentful of their trip across to Ostend, and while he was enjoying Ralegh's hospitality at Sherborne and receiving from him expressions of friendship written in the warmest terms, he was still trying to alienate Ralegh from his friends. To Sir George Carew, for instance, President of Munster, Cecil wrote, 'Believe me, two old friends use me unkindly, but I have covenanted with my heart not to know it, for in show we are great, and all my revenge shall be to heap coals upon their heads'. He begged Carew to take care what he wrote in his letters to Ralegh and Cobham because 'they show all men's letters to every man.'

At the same time, Cecil had to explain his friendship with Ralegh to James, who might otherwise have wondered what game he was playing. Cecil justified himself by saying that

> if I did not some time cast a stone into the mouth of these gaping crabs [i.e. Ralegh and Cobham], when they are in their prodigal humour of discourses, they would not stick to confess daily how contrary it is to their nature to be under your sovereignty; though they confess (Ralegh especially) that natural policy forceth them to keep on foot such a trade against the great day of mart. In all which light and sudden humours of his, though I do no way check him, because he shall not think I reject his freedom or his affection, but always use contestation with him . . . yet, under pretext of extraordinary care of his well doing, I have seemed to dissuade him from engaging himself too far.

Cecil's 'extraordinary care' for Ralegh's well doing was illustrated in November 1601 when James, evidently still under the impression that he could negotiate with Ralegh personally, sent the Duke of Lennox to London to see him, and Cobham, at Durham House.

Cecil, very alarmed, wanted to know who had been the intermediary for the meeting. James told him Sir Arthur Savage who, James said, was not to suffer for it. But Cecil need not have feared. Ralegh was not in the same class as a politician. He sent Lennox away with a flea in his ear. Innocently, he told Cecil that he had too much respect for the Queen and felt too much loyalty for her to think of treating elsewhere. Cecil commended him, and said he would have done the same himself. Ralegh then said he was going to tell the Queen 'what had been offered and what had been answered'. Appalled, Cecil managed to dissuade him. Subtly working on Ralegh's pride, he said the Queen might think Ralegh had been weak even to see Lennox, and, if he told her about their conversation now, at this late stage, the Queen might think Ralegh was trying to ingratiate himself with her. Ralegh agreed to keep silent, and one more round went to Cecil.

Cecil was seemingly terrified that James should think his friendship with Ralegh was genuine. His greatest fear was that Ralegh would say something favourable to James about him. He said

> Let me therefore presume thus far upon your Majesty's favour, that whatsoever he shall take upon him to say for me, upon any new humour of kindness, whereof sometime he will be replete (upon the receipt of private benefit) you will no more believe it (if it come in other shape) be it never so much in my commendation, then that his own conscience thought it needful for him to undertake to keep me from any humour of imanity, when, I thank God, my greatest adversaries and my own soul have ever acquitted me from that of all other vices. Would God I were as free from offense towards God, in seeking for private affection to support a person whom most religious men do hold anathema.

James must have heard of Ralegh's reputation for atheism and this sly, sideways reference to it was a most shrewd and damaging blow. If a narrow-minded Calvinist like James Stuart needed anything more to complete his disgust with and dislike of Ralegh, the imputation of atheism provided it.

But there was still more. 'But why do I thus far presume to trouble your ears so much with my poore private griefs at his ingratitude to me,' Cecil went on, 'when I resolved rather to record my private joys? I will therefore leave the best and worst of him, and other things, to 3's relation, in whose discretion and affection you may sleep secure.'

In the secret correspondence between Cecil and King James, '3' was the code number for Cecil's chief intermediary, Lord Henry Howard (just as '7' was Cobham, '2' was probably Ralegh, '10' was Cecil, '24' the Queen and '30' James himself). Lord Henry was a member of another, Catholic, branch of the Lord Admiral's family. It was somehow symbolic that one of the main instruments in poisoning James's mind against Ralegh and bringing about his downfall should be a Howard. His family's previous political careers had often ended in disaster: Lord Henry's brother, the Duke of Norfolk, was beheaded by Elizabeth for his treason on behalf of the Queen of Scots; his father the Earl of Surrey had been executed by Elizabeth's father, Henry VIII; and his nephew, the Earl of Arundel, had died in prison.

Lord Henry was mentally unbalanced and his neuroses came to a head in his violent hatred of Ralegh. There seemed no logical reason for this hatred. Ralegh had done Lord Henry no personal harm, nor seems ever to have had any dealings with him. But once Lord Henry had announced his hatred, it fed upon itself, and grew. Over months of correspondence with Cecil and with James, Lord Henry poured out a stream of vituperation, slander and innuendo against Ralegh, his wife, and his friend Cobham. 'Hell did never vomit up such a couple as Ralegh and Cobham.' He described Ralegh's hypocrisy, his 'duality', his malign influence on Cobham. Ralegh's pride 'exceedeth all men alive', and he countenanced 'a pride above the greatest Lucifer that lived in our age'. He had 'the soft voice of Jacob in courtly hypocrisy'. Hell, he told James, 'cannot afford such a like triplicity that denies the Trinity' – meaning Ralegh, Cobham, and the Earl of Northumberland. Lord Henry did not spare Lady Ralegh. She was 'as furious as Proserpina with failing of that restitution in Court which flattery had moved her to expect'. She was 'a dangerous woman', who bent 'her whole wits and industry to the disturbance of all motions, by counsel and encouragement, that may disturb the possibility of others' hopes'. Cobham Lord Henry seemed to see as a mere tool of Ralegh's, who was inspired by his own passions. The baleful influence of the Howards could be seen on all sides. Lord Henry, Lord Howard of Bindon from Dorset, Lady Frances, and the Lord Admiral were all ranged against Ralegh. When Lord Henry wrote to the Earl of Mar to tell him that the Lord Admiral wished with all his soul that he could level his cannon at Durham House just as he had, the year before, at Essex House, he was probably not exaggerating a great deal. Sometimes, Lord Henry's malice inspired him to accurate prophecy. 'The glass of time being very far run, the day of the Queen's death may be the day of their doom, if they do not agree with their adversary upon the way, lest he deliver them to the judge . . .'

The Earl of Northumberland, Ralegh's friend, did try to redress the situation in his own correspondence with James. He denied that Ralegh disputed James's right to the throne. Of Cobham, Northumberland said 'I know not how his heart is affected.' But of Ralegh he said,

> whom sixteen years acquaintance hath confirmed to me, I must needs affirm Ralegh's ever allowance of your right, and although I know him insolent, extremely heated, a man that desires to seem to be able to sway all men's fancies, all men's courses, and a man that ought of himself, when your time shall come, will never be able to do you much good or harm, yet must I needs confess what I know, that there is excellent good parts of nature in him, a man whose love is disadvantageous to me in some sort, which I cherish rather out of constancy than policy, and one whom I wish your Majesty not to lose, because I would not that one hair of a man's head should be against you that might be for you.

It was a generous letter. As Northumberland said, it was not to his advantage to be known as Ralegh's friend or to be associated with him in any way. But the harm had been irretrievably done. James was, as he said, 'exceeding far inamorat' of Ralegh and Cobham.

'Your suspicion,' he told Cecil, 'and your disgracing, shall be mine.'

Cecil played out his double game with Ralegh to the end. While continuing to foster James's suspicions against Ralegh, he acted towards Ralegh himself as a friend and a business partner. He consulted him, as he had so often done before, on affairs in Ireland and the treatment of the Munster rebels. In August 1601 Ralegh took over the supervision of Cecil's newly acquired estate of Rushworth, and advised Cecil on the disposal of estate timber and other matters. They had an arrangement together to import contraband cedar trees, if the Lord Admiral would order their seizure, whereupon Ralegh planned to make 'ciel cabinets' and boards, and many other delicate things. Cecil was Ralegh's partner in privateering ventures almost to the end of Elizabeth's reign. In 1602 he paid half the costs of an expedition's victualling, Ralegh and the Lord Admiral paying the other half between them. As late as January 1603, Cecil was investing with Ralegh, but imploring that his share be kept a secret. King James disliked privateering and any other enterprise that smacked of warfare, and Cecil did not want him to find out that his trusted servant had any part in such doings. 'I pray you,' Cecil wrote to Ralegh, 'as much as may be conceal our adventure, at the least my name above any others. For though I thank God I have no other meaning than becometh an honest man in any of my actions, yet that which were another man's *pater noster* would be accounted in me a charm.' Cecil was not as honest as he pretended. But Ralegh suspected nothing, and willingly kept Cecil's secret.

The Queen had been ill in the winter of 1602 but had recovered. In March she was sick again, with a fever. She fell into a coma and lay for two days and nights speechless and motionless, with her finger in her mouth. At last, at Richmond, in the early hours of 24th March 1603, the Queen died, 'mildly like a lamb, easily as a ripe apple from the tree'. A great reign had come peacefully to its end, and thanks to Cecil, another reign was peacefully about to begin.

The news of the Queen's death was taken north by Sir Robert Carey, who had placed relays of horses along the road to Edinburgh some days before. An official proclamation from Cecil soon followed. Still scarcely believing his luck, King James VI of Scotland and now I of England set out southwards on 5th April to enter upon his inheritance. On the way he set free some criminals and, just as arbitrarily, had others executed. He hunted hares, brought specially in baskets and released along the roadside. His prospects somewhat went to his head. He created over three hundred new knights, and granted lands and manors with abandon. At Newcastle he met the Bishop of Durham, listened to his sermons, exchanged jokes – and promised him the return of Durham House.

Ralegh was in the West Country when the Queen died but returned to London at once. Aubrey tells a dubious story that, at a consultation at Whitehall, Ralegh declared his opinion that ''twas the wisest way for them to keep the government in their owne hands, and sett up a commonwealth.' But there is no other support for the view that Ralegh was a republican; in fact his published opinions show him as a convinced monarchist. He was certainly one of those who signed a letter welcoming King James and, ignoring Cecil's proclamation that officers of the Crown should not go to meet the King, he rode north with

Sir Walter Ralegh, Captain of the Guard, in the funeral cortège of Elizabeth I, in 1603, from a contemporary painting by William Camden

hundreds of others to introduce himself to James. He said he urgently needed draft letters with the Royal signature, so as to continue the ordinary legal processes in the Duchy of Cornwall and to safeguard Crown woodlands.

Ralegh first met the King at the end of April, when James and his train had reached Cecil's house at Burghley in Northamptonshire. The meeting was inauspicious. According to Aubrey, when told that Sir Walter Ralegh was amongst those present, James said 'Ralegh. On my soul, mon, I have heard rawly of thee.' Ralegh was, as Aubrey says, 'such a person (every way) that a prince would rather be afrayd of then ashamed of. He had that awfulness and ascendency in his aspect over other mortalls, that the king –' Aubrey did not finish his comment, but anyone who saw the two men together would know at once that they were opposites in every way, in looks, manners, temperaments and beliefs. Ralegh's colour was black. James was mousy brown. Ralegh was over six feet tall. James barely reached five feet. Ralegh was dark, handsome, and glamorous. James was timid, pot-bellied, spindle-shanked. Ralegh had a bold face. James had flabby cheeks and a petulant, peevish, drawn-down mouth. Ralegh was known as a successful commander in the field. James wore heavily padded doublets, for fear of assassination. James was a Scot and Ralegh thought the Scots a 'needy beggerly nation'. Ralegh was a man of war, and James loathed war and warlike men. Ralegh was the chief enemy of Spain, with whom James was planning peace. Ralegh was one of the most notable privateers of his generation. James forbade privateering. Ralegh believed in free parliamentary speech. James mistrusted and prevented it. Ralegh had made tobacco fashionable. James abhorred tobacco.

The tomb of Queen Elizabeth I, engraving from Holland's *Herwologia*, 1620

Tumuli Elisabethæ Reginæ vera deliniatio

DIEV ET MON DROIT

The letters for the Duchy of Cornwall had been only an excuse, and James realized it. He told his secretary Sir Thomas Lake to write out the letters quickly, because they were 'all that Ralegh had to allege for excuse of his coming', so that Ralegh could go again. Lake wrote to Cecil on 25th April that Ralegh 'hath taken no great root here'. Ralegh was back in London for the Queen's funeral on 28th. It was already obvious to everyone at Court that Ralegh could never hope for any favour at James's hands.

It was obvious to everyone, except Ralegh himself. Aubrey records one of his earliest *faux pas* with James. 'It was a most stately sight, the glory of that reception of his majesty, where the nobility and gentry were in exceeding rich equippage, having enjoyed a long peace under the most excellent of queens.' They were indeed so splendid that they were a source of uneasiness.

'Their obedience,' said Aubrey, 'carried a secret dread with it.' James eventually identified the reason for the 'secret dread' in the person of Sir Walter Ralegh. 'King James did not inwardly like it, and with an inward envy sayd that, though so and so (as before), he doubted not but he should have been able on his owne strength (should the English have kept him out) been able to have dealt with them, and get his right. Sayd Sir Walter Ralegh to him. "Would to God that had been put to the tryall." "Why doe you wish that?" sayd the king. "Because," said Sir Walter, "that then you would have knowne your friends from your foes." But that reason of Sir Walter was never forgotten nor forgiven.' It is difficult to see how Ralegh's speech was offensive, unless matters had reached such a state where everything he said or did gave offence.

Ralegh met James again, on 3rd May, when the Court was at Theobalds, another of Cecil's great houses, in Hertfordshire. Ralegh was once again rebuffed. The Privy Council told him that he was to be replaced as Captain of the Guard by Sir Thomas Erskine. Though he cherished the office, Ralegh seems to have given it up with good grace. It was under-standable that the King would wish one of his fellow-countrymen and an old friend to have such an intimate position. But much worse was to follow. James recalled all monopolies granted by Elizabeth. Ralegh's farm of wines was eventually judged not to be a true mono-poly, but the levying of dues from it was forbidden, thus removing a large part of Ralegh's income. He was ordered to quit Durham House at once. He protested that he had spent more than £2,000 of his money on the place; he had food for forty people and hay for twenty horses laid in; he had been there for twenty years and even 'the poorest artificer in London hath a quarter's warning given him by his landlord'. The time-limit was extended, reluctantly, to Midsummer Day. Ralegh followed the Court to Greenwich and was one of the great crowd of nobility and gentry, estimated at between ten and twelve thousand, who jostled and elbowed each other to get the King's ear. Ralegh won one small success. He no longer had to pay the Crown an annual rent of £300 from his revenue as Governor of Jersey.

Even now, Ralegh remained oddly unaware of what was happening. He simply had not realized that his star was sinking. His 'springs of bounty' were all dried up. In July, when James was visiting Lady Ralegh's uncle, Sir Nicholas Carew, at Beddington in Surrey, Ralegh presented him with a pamphlet, *A Discourse touching a War with Spain, and of the*

Protecting of the Netherlands, and offered to lead an army of 2,000 men himself. James was appalled by any such suggestions. He had in mind peace with Spain, and he had no liking for the Dutch, or anyone else, who rebelled against a King. James's belief that Ralegh was war-like, dangerous and never to be trusted, was confirmed.

Later that month, probably on a day between the 12th and 16th, Ralegh went to Windsor to join the King in a hunting-party. While he was waiting on the terrace, Cecil (now Lord Cecil of Essandon) came up to him and told him that the King wished him to stay behind. The Privy Council had some questions they would like to ask him.

At the Council meeting, Ralegh was asked if he knew of a plot to seize the King's person, or of any communication between his friend Lord Cobham and Count Aremberg, the ambassador from the Spanish Netherlands. Ralegh denied any knowledge of either question. He was dismissed, but placed under house arrest, in Sir Thomas Bodley's house. From there he was taken to the Tower, later to be charged with high treason.

From the very beginning he was an awkward prisoner, insisting on his rights, sending five or six times a day for Sir John Peyton, Lieutenant of the Tower, 'in such passions,' Sir John said, 'as I see his fortitude is impotent to support his grief'. Ralegh already had foreknowledge of what awaited him. On 23rd July, Sir John Peyton wrote to Cecil, 'I never saw so strange a dejected mind as is in Sir Walter Ralegh.'

17. Trial for Treason

THERE CAN be no doubt that Ralegh knew something of a plot against King James. He may not actually have been a conspirator himself, and he may have been only on the fringe of affairs, with only the barest knowledge of the plot. But he did know something.

It was inevitable that his name should spring to mind as soon as any plot against James was discovered. Everyone knew the sad changes which had overtaken his fortunes since James came to the throne. Yet it was typical of the ironic fate which always pursued Ralegh that he should be arrested on suspicion of a plot about which he genuinely knew nothing. There were two plots, the 'Bye' or 'Surprising', and the 'Main', later called by the prosecutor, Coke, the 'Priests' Treason' and the 'Spanish Treason'. The 'Bye' was a Catholic plot to seize the King and force him to adopt religious policies more favourable to Catholics. The plot was known to Cecil in its early days and the conspirators – two Catholic priests called William Watson and Francis Clarke; Lord Grey, the son of Ralegh's old chief and adversary in Ireland; Sir Griffin Markham; Cobham's brother George Brooke; and Anthony Copley – were all arrested in the ten days before Ralegh's own arrest.

It was Brooke who implicated Ralegh, saying under questioning that he and his fellow conspirators had thought of Ralegh as 'a fit man' to have with them. This was quite untrue; if anything, the plotters had been particularly careful to keep their plot from Ralegh. But the mere mention of Ralegh's name was enough for Cecil. He had for some time been suspicious of what he thought were Ralegh's political meddlings; he could not afford to take any risks, now that he had James safely on the throne. Ralegh might be an old friend but Cecil could not help that. The safety of the State was paramount.

Ralegh was further implicated by the 'Main'. The principal figure in this plot was his very good friend Lord Cobham. Cobham disliked Cecil and King James and, as he never troubled to guard his tongue, he too became suspect in the Government's eyes. The precise shape of Cobham's plot will probably never now be made clear, but from Coke's later summing up it seems that Cobham intended to go to Spain to arrange a loan of between five and six hundred thousand crowns with which to finance the seditious activities of malcontent Catholics in England. He had already had some dealings with Count Aremberg, the ambassador from the Spanish Netherlands, to arrange the matter. He was to return by Jersey where he would confer with Ralegh. Back in England, the plan was to seize the King, 'to kill the fox and his cubs', and land a Spanish army at Milford Haven, to place the Lady Arabella Stuart on the throne.

It was of course absurd to suspect Ralegh, of all people, of plotting to land a Spanish army on English soil, and the Privy Council must have realized it. But they still could not bring themselves to believe that Ralegh knew nothing, as he said, of his friend's dealings with Count Aremberg. For instance, it was known that he and Cobham had had some correspondence while Ralegh was under house arrest, through Captain Keymis (who had also since been arrested). Ralegh had dined with Cobham at his house in Blackfriars, or Cobham had visited Durham House, on an evening when Count Aremberg's messenger, a merchant from Antwerp called La Renzi, had also been present.

Ralegh explained that Keymis had merely been carrying a great pearl and a diamond and other jewels worth £4,000 with which Cobham was going to buy a fee farm. He still said he knew nothing of Cobham's liaison with Aremberg. But, at last, he admitted that Cobham had offered him eight thousand crowns to assist in arranging a peace between England and Spain. Ralegh said he had not taken the offer seriously. He had thought it just one more of his friend's idle conceits. But to insist that he knew nothing, and then to admit that he did know something, even a little, made things look bad for Ralegh.

Ralegh seemed to be trapped in a circumstantial web and nothing he could do could get him free. He wrote to Cecil admitting some dealings with Cobham and saying that he had seen Cobham passing Durham House, on his way to visit La Renzi's lodgings, at St Mary Saviour's on the opposite bank. This was still not treasonable, and certainly not enough to bring Ralegh to trial, but when Cecil confronted Cobham with Ralegh's letter the situation changed completely. Cobham, in terror for his life and ready to do and say anything to save himself, cried, 'O villain! O traitor! I will now tell you all the truth.' He said that he had had dealings with Aremberg, but that it was Ralegh who was the chief instigator of the intrigue, Ralegh who had kept urging him on. Cobham later retracted his statement, then changed it, then retracted again, until nobody knew whether what he was saying bore any resemblance to the truth. But, in the meantime, he had said more than enough to damn Ralegh.

Ralegh was not uncomfortable in prison awaiting trial. Although Cecil was overstating it when he said that Ralegh was 'lodged and attended as well as in his own house', Ralegh had two small rooms to himself in the Bloody Tower, and two of his own servants to look after him. Nevertheless, he was in despair about the future. He well knew the cruelty of English law. Public State trials for treason were always foregone conclusions. They were only held when the Council had assured themselves of guilt, and had prepared the necessary evidence. Ralegh's real trial had been in front of the Privy Council, and he had failed to have himself acquitted there.

His pride writhed under the knowledge of how his enemies must be crowing over his downfall. In his wretched state of despair, and knowing himself innocent of treason, he attempted to draw sympathetic attention to himself. On 27th July, while dining with Sir John Peyton, he tried to commit suicide. He snatched up a knife from the table, tore open his shirt, and stabbed himself in the chest. Cecil was actually in the Tower at the time, examining prisoners, and when he was told of it, he found Ralegh 'in some agony, seeming to be unable to endure his misfortunes, and protesting innocency with carelessness of life.

In that humour he had wounded himself under the right pap, but no way mortally; being in truth rather a cut than a stab.' The knife had struck a rib a glancing blow and the wound was much less dangerous than it looked. It healed up in a few days. Ralegh's real wound was elsewhere, and the marks of it were his inability to endure his misfortunes and his protestations of innocence which Cecil noticed. Ralegh may seriously have intended to kill himself, and cheat the Crown of his property, which would be forfeit if he were convicted of treason. But it is more likely that he simply wished to attract attention. He failed. Cecil hushed up the incident, although Scaramelli, the Secretary to the Venetian Legation, heard of it and reported home. Cecil gave an account of the affair to Sir Thomas Parry, the ambassador in Paris, but no mention of it was made at Ralegh's trial.

Some time before his suicide attempt, possibly on the eve, Ralegh wrote a letter to his wife, revealing his intentions to her, and describing his feelings of hopelessness and frustration at great, and sometimes almost hysterical, length. The letter's authenticity has often been questioned. It is most probably genuine and gives an accurate reflection of Ralegh's state of mind as he awaited a humiliating public ordeal in court followed by – barring a miracle – a public execution.

> Receive from thy unfortunate husband, [he begins] these his last lines; these the last words that ever thou shalt receive from him. That I can live never to see thee and my child more! – I cannot. I have desired God and disputed with my reason, but nature and compassion hath the victory. That I can live to think how you are both left a spoil to my enemies, and that my name shall be a dishonour to my child – I cannot. I cannot endure the memory thereof. Unfortunate woman, unfortunate child, comfort yourselves; trust God, and be contented with your poor estate. I would have bettered it, if I had enjoyed a few years.
>
> Thou art a young woman, and forbear not to marry again. It is now nothing to me; thou art no more mine; nor I thine. To witness that thou didst love me once, take care that thou marry not to please sense, but to avoid poverty, and to preserve thy child. That thou didst also love me living, witness it to others; – to my poor daughter, to whom I have given nothing; for his sake, who will be cruel to himself to preserve thee. Be charitable to her, and teach thy son to love her for his father's sake.

The effect of such a letter on poor Bess must have been devastating. Her husband was here assuming that he was already a dead man, and making scarcely veiled allusions to his suicide by being 'cruel to himself to preserve thee'. Ralegh's bitterness at his situation quite overwhelmed him.

> For myself, I am left of all men that have done good to many. All my good turns forgotten; all my errors revived and expounded to all extremity of ill. All my services, hazards, and expenses for my country – plantings, discoveries, fights, councils, and whatsoever else – malice hath now covered over. I am now made an enemy and a traitor by the word of an unworthy man. He hath proclaimed me to be a partaker of

King James VI of Scotland and James I of England. He disliked everything he ever heard of, or saw about, Sir Walter Ralegh

his vain imaginations, notwithstanding the whole course of my life hath approved the contrary, as my death shall approve it. Woe, woe, woe, be unto him by whose falsehood we are lost. He hath separated us asunder. He hath slain my honour; my fortune. He hath robbed thee of thy husband, thy child of his father, and me of you both. O God! thou dost know my wrongs. Know, then, thou my wife, and child; – know, then, thou my Lord and King, that I ever thought them too honest to betray, and too good to conspire against.

Ralegh said he forgave Lord Henry Howard, 'my heavy enemy'. He forgave Cecil, too, though he thought 'he would never forsake me in extremity'. He proclaimed his own faith in God's mercy. He gave a list of some debts outstanding on his estate. There were also the wages of the men who were at that moment on another of Ralegh's expeditions to Virginia. The irony of the situation struck him very forcibly. 'Oh, what will my poor servants think, at their return, when they hear I am accused to be *Spanish* who sent them – at my great charge – to plant and discover upon his territory.'

Ralegh's bitterness welled up again.

Oh intolerable infamy! O God! I cannot resist these thoughts. I cannot live to think how I am derided, to think of the expectation of my enemies, the scorns I shall receive, the cruel words of lawyers, the infamous taunts and despites, to be made a wonder and a spectacle! O Death! hasten thou unto me that thou mayest destroy my memory which is my tormentor; my thoughts and my life cannot dwell in one body. But do thou forget me, poor wife, that thou mayest live to bring up my poor child.

He goes on to commend Adrian Gilbert to his wife and asks her to

be good to Kemis for he is a perfect honest man, and hath much wrong for my sake. For the rest, I commend me to them and them to God. And the Lord knows my sorrow to part from thee and my poor child. But part I must, by enemies and injuries; part with shame, and triumph of my detractors. And therefore be contented with this work of God, and forget me in all things, but thine own honour and the love of mine.

I bless my poor child, and let him know his father was no traitor. Be bold of my innocence, for God – to whom I offer life and soul – knows it. And whosoever thou choose again after me, let him be but thy politique husband. But let my son be thy beloved, for he is part of me and I live in him; and the difference is but in the number and not in the kind. And the Lord for ever keep thee and them, and give thee comfort in both worlds.

It is certainly not the letter of an atheist. It expresses convincingly Ralegh's rage and bitterness, his sense of humiliation, of opportunities and talents cut off and wasted. He had been one of the greatest spirits of his age. He had given his Queen and country so much. Now he was in real peril of dying a dishonourable death, and all through careless talk with worthless friends.

At one time during that summer it seemed that he might not be in so great a danger after all. He might possibly not even be brought to trial, for lack of firm evidence. In spite of the most determined interrogations of Sir William Waad and other officers of the Crown, it seemed that the case against Ralegh might well collapse. That it eventually did proceed to trial seems to have been largely at the instigation of Cecil. In October he said that Cobham's accusation of Ralegh was 'so well fortified with other demonstrative circumstances, and the retraction so blemished by the discovery of the intelligence which they had, as few men can conceive Sir Walter Ralegh's denial comes from a pure heart'. Cecil absolved himself from any personal responsibility. 'Always he shall be left to the law,' he wrote to James's Secretary of State, Sir Ralph Winwood, 'which is the right all men are born into.' Cecil must have known Ralegh's likely fate if he were left to English law at that time. Cecil suspected Ralegh of being a danger to James's reign. He would always be a danger. Therefore he must be deprived of all influence, of all ways of possibly interfering with the State. If such a political downfall meant execution for high treason, then so be it.

Ralegh was indicted at Staines on 21st September 1603, that

he did conspire, and go about to deprive the king of his Government; to raise up Sedition within the realm; to alter religion, to bring in the Roman Superstition and to procure foreign enemies to invade the kingdom. That the lord Cobham, the 9th of June last, did meet with the said sir Walter Ralegh in Durham-house, in the parish of St Martins in the Fields, and then and there had conference with him, how to advance Arabella Stuart to the crown and royal throne of this kingdom.

Ralegh's guilt was taken for granted, long before he was brought to trial. His Governorship of Jersey was declared forfeit and was given to the Governor of the Tower, Sir John Peyton. He was forced to resign his Lord Wardenship of the Stannaries in favour of Sir Francis Godolphin. King James's Scots toadies clamoured for scraps from Ralegh's dismembered fortunes. In October Cecil told Sir James Elphinstone that he was at least the twelfth man who had already applied for Sherborne. The Farm of Wines, Ralegh's main source of income, eventually went to the Lord Admiral, the Earl of Nottingham.

Ralegh's only hope, and that a very slim one, lay in Cobham. If Cobham could somehow be persuaded to retract all his accusations against Ralegh convincingly, and admit that his charges had been a false fabrication from start to finish, there might still be a chance of Ralegh escaping with his life. The two men were not lodged in the same place, and there were great difficulties in the way of the accused communicating with each other. But Ralegh overcame them. He succeeded in getting messages passed through Edward Cottrell, one of the Tower's servants. By sheer force of personality he also got John Peyton, the Governor's son, and young George, son of the new Governor, Sir George Harvey, to help him.

The methods Ralegh used were sometimes almost operatically sensational. Once he had a letter for Cobham tied by string to an apple, which was then thrown through Cobham's prison window in the Wendiski Tower, while the Governor was at dinner. The answer, when it came, was 'not to my contenting', and Ralegh tried again. This time the answer, when it was slipped under the door of Ralegh's cell, was 'a very good letter' and Ralegh kept it by for future use. Ralegh's pressure eventually did have its effect upon Cobham. On 24th October he wrote a letter to the Council asking for a personal hearing, and offering to absolve Ralegh of all complicity in any plot. But Harvey suppressed the letter and did not show it to the Council until some time after the trial, when his son was in trouble (for having helped Ralegh in the Tower).

The trials were delayed for some time after the indictments, possibly to allow the prosecution more time to assemble their evidence, and possibly because of the plague which was raging in London that summer, at its peak claiming some 2,000 victims a week. Because of the plague, the Court of the King's Bench sat that autumn at Winchester, in Wolvesey Castle. On 5th November Ralegh's keeper Sir William Waad was instructed to take his prisoner out of the Tower and bring him to Winchester for trial.

Ralegh set out on 10th November, travelling in his own coach in the charge of Sir Robert Mansel and Waad (who later told Cecil that he had found his prisoner 'much altered'). A party of Ralegh's friends and relatives waited by the roadside at Wimbledon to wish him luck as he passed by, but in general his reception was hostile. The mob had never liked him and now they had an excuse to abuse him. Those who hoped for favour from James, those who had for years resented the licensing of vintners under Ralegh's monopoly, those who disliked Court favourites – all Ralegh's enemies, the jealous, the envious, the mean-spirited, the louts and trouble-makers, all pressed around him to shout and abuse him, and to hurl tobacco pipes, stones, mud and anything they could lay their hands on. Waad had to place special watches by the roads, and travel as cautiously and inconspicuously as he could. They took two days to reach Bagshot, and another three to cover the thirty miles to Winchester. Even so, Waad wrote, 'if one hare-brained fellow amongst so great a multitude had begun to set upon him, as they were near to do it, no entreaty nor means could have prevailed; the fury and tumult of the people was so great'. The mob was further infuriated by Ralegh's disdain of them. He took no notice of their howlings, but sat calmly and impassively, puffing on his pipe. 'It was hab or nab,' Waad wrote to Cecil, 'whether or not he should have been brought alive through such multitudes of unruly people as did exclaim against him. He that had seen it would not think there had been any sickness in London.' The strength of popular feeling against Ralegh was expressed in doggerel:

> Now you may see the sudden fall
>   Of him that thought to climb full high,
> A man well known unto you all,
>   Whose state you see doth stand Rawly.

and

> For thy skance and pride,
> Thy bloody mind beside,
> And thy mouth gaping wide;
>   Mischievous Machiaevel!

250

Henry Howard, Ralegh's bitterest enemy. For years he poisoned James' mind against Ralegh with a vicious campaign of lies and misrepresentations

The two priests, George Brooke, Markham and the other lesser conspirators were tried on 15th November and all found guilty except Sir Edward Parham, who was acquitted through the efforts of the foreman of the jury and of Cecil; he was the first to be acquitted of high treason for more than forty years. Ralegh's trial was held two days later, on Thursday, 17th November. The two noblemen, Cobham and Grey, were to be tried last, on the following day.

The court was held under the King's Commission of Oyer and Terminer, 'to hear and to determine', and the appointed Commissioners were Lord Thomas Howard, now Lord Chamberlain and Earl of Suffolk; Lord Henry Howard, Ralegh's enemy; Charles Blount, Lord Mountjoy, Earl of Devonshire, who had been of Essex's faction; Lord Cecil; Lord Wotton of Morley, who was Cecil's man; Sir John Stanhope, Vice-Chamberlain, also Cecil's man; and Ralegh's gaoler, Waad. The professional lawyers on the Commission were Lord Chief Justice Popham, Chief Justice Anderson, and Justices Gawdy and Warburton. The court represented virtually the Establishment of the early part of King James's reign. They were the State personified. Their careers depended upon James. They were anxious to demonstrate their loyalty. There was no friend of Ralegh amongst them, and at least one bitter enemy.

The main hall of the old episcopal palace at Wolversey Castle had been converted for the trials. The Lord Chief Justice sat under a brocaded canopy in the centre of a raised platform, with the Lords Commissioners seated on either side of him. Opposite them sat Sir Edward Coke, the Attorney General, who was to lead the prosecution. Ralegh, after being brought to the bar, sat on a stool in a special place allotted for the prisoner. He knew people in the crowd, and it was noticed that he saluted his friends with a very steadfast and cheerful countenance. He stood up while the Lords of the Court were assembling but then asked permission to sit down, which was granted. The Commission was read out, while Ralegh held up his hand as he was bid. The trial, which was to last from eight in the morning until seven in the evening, then began with the indictment.

The indictment gave full details of the alleged correspondence between Ralegh and Cobham, and the financial assistance they hoped to get. Cobham was to negotiate with Aremberg for the 600,000 crowns. Arabella Stuart herself was to write to the King of Spain, the Archduke Albert and the Duke of Savoy, promising peace with Spain, Catholic toleration in England, and a Spanish marriage. Cobham and his brother had discussed their treason and agreed that 'there never would be a good world in England till the King and his cubs were taken away.' Furthermore, Ralegh had published a book, 'falsely written against the most just and Royal title of the king'. He had given it to Cobham who had passed it on to Brooke, thus giving them both confidence in the legality of their treason. Lastly, Cobham had offered him 8,000 of the 600,000 crowns from Spain.

Ralegh pleaded not guilty. He was asked if he objected to any of the jury. They were Sir Thomas Fowler, foreman, Sir Ralph Conisby, Sir Edward Peacock, and Sir William Rowe; Henry Goodyer, Thomas Walker, Roger Wood, Thomas Whitby, Esquires; Thomas Highgate, Robert Kempton, John Chawkey, and Robert Bromley, gentlemen. Ralegh said

Chief Justice Coke, prosecution for the Crown at Ralegh's trial. He was one of the most distinguished lawyers in English history, but his cross-examination of Ralegh was the one blot on his career

...ard Coke
...Chief Justice

he did not know any of them, but they were all Christians and honest gentlemen and he took no exception to any of them. However, he did ask one thing. His health and his memory were both bad. There was much to answer in the indictment, and there would probably be more in the evidence to be given. He asked, could he answer the points as they came up, and not have to carry them in his mind until the end of the Crown's case? (He was not allowed any defence counsel.) The request led to the first clash with Coke, who said that the King's evidence would lose much of its effect if it were 'broken or dismembered'. But Ralegh's point was allowed. He could answer after the evidence had been given.

The prosecution's case was opened by Sergeant Hele (the lawyer who had acted for Ralegh in his case against John Meere). Hele elaborated upon the indictment, indulging himself in some ponderous humour. The Lady Arabella Stuart, he said, 'hath no more title to the crown than I have, which before God I utterly renounce'. At least one man in court – Ralegh – smiled at the joke. 'Now, whether these things were bred in a hollow tree, I leave them to speak of, who can speak far better than myself.'

Hele sat down, giving way to one who could 'speak far better' – the chief prosecutor, Sir Edward Coke. It was Coke who prosecuted Essex and Southampton for treason. He was the most able lawyer of his generation and as Lord Chief Justice became one of the greatest judges in English legal history. The champion of the Common Law, he was himself to fall foul of James in the courts and in Parliament, and was himself imprisoned. But Coke's behaviour towards Ralegh was a disgraceful blot on his career. His manner towards the prisoner was so ferociously rancorous and so bitterly abusive that it eventually disgusted the spectators in the court-room, most of whom had come to enjoy Ralegh's downfall. Even John Aubrey said that Coke 'shewed himselfe too clownish and bitter in his carriage to Sir Walter Ralegh'. In mitigation of Coke, it can only be said that he must have known that the Crown's case was very weak, but his own career demanded that he make sure of a conviction.

Coke began with a lengthy discourse on the Bye plot, whose various treasons, he said 'were like Samson's foxes, which were joined in their tails, though their heads were severed'. Ralegh interrupted to remind the jury that he was not charged with the Bye. Coke took the point and went on to quote several historical precedents and examples of treasons. He seemed to be rambling, but he was coming closer to Ralegh and suddenly he struck. 'But to whom do you bear malice?' he asked. 'To the royal children?'

'To whom speak you this?' Ralegh replied, clearly taken aback. 'You tell me news I never heard of.'

'Oh sir, do I? I will then come closer to you. I will prove you the notoriest traitor that ever came to the bar. You, Sir Walter Ralegh, have followed them of the Bye in imitation. I will charge you with the words.'

'Your words cannot condemn me,' said Ralegh. 'My innocency is my defence. Prove one of these things wherewith you have charged me, and I will confess the whole indictment, and that I am the horriblest traitor that ever lived, and worthy to be crucified with a thousand thousand torments.'

'Nay, I will prove all,' said Coke. 'Thou art a monster. Thou hast an English face, but a Spanish heart.' This was, of course, a ludicrous remark to make of a man like Sir Walter Ralegh. 'I charge thee, Ralegh,' Coke went on, '*thou* incitedst Cobham to go unto Aremberg and deal with him for money, to raise rebellion in the kingdom.'

Ralegh at this point insisted on replying. Coke refused him. Ralegh pressed it, saying that it was his life at stake. Popham intervened to tell Ralegh to wait until Coke had completed his evidence.

Coke went on to describe Cobham's plot in some detail, but he returned again and again to Ralegh, to link him with the conspirators and to abuse him constantly. 'Your jargon was peace,' he told Ralegh sarcastically. 'What is that? Spanish invasion, Scottish subversion.'

Ralegh said once again that this was still news to him.

'Oh sir!' protested Coke. 'I am the more large, because I know with whom I deal. For we have to deal today with a man of *wit*.' It was intended as a back-handed compliment. Coke continued to insult Ralegh. He was 'odious', and 'a viper'. His policy was 'Machiavellian and devilish'. He indulged in 'the most horrible practices that ever came out of the bottomless pit of the lowest hell'.

Ralegh continued to deny all suggestions that he was a traitor. 'I will wash my hands of the indictment, and die a true man to the king.'

'You are the *absolutest* traitor that ever was!'

'*Your* phrases will not prove it.'

The distasteful exchanges continued, Coke shouting ever wilder insults, and Ralegh calmly replying to him.

'I do not hear yet that you have spoken one word against me,' said Ralegh. 'Here is no treason of mine done. If my Lord Cobham be a traitor, what is that to me?'

'All that he did was by thy instigation, thou viper, for I *thou* thee, thou traitor! I will prove thee the rankest traitor in all England.'

'No, no, Mr Attorney, I am no traitor. Whether I live or die, I shall stand as true a subject as any the King hath. You may call me traitor at your pleasure. Yet it becometh not a man of quality and virtue to call me so. But I take comfort in it, it is all you can do, for I do not yet hear that you charge me with any treason.'

'Sir Walter, I cannot blame you, though you be moved. Have I angered you?'

'Nay, you fall out with yourself. I have said nothing to you. I am in no case to be angry.'

Here the Lord Chief Justice intervened again, to remind Ralegh that Coke was acting out of professional duty in the service of the King, while Ralegh was speaking for his life. Popham told them both to be valiant.

Lord Cobham's Examination was now read out, the first one in which he called Ralegh a villain and traitor, and said that everything he had done had been done at Ralegh's instigation, and that Ralegh had urged him on.

Ralegh poured scorn on it. 'This is absolutely all the evidence can be brought against me! Poor shifts! *This* is that which must either condemn me or give me life, which must free me, or send my wife and children to beg their bread.'

Ralegh was now, at last, permitted to defend himself. He denied once again any connection with any of Cobham's plots. He made a superb speech, in which he demonstrated the sheer, fantastic improbability that he, of all the King's subjects, would ever conspire on behalf of Spain.

> Is it not strange for me to make myself Robin Hood, or a Kett or a Cade? I knowing England to be in better estate to defend itself than ever it was. I knew Scotland united; Ireland quieted, wherein of late our forces were dispersed; Denmark assured, which before was suspected. I knew, that having lost a lady whom time had surprised, we had now an active king, a lawful successor, who would himself be present in all his affairs. The state of Spain was not unknown to me: I had written a discourse, which I had intended to present to the King, against peace with Spain. I knew the Spaniards had six repulses; three in Ireland, and three at sea, and once in 1588, at Cadiz, by my Lord Admiral. I knew he was discouraged and dishonoured. I knew the king of Spain to be the proudest prince in Christendom; but now he cometh creeping to the king my master for peace. I knew, whereas before he had in his port six or seven score sail of ships, he hath now but six or seven. I knew of 25,000,000 he had from his Indies, he hath scarce one left. I knew him to be so poor, that the Jesuits in Spain, who were wont to have such large allowance, were fain to beg at the church-door.

As for Cobham and his plottings, Ralegh concluded, 'If I knew anything of these things, I would absolutely confess the indictment, and acknowledge myself worthy ten thousand deaths.'

A second of Cobham's Examinations was now read out, and there was some confused discussion about Cobham's character, and the value of his depositions as evidence. The foreman of the jury got up to ask for some clarification. He was answered by Cecil, who described the circumstances of the first questionings of Ralegh at Windsor. Cecil also defined his own feelings towards his former friend. He said there was 'a former dearness between me and him, tied so firm a knot of my conceit of his virtues, now broken by a discovery of his imperfections'. This was a clear insinuation, by one of the judges who was supposed to be hearing the case, that he already thought the accused guilty. It seems that Beaumont the French Ambassador was near the truth when he wrote to Henry IV before the trial opened that Cecil undertook and conducted the investigations against Ralegh 'with so much warmth, that it is said he acts more from interest and passion than for the good of the kingdom'.

Cecil also referred in his speech to Cobham. Cobham's name was recurring again and again: indeed the prosecution case began and ended with Cobham. Ralegh asked whether Cobham had really confessed to all these things; if he had, then Ralegh demanded to be allowed to confront his accuser face to face. Let Cobham appear in court in person and repeat his accusations. It was not as though he had to be fetched from a distance. He was here, in the same building. The court over-ruled Ralegh. Cobham was a party, they said, and

Sir Walter Ralegh, the Knight of Cadiz. A map of Cadiz can be seen above his right shoulder. Portrait dated 1598, artist unknown

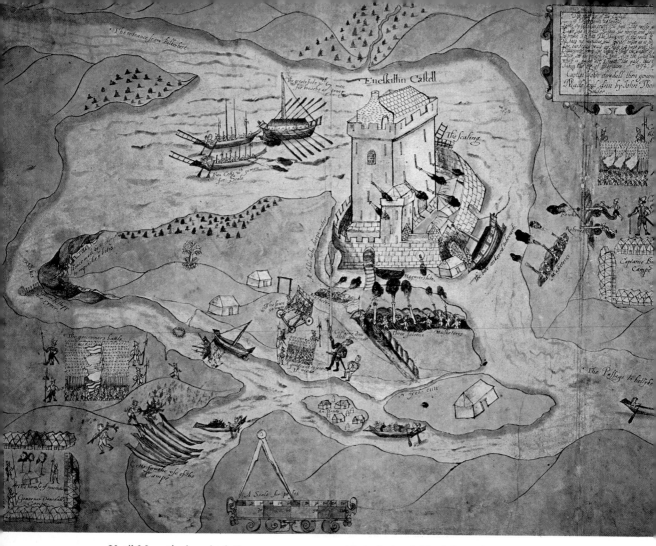

Until Mountjoy's arrival, there was constant trouble in Ireland. Hugh Maguire, an able lieutenant of Tyrone's, was besieged in Enniskillen Castle in 1592 by Sir Richard Bingham, Elizabeth's Governor in Connaught in one of the campaigns fought against the English in the 1590s

The *Prince Royal*, the ship built for Prince Henry by Phineas Pett, with Ralegh's encouragement and guidance. The arrival at Flushing of the *Prince Royal*, in 1613 with Frederick V, Elector Palatine, and his Consort Elizabeth, daughter of James I. Painting by Hendrick Vroom, *c.* 1623

could not appear.

Ralegh had had time to read some law while waiting in the Tower. He protested that he could not be tried without the testimony of two witnesses, and he cited statutes in support of his argument. The Lord Chief Justice replied that the statutes Ralegh had quoted had been repealed. 'It sufficeth now,' he said, 'if there be proofs, made either under hand, or by testimony of witnesses, or by oaths.' This was true but, in fact, misleading. The relevant statutes had indeed been repealed but the rights Ralegh referred to had been safeguarded under Common Law, and Popham must have known it.

Ralegh seemed to sense that the court were uneasy about their refusal. 'It may be an error in me,' he said, 'and if those laws be repealed, yet I hope the *equity* of them remains still. But if you affirm it, it must be a law to posterity. The proof of the Common Law is by witness and jury. Let Cobham be here. Let him speak it. Call my accuser before my face, and I have done.'

Coke then took the chance of another taunt at Ralegh's expense. 'You have read the letter of the law, but understand it not.' Ralegh retorted that if he ever read a word of the law or statutes before he was prisoner in the Tower, might God confound him.

But the court were still uncomfortable about Ralegh's demand to see his accuser face to face. Cecil raised the question again, but was told by Popham that it was not possible. Justice Gawdy said that the statute referred to had been 'found to be inconvenient' and had been therefore 'taken away'.

Ralegh stepped in again, perhaps seeing a chance of success. 'The common trial of England is by jury and witness,' he said.

This time, he was answered by the full weight of the heads of the legal profession. 'No,' replied Popham, 'by *examination*. If three conspire a treason, and they all confess it, here is never a witness, yet they are condemned.'

'I marvel, Sir Walter,' said Warburton, 'that you being of such experience and wit, should stand on this point.'

'I know not how you conceive the law,' said Ralegh.

'Nay, we do not *conceive* the law,' replied Popham, 'but we *know* the law.'

So Ralegh's life was to depend upon hearsay evidence. If this was the law, then, as he rightly said, 'you will have any man's life in a week'.

The trial continued, a confused medley of statements and questions, challenges and replies, interruptions and arguments and refutations. Extracts were read from examinations, confessions and additions from Copley, Watson, George Brooke, La Renzi, Ralegh himself, and, several times, from Cobham. Once again, Ralegh strongly objected to having his name coupled with some of those in the depositions. 'Do you bring the words of these hellish spiders, Clarke, Watson and others, against me?'

Coke was waiting. '*Thou* has a Spanish heart,' he told Ralegh, 'and *thyself* art a spider of hell.'

Poor Keymis's name came up again, as having carried messages from Ralegh to Cobham while Ralegh was in the Tower. Ralegh revealed that Keymis had been threatened with the rack, although the King had said that 'no rigour should be used'. This revelation greatly embarrassed the Lords Commissioners. Waad had to admit that although he had never expressly threatened Keymis with the rack, he had told him he deserved it. The Commissioners said they had known nothing of this.

Ralegh was taxed about a manuscript book by one Robert Snagge, concerning the right of Mary Queen of Scots (and hence of James) to the English throne. He said that he had borrowed it, without permission, from Lord Burghley's study in his house in the Strand, after his death. Cobham, too, had borrowed it without permission. Cecil jumped up to clear any possible slur on his family's name. His duty, and his father's duty, had been to examine such books; if anyone searched his study he would 'in all likelihood find all the notorious libels against the late queen'. He reproached Ralegh for taking the book and worked in another stab at him, saying he 'would have trusted Sir Walter Ralegh as soon as any man, though since for some infirmities, the bands of my affection to him have been broken'. Cecil was determined that there should be no suspicion left in anyone's mind that any of his friendship for Ralegh still lingered on.

Ralegh said that if anyone searched his study, they would probably find all the notorious libels against the late queen there, too. This gave Coke the chance of yet another unkind cut. '*You* were no privy counsellor, and I hope never shall be.'

This was too much even for Cecil. 'He was not a sworn counsellor of state,' he said, 'but he has been called to consultations.'

While this seemingly interminable discussion over the book was going on, Sir Robert Wroth was seen to whisper something. Coke stopped the case at once, to complain and to accuse Sir Robert of having said that the evidence was immaterial. Sir Robert denied it. Ralegh, too, was weary of the subject and betrayed a rare sign of irritation. 'Here is a book,' he said, 'supposed to be treasonable. I never read it, commended it, or delivered it, nor urged it.'

'Why, this is cunning,' said Coke.

'Every thing that doth make for me is cunning, and every thing that maketh against me is probable.' Ralegh must have known he had to keep his temper, but there were limits to his self-control.

At one point, there was a dramatic interruption, stage-managed by the prosecution. Lady Arabella Stuart appeared at the back of the court, on the arm of the Lord Admiral, the Earl of Nottingham. 'The lady doth here protest upon her salvation,' Nottingham said to the court, 'that she never dealt in any of these things, and so she willed me to tell the court.' So much for Ralegh's demand to be faced with his accusers.

In his anxiety to show proofs of Ralegh's treasons, Coke descended at times perilously near to farce. A ship's pilot called Dyer gave evidence that once when he was in Lisbon a Portuguese gentleman had asked him if the king of England had been crowned yet. Dyer said he thought not yet, but he would be shortly. Nay, said the Portuguese, he will never be crowned, for Don Ralegh and Don Cobham will cut his throat first.

Ralegh was, understandably, mystified. 'What infer you upon this?' he asked.

'That your treason hath wings!' replied Coke.

Coke continued to bait and bully Ralegh, using the most intemperate and hectoring language. He knew that Ralegh was unpopular, and he knew that the court was determined upon a conviction, and therefore he could insult and browbeat the prisoner with impunity. When Ralegh tried to point out that Coke had proved nothing against him directly, and that all the evidence was circumstantial, Coke interrupted him. 'Have you done? The king must have the last.'

'Nay, Mr Attorney, he which speaketh for his life must have the last. I appeal to God and the king in this point, whether Cobham's accusation be sufficient to condemn me.'

'The king's safety and your clearing cannot agree,' said Coke. 'I protest before God, I never knew a clearer treason.'

'I never had intelligence with Cobham since I came to the Tower.'

'Go to, I will lay thee on thy back, for the confidentest traitor that ever came to the bar.'

Cecil intervened here, to tell Coke not to be so impatient, and to give Ralegh a chance to speak. This so annoyed Coke that he sat down, and refused to go on with the case. The Commissioners begged him to continue. At last, after much ado, he did go on and gave the jury a long summing up of all the evidence, in which he several times repeated himself. This exasperated Ralegh, who interrupted, and protested that Coke was doing him wrong. There followed a typically acrimonious exchange between prosecutor and prisoner.

'Thou art the most vile and execrable traitor that ever lived,' said Coke.

'You speak indiscreetly, barbarously, and uncivilly.'

'I want words sufficient to express thy viperous treasons.'

'I think you want words indeed, for you have spoken one thing half a dozen times.'

'Thou art an odious fellow, thy name is hateful to all the realm of England for thy pride.'

'It will go near to prove a measuring cast between you and me, Mr Attorney.'

As the long day of the trial wore on, the mood of the court-room changed dramatically. The spectators tired of Coke, and his truculence, and his ceaseless insulting of the prisoner. They began to grow restless under the sound of his voice. Some even began to groan and hiss when he got up to speak again. At the same time, their feelings towards Ralegh changed from scorn and hatred to admiration. They had come to jeer, to gloat at the spectacle of one who had thought himself great being brought low in his pride. But they had seen the man answer his accusers with courage, patience, dignity and intelligence.

All surviving eye-witness accounts of the trial agree that Ralegh's behaviour under extreme provocation was magnificent. 'Never man spoke better for himself,' said Sir Toby Matthew. 'So worthily, so wisely, so temperately he behaved himself that in half a day the mind of all the company was changed from the extremest hate to the extremest pity.' Sir Thomas Overbury thought Ralegh's demeanour was perfect: 'to the Lords humble, yet not prostrate, to the jury affable, not fawning, rather showing love of life than fear of death, to the King's counsel patient, but not sensibly neglecting, not yielding to imputations laid against him in words'. One of his own countrymen reported to King James afterwards that 'whereas, when he saw Sir Walter Ralegh first, he was so led with the common hatred that he would have gone a hundred miles to see him hanged, he would, ere they parted, have gone a thousand to save his life'.

One perceptive observer, Sir Dudley Carleton, made a remark in a letter to John Chamberlain which seems to go to the core of Ralegh's nature. Ralegh, he wrote, 'answered with that temper, wit, learning, courage, and judgement, that, save that it went with the hazard of his life, it was the happiest day that ever he spent'. It was true that in some curious way Ralegh almost *enjoyed* his trial. He had the centre of the stage. People hung on his every word, and noted his every movement and expression. He relished the intellectual clash with his prosecutor; he liked to give the man the lie, to answer him point for point. Thus his vanity and his intellect were both exercised, as he fell naturally and easily into the great role of the noble innocent brought to bay by a pack of unworthy opponents.

Ralegh's composure seems to have been disturbed only once, towards the end of the proceedings, when Coke produced yet another of Cobham's Examinations. Cobham had made several statements and several retractions; one, as Ralegh said, he had retracted before he even reached 'the stair's foot'. But this one contained new information. Cobham protested, 'on his soul', that he spoke nothing but the truth. He reaffirmed that Ralegh had been the instigator of his plot. Ralegh had advised Cobham 'not to be overtaken with preachers, as Essex was' and to keep on denying everything. Furthermore, Ralegh was to have procured a pension of £1,500 from Spain.

Ralegh could only tell the Commissioners that they had 'heard a strange tale of a strange man'. When Popham asked him about the pension, Ralegh said that Cobham was 'a base dishonourable, poor soul'. The Commissioners evidently took the view that Ralegh should have mentioned the pension, even though he refused it. Popham said, 'I perceive you are not so clear a man, as you have protested all this while.'

The Spanish pension was proving to be a damaging piece of evidence, and to counter it, Ralegh took from his pocket the letter Cobham had written him, and which he had kept against this very emergency. He asked Cecil to read it, because he knew Cobham's handwriting and would recognize this as genuine.

> 'Seeing myself so near my end,' wrote Cobham, 'for the discharge of my own conscience, and freeing myself from your blood, which else will cry vengeance against me; I protest upon my salvation I never practised with Spain by your procurement; God so comfort me in this my affliction, as you are a true subject, for any thing that I know. God have mercy upon my soul, as I know no treason by you.'

Ralegh had been very much taken aback by Cobham's letter disclosing the pension offer. But his spirits had risen again. 'Now,' he cried, 'I wonder how many souls this man hath! He damns one in this letter, and another in that.'

It was the Commissioners' turn to be taken aback. There was a commotion. Coke said that the first letter was the true one, and Ralegh's had been 'politically and cunningly urged' from Cobham. Lord Mountjoy confirmed that Cobham had made the first statement voluntarily, and Popham told the jury that they could be satisfied on that point. This was

Sir John Popham, one of the judges of Ralegh's trial. He said, 'I hope I shall never see the like again'

the last evidence to be called.

The prosecution evidence had established that Ralegh knew Cobham well enough for Cobham to offer him 8,000 crowns if he would assist in arranging a peace with Spain; that Cobham had once borrowed a book from Ralegh without permission; that Ralegh had been offered a Spanish pension of £1,500. Ralegh had treated the 8,000 crowns as an idle conceit, and had refused the pension. (The pension had not been in the indictment, and in any case, to accept it would not have been treasonable; Cecil himself later had a Spanish pension of £1,000.) The Government's investigations may well have uncovered evidence of plots against King James, and some of that evidence may have incriminated Ralegh. But it was not put forward at his trial. On the actual evidence heard, the prosecution had no case at all against Ralegh. Nevertheless, the jury well knew that the Government thought Ralegh guilty and they took only fifteen minutes to bring in the same verdict themselves. Clearly, Ralegh had never at any time had any hope of being acquitted.

Asked if he had anything to say, Ralegh replied that he could say nothing why judgment should not proceed. But he repeated that he was not guilty, and asked that the king be told of the wrongs done him. Popham told Ralegh that he had had no wrong. Ralegh insisted once again that he never knew of Cobham's plans with Spain, never had any intention to put Arabella Stuart on the throne, never knew of Cobham's dealings with Aremberg, and knew nothing of the Bye plot.

But he could not convince Popham, who said that he was 'persuaded that Cobham hath accused you truly'. In passing sentence, Lord Chief Justice Popham made a speech which might be said fairly to represent the official view of Ralegh. He said that Ralegh ought to have been content with what he had, an income of £3,000, so Popham had heard. King James had deprived him of nothing but the Captainship of the Guard, and that was understandable enough. As for the Monopoly of Wines, the King's view was that 'It is a matter that offends my people, should I burden them for your private good.' Popham reproved Ralegh for the two vices of 'eager ambition', and 'corrupt covetousness'. He referred to the Spanish pension again and said that he was sorry to hear that a gentleman of Ralegh's wealth should become a Spanish spy for £1,500 a year. He deplored the 'heathenish, blasphemous, atheistical and profane opinions' which he had heard attributed to Ralegh. He advised him to renounce them, and not to let Hariot or any other 'doctor' persuade him that Heaven was not eternal, for if he thought thus, he would find eternity in hell-fire. 'I never saw the like trial,' said Popham, 'and hope I shall never see the like again.' He then pronounced the sentence for high treason.

> But since you have been found guilty of these horrible treasons, the judgment of this court is, That you shall be had from hence to the place whence you came, there to remain until the day of execution; and from thence you shall be drawn upon a hurdle through the open streets to the place of execution, there to be hanged and cut down alive, and your body shall be opened, your heart and bowels plucked out, and your privy members cut off, and thrown into the fire before your eyes; then your head to be stricken off from your body, and your body shall be divided into four quarters, to be disposed of at the king's pleasure: And God have mercy upon your soul.

18. Reprieve

FTER SENTENCE had been passed on him, Ralegh went forward to the bar of the court and asked the Earl of Devonshire and the other Lords whether they would intercede with the King on his behalf, that his death might be honourable and not ignominious. They promised to do so, and Ralegh was taken back to the castle as a prisoner, to await his execution.

According to one account, some members of the jury which convicted Ralegh were, 'after he was cast, so far touched in conscience as to demand of him pardon on their knees'. There is even an unlikely story that Coke himself, walking in the castle garden after the trial, was astonished when he heard the verdict, saying that 'I myself accused him but of misprision of treason.' Certainly, while the messengers rode to James at Wilton House with their reports of the trial, a reaction against the verdict had already set in. Ralegh's fate insulted the national sense of justice. Sir Francis Gawdy, one of the Justices at the trial, said on his death-bed two years later that 'Never before had the justice of England been so depraved and injured as in the condemnation of Sir Walter Ralegh.' His opinion would have had more weight if he had expressed it at the time.

Meanwhile, just or unjust, the verdict stood and, while waiting in prison for it to be carried out, Ralegh's high spirit cracked. It was one thing to stand up and be brave in open court, for one day of sensational drama. To sustain that courage in captivity, while the passing days brought death ever closer, was quite another. Ralegh's resolution failed him, and he began to plead for his life, abjectly and shamelessly. He wrote to Cecil, to the Lords of the Privy Council, and to the King. Much of Ralegh's language in his letters was conventionally exaggerated; the custom of his age demanded elaboration. In his letters to the King, Ralegh was addressing himself, not to James the man, but to King James, God's representative, and dispenser of divine justice upon earth. Nevertheless, even allowing for these excuses, Ralegh's letters were clearly written by a man in terror of the grave. It must have given James Stuart a great psychological satisfaction to see that even one of Elizabeth Tudor's great men could be brought to beg cravenly for his life, just like any other ordinary mortal.

To Cecil, Ralegh described himself as 'sumtyme your trew frind, and now a miserabell forsaken man'. He asked that 'if ought remayn of good, or love, or of cumpassion towards me, your Lordship will now shew it when I am now most unworthy of your love, and most unabell to deserve it'. In a postscript he said, 'Your Lordship will finde that I have bynn strangely practised agaynst, and that others have their lives promised to accuse me.' From the Lords Commissioners, Ralegh begged for time. 'If I may not begg a pardon or a life, yet lett me begg a tyme at the King's mercifull hands. Lett me have one yeare to geve to God in a prison and to serve Hyme. I trust his pitifull nature will have cumpassion on my sowle; and it is my sowle that beggeth a tyme of the Kinge.'

But it was to the King that Ralegh addressed his most abject pleadings. His letter is, even now, distasteful to read. Even in his extremity, Ralegh was talking of 'reward' for services rendered.

> I do therefore, on the knees of my hart, beseich your Majesty to take councell from your own sweet and mercifull disposition, and to remember that I have loved your Majesty now twenty yeares, for which your Majestie hath yett geven me no reward. And it is fitter that I should be indebted to my soverayne Lord, then the King to his poore vassall. [This was, at least, an ingenious way of pleading for pardon.] Save me, therefore, most mercifull Prince, that I may owe your Majesty my life itt sealf; then which ther cannot bee a greater debt. Lend it me att lest, my soverayne Lord, that I may pay it agayne for your service when your Majesty shall pleas. If the law distroy me, your Majesty shall put me out of your poure; and I shall have then none to feare, none to reverence, but the King of kings.

Ralegh signed himself 'Your Majesties most humble and penitent vassall'.

Bess, too, pleaded with her old friend Cecil. In the name of friendship, for the sake of times past, for the sake of their young families, for honour and sorrow and pity, she implored Cecil to deal with the King on Ralegh's behalf. 'Let the hole world prayes your love to my poour unfortunat hosban. For Cristis sake, wich rewardeth all mercies, pitti his just case; and God for his infeni marci bles you for ever, and work in the Keng merci. I am not abell, I protest before God, to stand on my trembling legs, otherwise I wold have waited now on you.'

It is not likely that Cecil or the other Lords Commissioners tried to save Ralegh's life, but others certainly did. Queen Anne of Denmark and the Spanish Ambassador both tried. Lady Pembroke, Sir Philip Sidney's sister, also tried; showing *veteris vestigia flammae,* 'remains of an old fervour', she sent her son to plead with James for Ralegh's life.

James was not a bloodthirsty man. He must have been impressed by the reports of Ralegh's behaviour at his trial. He debated openly whether Ralegh's life should be spared, himself arguing sometimes for, sometimes against. His chaplain, and most of his Scots courtiers, argued against. But there was still a chance that further interrogation, under the very shadow of the scaffold, might force more information out of the convicted men. King James seems to have decided in his labyrinthine mind on a cruel plan to play cat-and-mouse with his victims.

The two priests Watson and Clarke were executed on 29th November, their sentences being carried out with the full rigour of the law; they were both, according to Carleton, 'very bloodily handled'. George Brooke's sentence was commuted to beheading, and he was executed on 6th December, still saying that one day evidence would come to light which would prove him innocent. James, staying at Wilton House, signed warrants for Cobham,

Grey and Markham to be executed on Friday 10th December. Ralegh was to die the following Monday, the 13th.

That Friday was a dark and gloomy winter day. A cold steady rain fell on the scaffold, and on the spectators gathered on the castle green at Wolversey; as one of the eye-witnesses said, 'A fouler day could hardly have been picked out, or fitter for such a tragedy.' Ralegh's window looked out over the scene, and he was standing there watching when the first of the condemned men, Sir Griffin Markham, was led out at ten o'clock that morning. The spectators could see in his face 'the very picture of sorrow. But he seemed not to want resolution.' He did not, indeed. When a friend asked him if he wanted a napkin to cover his eyes, Markham said that he did not need it, that he could 'look upon death without blushing'. Markham said good-bye to his friends. He knelt in prayer for a little while. At such times, the pace of events was dictated by the wishes of the condemned man. At last, Markham was composed, and laid his head on the block. The executioner had raised his axe, when there was a disturbance in the crowd and a cry to stop the execution.

James had been almost too clever. He had signed the death warrants on 8th December and sent them to the Sheriff of Hampshire, Sir Benjamin Tichborne. But the day before, the 7th, he had drawn up a stay of execution. This he had given to one of his young Scots grooms of the bed-chamber, John Gibb, to take to the Sheriff. But because of his youth, Gibb was prevented from getting near the scaffold and was only able to call out at the last moment to attract the attention of one of the attending magistrates, Sir James Hayes. Hayes came down from the scaffold to receive the King's reprieve. He and Tichborne conferred. Markham was told he had been granted a stay of two hours. He was led away to the great hall of the castle, and locked in.

Grey was next. He prayed, with a cheerful and calm expression on his face, for about half an hour. He had evidently composed himself for death. Tichborne, who seemed to be entering into the spirit of the King's disgusting charade, then told Grey that he too had been granted a reprieve. Cobham was to be executed first. Grey was also led away, and locked in Arthur's Hall.

Cobham was brought out third. He was seen to be calmer than he had been for most of his trial; indeed he had almost an expression of boldness. He knelt with his friends to pray. He stayed praying, in the rain, for long after they had finished. He prayed for so long, in fact, that he disgusted some of the onlookers. 'He had a good mouth in a cry,' one of them complained, 'but was nothing single.' Significantly, he confirmed his accusations of Ralegh. He took it, he said, 'upon the hope of his soul's resurrection, that what he said of him was true'.

When Cobham had finished praying, the Sheriff told him there was still something that remained to be done. He ordered Markham and Lord Grey to be brought back to the scaffold. By this time, spectators and condemned were all thoroughly mystified by these strange proceedings. The most puzzled and concerned of all the spectators was Ralegh, at his window. He must have seen Gibb's arrival and the interruption of the executions. He had seen men praying, and being led away, and returning again. He could see, but hear nothing.

265

As Carleton said, he 'had hammers working in his head to beat out the meaning of this stratagem'.

On the scaffold, Tichborne was still acting out the King's obscene farce. When the three condemned men stood in front of him, he asked them whether their offences were not heinous, had they not been justly tried and lawfully condemned, and was not each of them subject to due execution, now to be performed? When all three had agreed, Tichborne's whole manner suddenly changed. 'Then,' he cried out, in a loud ringing voice, 'see the mercy of your Prince, who of himself hath sent hither a countermand, and hath given you your lives!' The final bewilderment for Ralegh was the sight and sound of everybody on the castle-green and on the scaffold clapping, cheering, and applauding the King's mercy. That evening he wrote to the Lords Commissioners, 'We have this day beheld a worke of so great mercy, and for so great offences, as the like hath byne seldome if ever known.' In the event, Markham and Copley were exiled, Grey and Cobham imprisoned.

Ralegh could only now nurse the faint hope that the great work of mercy might be extended to include him. But there was no sign of it, and meanwhile he had that week-end to prepare himself for the scaffold (which was still left in position outside his window). As he summoned his spirits to meet his last hour, he regretted that he had earlier pleaded so shamelessly for his life. In his last letter to his wife, he asked her to try to get his letters back. It was a letter of love, and of resignation. The time for rancour and recrimination was past, although he was still firmly enough in the world to remind Bess of a few financial details outstanding. He was writing, late at night, when all were asleep.

You shall receave, deare wief, my last words in these my last lynes. My love I send you, that you may keepe it when I am dead; and my councell, that you may remember it when I am noe more. I would not with my last Will present you with sorrowes, dear Besse. Lett them goe to the grave with me, and be buried in the dust. And, seeing it is not the will of God that ever I shall see you in this lief, beare my destruccion gentlie and with a hart like yourself.

First, I send you all the thanks my hart cann conceive, or my penn expresse, for your many troubles and cares taken for me, which – though they have not taken effect as you wished – yet my debt is to you never the lesse, but pay it I never shall in this world.

Secondlie, I beseich you, for the love you bare me living, that you doe not hide yourself many dayes, but by your travell seeke to helpe your miserable fortunes, and the right of your poore childe. Your mourning cannot avayle me that am but dust.

You shall understand that my lands were conveyed to my child, *bonâ fide*. The wrightings were drawn at Mid-summer was twelvemonethes, as divers can witnesse.

My honest cosen Brett can testifie so much, and Dalberie, too, cann remember some what therein. And I trust my bloud will quench their mallice that desire my slaughter; and that they will not alsoe seeke to kill you and yours with extreame poverty. To what frind to direct thee I knowe not, for all mine have left mee in the true tyme of triall: and I plainly perceive that my death was determyned from the first day. Most sorry I am (as God knoweth) that, being thus surprised with death, I can leave you noe better estate. I meant you all

266

myne office of wynes, or that I could purchase by selling it; half my stuffe, and jewells, but some few, for my boy. But God hath prevented all my determinations; the great God that worketh all in all. If you can live free from want, care for no more; for the rest is but vanity. Love God, and beginne betymes to repose yourself on Him; therein shall you find true and lastinge ritches, and endles comfort. For the best, when you have travelled and wearied your thoughts on all sorts of worldly cogitacions, you shall sit downe by Sorrow in the end. Teach your sonne alsoe to serve and feare God, while he is young; that the feare of God may grow upp in him. Then will God be a husband unto you, and a father unto him; a husband and a father which can never be taken from you.

Bayly oweth me two hundred pounds, and Adrion six hundred pounds. In Gersey, alsoe, I have much owinge me. The arrearages of the wynes will pay my debts. And, howso-ever, for my soul's healthe, I beseech you pay all poore men. When I am gonne, no doubt you shalbe sought unto by many, for the world thinks that I was very ritch; but take heed of the pretences of men and of their affections; for they laste but in honest and worthy men. And no greater misery cann befall you in this life then to become a pray, and after to be despised. I expect it (God knows) not to disswad you from marriage for that wilbe best for you – both in respect of God and the world. As for me, I am no more your's nor you myne. Death hath cutt us asunder; and God hath devided me from the world, and you from me.

Remember your poore childe for his father's sake, that comforted you and loved you in his happiest tymes. Get those letters (if it bee possible) which I writt to the Lords, wherein I sued for my lief, but God knoweth that itt was for you and yours that I desired it, but itt is true that I disdaine myself for begging itt. And know itt (deare wief) that your sonne is the childe of a true man, and who, in his own respect, despiseth Death, and all his misshapen and ouglie formes.

I cannot wright much. God knowes howe hardlie I stole this tyme, when all sleep; and it is tyme to separate my thoughts from the world. Begg my dead body, which living was denyed you; and either lay itt at Sherborne if the land continue, or in Exiter church, by my father and mother. I can wright noe more. Tyme and Death call me awaye.

The everlasting, infinite powerfull, and inscrutable God, that Almightie God that is goodness itself, mercy itself, the true lief and light, keep you and yours, and have mercy on me, and teach me to forgeve my persecutors and false accusers; and send us to meete in His glorious kingdome. My true wief, farewell. Blesse my poore boye; pray for me. My true God hold you both in His armes.

Written with the dyeing hand of sometyme thy husband, but now (alasse!) overthrowne. Your's that was, but now but my owne,

W. Ralegh

Ralegh was attended in prison by Thomas Bilson, Bishop of Winchester, whom James had appointed to console him and to obtain his confession (preferably, one which tallied with that of Cobham). The two men seem to have respected each other. Ralegh was impressed by the Bishop's gravity and scholarship, while the Bishop satisfied himself that Ralegh was 'settled and resolved to die a Christian and a good Protestant'. But Ralegh would admit nothing fresh concerning the Main Plot. They discussed the Spanish pension 'once, but it was not proceeded with'.

With the shadow of death hanging over him, Ralegh wrote one of the greatest poems in the language, in which two appropriate images, of the pilgrimage and the court of law, are powerfully combined, 'The Passionate Man's Pilgrimage':

> Giue me my Scallop shell of quiet,
> My staffe of Faith to walke vpon,
> My Script of Ioy, Immortall diet,
> My bottle of saluation:
> My Gowne of Glory, hopes true gage,
> And thus Ile take my pilgrimage.
>
> Blood must be my bodies balmer,
> No other blame will there be giuen
> Whilst my soule like a white Palmer
> Trauels to the land of heauen,
> Ouer the siluer mountaines,
> Where spring the Nectar fountaines:
> And there Ile kisse
> The Bowle of blisse,
> And drink my eternall fill
> On euery milken hill.
> My soule will be a drie before,
> But after it, will nere thirst more.
>
> And by the happie blisfull way
> More peacefull Pilgrims I shall see,
> That haue shooke off their gownes of clay,
> And goe appareld fresh like mee.
> Ile bring them first
> To slake their thirst,
> And then to tast those Nectar suckets
> At the cleare wells
> Where sweetnes dwells,
> Drawne vp by Saints in Christall buckets.
>
> And when our bottles and all we,
> Are fild with immortalitie:
> Then the holy paths weele trauell
> Strewde with Rubies thick as grauell,
> Seelings of Diamonds, Saphire floores,
> High walles of Corall and Pearle Bowres.

From thence to heauens Bribeles hall
Where no corrupted voyces brall,
No Conscience molten into gold,
Nor forg'd accusers bought and sold,
No cause deferd, nor vaine spent Iorney,
For there Christ is the Kings Atturney:
Who pleades for all without degrees,
And he hath Angells', but no fees.

When the grand twelue million Iury,
Of our sinnes and sinfull fury,
Gainst our soules blacke verdicts giue,
Christ pleades his death, and then we liue,
Be thou my speaker taintles pleader,
Vnblotted Lawer, true proceeder,
Thou mouest saluation euen for almes:
Not with a bribed Lawyers palmes.

And this is my eternall plea,
To him that made Heauen, Earth and Sea,
Seeing my flesh must die so soone,
And want a head to dine next noone,
Iust at the stroke when my vaines start and spred
Set on my soule an euerlasting head.
Then am I readie like a palmer fit,
To tread those blest paths which before I writ.

At Wilton House, James's tortuous communings with his conscience worked themselves out to a conclusion. 'And therefore,' he told his courtiers triumphantly, 'I have saved the lives of them *all*.' Therefore Ralegh was also reprieved, and was removed to the Tower of London. He was lodged in the Bloody Tower on 16th December 1603, and was a prisoner for the next thirteen years.

Ralegh's reputation as a man of endless resource and Machiavellian subtlety, able to exert hidden influence on events, died hard. Even in the Tower, he was suspected of having somehow engineered his reprieve. Henry IV of France was sceptical of James's motives. He believed 'Spanish gold' might have been concerned, and he wrote to his ambassador Beaumont to ask if Don Juan de Taxis or Cecil had influenced the reprieves, 'for it is rumoured that these persons, backed by money expended by Ralegh, brought the thing about'.

One of Ralegh's first acts in the Tower was to write to King James to thank him for the gift of life. He wrote gratefully, almost obsequiously, although once again allowances must be made for the literary conventions of the time. 'Most Mighty and Most Mercifull Kinge,' wrote Ralegh, 'Seing it hath pleased your Majestye to breathe into dead yearth a new life, I amonge others do presume to offer my humblest thancks and acknowledgements, which

269

(God knowes) can neather in words be exprest or presented . . .' Ralegh went further than merely thanking the King. He offered him his services. In every civic sense, Ralegh was a dead man. He had no future. Yet here he was, irrepressibly offering that future to the King's service. Those early letters to the King give a hint of things to come. King James was soon to discover that Ralegh was not one to accept his sentence and settle down quietly in his cell to wait for death to overtake him. On the contrary, Ralegh was tirelessly determined to press his innocence, to plead his case for release, to proclaim the injustices done him, and to try to influence anybody and anything that could possibly work towards his release from the Tower. As the years went by, King James was to find that in Ralegh he had possibly the most restless, talkative, worrying, and generally most embarrassing political prisoner any political leader was ever plagued by.

Legally, Ralegh was dead. In a letter to King James he actually referred to himself as a dead man. But though he wrote it, he could not accept it in his mind. He simply could not bring himself to believe that his imprisonment was anything but temporary. He was innocent. He knew it, the Lords knew it, everybody knew it, and in a very short time he was writing to Cecil about a pardon, and suggesting how he might be employed, unobtrusively, out of prison. If he could not be here in London ('which God cast my sowle into hell if I desire,' he said) then he would be content to be confined to the Hundred of Sherborne. Or if not so much as that, then he would not mind living in Holland, where he might get some employment to do with the Indies. Failing that, 'if I be apoyncted to any bishope or other gentleman or nobel man, or that your Lordship would lett me keep but a park of yours – which I will buy from sume one that hath it.' Ralegh went on plaintively to say that 'God douth know that if I cannot go to the Bathe this fall I am undun, for my health; and shalbe dead, or disabled for ever.'

Ralegh did not say how he could have paid for the park from Cecil. At that time he was financially almost helpless. He certainly could not have purchased his reprieve, as Henry of Navarre had suspected. In fact, he could hardly, as he said himself, buy bread and clothes for his family. His great fortune was wrecked. On 14th February 1604, all his goods and chattels and the moneys due to him were assigned to trustees, Robert Smythe and John Shelbury (who was Ralegh's steward), to pay his debts and maintain his family. On 30th July that year, Sherborne Castle and ten named manors in Dorset and Somerset were conveyed to Sir Alexander Brett, George Hall and others for sixty years ('should Sir Walter so long live') in trust for Lady Ralegh and young Walter. His main sources of income were cut off when he was stripped of the offices of Governor of Jersey, the Wardenship of the Stanneries, the wine patents, the Rangership of Gillingham Forest and the Lieutenantcy of Portland Castle (although the last two went to his brother Sir Carew Ralegh, and so they did not leave the family). With great reluctance, he returned the seal of the Duchy of Cornwall to Cecil.

Commissioners had moved in to seize and despoil Sherborne and its estates. Amongst them was, in Ralegh's own words, that 'infamus and detested a wrech', John Meere, who rooted up Ralegh's 'copps-woods' and proposed to pay off his own creditors with the proceeds of

At Easter, 1604, King James and Queen Anne went to a bull-baiting at the Tower. Ralegh hoped to be released by Royal Amnesty for the occasion, but he was removed to Fleet Prison instead

Sherborne. As for the rest, the tenants refused to pay Lady Ralegh. Everything was going to ruin. The woods were being cut down, the grounds laid waste, the stock sold. As he said to Cecil, 'I perishe every waye.' They had even begun to dismantle the castle.

Ralegh estimated that he had lost £3,000 a year income from the offices taken from him. Worse still, the Lord Admiral not only had the wine patent but also insisted on being paid arrears of some £6,000. In desperation, Lady Ralegh appealed to Cecil and, for once, Cecil did his best for the Raleghs. He stopped the pillage of Sherborne, and he seems to have 'spoken the one word' Bess Ralegh asked, for the Lord Admiral moderated his demands.

Ralegh had £300 from Sherborne but, he said, was over £3,000 in debt there. He drew up a statement (with arithmetical errors) of his rent income from his Sherborne estate, for the Treasurer, Lord Buckhurst. Ralegh put the value of all the goods he had in the world at no more than a thousand marks, if that. He had to pay the Bishop of Salisbury £260 a year. In fees, pensions, the provision of the King's house, the maintenance of maimed soldiers and the poor, he paid £50 a year. He had sold all his rich hangings to the Lord Admiral for £500. He had only one rich bed, which he had sold to Cobham. All his plate, which was 'very fayre', was now lost or 'eaten out with interest' at Cheynies', the goldsmith, in Lombard Street. He had, as he said, 'a miserabell estat, God knowes'. He even had to pay for his keep, and for his wife, child and two servants in the Tower. It cost him £4 a week – later it was £5.

Ralegh had a brief hope of release in March 1604, his first Eastertide in prison, when King James made his formal procession through London. He and his Queen visited the Tower for a bull-baiting on the 26th. Often, at such times, the prisoners in the Tower were released, as a sign of royal clemency. So they were on this occasion. But Ralegh, Grey and Cobham had previously been moved to the Fleet Prison. When they returned, they found the plague in the Tower, and Ralegh did not hesitate to complain vehemently. 'The plaug being cum at the next dore unto mee,' he wrote to Cecil, now Viscount Cranborne, 'only the narrow passage of the way between. My poore child having lien this 14 dayes next to a woman with a running plaug sore, and but a paper wall between, – and those childe is also this Thursday dead of the plauge. So as now my wife and child, and others in whom I had cumfort, have abandoned me; and in what fearful estate, the Lord knowes.' In fact, Lady Ralegh had moved from the Tower, very sensibly, because of the plague and had rented a house on Tower Hill. It was most probably there that she gave birth that winter of 1604 to another son, christened Carew Ralegh in the Tower Chapel on 15th February 1605.

Ralegh was constantly anxious about his health. Deprived of his annual resort to the waters of Bath, he was all the more susceptible to the damp and cold of the Tower. He was, he said, 'dayly in danger of death by the palsey; nightly, of suffocation, by wasted and obstructed lungs'. There was a steady physical deterioration. A year later, he was telling Cecil that he was on 'every second or third night in danger ether of suddayne death or of the loss of my lymes and sense, being sume tyme two hores without feeling or motion of my hand and whole arm. I complayn not of it,' he added, untruthfully. His condition was confirmed by his doctor, Peter Turner, who reported in March 1606 that Ralegh's left side was cold and numb, the fingers of his left hand were enfeebled, and his tongue was affected. Turner, speaking as a physician, recommended that his patient be moved from his present cold lodgings to somewhere warmer. He suggested the little room which Ralegh had built in the Tower garden, next to his still-house. Certainly, Ralegh was later allowed to move.

Ralegh's other great anxiety was Sherborne. During the investigations into his financial affairs after his conviction, a suspicion arose about the validity of the deed transferring Sherborne to young Wat Ralegh which was drawn up by Sir John Doddridge at Midsummer 1602; this was the deed which Ralegh himself referred to in a letter to Cecil as being good, if Sir John had 'law or honesty'. But Ralegh was almost superstitiously uneasy about his ownership of Sherborne. Now, his worst fears were about to be realized. Popham and Coke, two of the finest legal brains in England, examined the document and in June 1605 they reported to Cecil that it was invalid. The engrossing clerk had omitted some crucial words, that the trustees 'shall and will from henceforth stand and be thereof seised'. It was no more than a clerical error, a mere slip of the pen. But it was enough to invalidate the transfer – and also the transfer to Brett dated July 1603. Sherborne had legally still belonged to Ralegh himself at the time of his attainder, and now passed to the Crown with the rest of his estate.

This misfortune, coming on top of everything else, was too much for Lady Ralegh. She blamed Ralegh for his carelessness. The Raleghs seem to have had the worst quarrel of their married life.

> I shalbe made more then weary of my life by her crijng and bewayling, [Ralegh wrote to Cecil] who will return in post when shee heares of your Lordship's departure, and nothing don. Shee hath alreddy brought her eldest sonne in one hand and her sucking child in another, crijng out of her and their destruction; charging mee with unnaturell negligence, and that having provided for myne own life I am without sense and compassion of theirs.

Bess must have been very angry. She could have said nothing more hurtful to her husband than to accuse him of looking after himself at his family's expense.

Ralegh begged Cecil to save his estate, but Cecil ignored the appeal. Lady Ralegh then appealed to the King. His sense of justice was touched and he agreed that the estate should not be forfeited through a clerk's carelessness. He instructed Cecil to have a new draft correctly drawn up. But Cecil ignored this, too, with most unfortunate results for the Raleghs.

Lady Ralegh continued to visit Sherborne and to treat it as their home. She was there in September 1605, and later brought suspicion on herself and her husband when it was reported that she had had the rusty armour scoured. The ownership of Sherborne remained undecided until 1607, when James was looking for an estate to give his favourite Sir Robert Carr, later to be Earl of Somerset. Cecil reminded James of 'yon manor of Sherborne', and in the autumn of 1607 James began an action in the Court of Exchequer, which in January

1608 required Ralegh to show his proper title by which Sherborne should revert to his heirs. Ralegh had no defence except the faulty conveyance. On 27th October the Court duly gave judgment for the King, who behaved with commendable magnaminity. He offered Lady Ralegh £5,000 in exchange for her interest and young Wat's during her husband's lifetime. Later, he appointed Keymis as a surveyor, and Sir Arthur Throckmorton as a trustee. He withdrew the offer of £5,000 but agreed to pay Lady Ralegh and her son a pension of £400 for the duration of their lives. He also agreed to pay a capital sum of £8,000.

The Raleghs had not much choice but to agree (although the pension was not paid regularly). However, they did not give up without a struggle. Ralegh wrote to Carr, pleading with him not 'to geve me and myne our last fatall blowe, by obtayninge from his Majestie the inheritaunce of my children and nephewes, lost in law for want of wordes'. Needless to say, Carr ignored the appeal. Lady Ralegh fell on her knees in front of James at Hampton Court and begged him to have mercy on her and hers. James muttered, 'I maun hae the land, I maun hae it for Carr' and walked on. Thus, on 9th January 1609, Sherborne became the property of Robert Carr. Chamberlain wrote to Carleton the following day to tell him the news. Lady Ralegh, he said, 'had been an importunate suitor all these holidays in her husband's behalf', but to no avail. Ralegh would have now to say with Job, 'Naked came I into the world, and naked will I go out.' It is interesting to note that his name was still tainted with atheism, and any misfortune that befell him was attributed to divine vengeance. 'One thing is to be noticed,' wrote Chamberlain, 'that the error or oversight is said to be gross, that men do merely ascribe it to God's own hand that blinded him and his counsel.'

Ralegh was one of the most sociable and sought-after prisoners. He had his own family with him and his servants, John Talbot and Peter Dean. He was visited by John Shelbury, his steward, by Thomas Hariot, his cousin George Carew, Dr Peter Turner, a surgeon Dr John and a clergyman called Hawthorn. His boatman Owen brought him beer and ale. He had a chest of books and papers (of which Cecil had kept some for checking). His two rooms were on the second floor of the Bloody Tower, which was part of the inner wall of the fortress; inwards, the tower looked over the Green to the main entrance of the White Tower, and across to the Chapel of St Peter ad Vincula. Outwards, Ralegh's room looked on the back of St Thomas's Tower and Traitors' Gate, facing the Thames. There was a terrace for him to walk on and take the air. He could be seen from the river, and the crews of passing ships used to wave to him. The Lieutenant of the Tower at that time, Ralegh's friend Sir George Harvey, very obligingly left the door of the Bloody Tower permanently open, and gave Ralegh the freedom of his garden. There, Ralegh had a small lath and plaster out-building, once the prison of Bishop Latimer, more recently a hen-house, which he used to store equipment and carry out experiments.

Ralegh was eternally curious, and endlessly busy, on all manner of new projects. He grew herbs in his garden. He kept a stock of spices, and dispensed drugs, and made up pills. He assayed minerals, and he had a small furnace for testing metals. He experimented with ways of distilling fresh water from salt, and he tried out methods of preserving meat for long sea voyages. He cured his own tobacco. He concocted a tonic made of strawberries. His

The Gunpowder Plot conspirators. When the plot was uncovered, Ralegh was at once interrogated about it, as he was several times in political crisis during his imprisonment. Anonymous engraving

'Great Cordial' was internationally famous. It was a complicated recipe of bezoar stone, hart's horn (ammonia), ground pearl, musk, spirits of wine, with mint, borage, gentian, sugar, sassafras, and assorted spices. James's Queen, Anne of Denmark, took it, and thought very highly of it.

Although he was shut away in prison, people never forgot Ralegh. He was out of sight but by no means out of mind. People were always curious about his doings, enquiring about him, gossiping and discussing him. The image of the old wizard, the fox, the 'witch', still working away at his schemes in the Tower, had a powerful effect on the popular mind. Like the lions, he became one of the sights of the Tower. One day in 1605 Madame de Beaumont, wife of the French Ambassador, visited the Tower to see the lions, accompanied by Lady Howard of Effingham. She saw Ralegh working in his garden and sent a message to ask him if she could have some of his 'Balsam of Guiana'.

Ralegh was very pleased to oblige the ladies, and sent some of the ointment by a Captain Whitelocke, who was attending them on that day. But such was Ralegh's reputation that even this innocent event had serious repercussions for him. In November 1605, the Gunpowder Plot was discovered. At once, all hope of toleration for Catholics vanished for centuries. All James's old and only half-lulled terrors of assassination were revived. One of the first names that must have occurred to him was that of the dark and treacherous Machiavellian plotter in the Tower. It was remembered that Whitelocke had been seen in the retinue of the Archduke Albert that summer, and Whitelocke had recently had dealings with Ralegh. Ralegh was interrogated by special commissioners about Whitelocke, and about his own dealings with Northumberland, who was also in the Tower on suspicion of implication in the Plot. It was then that Lady Ralegh's scouring of the rusty armour at Sherborne was thought to be suspicious.

The commissioners found it difficult to believe that Ralegh's relations with Whitelocke only concerned the balsam of Guiana, and that he had recently had very little to do with Northumberland. This suspicion of Ralegh lasted almost to the end of his imprisonment. The slightest breath of scandal or treason anywhere was enough to bring him once more into an enquiry. He appeared in 1607, answering questions about the custodianship of Sir George Harvey at the Tower, and about the behaviour of the Tower servant Edward Cottrell (who had actually been living at Sherborne for some time, on a pension from the Raleghs). Three years later, the Council again sat at the Tower, to accuse Ralegh of some undisclosed offence. Lady Ralegh was told to leave the Tower and live in her house on Tower Hill. Ralegh himself was officially reprimanded by Cecil (now Earl of Salisbury) and was kept in closer confinement for over three months. His offence was never made public, possibly because it might have made the Government look ridiculous. In July 1611 yet another enquiry investigated more rumours about Ralegh's behaviour. One of the investigators was Ralegh's enemy, the Lord Chamberlain, Lord Henry Howard, now Earl of Northampton. Howard reported that he and his fellow commissioner had 'had a bout with Sir Walter Ralegh, in whom we find no change, but the same boldness, pride and passion, that heretofore hath wrought more violently, but never expended itself in a stronger passion'.

That Ralegh had not changed was a tribute to his astonishing resilience of spirit. He was as closely imprisoned when Howard visited him, after eight years in the Tower, as on his first day – or rather, since the arrival of Sir William Waad, who relieved Harvey in August 1605. The mean-spirited Waad resented the manner in which the Raleghs were making the best of their circumstances. He subjected them to a multitude of petty restrictions and regulations, almost as though he had somehow got the impression that the Raleghs believed that the Tower of London was being run for their benefit and he was determined to disillusion them. He removed the low, wooden fence around Ralegh's little garden and built a high, brick wall in its place, so that Ralegh could not look out. He had a silly curfew bell rung in the afternoon, when all prisoners, with their families and servants, had to retire indoors, and the gates were locked. He forbade Lady Ralegh to drive through the gates of the Tower in her coach. He did his best to make the Raleghs' imprisonment as unpleasant as he could with a series of pin-pricks to the limit of his authority.

The Earl of Northumberland, who became known as the Wizard Earl, was a notable addition to the captives' society in the Tower. He set up a kind of noble residence in Martin Tower, where he had an establishment of his own servants, and lived on his own victualling – he paid Waad £100 a year not to have to eat the official Tower food. Northumberland enlarged his rooms, furnished them, put in bigger and more windows. He too had a garden, in which he built a still-room and laid out paths and a bowling alley. Northumberland introduced what was almost a university atmosphere into the Tower. He was attended by his

Henry, Earl of Northumberland, 'The Wizard Earl', also imprisoned with Ralegh in the Tower

Henry, Prince of Wales. Miniature by Isaac Oliver. Henry said of his father's treatment of Ralegh, 'Only my father could keep such a bird in a cage'

'Three Magi', the scholars and mathematicians Robert Hues, William Warner, and Thomas Hariot. Hariot was working on optics at the time, and he may have made the sun-dial on the south wall of Martin Tower for Northumberland. He had a yearly pension from the Earl, and seems to have acted as his agent and general link with the outside world.

Ralegh, too, kept his links with the world outside the Tower. He continued to write to Cecil, complaining about his living conditions and pointedly reminding the Earl of his innocence. He corresponded with the scholars of his day. He offered his services to Queen Anne, who seemed to be intrigued by his personality. He and Hariot gave advice on the planning of new expeditions to Virginia.

Ralegh's own rights and patent in Virginia had reverted to the Crown, but though he had been forced to the side-lines, others were planning new ventures. At one time the Earl of Southampton had loose plans for a Catholic colony, but nothing came of them. The main serious contenders were some London merchants headed by one of Ralegh's former City associates, Sir Robert Smythe, a group of Bristol merchants who had the advice and encouragement of Richard Hakluyt, and a West-Country group including Sir Ferdinando Gorges, the Lord Chief Justice Popham, and Sir Humphrey Gilbert's sons. Two companies were formed from the interested parties, the Plymouth Company to exploit North Virginia, and the London Company of South Virginia. A Council of Virginia was set up under a Royal Charter of April 1606. Both companies sent out expeditions in 1607. There were many disappointments and deaths ahead, but permanent colonies were eventually established. Ralegh continued his interest. In 1609, to the alarm of the Spanish Ambassador, he was writing a paper for the Council giving his advice on how to settle colonies in Virginia.

In the same year of the first of the new expeditions to Virginia, the Queen's brother King Christian IV of Denmark visited London. He had a Viking's thirst, and a wish to have Ralegh as admiral of his fleet. His brother-in-law indulged the first, in a round of parties, tourneys, hunts, bear-baitings and tremendous drinking bouts, but refused the second.

Ralegh meanwhile was preoccupied with another royal visitor, whose personality was to be the main influence on his later years in the Tower. He was King James's own son, Prince Henry, who was the great hope of his country, and of Sir Walter Ralegh.

19. Prisoner in the Tower

PRINCE HENRY'S celebrated remark about King James and Ralegh's imprisonment, that 'No one but my father would keep such a bird in a cage', aptly illustrates the young man's attitude towards his father. Henry did not like James, and was not like him. Prince Henry's choice of friends, his tastes, his general way of life, might almost have been specially chosen to advertise the differences between father and son. He was high-spirited, brave, honest and intelligent, direct in speech, open in outlook and healthy in body. The Venetian Ambassador described him as 'little of body, and quick of spirit, ceremonious beyond his years, and with great gravity'. He loved sports, except hunting, his father's greatest love. He could not abide his father's young male favourites such as Robert Carr. He abhorred foul language, and had swear-boxes in his households (which would soon have bankrupted the coarse-mouthed James). He was a liberal and discerning patron of the arts. Ralegh's kinsman Sir Arthur Gorges had a 'place of right good trust' in the Prince's service. Ralegh himself, a foul, atheistic, tobacco-smoking traitor to James, was both a trusted friend and a respected teacher to Prince Henry.

It was probably in about 1607, when the Prince was thirteen years old, that he was first brought by Queen Anne to the Tower to meet Ralegh. Like his mother, Henry was first intrigued, then charmed and captivated by Ralegh's personality. To the young prince, Ralegh was an enchanting figure from England's past, a living legend. He had fought the Spaniard on both sides of the Atlantic. He was a survivor of '88. He had known and befriended Spenser and Marlowe. He had been the late Queen's favourite. All the soldiers, courtiers, politicians, prelates, poets and explorers of the last thirty years – Ralegh had known them personally. It was as though three decades of English history were embodied in one man, now reduced to pacing up and down his cell in the Tower.

Ralegh for his part was pleased and flattered by Prince Henry's friendship. He was pleased to rub his intellect against another's, and especially one so young and eager and vigorous. He was flattered to know that as their friendship ripened and deepened he was entrusted with a major part in what was virtually the higher education of the heir to the throne. He knew also that in Prince Henry's friendship lay his best hope of eventual release from the Tower.

Sir William Waad's curfew at five o'clock in the evening, when wives had to leave the Tower and prisoners had to retire into their quarters, left Ralegh with the leisure for reading and study. In the Tower he wrote on a variety of subjects and much of his writing was for the instruction and entertainment of the Prince of Wales. Their enthusiasms chimed at many points. Ralegh fostered the Prince's interest in one of his own great loves, ship-building.

In 1608 Prince Henry engaged the best naval architect of his day, Phineas Pett, to build him a ship, the *Prince Royal*. The old *Ark Royal* was also converted, and renamed the *Anne Royal*.

Prince Henry and Queen Anne were present at Woolwich to see the launch of the *Prince Royal* in September 1610. There was some difficulty in getting the ship afloat, but that was not her fault; she was of sound design and, years afterwards, Henry's younger brother Charles survived a Channel storm in her when many other ships were sunk.

For Prince Henry, Ralegh wrote *A Discourse of the Invention of Ships, Anchor, Compass, etc.* and *Observations on the Royal Navy and Sea Service* which may now be the only surviving parts of his treatise on *The Art of War by Sea*. In October 1618, shortly before his execution, Ralegh wrote from the Tower to Lady Ralegh asking her to make up into a bundle some papers from a 'sedar chist' and send them to him. They were his *The Art of War by Sea* and some notes belonging to it which have been lost.

On occasion, Ralegh's writings were intended for the eye of the King himself. In James's reign, the old anti-Spanish temper of the Elizabethans had dwindled away, and had been replaced by pro-Spanish sentiments. James had concluded a peace with Spain in 1604. Some of the most prominent members of James's Court and Government received Spanish pensions from Philip III. The Queen was a Catholic. For some time after James's accession, the Pope had looked forward eagerly to his conversion to Catholicism. In 1611 James considered a suggestion for a double Royal marriage which would have favoured Spanish and Catholic interests. Duke Charles Emmanuel I of Savoy proposed that James's daughter the Princess Elizabeth should marry his second son Don Philibert, and Prince Henry should marry the Duke's eldest daughter.

At Prince Henry's request, Ralegh examined the possibilities of both matches. He reported that he could find nothing good to recommend either of them. In his two essays, *On a Match between the Lady Elizabeth and the Prince of Piedmont*, and *On a Marriage between Prince Henry and a Daughter of Savoy*, Ralegh made it clear that in his opinion Savoy was a hopeless alliance. Savoy was a long way from England, and was geographically, politically and religiously much closer to Spain. England could never defend Savoyard interests against Spain (if in fact Savoy could ever be prevailed upon ever to resist Spain). Savoy herself could never give any assistance to England. Furthermore, an alliance with Savoy might force England to remain neutral in any future war between the Netherlands and Spain.

Both essays showed that Ralegh had lost none of his talent for fine invective against Spain. 'It is the *Spaniard* that is to be feared,' he insisted, 'the Spaniard, who layeth his pretences and practices with a long hand.' Spain, he repeated, was never as strong as was feared. The Spaniards themselves had a proverb that 'the lion is not so fierce as he is painted.' If Queen Elizabeth had believed her men of war (Ralegh himself, by inference) as she did her scribes (clearly, such as Cecil), 'we had in her time beaten that great empire to pieces, and made their kings kings of figs and oranges, as in old times'. The proposed marriages would be of mixed religions. England would lose her pre-eminence as the foremost Protestant country in Europe. The Prince was still young. While Henry was still a bachelor, James would have a strong political card to play. Ralegh advised that the Prince stay unmarried for the time being and, when the time came, he should consider the King of France's daughter. As for the Princess Elizabeth, Ralegh suggested that she marry a Protestant prince, such as the Prince Palatine of the Rhine. Ralegh would value such an alliance more than 'ten dukes of Savoy'.

Neither the King nor his chief minister Cecil welcomed such pungently expressed advice from a prisoner who was supposed to be dead and forgotten in the Tower. The advice was all the more unpalatable because it was politically sound. The Savoyard marriage proposals came to nothing. Elizabeth married Frederick the Elector Palatine in 1613, and became Queen of Bohemia (the 'Queen of Hearts', and the 'Mistris' of Sir Henry Wotton's poem).

The treatises which Ralegh wrote in the Tower, none of which was published until after his death, were priceless mental exercises for him. They helped to keep his intellect keen through the years of his imprisonment. They also showed his progress towards a mastery of English prose. Ralegh may have been a minor poet, but as a prose-writer he had a major talent. At his best he was sublime, and even when he was dull he was magnificently dull. He wrote on politics and economics, philosophy, ethics and metaphysical problems, and history. No matter what his subject, he was never at a loss for the apt illustration or anecdote drawn from history or his own experience; names, places, incidents, seemed to spring to his aid whenever he needed them.

His writings reveal much about Ralegh's political thinking and his religious beliefs. He was not a democrat. He was a monarchist who firmly believed that kings should rule by divine right as benevolent despots. A king should be approachable but unaccountable. He was the Law and yet he was more than the Law. Ralegh went so far in his *Prerogative of Parliaments* as to defend King John for resisting Magna Carta; in Ralegh's view, it was Bishop Langton, who drew up the charter, who was a traitor, and the barons who were outrageous rebels.

At the same time, Ralegh believed in a political system of checks and balances. A king should establish a proper relationship between himself and his people. Ralegh set out some strict rules for the behaviour of kings. If much was granted a king, then much was required of him. 'Mischievous Matchivel' was one of the epithets hurled at Ralegh, and ironically he had indeed given the writings of Machiavelli very close study. In his essay on *The Cabinet Council* (which so impressed John Milton that he had it printed, for the first time, in 1658) Ralegh laid down the qualities needed by a successful king. People follow the example of their King, he said. They study with a learned king, and get drunk with a drunken king. 'The virtuous and vicious examples of princes incite subjects to imitate the same qualities.' Therefore a king should be brave, and wise, and good, and just. Often Ralegh gives the impression (at least, to a modern reader) that he is listing the very qualities and recommending the very courses of action which King James did not have or refused to adopt. Very occasionally, it seems that Ralegh could not resist a surreptitious dig at James. 'The way whereby a prince eschews the hate of his subjects,' he wrote, 'is not to take from them their lands or goods.' He also had a most unfortunate tendency to hark back tactlessly (or perhaps intentionally) to the good old days of the former reign. 'A little money went far in those days,' he says, wistfully, recalling his efforts in Parliament on behalf of the poor, 'in the time of Queen Elizabeth, who desired much to spare the common people, and I did it by her commandment.' He talked of 'our late dear sovereign' and remembered that 'queen Elizabeth would set the reason of a mean man before the authority of the greatest counsellor she had' because she was 'a queen of the small, as well as of the great, and would hear their complaints'. When Ralegh suggested in his *Maxims of State* that, for instance, a king should show himself often to his people, should sit in open courts, should not favour courtiers at the commons' expense, should not borrow money needlessly, and should 'be well furnished with warlike provision', it is not impossible that he was really suggesting that James was afraid to show himself or to sit in open courts, that he did favour courtiers unduly, that he did borrow money needlessly, and that he was unfurnished with warlike provision.

Ralegh also wrote for his own son Wat, who was about the same age as Prince Henry. Wat was a chip off the old block, with his father's 'pig-eye' and his father's attitude to life, being 'a handsome lusty stout fellow, very bold and apt to affront'. He had years before been betrothed to Elizabeth Bassett, a ward of Cobham's, who had an income of £3,000 a year, but that was long since cancelled. Ralegh sent him to Corpus Christi College, Oxford, and warned his tutor, Dr Daniel Featley, of his son's interest in violent physical exercise and what he called 'strange company'. Young Wat graduated on 30th October 1607. His father sent him to Paris, with Ben Jonson as his governor, to learn some of the accomplishments of a young gentleman. It was then Jonson's duty to try to control his charge's 'planetary and irregular motions'. He was not very successful, as the story of the wheelbarrow shows. For Wat, Ralegh wrote a humourless, forbidding and slightly sanctimonious tract, his *Instructions to his Son and to Posterity*, in which he frequently offers his son advice which he did not take himself. Wat was advised to choose only virtuous persons as his friends, to take great care in choosing a wife, to beware flatterers, avoid quarrels, look after his goods and belongings, eschew wine, and to trust to God. He should beware of talking too much, of laughing at the mentally afflicted, of making false accusations, of lying, of buying and wearing extravagant clothes, and of putting temptation in the way of servants. The advice was excellent, but it was somewhat solemnly and pompously offered.

Evidently Wat ignored most of his father's cautions, for one of the oddest stories in Aubrey concerns a dinner party attended by Ralegh and his son. On the way, Ralegh told Wat to behave himself, saying 'thou art such a quarrelsome, affronting . . . that I am ashamed to have such a beare in my company'. However, Wat humbled himself to his father and promised he would mend his manners. He sat next to his father and was very demure 'at least halfe dinner time'. Ralegh was beginning to breathe a sigh of relief, when Wat suddenly said 'I, this morning, not having the feare of God before my eies but by the instigation of the devill, went to a whore. I was very eager of her, kissed and embraced her, and went to enjoy her, but she thrust me from her, and vowed I should not, for your Father lay with me but an hower ago.'

Ralegh must have been the first at the table to recover from this sensational statement. 'Strangely surprised and putt out of his countenance at so great a table,' he gave Wat a 'damned blow over his face'. 'His son, as rude as he was, would not strike his father, but strikes over the face the gentleman that sate next to him and sayd "Box about: 'twill come to my father anon."' Wat Ralegh's table manners were evidently on a par with his behaviour in the field. Aubrey says that Wat 'was a notable disputent and courser, and would never be out of countenance nor baffled; fight lustily; and, one time coursing, putt a turd in a box, and besmeared it about his antagonist's face.'

Ralegh's major prose work in the Tower, and the only one of his copyright works to be published while he was a prisoner, was an undertaking of typically Elizabethan industry and Raleghan audacity. He set out to write a history, not just of his own times, nor of Elizabeth's reign, nor even a history of England, but a history of the whole world, no less. He proposed to assuage 'those inmost and soul-piercing wounds which are ever aching while uncured' by summoning up a lifetime's reading, learning and experience and arranging them in one great 'story of all ages past'. He would begin at the beginning of the world and bring the story up to modern times, or almost to modern times. He recognized that there would be political dangers in being too topical. He knew that his readers would take double meanings if they possibly could, and in a witty disclaimer in the Preface he tried to forestall future accusations that he was using the examples of the dead to criticize the living. 'Certainly,' he said, 'if there be any, that finding themselves *spotted like the Tigers of old time*, shall find fault with me for painting them over a new; they shall therein accuse themselves justly, and me falsely.'

Ralegh began work on his *History* probably as early as 1607. The book was intended for Prince Henry, and was dedicated to him. 'For it was for the service of that inestimable Prince Henry, the successive hope, and one of the greatest of the Christian World, that I undertook this Work. It pleased him to peruse some part thereof, and to pardon what was amiss.'

In writing such a colossal work (in which, for example, some six hundred and sixty sources are quoted as authorities) Ralegh had the assistance of what Ben Jonson called 'the best wits of England'. The antiquary Sir Robert Cotton lent him books from his library. Ben Jonson himself wrote a draft, later amended by Ralegh, of a section dealing with the Punic Wars. Ralegh had no Hebrew and preferred to read Greek in Latin translation. He was greatly assisted in these two languages by the scholar and divine Dr Robert Burhill; Burhill's widow told Aubrey that her husband performed 'all or the greatest part of the drudgery of his book, for criticisms, chronology, and reading of Greek and Hebrew authors'. No doubt Hariot and the other Magi of the Wizard Earl also contributed to sections on their own subjects.

Ralegh may have had help, but his book was his own. It is a plain statement, though built up like a great structure buttressed by innumerable examples, of Ralegh's belief that the Hand of God was the prime mover in all things, and that 'the end and scope of all history' was 'to teach by example of times past such wisdom as may guide our desires and actions'. Ralegh's providential view of history, the range of his historical knowledge, and his genius for superb, rhythmical prose are shown on almost every page.

Ben Jonson, Poet Laureate, who contributed a chapter on the Punic Wars to Ralegh's *History of the World*, and was tutor to his son, Wat. Painting after A. Blyenberch

FAMA BONA
FAMA MALA
THE HISTORY OF THE WORLD
MAGISTRA VITÆ
TESTIS TEMPORV
EXPERIENTIA
LVX VERITATIS
VERITAS
MORS
OBLIVIO
At London Printed for WALTER BVRRE.
1614

THE HISTORY OF THE WORLD.

In Fiue Bookes.

1. Intreating of the Beginning and first Ages of the same from the Creation vnto Abraham.
2. Of the Times from the Birth of Abraham, to the destruction of the Temple of Salomon.
3. From the destruction of Ierusalem, to the time of Philip of Macedon.
4. From the Reigne of Philip of Macedon, to the establishing of that Kingdome, in the Race of Antigonus.
5. From the setled rule of Alexanders successors in the East, vntill the Romans (preuailing ouer all) made Conquest of Asia and Macedon.

By Sir Walter Ralegh, Knight.

VERA EFFIGIES CLARISSIMI VIRI DOM GUALTHERI RALEGH EQV. AUR. &c.
The true and liuely portraiture of the honourable and learned Knight S^r. Walter Ralegh

Left: Frontispiece of Ralegh's *History of the World*, engraved by Elstrach, and published anonymously in March 1614 by Walter Burre, London
Right: The second edition of Ralegh's *History of the World* appeared in 1617, this time with his name and portrait

No suspicions that Ralegh was an atheist can survive a reading of the opening of the first chapter:

> GOD, whom the wisest men acknowledge to be a power uneffable, and virtue infinite; a light by abundant clarity invisible; an understanding which itself can only comprehend; an essence eternal and spiritual, of absolute pureness and simplicity; was and is pleased to make himself known by the work of the world: in the wonderful magnitude whereof, (all which he embraceth, filleth, and sustaineth,) we behold the image of that glory which cannot be measured, and withal, that one, and yet

universal nature which cannot be defined. In the glorious lights of heaven we perceive a shadow of his divine countenance; in his merciful provision for all that live, his manifold goodness; and lastly, in creating and making existent the world universal, by the absolute art of his own word, his power and almightiness; which power, light, virtue, wisdom, and goodness, being all but attributes of one simple essence, and one God, we in all admire, and in part discern *per speculum creaturarum*, that is, in the disposition, order, and variety of celestial and terrestrial bodies: terrestrial, in their strange and manifold diversities; celestial, in their beauty and magnitude; which, in their continual and contrary motions, are neither repugnant, intermixed, nor confounded. By these potent effects we approach to the knowledge of the omnipotent Cause, and by these motions, their almighty Mover.

Ralegh intended his great work to be in three parts, but only the first part was published, in five books, which take the history of the world from the Creation up to the Roman conquest of Macedonia in 133 BC. With immense scholarship and erudition, Ralegh chronicles the rise and fall of empires and dynasties, in Persia, in Babylon, in Egypt, Greece, Macedonia, Carthage and Rome. In stately, leisurely (and occasionally in Books I and II somewhat tedious) detail, Ralegh tells how one people subjugated others and was itself enslaved, of how one ruler seized power and was himself deposed and ruined. He ranges freely from ancient to modern, from epic to domestic, from the fall and sack of Troy to the capture by a trick of the Channel Island of Sark. He traces out the wars and wanderings of the Ten Tribes of Israel, the campaigns of Alexander the Great, the rise to power of the Roman Empire.

In Books I and II, from the Creation to the destruction of Jerusalem, Ralegh deals with the history of the Old Testament. He accepts uncritically the biblical version of events. He does not dispute its truth. His concern is to interpret and comment upon it, as fact. But he informs his narrative with references to his own experience. He writes about Noah's Ark, for instance, with the expertise of a seaman, speculating knowledgeably about the distance which the Ark probably drifted during the rains, about the wood probably used for its construction, and the caulking of its seams (when he remembers and recommends again the excellent pitch he saw when he was in Trinidad).

Ralegh had strong likes and dislikes. Those who knew Xerxes well 'might easily discern his faint heart, through his painted looks'. But for the Greek commander Epaminondas, struck down and dying during the battle against the Spartans at Mantinea, Ralegh had nothing but admiration, and he wrote a noble epitaph for him:

So died Epaminondas, the worthiest man that ever was bred in that nation of Greece, and hardly to be matched in any age or country; for he equalled all others in the several virtues which in each of them were singular. His justice and sincerity, his temperance, wisdom, and high magnanimity were no way inferior to his military virtue; in every part whereof he so excelled, that he could not properly be called a wary, a valiant, a politic, a bountiful, or an industrious and a provident captain; all these titles, and many others, being due unto him, which, with his notable discipline and good conduct, made a perfect composition of an heroic general.

When Ralegh reached the histories of Greece and Rome, in Books III–V, his interest and consequently the pace of his narrative seem to quicken. There are many more personal interpolations (although still tantalizingly few) in which he makes comparisons or draws morals from his own service, for example, in France or in the Islands Voyage, or from Norris's expedition to Lisbon in 1589. He interrupts a discussion on Roman naval tactics to expound his views about Howard's defeat of the Armada and to give a short dissertation on naval warfare in general. He praises the courage of the Roman and Macedonian soldiers but, in a celebrated passage, prefers the 'golden metal' of the incomparable English soldier, quoting from the French historian John de Serres that 'the English come with a conquering bravery, as he, that was accustomed to gain everywhere, without any stay: he forceth our guard, placed upon the bridge, to keep the passage.'

Ralegh lost all interest in writing his *History* after the death of the Prince of Wales in 1612. He seems to have stopped work abruptly, decided to publish what was already written, and to leave the rest. In the last sentence of the last chapter of the last book he wrote that the title of his book implied 'a second and third volume, which I also intended, and have hewn out; besides many other discouragements persuading my silence, it hath pleased God to take that glorious prince out of the world to whom they were directed, whose unspeakable and never enough lamented loss hath taught me to say with Job, *Versa est in luctum cithara mea, et organum meum in vocem flentium* – "My harp is also turned to mourning, and my organ into the voice of them that weep."' His treatise on *War at Sea* was also left unfinished, and lost. Although, as he said himself, it was an unusual subject, 'never handled by any man, ancient or modern', 'God hath spared me the labour of finishing it, by his loss; by the loss of that brave Prince, of which, like an eclipse of the sun, we shall find the effects hereafter. Impossible it is to equal words and sorrows.'

Prince Henry had fallen ill during the lavish celebrations for the wedding of his sister the Princess Elizabeth to Frederick the Elector Palatine. His doctors said he had 'a malicious extraordinary burning fever; a putrid fever'. They treated him by cutting a live cock in half and putting it to his forehead. Prince Henry was delirious, moaning for his Elizabeth, 'O where is my sweet sister?'. As he lay dying, there were ominous weather signs. A rainbow ringed the moon over St James's Palace. As the doctors prevaricated and delayed, a distraught Queen Anne sent a messenger to the Tower to ask Ralegh for some of his Great Cordial. He sent it, with instructions that it should be administered at once. He believed it would cure the Prince, unless he had been poisoned. But the King was out of London, hunting. The Privy Council shirked the responsibility of giving such a remedy to the heir to the throne. The doctors tried it out on dogs, on themselves, even on the Privy Council. They tried to find out what it was made of. As the dogs, the doctors, and the Privy Council still survived, they at last gave the medicine to the Prince. It was too late. He revived briefly but relapsed and in the evening of 6th November he died, of what is now known to be typhoid fever.

Lady Ralegh in later days, her face showing the strains and stresses of being Sir Walter's wife

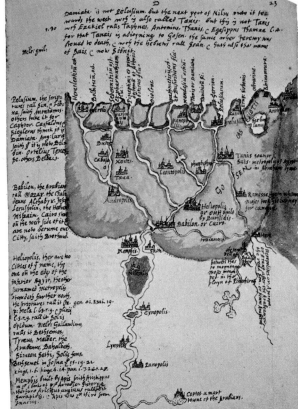

Page from a notebook of Ralegh's which he used, while working on the *History of the World*, in the Tower – the notes and map are in Ralegh's hand

Ralegh encouraged Prince Henry's interests in shipbuilding. It was one of the many subjects on which his and the young prince's interests agreed. Two Elizabethan ship designers, from Mathew Baker's *The Ancient Art of Shipwrightary*

Design for a ship, from an Elizabethan manual *The Ancient Art of Shipwrightary* by Mathew Baker

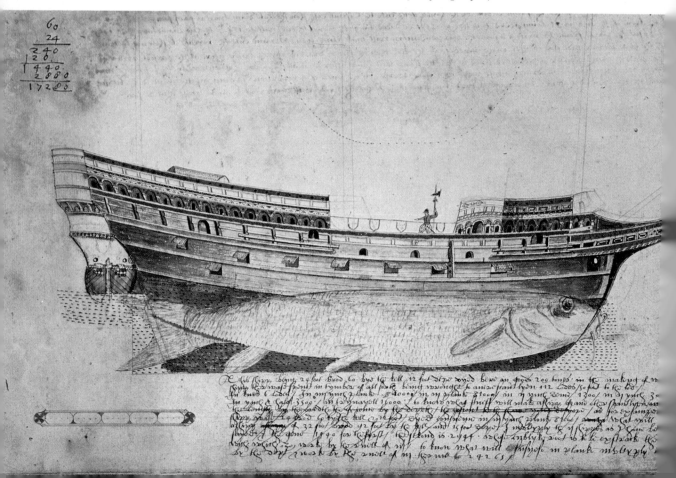

There was another death in that year of 1612, for which Ralegh wrote (or at least has been credited with writing) a quite different kind of commemorative verse:

Epitaph on the Earl of Salisbvry

HERE lies Hobinall, our Pastor while ere,
That once in a Quarter our Fleeces did sheare.
To please us, his Curre he kept under Clog,
And was ever after both Shepherd and Dog.
For Oblation to Pan his custome was thus,
He first give a Trifle, then offer'd up Us:
And through his false worship such power he did gaine,
As kept him o'th' Mountaine, and us on the plaine.
Where many a Horne-pipe he tun'd to his Phyllis,
And sweetly sung Walsingham to's Amaryllis.
Till Atropos clapt him, a Pox on the Drab,
For (spight of his Tarbox) he died of the Scab.

Cecil, now Earl of Salisbury, had been in bad health for some time. He was sick of the ague, racked with rheumatism and possibly, as the epitaph suggested, also suffering from venereal disease. In the early summer of 1612 he went to Bath to take the medicinal waters. As his health declined, so did his influence at Court and in the Government. Even James had said cruelly that 'we'll no need the little man the noo'.' Though he was still very ill, Cecil roused himself and set out from Bath to return to London intending, as he said, 'to countermine my underminers and cast dust in their eyes'. But on 24th May, when he had reached Marlborough in Wiltshire, he became so ill that he had to be carried from his coach to the parsonage in the town. There he died that evening, in a strange house, amongst strangers. He was forty-eight years old. From a position of immense power and fortune he had plunged to decline and death, like any one of a dozen characters in Ralegh's *History*.

Ralegh's book was published on 29th March 1614 by Walter Burre, of the sign of the Crane in St Paul's Churchyard, with a commendatory verse 'The Minde of the Front' by Ben Jonson, and a handsomely elaborate title page engraved by Renold Elstracke to Ralegh's own design. The book was published anonymously, but nobody had any doubts about its authorship, and it was an immediate success. The first folio edition, which cost between twenty and thirty shillings, was published in two issues, the errata of the first being corrected in the second. It was quickly sold out. Two more editions were printed in 1617, and there were in all ten editions of the work in the seventeenth century. Princess Elizabeth took a copy with her to Prague, where it was captured by the Spaniards in 1620, and recovered by the Swedes in 1648. John Hampden read it with delight and for instruction. John Milton admired Ralegh's prose, and made notes from the *History*. Oliver Cromwell read it and told his son Richard to read it. Ralegh's view of history as God's instrument for the moral improvement of man was acclaimed by many of the men of Parliament who were to lead the rebellion against the King. It is one of the more ironical paradoxes of Ralegh's life that

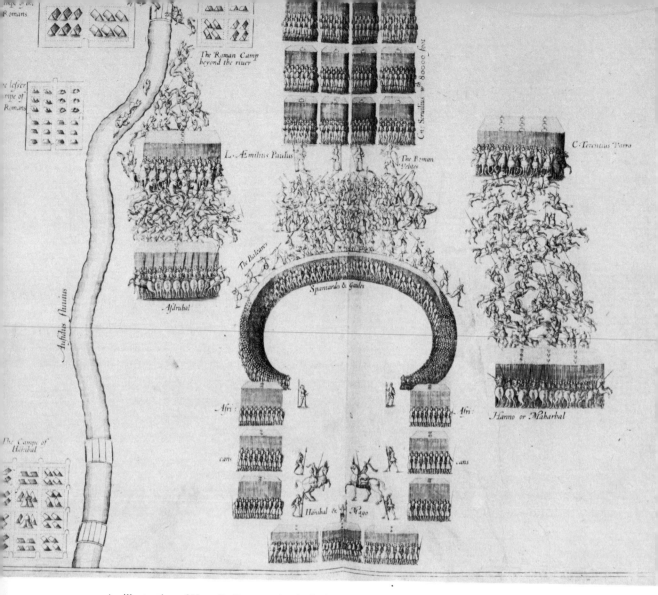

An illustration of Hannibal's campaign in Italy, from the 1614 edition of Ralegh's *History of the World*, published anonymously in March 1614 by Walter Burre, London

the writings of such a convinced supporter of the monarch should have had such an appeal for republicans, and that the man who was accused of causing Essex's death should be a source of such comfort and instruction for Puritans. Ralegh was the archetypal Elizabethan, but he survived into the seventeenth century, and was not out of place in it. His writings, and especially his *History*, had an important influence on the intellectual and moral arguments which led up to the Civil War. He was so often called an atheist. Yet it was in his philosophies that men found some of the moral justification they needed to be able to resist, and eventually to behead, their King in the name of their God. It was an irony that Ralegh himself would have appreciated.

Everybody enjoyed Ralegh's book except King James, the one man whom the author should have tried to impress most. Although he probably only read the Preface, James disliked the book, and for a time tried to suppress it. On 5th January 1615, Chamberlain was writing to Carleton that 'Sir Walter Ralegh's book is called in by the King's commandment, for divers exceptions, but specially for being too saucy in censuring princes. I hear he takes it much to heart, for he thought he had won his spurs, and pleased the King extraordinarily.'

If Chamberlain was accurately reporting Ralegh's feelings, then Ralegh was surely being a trifle naïve. He must have known that James was touchy on the subject of kings and their privileges, and he had gone out of his way to criticize several English kings in his Preface. When King James was actually asked what fault he found with Ralegh's book, he acted as though surprised that anybody should be in any doubt, and gave the astonishing reason that Ralegh had spoken irreverently about Henry VIII, a king whom James himself had often criticized! Normally, James could have been expected to agree with Ralegh's opinion of Henry VIII that 'if all the pictures and patterns of a merciless Prince were lost in the world, they might all again be painted to the life, out of the story of this King'.

In fact, it is very likely that King James was one of those 'spotted tigers of old time' who fancied he saw himself painted anew in Ralegh's book. He may have recognized himself in King Rehoboam, 'transported by his familiars and favourites', or in Ninias, who succeeded the great Queen Semiramis and who performed nothing of any moment, 'being esteemed no man of war at all, but altogether feminine, and subjected to ease and delicacy'.

The Archbishop of Canterbury wrote to the Stationers Company on 22nd December 1614, to tell them 'that the booke latelie published by Sr Walter Rawleigh, nowe prisoner in the Tower, should be suppressed, and not suffered for hereafter to be sould'. However, the censorship was only temporary. Of the two editions published in 1617, Ralegh's name and portrait were included on the title page of the second. By that time, Ralegh had at last been released from the Tower.

20. Release

WHEN RALEGH dedicated to King James his essay on politics, *The Prerogative of Parliaments*, in which he offered the King much sound but unwanted advice on how he should behave, he also mentioned that the arms and hands that had abused the King's authority to fling stones at himself were 'most of them already rotten'. It was true. Time was working its revenge upon some of those who had been most closely involved in Ralegh's trial and disgrace. Cecil was already dead. So was Justice Gawdy, of apoplexy. Lord Henry Howard died in June 1614. Lord Grey died in the Tower the same year; he hoped to the end for release, and died still offering to serve against Spain in the Low Countries. Cobham lingered on for a few more years. He was released from the Tower in 1617, but soon came to a miserable and lonely end. He was lying paralysed, starving, and penniless in an upper room of a laundry in the City of London when he died in January 1619.

Another sad victim of the Main Plot, dragging out a wasted existence in captivity, was the Lady Arabella Stuart. She had secretly and injudiciously married William Seymour in 1610, thus uniting two families who provided two possible claimants to James's throne. James was so alarmed to discover this that he sent Arbell to the Tower the following year. She was always strongly influenced by her formidable grandmother, the Countess of Shrewsbury, 'Bess of Hardwick'. She herself had no taste for politics and it is very unlikely that she ever took any part in any of the intrigues set afoot in her name. A mild-tempered, amiable woman, she seems to have endured her imprisonment meekly, with only her personal jewels and clothes to console her. She was forty years old, and slightly out of her wits, when she died, still in the Tower, in September 1615. In December Ralegh and others were required by the Privy Council to deliver up any of Arbell's clothes and jewels still in their possession. Ralegh had always had an eye for fine jewels, and evidently Arbell had consulted him about the value, or perhaps the disposal, of some of hers.

Ralegh had by now given up all hope of owning Sherborne again. After Prince Henry's death the house and estate reverted to King James. He sold them back to Robert Carr for £25,000, thus showing a profit on his transactions. But the Bishop of Salisbury's old curse was still apparently laid upon anyone who held Sherborne unrightfully. Carr might have done better to have obeyed Ralegh's plea 'not to begynne your first buildings upon the ruyns of the innocent' for he only held the property for about two years. By March 1616 he too was in the Tower, for his part in the poisoning of Sir Thomas Overbury.

The guiltiest party in the Overbury murder was Frances Howard, Robert Carr's venomous little wife. He was her second husband. She had divorced her first, the 3rd Earl of Essex, in scandalous circumstances. She had drugged him into impotence, and then had produced for the special divorce commissioners a mass of false and obscene evidence on the nature of their sexual life. Overbury was a young courtier, Carr's friend and one-time secretary, who made no secret of his dislike and contempt for Frances Howard. When hurt, Frances Howard could strike like a snake. She virtually slandered Overbury into the Tower, where she arranged for his murder. Sir William Waad was replaced as Lieutenant of the Tower by Sir Gervase Elwys; Waad was an unpleasant man, but not a dishonest one, and the Howards needed a more malleable Governor. Poison was introduced into Overbury's food over a period of time and he eventually died of its effects, in September 1613.

Despite Lord Henry Howard's efforts to conceal it, the crime was discovered the following year. By that time, Sir Ralph Winwood, anti-Spanish, no friend of either Carr or the Howards, was in Cecil's office as Secretary of State. The Governor of the Tower confessed, and was executed, along with several others. Carr and Frances Howard were condemned to death, but their sentences were commuted to imprisonment because of their rank.

The murder of Sir Thomas Overbury was the great Court scandal of King James's reign. It was a social and political bombshell, which had a widespread effect. James learned for the first time that Howard had been implicated, and, further, that he had been receiving a pension from the King of Spain – the very accusation which had been so damning for Ralegh at his trial. James learned, too, that his faithful and trusted servant, the 'wee mon' Cecil, had also received a Spanish pension. If Howard and Cecil had lived until the Overbury cases came to trial, it is not inconceivable that they would both have joined Ralegh in the Tower.

The Overbury murder had its effect upon James himself. He became even more wary, and more sensitive to public opinion. This unsavoury case, coupled with many other aspects of James's Court, alienated and disgusted a large section of the prosperous middle classes, and especially the Puritans. King James became even less ready to show himself publicly amongst his subjects, even more suspicious of the common people, and even less tolerant of free speech, whether it was in Parliament or anywhere else.

Perhaps one of the least expected results of the Overbury affair was that it helped indirectly to speed Ralegh's release from the Tower. Carr was ruined, and replaced by the King's new favourite boy, the young and beautiful George Villiers. Sir Ralph Winwood was able thoroughly to exorcize the ghosts of Cecil and his policies. The Howards were disgraced. The old pro-Spanish faction, hostile to Ralegh, was discredited and supplanted at Court by a new anti-Spanish feeling, which was at least not unfriendly to Ralegh. As his enemies' fortunes declined, so naturally Ralegh's chances of release became much better.

Well aware of this favourable change in the political climate, Ralegh redoubled his efforts to obtain his freedom. In particular, he pressed forward his plans for another expedition to Guiana. He had never really forgotten that large, rich and beautiful empire in the west, with its mountains and mines of gold. Now, in the new and hopeful atmosphere at Court, and with King James as always short of money, there was a real chance that the gold of Guiana would do for Ralegh what the *Madre de Dios* had done more than twenty years before.

ARBELLA STVARTA
COMITISSA LEVINIÆ
ÆTATIS SVÆ 13 ET
ANNO DÑI 1589

Ralegh had sent Keymis back to Guiana in 1596. Keymis had found a Spanish settlement at San Thomé blocking the way up the Caroni river. He had not been able to find Chief Putjima, but he returned as convinced as ever that the gold-mines were there. English, Dutch and French ships were already trading with the Spaniards at Port of Spain in Trinidad. The Dutch had gone further, sending out exploration ships to Guiana, and trading as far up the river as San Thomé. Henry of Navarre issued letters patent for the exploration of Guiana, and the French settled a colony of about 400 people, who were in the end wiped out by Indians. Ralegh's patents had passed to King James on his attainder, and in 1604 Charles Leigh sailed for South America with the King's authority. In May he reached the mouth of the Wyapoco, a river to the south of Guiana. He tried to establish a small colony but it failed for lack of support and supplies.

Meanwhile, even from his cell in the Tower, Ralegh tried to maintain interest in Guiana and to keep its possibilities always in the public eye. He refined some of the ore he had brought back in 1595, and delightedly published the results of his assays when he found gold in small quantities. He sent messages (and suits of English wool) to the Indians of the Wyapoco. He whipped up Prince Henry's enthusiasm for Guiana, but failed to keep Cecil's interest. Cecil always trod very softly when there was any likelihood of offending Spain, and soon Ralegh was complaining that Cecil had lost interest and had retreated into his 'arrière-boutique'.

Some of the Wyapoco natives were actually wearing Ralegh's clothes when they climbed on board the ship of the next explorer, Robert Harcourt, in 1609. Prince Henry had succeeded in getting his father to authorize a new expedition, to take possession in King James's name, as Harcourt's warrant said, of all land between the Amazon and the Orinoco, 'not being actually possessed and inhabited by any Christian Prince or State'. Harcourt found himself borne along on a tide of goodwill towards Ralegh. The Indians had looked forward to his coming and were very disappointed to find that he was not in command of the expedition. Harcourt was impressed by the country which, he said, gave him 'satisfaction that there be richer Mynes in the Country to be found'.

Ralegh himself subscribed £600 to the next expedition, commanded by Sir Thomas Roe, which set out in 1610. Roe spent about thirteen months off the coast, gaining invaluable navigational information. He was horrified by the atrocities committed by the Spaniards upon the Indians and upon European traders who fell into their hands. However, he was not convinced that either Manoa or El Dorado really existed.

Ralegh refused to be discouraged. Soon he was writing to Queen Anne, complaining that nothing much seemed to be happening about Guiana. Ingeniously, he rejected the notion that he was suggesting a Guiana voyage as a device for getting himself out of the Tower. 'The ever living God doth witness,' he protested, 'that I never sought such an imployment, for all the gold in the earth could not invite me to travell after miserie and death.' He appealed once again to her tender-heartedness, reminding her that his health was very bad. 'My extreeme shortnes of breath doth grow so fast on me, with the dispaire of obtayning so mich grace to walke with my keeper up the hill within the tower.'

Lady Arabella Stuart. It is very unlikely that 'Arbell' ever had anything to do with any of the plots arranged in her name. One of them helped to bring Ralegh down. Portrait by Carl van Mander, 1589

He wrote to the Lords of the Council, to tell them that a Captain Moate, one of Sir John Watts's men, had come back from the Orinoco with a report of the Spanish strength at San Thomé. It might be feasible for Keymis and other captains to force a way past the Spaniards and reach the mine up-river. Ralegh proposed a bargain. If Keymis went, and failed to bring back to England 'half a tunne, or as much more as he shall be able to take upp of that slate gold ore whereof I gave a sample to my Lord Knevett' then Ralegh himself would bear the entire costs of the expedition, and say no more. It would be very difficult 'for any man to find the same acre of ground againe in a country desolate and overgrowne which he hath seene but once, and that sixteen yeares since'. It would be hard enough to do on Salisbury Plain, let alone Guiana. But if Keymis *did* succeed, and brought home half a ton of 'that former oare', then Ralegh should have his liberty. Their Lordships appear to have ignored this request, at least for the time being.

Ralegh wrote to Secretary Winwood, enclosing copies of some of his plans for Guiana, and also taking the opportunity of once more proclaiming his innocence. Prince Henry, the Queen, and the Queen's brother, the King of Denmark, were all convinced, he said. 'The wife, the brother, and the son of a king do not use to sue for men suspect.' It was a good point, though it was probably tiresome for King James to hear it made once again, but Ralegh went on to suggest to Winwood that if King James had known him better, much embarrassment and misunderstanding would have been avoided. The trouble, Ralegh said, was that two or three of His Majesty's Privy Council knew him all too well.

> For had his Majesty known me, I had never been here where I now am; or had I known his Majestie, they had never been so long there where they now are. His Majestie not knowing of me, hath been my ruine; and His Majestie misknowing of them, hath been the ruine of a goodly part of his estate. [After which sly jabs at some members of the Privy Council, Ralegh came to the point] To die for the King, and not by the King, is all the ambition I have in the world.

In other words, let me go to Guiana.

Ralegh's constant pressure began, at last, to have an effect. By now King James must have been heartily sick of the very sound of Ralegh's name. Since his earliest days in the Tower, and through all the years of imprisonment, Ralegh had never ceased bombarding James with unwanted advice, requests, admonishments, and lectures – on Guiana, on Sherborne, on freedom, on politics, on Parliament, on the liberty of the subject, on the marriage of the Royal children, and, most of all, on his innocence. To let Ralegh out of the Tower would be like ridding oneself of the most persistent and objectionable type of bore.

There were also some other, less subjective, reasons for releasing Ralegh. His presence at large would remind the King of Spain that the King of England and Scotland was still an independent and powerful sovereign. Winwood, the new favourite Villiers, and the anti-Spanish faction could think of no sharper rebuff to the Earl of Somerset and the pro-Spanish party than to set loose once more 'Guateral' the man the Spaniards dreaded more than anyone else except Sir Francis Drake himself. Besides, Ralegh might actually find the

Map of South America, showing Guiana at the top, and the Straits of Magellan, bottom. Engraving from L. Hulsius, a German edition of the discovery of Guiana, 1599

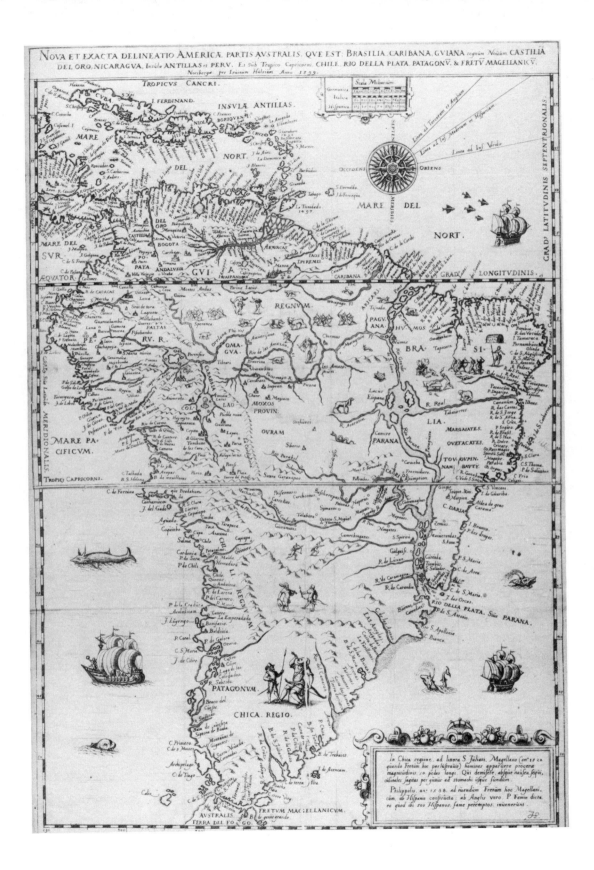

gold-mines of Guiana. King James was undergoing yet another financial crisis and yet another tussle with an unco-operative House of Commons. Any addition to the exchequer would be most welcome. If Ralegh did bring back Guianan gold, then the King would be the richer by his share of it. If not, then Ralegh would be exposed as a liar and a knave, and the King would be no worse off.

Even so, it is likely that Ralegh still had to lubricate the last lock on his cell-door himself to gain release. He very probably did bribe Sir William St John and Sir Edward Villiers, the favourite's half-brother, with £750 each to persuade 'Steenie' to intercede with King James on his behalf. But it worked. On 17th March 1616, Ralegh wrote to Villiers, 'You have, by your mediation, put me again into the world.' Two days later, the Privy Council reminded him that the King had graciously allowed him to go abroad with a keeper and to prepare for his intended journey, and admonished him that he was not to go to Court or attend any public function without the King's permission.

He was not wholly a free man; he still had to be accompanied by a keeper. But at least he could leave the Tower, after being a prisoner for nearly thirteen years. On 27th March Chamberlain wrote to Carleton that Ralegh was 'freed out of the Tower last week and goes up and down seeing sights and places built or bettered since his imprisonment'. He must have seen the New Exchange, built by Cecil close to Durham House, and the new Banqueting Hall in Whitehall, replacing the old Elizabethan building, the scene of many social functions attended by Ralegh and the old Queen, which had been pulled down in 1606. He must have visited Westminster Abbey and seen there the memorials to his old comrades-in-arms, Sir John Norris and Sir Francis Vere. He must also have seen the elaborately-carved canopy over the inscription: 'Together on the throne and in the grave, here sleep the sisters Elizabeth and Mary, in hope of the Resurrection.'

Ralegh must himself have attracted attention as he walked along stiffly, with the help of a stick. He was in his sixties, grey-haired, short of breath. He had suffered a stroke shortly before his release. He was stooped and bent from ague and rheumatism. He had bad legs and bad lungs. His face was aged and lined, but there would be still some quality in it, some flash in the eyes, which would make passers-by stop in their stride and look after him, with a question on their lips, 'Could that be . . . ?'

In an arrangement typical of King James, Ralegh was free and yet not quite free. He was not completely at liberty to come and go as he wished until 30th January 1617, when King James signed a warrant 'fully and wholly enlarging him'. Meanwhile, he probably stayed at Lady Ralegh's house in Broad Street. Within a few days of his release he paid Phineas Pett £500 on account for a new ship, to be called the *Destiny*, and began to make plans for his expedition. Ralegh had not entirely given up all thoughts of colonizing – he would never do that – but this was to be a venture in search of gold.

The spectre of Sir Walter Ralegh sailing the high seas in search of gold, *Spanish* gold, naturally horrified the Spaniards. However Ralegh might wrap up his purposes in excuses, the Spaniards would never believe that he was engaged in anything else but a plain piratical assault upon their possessions. At that time the King of Spain was represented in London by

Count Gondomar, attributed to A. Blyenberch. Gondomar was the Spanish Ambassador at the court of James I, and Ralegh's formidable enemy

a particularly able ambassador, Don Diego Sarmiento de Acuna, better known by his later title of Count Gondomar. Gondomar was Ralegh's formidable enemy. He may just possibly have been related to the Sarmiento who had been Ralegh's prisoner years before, and so bore Ralegh a family grudge; but it is much more likely that he hated and feared Ralegh simply because he regarded him as a very dangerous threat to Spanish interests.

Gondomar was a courtier, a scholar, a collector of *objets d'art*, an intriguer, an intellectual, a brilliant conversationalist and a surpassingly fine diplomat. He could joke with King James, make up the dog Latin phrases James loved to exchange, flatter James's scholarship, play upon him as on an instrument. In time Gondomar established an extraordinary mental ascendancy over King James, and he used his influence to try to steer James away from his support of the French, Dutch and German Protestant princes. He was a most capable politician and he took advantage of every shift in the European political scene. He advocated especially keenly a marriage between Prince Charles and the Spanish Infanta. The match had at least one powerful incentive for King James. Spain offered a dowry of £600,000.

Gondomar exerted himself to stop Ralegh's expedition. He first offered Ralegh a safe conduct to the mine. If gold was really all Ralegh wanted, then he could dig for it to his heart's content, under Spanish protection, and return with whatever he had mined. But Ralegh refused. He knew Spanish 'protection' of old. To be protected by Spain often meant having one's throat cut. Even King James jibbed at the notion of a Spanish escort. It would concede the Spaniards' claim that they were the rightful owners of Guiana. Ralegh maintained that Guiana was English by right of his former occupation, and that it was the Spaniards who were intruding upon English soil. Quite possibly King James also believed this.

King James would have taken Ralegh's side with much more conviction had Ralegh returned with enough gold. Sir Francis Bacon related a conversation with Ralegh at this time, in which Ralegh was asked if he would take prizes if he could do it 'handsomely'. Ralegh replied that he certainly would; if he could light upon the Plate Fleet, people would think him mad not to seize it. Bacon said that that would make Ralegh a pirate. Ralegh is supposed to have replied, 'Did you hear of any that was counted a pirate for taking millions?' It is unlikely that even Ralegh would ever have spoken so indiscreetly to Bacon, who was Winwood's political opponent, but the anecdote makes a valid point. Gold was the key. Ralegh would be forgiven anything, could he bring home enough of it. As a matter of interest, the Plate Fleet in 1618 was worth £2,545,454. Had Ralegh brought home even a fraction of that, he would never have gone to the scaffold.

Gondomar could not stop Ralegh going, but he made it virtually impossible for him to succeed. He persuaded King James to promise that if Ralegh damaged Spanish property or subjects he would be delivered up to the Spanish authorities in Madrid for punishment – which, of course, would mean execution. King James demanded to know the number and size of Ralegh's ships, their armament, the ports he intended to call at, and the dates – in short, all Ralegh's plans, to the last detail. King James then gave this information to Gondomar, who passed it on to Madrid.

Ralegh knew of this, but was not dismayed. His cousin Carew wrote to Sir Thomas Roe, who was by then ambassador to the Great Mogul in India, 'The alarm of his journey is flown into Spain, and, as he tells me, sea forces are prepared to lie for him, but he is nothing appalled with the report, for he will be a good fleet and well manned.' Ralegh said he was as confident of finding Guiana gold as he was 'of not missing his way from his dining-room to his bed-chamber'.

King James refused to pardon Ralegh, whose commission in August 1616 was sealed with the Privy Seal, not the Great Seal. The King himself scratched out the customary words to the addressee 'trusty and well-beloved'. Ralegh was 'under the peril of the law', and investors had to be reassured that he was licensed to carry the King's subjects to South America. The King reserved a fifth part of the gold, silver, pearls and precious stones to himself, but he constituted Ralegh 'sole commander, to punish, pardon, and rule according to such orders as he shall establish in cases capital, criminal, and civil, and to exercise martial law in as ample a manner as our lieutenant-general by sea or land'. Thus, paradoxically, a man convicted of high treason against the King now became the King's lieutenant-general. Ralegh could pardon others, though he was unpardoned himself. He had power of life and death over others, though lying under sentence of death himself.

King James could have pardoned Ralegh (and Bacon as Lord Chancellor actually argued that a commission from the Crown implicity carried a pardon) but, according to the Declaration published after Ralegh's execution (written by Bacon), the King, 'the better to contain Sir Walter Ralegh, and to hold him upon his good behaviour, denied, though much sued unto for the same, to grant him pardon for his former treasons'. The shabby little excuse, and the cat-and-mouse behaviour, were both very typical of James.

Gondomar's manipulation of King James resulted in an impossible situation for Ralegh. He was to be sent with an ostentatiously armed force into disputed territory, where the political atmosphere was known to be highly charged. The target gold-mine might, as Keymis believed and reported, be some distance away from any Spanish settlement. But the Spaniards would be waiting for Ralegh. They would know where and when he was coming. They would certainly resist his approach and any attempt to pass. And yet, if a single Spaniard was hurt or a single item of Spanish property damaged, then Ralegh's life was forfeit.

Spain was not the only European country anxious to know of Ralegh's intentions, nor had King Christian of Denmark been the only ruler who had ever considered using Ralegh at sea. Ralegh's name was always enough to set the diplomatic pigeons fluttering, as though a great cat had got amongst them. The Doge of Venice always wished to be kept informed about Ralegh, and the Venetian ambassador constantly reported on his doings. The Duke of Savoy, at war with Spain, sent his ambassador Count Scarnafassi to have conversations with Winwood and Ralegh over a proposition that Ralegh should lead a squadron of English, Dutch and Huguenot ships against the port of Genoa. Ralegh might possibly have agreed to carry out an attack on such a rich city but the project came to nothing. King James was by then enthusiastic over the Spanish marriage and did not want to offend Spain. He preferred to send Ralegh to Guiana. He also seems to have doubted that Ralegh would give him his share of Genoese booty.

Cardinal Richelieu thought Ralegh a 'great sailor but a bad captain'. He was concerned that Ralegh might lead a raiding squadron of Huguenot ships against St Valéry and other French ports. Yet another ambassador, the French Comte des Marêts, came to London to find out Ralegh's intentions. In March 1617 he visited the *Destiny*, fitting out in the Thames, to sound Ralegh's views. He also sympathized with Ralegh over the King's recent gift of Sherborne to Sir John Digby, the English ambassador to the Spanish court. Ralegh, of course, had no offensive plans in French waters. Neither did he wish to accept any offered French commissions. He had dealings with one Frenchman, Captain Faige, who actually sailed with Ralegh from the Thames to Plymouth. Ralegh appears to have tried to reach some agreement to use French troops and ships in Guiana. They might possibly prevent direct confrontations with the Spaniards. At one time he had hopes of a licence to bring his ships and treasure into a French port on his return from Guiana. But the hopes came to nothing and these plans, like the earlier arrangements, were soon made known to the Spaniards through an untrustworthy associate. Ralegh was often unfortunate in his choice of partners.

His forthcoming voyage was a gift to the gossips. His reputation, still potent even after so many years, his sudden and somewhat mysterious release from the Tower, that fleet of armed ships unmistakably fitting out in the Thames, the choice of their possible destinations, all were food for rumour. People said he would turn pirate. They said he would never return to England. They said he would go to the French Court, or to Venice, or to Virginia. King James and his Court, Winwood and the Privy Council, foreign rulers and their embassies – anybody who had political or personal ends to further by speculating about Ralegh was free to do so, and they did so. The web of innuendo and rumour and intrigue is impossible to disentangle now. Everyone had his say about Ralegh and his voyage, everyone left his commitment open – everybody except Ralegh himself, who was never given the benefit of any doubt and who was bound to keep an impossible bargain. But it is very doubtful if the old man ever fully realized how his name was being exploited.

The 'great ship' *Destiny* was launched on 16th December 1616. Phineas Pett delivered her, as he said, 'on float and in good order and fashion' but he later complained that he lost £700 on her and was never compensated for his loss. In the circumstances, Phineas Pett was lucky to have received what he already had on account. America had fallen out of favour with speculators, and there was no great rush to invest in Ralegh's expedition. The total investment was nearly £30,000 of which Ralegh himself raised about a third. To do it, he had to sell or pledge almost everything he and his family had; when he left London, he said, he had only a hundred pieces, of which he gave Bess forty-five and took fifty-five with him. He called in £3,000 of a £5,000 family loan to the Countess of Bedford. Lady Ralegh sold a house and estate in Mitcham to Mr Thomas Plumer, Member of Parliament for Hertfordshire, for £2,500. The Crown contributed £175 in tonnage money under an Act of Parliament passed for the encouragement of ship-building. Somehow the money was

Phineas Pett, First Master of the Shipwright's Company. He built the *Destiny* in 1616, in which Ralegh sailed to Guiana on the voyage of 1617. He said he was never paid for the *Destiny*

raised. Friends and relatives rallied round. The Earl of Pembroke invested some money. So did Lady Ralegh's cousin the Earl of Huntingdon, who also presented a pair of cannons to be fitted in the *Destiny*. Some of the gentlemen volunteers in the voyage subscribed up to £50 each. It was impolitic for Queen Anne to put up any money, but she sent her good wishes, and would have liked to visit the *Destiny* if she had been permitted to.

By mid-March 1617 Ralegh was ready and anxious to get under way. At any moment Gondomar might persuade James to cancel the expedition. For a voyage ostensibly of geological research, Ralegh had a large and well-armed force. On 15th March, when his fleet was surveyed by officers appointed by the Lord High Admiral, he had the *Destiny*, of 440 tons, 36 guns, with himself as General, his son Wat as Captain, Robert Burwick as Master, 100 sailors, 20 watermen, 80 gentlemen, the rest servants and labourers; the *Star* (or *Jason*), 240 tons, Captain John Pennington, 25 guns; the *Encounter*, 160 tons, Captain Edward Hastings, 17 guns; the *John and Francis* (or *Thunder*), 150 tons, Sir William St Leger, 20 guns; the *Flying Joan*, 120 tons, Captain John Chidley, 14 guns; the *Husband* (or *Southampton*), 80 tons, Captain John Bayley, six guns; and the 25-ton pinnace *Page*, Captain James Barker, armed with three brass robinets.

As so often on past ventures, the men who went with Ralegh were his kinsmen, or friends of the family. His son commanded the *Destiny*; his nephew George Ralegh was also on board, with his cousin William Herbert, a relative of the Earl of Pembroke; Edward Hastings, in the *Encounter*, was a relative of the Earl of Huntingdon. Sir William St Leger was the son of Sir Warham, who served with Ralegh years before in Ireland. Captain North, brother of Lord North, was also on the expedition.

But many of the rest were as Ralegh himself described them, 'the very scum of the world, drunkards, blasphemers, and such others as their fathers, brothers, and friends thought it an exceeding good gain to be discharged of, with the hazard of some thirty, forty or fifty pounds'. Some were so disgracefully behaved they were discharged even before sailing. Of them one observer commented that 'it will cause the King to be at some charge in buying halters to save them from drowning'.

Ralegh's London force was 1,215 tons of shipping, 121 guns, and 431 men – including gentlemen, soldiers, sailors, watermen, servants, labourers, and assayers – but, oddly for a mining expedition, there were apparently no miners on board.

Ralegh was desperately keen to make away, in Chamberlain's phrase, 'with all speed for fear of a countermand'. The *Destiny* dropped down the river to the Downs on 26th March. Ralegh rode overland to meet her at Dover on the 29th. 'I fear,' said Chamberlain, 'he doth but go (as children are wont to tell their tales) to seek his fortune.' But George Carew spoke for all those who loved Ralegh and who wished him well. 'God grant he may return deep loaded with Guianan gold ore!'

They were to meet more of Ralegh's ships at Plymouth, but troubles began long before they saw Plymouth Hoe. While still in the Thames, the *Southampton*'s anchor cable fouled the *Destiny*'s and John Bayley was offended when Ralegh ordered it to be cut. On passage Bayley married a girl in the Isle of Wight. Later he only consented to sail with the expedition on condition he could be the first to bring news home. It would have been better if Ralegh had refused; John Bayley's lies and trouble-making were to cause constant anxiety.

But Bayley was not the only one. Pennington in the *Star* reached the Isle of Wight and then could not pay for bread for his ship's company. He rode to London, where Lady Ralegh gave him letters of credit, to cash in Portsmouth. Ralegh had to sell some of his plate to victual Thomas Whitney's sailors in the *Encounter*.

At Plymouth, Ralegh found four more of his ships. Their captains were Sir John Ferne (for whom Ralegh had to raise £300 for victualling); Richard Wollaston, a part-time pirate, in the *Confidence*; and two old and trusted friends, Samuel King commanding a flyboat, and Laurence Keymis, in command of the *Convertine*. Keymis was now in his fifties. He was described on this voyage as tall and slim, with a cast in one eye, but obviously a gentleman. He at least was someone Ralegh felt he could rely on, whatever happened.

On 3rd May 1617, at Plymouth, Ralegh issued his Orders to be observed by the Commanders of the Fleet and Land Companies. They were models of good manners, sound seamanship, proven fighting tactics, and common sense. Divine service was to be held on board morning and evening. There was to be no swearing, stealing, gambling, smoking between decks, or eating or drinking between meals. There were instructions about firefighting, damage control, gun drill, station-keeping by day and by night, action to be taken on sighting a strange ship, and on signalling in emergency. No man was to strike a superior officer or rape an Indian woman, on pain of death. The hands were not to eat unsalted meat, or unidentified fruit, and were not to swim in rivers, except where the Indians swam, for fear of alligators. The tone of Ralegh's Orders is moral, judicious, stern, imbued with a deep concern for the welfare of the men entrusted to his care.

On 12th June Ralegh sailed from Plymouth with seven ships and three pinnaces. Outside he was joined by stragglers to bring his strength up to thirteen vessels, and nearly a thousand men. But by the 16th they had been driven back to Falmouth to shelter from a gale. There were continual quarrels and fighting on board the ships, and everybody hoped it would be quieter when at last they got properly to sea. Ralegh seemed to think he would be away for over a year, and landed a number of men, to save victuals. Later in the month, his fleet put to sea again, and again, on the 25th, they were forced to seek harbour, this time in Cork. One of the pinnaces was sunk in heavy seas off the Irish coast.

At Cork, Ralegh was fêted and feasted by all, old friends and old enemies alike. The Lords Barry and Roche came to see him. He flew hawks, bought a share in a copper-mine, borrowed £350 from Richard (now Lord) Boyle, who kept open house for him for weeks, gave him a thirty-two-gallon cask of whisky, and supplied his ships with oxen, beer, biscuits and iron ballast to the value of six hundred marks. In return, Ralegh said he would abandon any remaining claim he might have had on the estates he sold to Boyle (which were, in any case, now worth far more than they had been in Ralegh's day). He also helped Boyle in a law case against that old bugbear, Henry Pyne.

Bad weather kept Ralegh in Cork until August. He was criticized for this but, as he said, 'they must accuse the clouds, and not me, for our stay there, for I lost not a day of a good wind'. He sailed at last on the 19th, in 'a frank gale of wind', and stood to the southward – and to fresh trouble and controversy.

Off Cape St Vincent they chased four ships, and came up with them on 30th August. They proved to be four Frenchmen, loaded with fish and oil. John Bayley boarded them and took a seine fishing net, a pinnace, and several barrels of oil, saying that the Frenchmen and their cargoes were fair game for plunder, because they themselves had robbed from the Spaniards in the West Indies. Ralegh disagreed, and to Bayley's great indignation insisted on paying the Frenchmen sixty-one crowns for the goods taken; the French, he said, had as much right to plunder beyond the 'line' – which ran south of the Canaries and west of the Azores – as anybody else.

With a good wind behind them, they reached Lancerota in the Greater Canaries on 6th September. Ralegh only wanted to water and victual his ships there, but the island had just been raided by Barbary pirates and was still in a state of fear. The islanders mistook Ralegh's ships for the 'Turks', and when a party went ashore, it was attacked and one man was killed. After much prevarication, the Governor of the island promised food and water, but Ralegh's landing-party was ambushed again and two more men were killed. Some of Ralegh's captains called for revenge, but Ralegh restrained them. He knew that reprisals would be taken against the captain of an English ship then in the harbour. This was too much for John Bayley, who deserted the expedition and went back to England, where he spread the libels that Ralegh was behaving disgracefully, and was about to turn pirate. At Lancerota, and elsewhere, Ralegh made every effort to avoid just such an accusation, by keeping the peace, by avoiding damage to property, and by paying in full for anything he used (even, once, paying eight ducats for six ducats' worth of fish). The English captain at Lancerota, a Mr Reeks of Ratcliffe, eventually reached home early the next year and testified to Ralegh's good conduct. But it was too late. The harm had been done. The word had been eagerly accepted, in London and in Madrid, that Ralegh had turned pirate. Gondomar complained again, and was again reassured that Ralegh would be properly dealt with. In October Sir Thomas Lake wrote to tell him that he had heard from Sir Thomas Erskine, Captain of His Majesty's Guard, that the King was 'very disposed and determined against Ralegh, and will join the King of Spain in ruining him, but he wishes this resolution to be kept secret for some little while, in order that, in the interim, he may keep an eye on the disposition of some of the people here.' In December 1618 John Bayley was completely discredited and proved to be a liar, but not in time to save Ralegh's name. In any case, probably nothing on earth could have changed James's mind about Ralegh.

There was a shortage of water at Lancerota, and Ralegh moved his fleet on to Gomera, an island in the Lesser Canaries. Here, too, there was initial suspicion, but the Governor was persuaded to provide food and water. Ralegh sent a present of gloves to the Governor's wife, who was an Englishwoman of the Stafford family. Charmed, she replied with fruit, sugar and rusks. Not to be outdone, Ralegh sent more gifts, of amber, ambergris, rose-water, an excellent cut-work ruff, and a picture of Mary Magdalene. The Governor's wife sent back various fruits, live hens, and fresh bread. The Governor gave Ralegh a letter for

News of Ralegh's expedition to Guiana was published in London before he returned

NEVVES
Of Sr. VValter Rauleigh.

a. 607.

tobt. g

6d

c. 3739.

WITH
The true Description of GVIANA:

As also a Relation of the excellent Gouernment, and much hope of the prosperity of the Voyage.

Sent from a Gentleman of his Fleet, to a most especiall Friend of his in London.

From the Riuer of Caliana, on the Coast of Guiana, Nouemb. 17. 1617.

LONDON,
Printed for H. G. and are to be sold by I. Wright, at the signe of the
Bible without New-gate. 1618.

Gondomar vouching for his good behaviour during his visit.

The charming exchange of civilities at Gomera was almost the only pleasant episode in a voyage which was becoming ever more sad and dark. The fleet battled through gales and heavy seas to the Isle of Bravo in the Cape Verde Islands, taking six weeks instead of a normal fortnight. Many of the ship's company fell sick, probably of scurvy. Forty-two men died in the *Destiny* alone, including many men of chief importance to the expedition: Mr Fowler, the principal refiner, Mr W. Steed, the provost marshal, Captain Piggot the best land-general, Mr Moon, governor of the Burmudas, Mr Newhall, the master surgeon, and Mr John Talbot, a very old friend of Ralegh's, 'who had lived with me eleven years in the Tower, an excellent general scholar, and a faithful true man as lived'. One of Ralegh's most endearing qualities was his ability to write the most touching epitaphs for his friends. This one to John Talbot, from the *Journal* of the voyage Ralegh kept from 19th August onwards, ranks with anything in his *History*.

Ralegh's fleet sailed from Bravo on 3rd October, on the last stretch to Guiana, and now even the elements began to combine to cast omens of disaster. There were days of sweltering calm, and then two days of great darkness. The crews had to light candles to steer by, at midday. The sea was copper-coloured, and the sun went down behind a horizon overcast with dark clouds, arched and overshot with gloomy discolorations. By night, St Elmo's ghostly fire burned on the masts and yards. On one day, they saw two water-spouts arising from the sea, and no less than fifteen rainbows, one of them describing a perfect whole circle in the sky. Then it rained heavily. The morning rainbow, Ralegh noted in his Journal, did not produce a fair day as in England. They caught the rain in hogsheads and drank it – 'all quenched their thirst with great cans of this bitter draught.'

Ralegh himself fell sick on the last day of October. 'Rising out of bed, being in a great sweat, by reason of a sudden gust and much clamour in the ship before they could get down the sails', Ralegh went up on deck and caught a cold, which soon became a burning fever. For twenty days, he ate nothing 'but now and then a stewed prune'. He drank every hour, day and night, and was sweating so much he had to change his shirt three times a day and three times a night. The oranges and other fruit given him by the Governor's lady at Gomera saved his life. He had carefully preserved them in sand, 'to his great refreshment', and without them he could not have lived. His usual servants were themselves sick (his valet Crab, and his personal cook Francis died) but he was looked after by his pages.

He was still sick in his bunk when his fleet arrived off the mouth of the Wyapoco on 11th November. He sent a boat inshore for the local *cacique*, his old servant Leonard the Indian, who had been in England for three or four years with him. But Leonard was up-country and could not be traced, and so the fleet sailed northwards to Caliana (Cayenne), where the *cacique* Harry was also Ralegh's friend.

Here, Ralegh and his men began to recover after their foul voyage. They buried their dead, who now included the sergeant-major Mr Hart, and Edward Hastings (who, Ralegh said, would have died even at home 'for both his liver, spleen, and brains were rotten'). The men recovered from their fevers, cleaned out the ships, repaired the pinnaces, mended torn sails and damaged rigging, filled the water-casks, collected fresh fruit and meat, and built a forge on shore to repair metal gear and tackle.

Ralegh himself was joyfully welcomed by Harry and his Indians, some of whom remembered his name from 1595. They set up a tent for him on the beach, and brought him cassava bread, roasted mullet, plantains, pistachio nuts and pineapples. After a day or two's rest Ralegh ventured to try some of the pineapple, and, with a little armadillo meat and pork, he began to recover his strength. It was balm to his spirit to be so royally received by the Indians. 'To tell you I might be here King of the Indians were a vanity; but my name hath still lived among them,' he wrote gratefully and proudly to Lady Ralegh, from Cayenne, on 14th November. 'Here they feed me with fresh meat, and all that the country yields; all offer to obey me.'

The rest of the letter was not quite so cheerful in tone.

> Sweetheart, [he began] I can yet write unto you but with a weak hand, for I have suffered the most violent calenture, for fifteen days, that ever man did, and lived: but God that gave me a strong heart in all my adversities, hath also now strengthened it in the hell-fire of heat.

Their son Wat 'had never so good health, having no distemper, in all the heat under the Line'. But there was still a long list of casualties. Ralegh was not going to write to Lord Carew or Winwood just yet, 'for I can write of nought but miseries yet.'

Ralegh's letter was taken home by one of his captains, Peter Alley, whom Ralegh sent back to England because he was suffering from what Ralegh called 'infirmitie of his head', probably vertigo. He took passage in a Dutch ship and eventually reached Portsmouth in February 1618. He also took with him an account of the expedition so far, written by one of the gentleman adventurers, which painted a generally optimistic and complimentary picture both of Ralegh and of Guiana. Called 'Newes of Sr. Walter Rauleigh, with the true Description of Guiana, from the River of Caliana, November 17. 1617', it was published in London as a pamphlet late in 1618 – too late to counteract the personal effect of the vertiginous Alley who presented himself as a doleful and dismal victim of Ralegh's expedition. So, once again, as in the case of John Bayley, the bad account of Ralegh's conduct outpaced and outweighed the good.

After about three weeks, the health of most of Ralegh's men had recovered enough for them to go on. On 4th December the fleet sailed north and west to the Triangle Islands, off the Orinoco mouth. From here, the expedition to the gold-mine would be launched.

21. Return to Eldorado

HAD RALEGH himself commanded the expedition up-river, matters might have turned out very differently. But he was too ill to go, and in any case, he was required to stay with the ships at the Orinoco entrance. There were Indian rumours of a Spanish fleet off the coast. Ralegh's men were afraid of Spanish reprisals. Whoever they left behind must be absolutely trustworthy. Everyone knew that Ralegh would never desert them. Piggot, who should have commanded on land, was dead. St Leger, who was next in line, was still sick and was not expected to recover. So command was given to Laurence Keymis.

Keymis was by no means a rough old sea-dog, a sturdy but uneducated mariner. He was a scholar of Balliol, a composer of accomplished Latin verses, a writer of a fair and readable prose. To call him, as another member of the expedition, Captain Parker, did later, 'false to all men', 'a hateful fellow', 'a mere Machiavel', was cruelly unjust. Keymis loved and served Ralegh for many years and with all his heart. Unfortunately, he was one of those fated men who with the best of intentions bring bad luck to their friends. His evidence at Ralegh's trial was, to put it charitably, unhelpful. His insistence that he knew where there was a gold-mine in Guiana had sustained, but badly misled, Ralegh through all those years in the Tower. When the critical moment came, Keymis disobeyed his orders, and brought ruin upon Ralegh and upon himself.

There were, apparently, *two* gold-mines in Guiana and nobody was ever quite sure which of the two Ralegh or Keymis was talking about at any one time. The first, Ralegh believed, was where he had found some gold-bearing stones in 1595, about three or four miles away from the site of the town of San Thomé in 1618, near a mountain called Iconuri. The second mine, Keymis believed, was some twenty miles downstream and to the east of the first, near a mountain called Aio; Putjima had talked of it in 1595, and Keymis had heard of it again in 1596. Ralegh had only discussed one mine when he was in England; it was hard enough to convince people of the existence of one, and he did not wish to confuse the situation by talking of two. But he certainly had the Mount Aio mine in mind when he wrote out his orders for Keymis.

Keymis was to take his captains and companies of English to the west of Mount Aio, which was about three miles from the mine. He was to place his forces between the mine and the Spanish town (if there was a town there). This was a purely defensive measure while Keymis made 'trial what depth and breadth the mine holds, and whether or no it answer our hopes'. If the mine was found to be 'royal', and the Spaniards attacked, then the sergeant-major had permission to repel them and drive them off as far as he could.

But if the mine was not so rich as to be worth defending, then Keymis was to bring back 'but a basket or two', just enough to satisfy the King that the mine was not imaginary. Ralegh, after all, had never said how rich the mine was, only that there was a mine there.

Ralegh stressed the need for Keymis to take care. He told him to be well advised how he landed, if the passage was defended, because he knew (a few gentlemen excepted) 'what scum of men' Keymis had. He reminded Keymis that George Ralegh, who was in charge of the land forces, was only a young man and he, Ralegh, therefore relied greatly upon Keymis's judgment. Ralegh himself had to stay with the ships, as he said, because he was sick and because the galleons of Spain were expected daily. 'Let me hear from you as soon as you can,' Ralegh said. 'You shall find me at Puncto Gallo, dead or alive; and if you find not my ships there, yet you shall find their ashes; for I will fire with the galleons if it come to extremity, but run away I will never.'

With that firm pledge, Keymis embarked with 250 soldiers and 150 sailors on 10th December in five of the shallowest draught vessels: the *Encounter*, commanded by Whitney, the *Confidence*, commanded by Wollaston, two flyboats commanded by Samuel King and Robert Smith, and a carvil commanded by Captain Hall. Wat Ralegh was one of the company commanders as were Captain Charles Parker, and Captain Roger North.

While Keymis and his party were away, Ralegh patrolled off Punto Gallo, the south-west tip of Trinidad, watching for the expected Spanish fleet. He visited the great lake of pitch he had noticed on his previous voyage. He collected balsams and other herbs. He tried to trade with the Spaniards, but only succeeded in having two of his men shot by snipers. Thereafter he ignored the desultory Spanish sniping from on shore, while he waited for news of Keymis. He heard disquieting rumours from Indians coming down to the coast in their canoes. It seemed there had been some trouble up river. There were tales of some sort of affray between the English and the Spanish at San Thomé. At last, on 13th February, significantly the day on which his *Journal* entries stopped abruptly, Ralegh had a letter from Keymis, dated 7th January. Every word in it was like a stab in Ralegh's heart. It was the worst of all possible news. Keymis had occupied San Thomé. There had been some skirmishing in which English and Spanish had been killed. Young Wat Ralegh was dead. It was the end of all hopes for Ralegh. His beloved son was dead, and his own life would be forfeit when he returned to England.

As he read that letter, Ralegh must have realized bitterly that, whatever arguments had been against it, he should have led the expedition himself. He had always justified his expedition on the grounds that the territory legally belonged to the King of England; that the gold-mine was some way from any Spanish settlement; and that action against the Spaniards would only be taken as a last resort, in self-defence. Finally, there was the argument that if there were any Spanish casualties, gold in sufficient quantities would excuse them.

But Keymis had destroyed all Ralegh's lines of defence. Under his leadership the expedition had gone catastrophically, irretrievably, wrong. He had obviously heard from Indians that some of the Spanish in San Thomé were favourably disposed towards the English and were anxious to trade with them. Keymis probably remembered Sir Thomas Roe's reports

Manoa, the fabulous city of El Dorado, which Ralegh spent so much time, money and effort in trying to reach. Engraving from L. Hulsius, 1599

of some years before, that the Spanish were unpopular along the Orinoco, and he may have hoped for an Indian rising in his favour. He disobeyed his instructions, and instead of sending a party overland to Mount Aio he had, on 2nd January, landed troops only a few miles down-river of San Thomé. But the military commander in the town, Don Diego Palomeque de Acuna (possibly a relative of Gondomar's) was determined to oppose any advance by the English. He had been supplied with full details of Ralegh's strength and intentions – the very information Ralegh had been forced to give the King, passed from Gondomar to Madrid. When Keymis, somewhat provocatively, sent his three ships (Whitney and Wollaston had not yet arrived) up-river to anchor off the town that evening, Palomeque's troops fired on them. It was clear that, if Keymis had ever hoped for an easy entry into San Thomé, he was to be disappointed.

Much worse was to follow. Possibly, as Ralegh later claimed, the English soldiers ashore were much closer to San Thomé than Keymis realized. Possibly Keymis really had intended to stay peaceably where he was for the night and then, in the morning, lead his party carefully around the town on its way to the mine. Whatever the English intentions, their presence so

Warring Indians in Guiana; engraving from L. Hulsius, a German edition of the discovery of Guiana, 1599

close to the town was regarded by the Spaniards as a threat. Later that night, the English camp was ambushed by a Spanish force of about forty soldiers led by one Geronimo de Gradas, all shouting 'English dogs!'

In the darkness and confusion, the surprised English were close to panic and they were only rallied by the determined action of their officers, amongst whom young Wat Ralegh was outstanding. He may have been rash and hot-tempered – the ungenerous Captain Parker called his behaviour 'unadvised daringness' – but he showed the most daring leadership in the wild and scrappy fighting which followed the Spanish attack. Crying 'Come on my hearts! This is the mine you must expect! They that look for any other are fools!', he led a counter-attack which drove the Spaniards back to the outskirts of the town, where Palomeque and the main body of Spanish troops were waiting.

Now thoroughly roused, the English followed Wat Ralegh into the streets of San Thomé and scattered Palomeque and his troops. It was here that Wat was mortally wounded. But though dying, he still encouraged his men, shouting to them, 'Go on, go on!' To himself he added, 'The Lord have mercy upon me, and prosper your enterprise.'

Indians out hunting the armadillo, and other game. Engraving from L. Hulsius, a German edition of the discovery of Guiana, 1599

Keymis was now hopelessly committed. He could do nothing but go on and take the town. The English stormed the monastery of St Francis, where some of the garrison had taken refuge, but most of the Spaniards retreated to the fortified island of Seiba, in the Orinoco channel.

When the sun came up, the English counted four casualties, besides Wat Ralegh. They buried Wat and Captain Cosmor before the altar of the church of St Thomas. Whitney and Wollaston arrived belatedly on the day of the funeral. The Spaniards, too, had losses, including Palomeque himself.

Keymis had San Thomé, and he could now search for the mine. For more than twenty years he had been saying that there was a gold-mine and that he knew where it was. This was his chance to prove it. But Keymis did not know where the mine was, nor even what to do next. He waited for several days, evidently turning over in his mind what he should say, phrasing and rephrasing a letter to Ralegh, before sending it off. He referred to Wat's 'extraordinary valour and forwardness' and his 'vigour of mind'. He said that the best houses in San Thomé were refiners' houses, but he had not seen one piece of coin, or bullion, neither gold nor silver. Keymis sent his letter by hand of Peter Andrews, with an Indian guide. He also sent a 'parcel of scattered papers' (leaving, he said, a cart-load behind), a roll of tobacco, a tortoise, and some oranges and limes. The papers included one dated 17th March 1617, before Ralegh left the Thames; it was from the King of Spain and gave full details of Ralegh's intended voyage.

Keymis tried to excuse himself by saying that the town of San Thomé had been moved some twenty miles downstream of the point where he thought it was. He had therefore stumbled upon it accidentally in the dark, while searching for Mount Aio. Ralegh believed, or seemed to believe, this explanation and repeated it, so that he too was later accused of being a liar.

At last, Keymis took a party in two boats to look for the mine, which he said was only eight miles off. But they were fired on from Seiba, and lost nine men killed or wounded. They turned back, Keymis afterwards saying that the fire was from the mainland and showed that the Spanish were in too great a strength to allow him to land and search for the mine.

Keymis and George Ralegh then went on an extended exploration up-river. They were away for about three weeks and probably went about 150 miles, although the Spaniards said 300. While they were away, the men left behind were subjected to constant harassment and sniping attacks by the Spaniards. When Keymis returned, he found that his men had burned San Thomé down.

So far, Keymis had made no attempt to find the mine near Mount Aio. Now, he half-heartedly suggested that there was another way to the mine, and proposed an expedition overland to find it. But Keymis had lost all credibility as a leader. If this mine really was at Mount Aio some twenty miles downstream of San Thomé, then why, his men asked with some justification, had Keymis just spent so much time ostensibly searching for the mine many miles upstream? Weary, disheartened, and abusing Keymis, the English left San Thomé on 1st February, taking with them loot estimated at 40,000 *reals*, including church ornaments, two gold ingots intended for the King of Spain, and a large amount of tobacco. Keymis had lost over half of his men to Spanish and Indian attacks. Only 150 of his original 400 survived to rejoin Ralegh on the coast on 2nd March.

Ralegh had always been a magnanimous man, and a generous and considerate commander, prepared to shoulder responsibility and refrain from reproaching a subordinate. But grief and bitterness at Keymis's conduct overwhelmed him. The more he heard of Keymis's behaviour on the expedition, the more appalled he was. If Keymis had positively set out to ruin him, he could not have done it better.

In his remorse and desperation, Keymis was driven to advance some astonishing excuses. He said the country round about the mine had steep hills and thick woods, and was almost impassable. He said they would not have been able to take with them enough food to sustain them. The Spaniards were there in such force that they could not have penetrated to the mine without great loss. Keymis had been afraid that Ralegh was dead, either of sickness, or of grief on hearing of Wat's death. To find the mine then, would only mean disclosing its whereabouts to the Spaniards.

Ralegh rejected these excuses out of hand. He said that a blind man could have found his way to the mine from the directions that Keymis himself had given. He did not believe that Keymis had had any care for the men he might have lost in the woods. As for Ralegh himself, as he wrote to Winwood, he told Keymis 'that seeing my son was lost, I cared not if he had lost an hundred more in opening the mine, so my credit had been saved'. Ralegh said that Keymis had gone his own way and disobeyed Ralegh. He hoped Keymis would be able to satisfy the King and the Privy Council. He could expect no justification or support from Ralegh.

With that Keymis 'seemed greatly discontent, and so he continued divers days'. Then he came to Ralegh's cabin and showed him a letter he had written to the Earl of Arundel. He asked Ralegh to accept it as his apology. Although the letter only set out the same arguments and excuses as before, the Ralegh of former days would have accepted the apology, embraced his friend and forgiven him. But now Ralegh merely told Keymis that he had undone him by his obstinacy. Ralegh refused to favour or colour in any sort Keymis's former folly. Keymis asked whether that was Ralegh's resolution. Ralegh said that it was. Keymis said, 'I know then, sir, what course to take.'

Keymis went back to his own cabin, and almost at once there was a pistol shot. Not suspecting anything, Ralegh sent up to know who had fired a pistol. Keymis himself replied, lying on his bed, that it was he; the pistol had been loaded for a long time. Ralegh was satisfied with that. But about half an hour later, Keymis's cabin boy went in and found Keymis lying on his bed, with a long knife through his heart. The bullet had only glanced off a rib, and Keymis had completed the suicide with a thrust under his left breast. 'Some puppies,' as Ralegh wrote, said that Keymis committed suicide because he had 'seduced so many gentlemen and others with an imaginary mine'. But Keymis was an imaginative man. He realized the magnitude of the disaster he had brought down on Ralegh's head. He cared for no man's opinion except Ralegh's, and without Ralegh's good opinion he could not go on living. Ralegh wrote no affectionate epitaph for Laurence Keymis.

Ralegh was all the more bitter against Keymis when he discovered from the captured Spanish documents Keymis had brought back that there genuinely were gold-mines in the area. Apparently, there was one only two hours' journey from San Thomé. It seemed that work had stopped temporarily because of troubles over labour shortages. Ralegh tentatively suggested a return to the Orinoco. But his captains would have none of it. Ralegh was not the force he had been. His authority had been seriously weakened by the fiasco up-river. His son's death, the failure of the expedition, and Keymis's suicide, all combined to extinguish some vital spirit in Ralegh. Discipline in his fleet began to crumble. One of his pages had already spread an absurd story that Ralegh kept 24,000 guineas in coin hidden in his cabin; there had been rumours of a wild plan to maroon Ralegh ashore in Trinidad and sail off with the money. Wollaston and Whitney deserted at Grenada, both going to lie in wait for Spanish ships homeward bound. They advised Ralegh to join them. They told him crudely (but truthfully) that if he returned to England and King James he was a dead man.

Discontent in the fleet came to a head at St Christopher's (St Kitts) in the Leeward Islands. Ralegh put the most dissident elements in a flyboat and sent them home under the command of his cousin William Herbert. Captain Roger North also left for England at about the same time. The fleet was disintegrating. Ralegh had lost control, and the plans he announced for the future became ever more widely divorced from reality; he would go to Newfoundland to clean and revictual, paying his way with the tobacco taken from San Thomé; he would return to the Orinoco, in spite of anything anybody said; he would lie in wait off Mexico for the homebound Plate Fleet; he would prey upon Spanish shipping and take his prizes home to French ports; he hinted that he had a French commission but nobody had ever seen it. The hard truth was that Ralegh had only one destination, and he knew it. His captains fled from him, as from a man who had a sign on him.

Ralegh wrote some letters at St Christopher's and sent them home with Roger North. In one to Sir Ralph Winwood, dated 21st March, Ralegh gave an account of the events leading up to the failure of the expedition, and the circumstances of Keymis's suicide. He was dismayed that the King had thought so little of him that he had given details of his voyage to the Spaniards; and he had a thought for his own future, 'What shall become of me now, I know not; I am unpardoned in England, and my poore estate consumed; and whether any other Prince or State will give me bread, I know not.' Ralegh implored Winwood to disregard anything said by the 'diverse other unworthy persons, good for nothing' who were coming home with Herbert. 'I beseech your Honor that this scumme of men may not be beleeved of me, who have taken more paine, and suffered more then the meanest rascall in the ship.'

But all Ralegh's pleas were quite wasted. Winwood had died very suddenly the previous October. Ralegh's letter was read by Winwood's far less sympathetic successor, Sir Robert Naunton.

Ralegh also wrote to Bess, on the following day.

I was loathe to write, because I knewe not how to comforte you; and, God knowes, I never knewe what sorrow meant till nowe. All that I can say to you is, that you must obey the will and providence of God; and remember, that the Queene's Majestie bare the losse of Prince Henry with a magnanimous harte, and the Lady Harrington of her onely sonne. Comfort your hart (deerest Besse), I shall sorrow for us bothe. I shall sorrow the lesse, because I have not longe to sorrowe, because not longe to live. I referr you to Mr Secretary Winwood's letter, who will give you a coppy of it, if you sende for it. Therein you shall know what hath passed. I have written that letter, for my braynes are broken, and it is a torment for mee to write, and espetially of misery. I have desired Mr Seacretary to give my Lord Carewe a coppy of his letter. I have clensed my shipp of sicke men, and sent them home. I hope God will send us somewhat ere wee returne. Comend mee to all at Loathbury. You shall heare from mee, if I live, from the Newefoundland; where I meane to make cleane my shipps and revittle; for I have tobacco enough to pay for it. The Lord blesse and comfort you, that you may bear patiently the death of your valiant sonne.

Ralegh's grief and bitterness then took charge of him again and in a long postscript he poured out his feelings about the things which had hurt him most deeply: Wat's death, Keymis's betrayal, the débâcle on the Orinoco, and the King's curious conduct.

My braynes are broken, [he ended] and I cannot write much. I live yet, and I have told you why. Whitney, for whome I sold my plate at Plymouth, and to whome I gave more creditt and countenance then all the captaines of my fleete, ran from mee at the Granadoes, and Woolaston with him; soe as I am nowe but five shipps, and one of those I have sent home – my fly-boate – and in her a rable of idle rascalls, which I knowe will not spare to wounde mee; but I care not. I am sure there is never a base slave in the fleete hath taken the paines and care that I have done; hath slept so little, and travilled so much. My frends will not beleive them; and for the rest I care not. Go in heaven blesse you and strengthen your hart.'

Perhaps Ralegh protested too much that he did not care what his enemies said of him. He did care. It was his fate to be betrayed by such as Whitney and Wollaston. Perhaps it was a lifelong weakness in Ralegh, and a symptom of his inner insecurity, that he was always upset by worthless accusations from worthless people, and went to great trouble to refute them, thus giving them undue importance; often he might have done better to have remained loftily silent.

The rest of Ralegh's captains left him at St Kitts and he set out for Newfoundland with the *Destiny* alone. But he never reached it. On passage he discovered that about a hundred of his crew (including some 'gentlemen', he noted) planned to seize the best English ship there on arrival, and take to piracy. Ralegh was forced to parley with the mutineers. They would not return to England, nor to Guiana. At last, they agreed to go to Ireland, if Ralegh would obtain their pardons. Ralegh was by this time sick of the pleurisy which had attacked him in the Tower, so that he could hardly hold a pen. He could barely see for lack of sleep, having stayed awake all night for fear of being surprised and captured by the mutineers.

The *Destiny* arrived at Kinsale in Ireland on 26th May. Three of Ralegh's ships, commanded by Ferne, Pennington and King, were already in the harbour. King was the only one still loyal to Ralegh. There was no welcome from the others, nor from Boyle or any of the Irish chieftains. There was no feasting, hawking or whisky this time. The story of Ralegh's failure and the burning of San Thomé, and the King's reaction, were known by all. Roger North had given King James a full account, and had tried to put as favourable a gloss as he could on it. But the harm was already done. Gondomar had had the story from Madrid. He had asked for an immediate audience with the King. Hardly waiting to be announced, he had burst into the King's presence, repeating the one accusing word, 'Pirates! Pirates! Pirates!' He reminded the King of his promise to punish Ralegh, and to send him to Madrid to be properly dealt with. The King was preoccupied with negotiations for the Spanish marriage,

Ralegh's son Wat, killed leading English troops in an attack on San Thomé. When he heard the news, Ralegh wrote to Bess, 'I never knew what sorrow meant until now'

which were at a particularly delicate stage. He was very anxious not to offend the King of Spain. On 9th June he signed a public declaration of his 'utter mislike and detestation' of Ralegh's insolences and excesses. Although King James admitted that he had only heard of them 'by a common fame', he required anybody who knew of Ralegh's scandalous and enormous outrages to inform the Privy Council without delay. The declaration was published on 11th June, and on the next day the Lord High Admiral issued an order to Sir Lewis Stukeley to arrest Ralegh, and bring him to London.

The *Destiny* sailed into Plymouth Sound on 21st June. On arrival Ralegh had her moored securely, and sent her sails and tackle ashore. Clearly, he did not intend to make a quick escape. He wrote to Carew on the same day, pointing out that he could have turned pirate, as so many people expected him to do. He had a magnificent ship, 'there is no better in the world,' he said, and the men to do it. As a commerce raider he could have made, he estimated, a hundred thousand pounds in three months, and he could have collected a company which would have impeded the traffic of Europe. But he had not done that. For better or worse, he was home.

There was no rush to arrest Ralegh. It does appear that everybody from King James downwards hoped that Ralegh would take the hint, and make use of the respite to escape to France. Lady Ralegh went down to Plymouth to meet him, and they stayed at Sir Christopher Harris's house, and then at the home of Mr Drake. Ralegh seems to have had the time and liberty to begin to dispose of the *Destiny*'s tobacco and other ship's stores, and generally to wind up his affairs after the voyage. The Raleghs did not leave for London until about the second week in July. They had reached the town of Ashburton, a little more than twenty miles from Plymouth on the London road, when Sir Lewis Stukeley met them and said he had authority to arrest Ralegh. Stukeley did not have a formal written warrant, but Ralegh took his word and returned with him to Plymouth. Stukeley was Vice-Admiral of Devon, an office which he had purchased for £600. He was Sir Richard Grenville's nephew and thus a cousin of Ralegh's. His father Sir John had taken part in one of the Virginia voyages.

At Plymouth, there was again a strange lull of several days, while everybody seemed to be waiting for Ralegh to take the initiative. Meanwhile, Stukeley set about completing the sale of the tobacco and other goods, pocketing the proceeds himself.

There seemed nothing to prevent Ralegh escaping, and it would have been a great relief to everyone if he had. Some such thoughts occurred to Lady Ralegh and to Samuel King. Bess urged her husband to try, and King arranged with two French captains from La Rochelle, Flory and Le Grand, to have Ralegh carried across the Channel by night. King and Ralegh actually set off one night to row to Flory's ship and were only a quarter of a mile from her when Ralegh changed his mind. He may have revolted from the prospect of ignominious flight, followed by exile from his native land. Maybe he realized that it made no sort of sense for a man of honour to escape like a criminal in the night, when he had already failed to take his chance while in command of a ship and a crew. Ralegh turned back.

The rumour in London was that Ralegh was too sick to travel. Perhaps he was, or, anyway, perhaps Stukeley believed he was. But by 23rd July the Privy Council had lost patience.

They would hear of no more delay. They directed Stukeley in unequivocal terms to bring Ralegh to London forthwith. On 25th July they set off: Ralegh, Lady Ralegh, Stukeley, the faithful Samuel King, and servants. The one strange and unexpected member of the party was a Dr Manourie, a French medical practitioner of sorts, probably a quack, and possibly a spy engaged by Stukeley.

Manourie watched and later reported Ralegh's sometimes pathetic and often bizarre behaviour during that last journey up to London. On Sunday 26th July Ralegh stayed the night at Poyntington Manor, outside Sherborne. Passing the castle, he is supposed to have said to Manourie, sighing and looking around him, that all this had been his, and the King had unjustly taken it from him. At Salisbury, Ralegh heard that the King was on his summer Progress nearby. He needed time to write down a defence of his actions, and so faked an illness. He asked Manourie to give him an emetic.

> I know [he said] that it is good for me to evacuate many bad humours, and by this means I gain time to work my friends, give order for my affairs, and, it may be, pacify his Majesty before my coming to London; for I know well, that as soon as I come there I shall go to the Tower, and that they will cut off my head if I use no means to escape it.

That night after supper Ralegh complained of clouded vision and dizziness. He stumbled and hit his head against a gallery post outside his room.

The next day Ralegh sent on Lady Ralegh, Samuel King and most of the servants to London. He stayed in his room, where one of his servants found him, crouched on all fours, naked except for a shirt, scratching and biting at the rushes strewn on the floorboards. The servant called Stukeley, who arrived just as Ralegh was vomiting. His leg and arm muscles contracted, and Stukeley had to call for help to pull Ralegh's limbs straight. Ralegh is then supposed to have laughed and said that he had 'well exercised Sir Lewis Stukeley and taught him to be a physician'.

Ralegh asked Manourie if he could supply him with some ointment which would make him 'horrible and loathsome outwardly, without offending his principal parts, or making him sick inwardly'. The emetic, it seemed, 'had done nothing as yet'. Manourie supplied some ointment to make Ralegh look like a leper. It certainly had an alarming effect when Ralegh smeared it on himself, making him 'all pimpled', 'full of great blisters' with a touch of yellow, and 'round about like a purple colour', as though his skin were dangerously inflamed. Stukeley was not in the conspiracy (according to Manourie) and became alarmed for the prisoner. He went to consult Lancelot Andrewes, the Bishop of Winchester, who sent three of his physicians. They were mystified by the patient's condition, but certified that he was too ill to be moved. Manourie countersigned their statement.

It occurred to Ralegh that the doctors might ask to see his water. Manourie rubbed round the inside of Ralegh's urinal with some substance that made the urine turn 'all into an earthy humour, of a blackish colour'. To maintain the pretence that he was sick, Ralegh gave out that he had eaten nothing for three days. In fact, Manourie had been to the

White Hart in Salisbury and bought him a leg of mutton and three loaves.

Manourie wrote much more in his report, discreditable to Ralegh: that he had twice tried to bribe Manourie, and was rehearsing various schemes of escape. Manourie's evidence was incorporated in King James's *Declaration*, which was an attempt to justify Ralegh's execution. Manourie's was obviously an exaggerated account of what happened, but there is no doubt that Ralegh did behave in an extraordinary manner to gain time at Salisbury. He excused himself by quoting from the First Book of Samuel, when King David had feigned madness, and dribbled on his beard, to save himself from his enemies. Ralegh wrote his *Apology*, but the King never saw it, at least during Ralegh's lifetime. Manourie left the party at Staines, his work presumably accomplished.

At an inn at Brentford, near London, Ralegh met a Frenchman, David de Novion, who had a message from the French Ambassador, Le Clerc. The meeting was possibly pre-arranged. Ralegh might have sent Samuel King on from Salisbury to prepare plans for an escape. At last, Ralegh may have been rousing himself from his state of shocked emotional numbness which had lasted since he heard the news of Wat's death. Now, when the Tower doors were opening for him, with the block and the grave beyond them, Ralegh might have awoken to a knowledge of what surely lay in store for him. It was not too late – not quite.

De Novion's message was that Le Clerc wished to see Ralegh. Ralegh agreed. He arrived at the house in Broad Street in the evening of Friday, 7th August. The following night, on Saturday the 8th, Le Clerc and de Novion came to the house to see Ralegh. There was no secrecy about the meeting, which was held in the presence of about a dozen of Ralegh's friends. The Privy Council in any case knew of this French 'plot', if it could be called a plot, but evidently had decided to let it run on for the information it might reveal.

Le Clerc said that Ralegh would be welcome in France. The King of France could employ him to prevent the Anglo-Spanish alliance, which might be concluded at any moment with a Spanish marriage. Queen Anne was known to be against the Spanish marriage, and to have tried to intercede with the King on Ralegh's behalf (although Anne's influence with James was by now almost nil). In France, Ralegh would be able to carry on the struggle against the old enemy, Spain.

Ralegh agreed to go to France, but not in a French ship. He preferred to use the escape route planned for him by Samuel King. A man called Hart, who had once been King's boatswain, had a ketch down-river at Gravesend. Edward Cottrell had agreed to brief Hart, and to provide wherries to take the party down the Thames. This was the same Cottrell who had once been of service to Ralegh in the Tower. He had given evidence compromising Ralegh before, and he was willing to betray Ralegh now. He and Stukeley revealed their plans to William Herbert, one of Stukeley's relatives, and to Sir William St John; he, too, had once been willing to help Ralegh, if bribed, and was now equally willing to betray him.

Cottrell had two wherries waiting at Tower dock on Sunday night. Ralegh, wearing a hat with a green hat-band and, ludicrously, a false beard, carried his cloak-bag and four pistols. Stukeley was there, with his son, and one of Ralegh's pages, and King. Before they got into the boats, Stukeley smugly asked King whether he would not agree that he, Stukeley, was an honest man after all? King merely said he hoped so.

Ralegh gave two of his pistols to Stukeley, and they all embarked, Stukeley and Ralegh in one wherry, Hart, King and young Stukeley in the other. The boatmen had not pulled twenty strokes from the jetty when Ralegh saw another, larger boat. It was actually Herbert's and it turned downstream to follow them. Ralegh was very alarmed and was sure they were betrayed, but Stukeley reassured him. Ralegh then asked the boatmen whether they would still go on, even if someone called upon them to stop in the King's name. This was an extremely stupid thing to say. 'The great boobies' were so frightened they stopped rowing at once. Ralegh said that a 'brabbling matter' with the Spanish ambassador had caused him to go to Tilbury, to embark for the Low Countries. He offered the boatmen ten gold pieces for their pains, if they would go on.

Stukeley, playing his part, then began to curse and call himself a fool for ever allowing himself to be involved in an affair like this, with a man so fearful and suspicious as Ralegh. He swore he would kill the boatmen if they did not row on. He told Ralegh there was nothing to fear. Samuel King seemed to agree with him. They had reached Greenwich when another wherry passed close to them. Ralegh was sure it had come to arrest them.

By now they had delayed so long that the boatmen said they would not be able to reach Gravesend by the morning on that tide. There was some discussion about going on by horse. They were by this time about a mile beyond Woolwich, in Galleon's Reach off Plumstead. There were two or three ketches in the river, but Hart said he was not sure which was his. This was the last straw for Ralegh. He was convinced they were all betrayed.

And so they were. They rowed to the shore at Greenwich, where Stukeley told Ralegh and King that he was arresting them in His Majesty's name. After that, they all went, astonishingly, into a tavern where Ralegh reproached Stukeley saying 'these actions will not turn out to your credit'. It was, in the circumstances, a very mild reproof. But it turned out to be accurate. Stukeley was paid £1,000 for his treachery. Afterwards he complained to King James that men were criticizing him for his conduct. King James retorted that there was nothing he could do about that. 'If I should hang all that speak ill of thee, all the trees in my kingdom would not suffice.' Stukeley and Manourie were later convicted of clipping the coinage and sentenced to death. Stukeley's sentence was commuted to imprisonment. He died, a raving madman, on the Isle of Lundy in the Bristol Channel in August 1620.

Ralegh was taken to the Tower of London, for the third and last time, on the morning of 10th August 1618. The faithful King went with him, although he was afterwards discharged. Ralegh told King that he had been betrayed by Cottrell and Stukeley. 'For your part, you need be in fear of no danger,' he said to King, 'but as for me, it is *I* am the mark that is shot at.'

22. *The End*

ACCORDING TO John Aubrey, King James used to say that Ralegh 'was a Coward to be taken and conveyed, for els he might easily have made his escape from so slight a guard'. The guard may have been slight, as James said, but there had never been a chance of escape for Ralegh that night on the Thames and, as the boats came alongside each other in mid-river, Ralegh must wearily have acknowledged it. The whole escape plan had been betrayed. Sir Lewis Stukeley, 'Sir Judas' as he came to be called, was an agent of the Government. He had been briefed by Naunton to win Ralegh's confidence, and then betray him. Ralegh the fox was in a trap. One of the greatest of Elizabethans had been brought down by worthless trash such as Stukeley and Manourie. Everyone, friends and enemies alike, thought this was the end for Ralegh.

Gondomar certainly thought so. He had been about to leave England for Madrid in June when he heard the news of Ralegh's return. He had a letter at Greenwich from Villiers, dated 26th June. It said that 'His Majesty will be as severe in punishing them as if they had done the like spoil in any of the cities of England.' The letter promised that all the offenders would be properly punished, and if Ralegh had come back with a ship full of gold, the treasure too would have been returned to Spain.

The letter demonstrates Gondomar's moral ascendancy over the King. He had taken a lofty line with King James from the first. The ship bringing him to England had failed to dip its ensign to English ships and Gondomar was roughly handled by the Governor of Plymouth. He demanded, and got, an apology. The Governor was reprimanded for conducting himself in a discourteous manner. Throughout the negotiations for the Spanish marriage, Gondomar handled the King with consummate diplomatic skill. James was greedy for the Infanta's dowry, and Gondomar played upon his greed, now threatening him, now wheedling him. When Ralegh returned, Gondomar lectured the Privy Council on their obligations to Spain, reminded James of his promises about Ralegh's fate, and of the likely consequences of the King of Spain's displeasure. He even got James to publish again his threatening proclamation against Ralegh.

Gondomar had been ordered to stay until he had witnessed the 'thorough completion' of Ralegh's punishment. When he left London on 15th July, he must have felt he had done his duty; all was arranged, except the axe-stroke itself. King James and his Privy Council seemed suitably impressed with a sense of their obligations to the King of Spain. The negotiations for the marriage were well in hand. Ralegh's head would neatly seal the agreement.

But, as happened so often in Ralegh's career, matters were not nearly so simple as they looked. Ralegh had vanished into the Tower. The days passed, there was no announcement.

London buzzed with rumours. Ralegh was to be executed at once, for his old crimes. Ralegh was to be executed at once for his new crimes. Ralegh was to be imprisoned for a time, and then executed. He was to be pardoned, by the Queen's intercession, and then to live abroad. He was to be pardoned provided he gave information on the misappropriation of money and property belonging to the Crown during the administration of the late Cecil, Lord Salisbury, as Lord Treasurer.

On 17th August, and on two later occasions, Ralegh was questioned by a Committee of the Privy Council consisting of Lord Chancellor Bacon, Archbishop Abbott, the Earl of Worcester, Sir Edward Coke, Sir Julius Caesar and Sir Robert Naunton. The committee found that they had some knotty points to unravel. For example, it could be argued that the King himself was as legally guilty for what had happened in Guiana as Ralegh was. Ralegh had offended by damaging Spanish property and killing Spanish subjects on supposedly Spanish soil. But if the scene of the offence was in Spanish territory and King James had known it was Spanish territory, then why had he allowed an armed expedition to go there? And if the territory in question were not Spanish, but English, then surely Ralegh had committed no offence? There were many other puzzling questions. Had Ralegh ever meant to go to the gold-mine? The committee seemed convinced that he had not. Some members of the expedition thought Ralegh had made fools of them, by taking them on a wild-goose chase after a mine he knew did not exist. Had Laurence Keymis been a party to some secret arrangement, and was that why he had hesitated so incompetently, and made no real effort to find a mine? Had Ralegh himself been a party to some secret agreement? And was it with the King? When Ralegh had first arrived at Plymouth he had written to George Carew, explaining what had happened, and seeming surprised by the King's displeasure that he had attacked San Thomé. 'Since my arrival in Ireland,' he wrote, 'I have been alarmed not a little, and have been told that I have fallen into the grave displeasure of His Majesty for having taken a town in Guiana which was in the possession of Spaniards.' The wording possibly hints at a degree of collusion.

The committee clearly would need time to consider these and other questions. Meanwhile they interrogated many more people connected with the Guiana voyage, and with the abortive attempt at escape on the Thames. They questioned de Novion, and attempted to question Le Clerc who, however, stood upon his diplomatic rights and refused to attend. He was confined to his house. The treatment of Le Clerc brought relations with the French to a low point. But his failure to provide any information meant that the Privy Council had to rely more than ever on a confession from Ralegh himself.

When he was admitted to the Tower on 10th August, Ralegh was searched and an inventory was made of his personal belongings. He had with him charts of Guiana, Nova Regnia, the Orinoco river, and Panama, a 'Tryall of Guiana oare, with a description thereof', and five assay reports of a silver mine. He also had about £50 in gold; a 'Guiana idoll' of gold and copper; a jacinth seal, set in gold, with Neptune engraved on it, with certain 'Guiana oare' tied to it; a 'Symson' stone, set in gold; a loadstone in a scarlet purse; a seal of his own coat of arms, in silver; a wedge of fine gold at 22 carats; another stub of

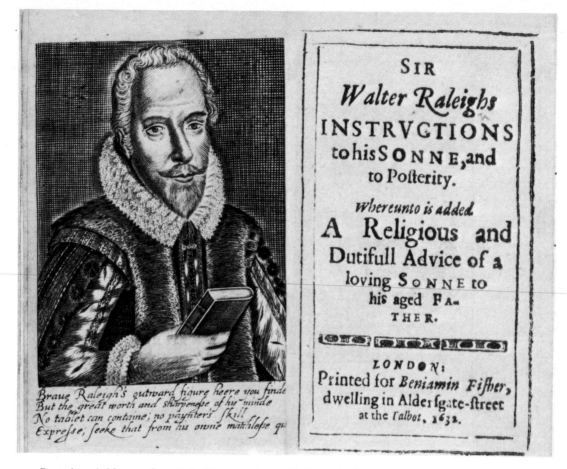

Portrait and title page from Ralegh's *Instructions to His Son, and to Posterity* published in 1632

coarser gold; sixty-three gold buttons with 'sparks' of diamonds; a gold chain, with sparks of diamonds; a diamond ring, of nine sparks; a gold whistle, set out with small diamonds; a gold picture case, set with diamonds; a 'sprigg jewell', set with soft stones and a ruby in the middle; and a diamond ring which he wore on his finger, given him by the late Queen. The jewels and the gold objects, all easily portable and readily saleable, and the charts, taken along possibly to persuade some future French investor, do suggest that at least Ralegh genuinely believed that he had a real chance of escaping to France.

The Lieutenant of the Tower at that time was Sir Allen Apsley, who had served in Ireland, and on the Cadiz expedition in 1596. His previous wife (he had three) had been a niece of Lord Carew. His present wife, his third, had a great admiration for Ralegh, and the Apsleys made Ralegh welcome and comfortable in their own house, before he moved in a few days to quarters in the Wardrobe Tower.

Unfortunately, these pleasant arrangements did not last long. The Privy Council committee were themselves quite unable to reach any decision about Ralegh and on 11th September they appointed a special gaoler, Sir Thomas Wilson, Keeper of the State Paper Office, whose task it was to obtain from Ralegh some self-incriminating statement. Wilson was given complete control over Ralegh's life in prison, with authority to question his prisoner on any subject he liked, and for as long as he liked. Wilson was with Ralegh every day, and all day, from morning to night. He ate with Ralegh, talked with Ralegh, lived close to Ralegh, for days. Nobody else could see or talk to Ralegh without Wilson's permission or presence. Wilson took notes of everything Ralegh said and reported it in copious detail to Naunton and the Privy Council. Wilson knew, and wrote it down, that everybody in the Tower looked upon him as the 'messenger of death'.

For day after day, Wilson subjected Ralegh to a seemingly never-ending cross-questioning. Calling himself a simple man, he threw up his hands at what he termed Ralegh's 'subtlety'. He called Ralegh an 'arch hypocrite' and an 'arch imposter'. He suggested that the only ways to get the truth out of such a man were by 'the rack or the halter'. Wilson, a pious, intellectually arrogant but narrow-minded and suspicious man, was indeed too simple for Ralegh, who was quite uncharacteristically discreet with him. Ralegh began by talking freely of his life and career, but soon realized what manner of man he had to deal with and became much more circumspect. From direct questioning, Wilson soon moved to shabby hints that Ralegh might profit if he gave some information, although he reported that Ralegh said 'that the more he confessed, the sooner he should be hanged'. He told Ralegh that 'if he would but discover what he knew, the King would forgive him, and do him all favours'. But Ralegh was not moved, and declined to make any incriminating admissions. There had been no 'French plot'. It was true that he had a French commission, but that was from Admiral de Montmorencie in person, and not from the French government. It was true that de Novion and Le Clerc had visited him at Broad Street, but they had discussed his escape, and nothing else. Ralegh would not admit that Guiana belonged to Spain, nor that anybody in England had ever conceded that Guiana had ever belonged to Spain.

Wilson found himself baffled by Ralegh. He could make no impression on him. Whenever he felt himself on the verge of discovering some damaging statement, Ralegh seemed to slip away from him. Wilson constantly underestimated his man. They discussed suicides, in the 'nobel Roman' fashion. But Wilson reported that Ralegh had not 'such Roman courage' as to take his own life. He took away Ralegh's chemicals and drugs, just in case, but Ralegh retorted that if he wanted to commit suicide he could run his head against a post. Wilson was mystified by Ralegh's experiments. He could not bring himself to believe that Ralegh was actually able to distil fresh water from salt, using his apparatus of copper pipes and vessels.

Wilson removed Ralegh from his comparative comfort in the Wardrobe Tower and put him in a tiny cell at the top of the Brick Tower. 'Though it seemeth nearer Heaven,' he wrote to Naunton, 'yet is there no means to escape but into Hell.' He was also unnecessarily cruel to Ralegh by refusing to believe that he was sick. He thought of him as a hypochondriac, and scoffed at his 'puling, pining and groaning'. Although Ralegh would never have made light of his ailments, he genuinely was a sick man. He had painful sores all over his body, which needed a servant to dress them daily. He suffered from periodical fits of ague, he was still lame from his Cadiz wound, and his liver and left side were swollen. 'I am sycke and weak,' he wrote to Lady Ralegh. 'This honest gentleman, Mr Edward Wilson, is my keeper, and takes much payne with me. My swolne syde keeps me in perpetual paine and unrest. God comfort us!' Bess was sympathetic, but could only suggest a somewhat humdrum reason for the pain in her husband's side, 'Tis meerly sorrow and greaf that with *wynd* hath gathered into your syde.'

Wilson could not resist a reference to the old accusation of atheism. He told Naunton that the things Ralegh 'seems to make most reckoning of are his chemical stuffs, amongst which there is so many spirits of things, that I think there is none wanting that ever I heard of, unless it be the Spirit of God'. Wilson could make such cheap jokes, but time was passing, and he was no nearer success in his examination of Ralegh. After some days of his attentions, he and the Privy Council allowed Ralegh to write directly to the King. Naunton called it 'soaring and tedious' but the letter, dated 24th September, is a clear and vigorous statement of Ralegh's position. If the Privy Council had ever hoped for some damaging admission, they were to be disappointed.

> If in my jorny outward bound I had of my men murthered at the Ilands, and spared to take revenge; if I did discharge some Spanish barkes taken, without spoile; if I forbare all partes of the Spanish Indies, wherin I might have taken twentye of their townes on the sea cost, and did only follow the enterprise which I undertooke for Guiana, – where, without any direccion from me, a Spanish village was burnt, which was newly sett up within three miles of the mine – by your Majesties favor I finde noe reason whie the Spanish Embassadore should complaine of me. If it were lawfull for the Spanish to murther 26 Englishmen, tyenge them back to backe, and then to cutt theire throtes, when they had traded with them a whole moneth, and came to them on the land without so much as one sword amongst them all; – and that it may not be lawfull for your Majesties subjects, beinge forced by them, to repell force by force; we may justly say, 'O miserable English!'
>
> If Parker and Mutton took Campeach and other places in the Honduraes, seated in the hart of the Spanish Indies; burnt townes, killed the Spaniards; and had nothing sayed to them at their returne, – and that my selfe forbore to looke into the Indies, because I would not offend, I may as justly say, 'O miserable Sir Walter Ralegh!'
>
> If I had spent my poore estate, lost my sonne, suffred, by sicknes and otherwise, a world of miseries; if I had resisted with the manifest hazard of my life the rebels and spoiles which my companyes would have made; if when I was poore I could have mad my selfe rich; if when I had gotten my libertye, which all men and Nature it selfe doth

so much prize, I voluntarilie lost it; if when I was master of my life I rendred it againe; if, I might elsewhere have sould my shipp and goods, and put five or six thousand pounds in my purse, I have brought her into England; I beseech your Majestie to beleeve, that all this I have done because it should not be sayed to your Majestie that your Majestie had given libertie and trust to a man whose ende was but the recovery of his libertie, and whoe had betrayed your Majesties trust.

My mutiners tould me, that if I returned for England I should be undone; but I beleeved more in your Majesty's goodnes then in their arguments. Sure I am, that I am the first who, being free and able to inrich my selfe, hath embraced povertie. And as sure I am that my example shall make me the last. But your Majesties wisdome and goodnes I have made my judges, whoe have ever bine, and shall remain, Your Majesty's most humble vassall.

But Ralegh was arguing a lost cause, and the Privy Council were growing impatient. Wilson and Lady Wilson ('your fellow prisoner', as Naunton jocularly called her), who was empowered to question Ralegh with her husband, were instructed to examine Lady Ralegh.

She had been under virtual house arrest since 20th August. Now, she was questioned by Wilson, and her actions were placed under his supervision. Her letters to Ralegh, and his to her, were intercepted. But neither the questions, nor the spying, nor the letters, revealed anything suspicious. There was no case against Lady Ralegh.

By now, there seemed no case against Ralegh either. On 3rd October, Sir Edward Harwood wrote to Carleton that 'the King is much inclined to hang Ralegh; but it cannot handsomely be done; and he is likely to live out his days'. Wilson asked to be released from his duties and on 15th October was back in his own house.

Ralegh left his cramped little cell in the Brick Tower on 11th October, and returned to the more congenial custody and company of the Apsleys for the last few days of his life. Public opinion had changed while he had been imprisoned. It was not now politically possible to send him to Madrid for execution. The people of England would not have stood for it. There had always been a party in the Privy Council who were strongly against it. On 15th October the news arrived that the King of Spain himself was also against Ralegh being sent to Spain for punishment. Shrewdly, Philip III was evading any possibility that he might be held responsible for the legal murder of a gallant opponent. King James had no such scruples. It did not matter to him whether Ralegh lost his head in London or in Madrid. His problem was not where, but how. No means had yet been devised for giving Ralegh's execution a legal gloss.

The Law Lords and the committee of the Privy Council, under Bacon, had been considering the question, and they reported their unanimous opinion to the King on 18th October. Ralegh had been convicted of high treason in 1603. He could not legitimately be tried on any charge arising out of an action committed since. He was, and always had been, civicly dead. Therefore the King had a choice of two courses of action. He could simply issue a warrant for Ralegh's execution under the old conviction of 1603. To execute an old man, more than fifteen years after his sentence, would appear cold-blooded and vindictive. The King would probably have to excuse his action by publishing an account of Ralegh's fresh crimes (although legally, of course, they would have nothing to do with Ralegh's conviction). Alternatively, the King could order Ralegh to be examined publicly by a full Council of State, augmented by the Law Lords, and other noblemen and prominent people. Witnesses could be called, evidence given, cross-examination permitted. It would be, in fact if not in name, another public trial, on new charges arising out of Ralegh's conduct on the Guiana voyage.

Of the two, the Law Lords were 'rather inclined' to the second, because it was the one 'nearest to a legal procedure'. King James agreed, although he objected to the hearing being in public. He was afraid that it would make Ralegh too popular, 'as was found by experiment at the arraignment at Winchester, where by his wit he turned the hatred of men into compassion'. King James also felt that a full public hearing of peers, on the lines of a previous precedent for the Countess of Shrewsbury, was doing too much honour to a man like Ralegh.

In the event, the hearing was conducted in private by the same committee of six, headed by Bacon, which had first begun the examinations in August. They summoned Ralegh to appear before them on 22nd October, and they questioned him for four hours. The only record of the hearing is from rough notes, unlikely to be wholly unbiased, made by Sir Julius Caesar.

The prosecution was opened by Henry Yelverton, the Attorney General. He led his hearers over some very familiar ground. Ralegh had, he said, deceived the King into thinking there was a gold-mine in Guiana. Ralegh had never really intended to look for a mine. If he had, then why had he no miners in his expedition? Ralegh had a French commission, which he had used to attack the Spaniards. Not content with his acts of hostility in Guiana, he had intended to go on and attack the Plate Fleet. Worst of all, Ralegh had (this was tittle-tattle from Manourie and Stukeley) made vile and dishonourable speeches against the King.

Almost for the last time, Ralegh summoned himself to fight across the same old battle-field. He had believed, he said, that the King had cleared him in all conscience. He had heard that the King himself had said of his trial that he would not wish to be tried by a Middlesex jury. He denied absolutely the slanders of Manourie and Stukeley. He only admitted that he had once said that his confidence in the King had been deceived. As to miners, he had refiners, mining tools, and assaying equipment worth £2,000 with him on the expedition; that hardly showed a lack of interest in gold-prospecting. As to aggressive acts against Spain, it was the Spaniards who had attacked first.

To add conviction to the evidence of intention to attack the Plate Fleet, the committee confronted Ralegh with two of his captains, St Leger and Pennington, who both said they had heard him planning such an attack. Wearily Ralegh explained that he had only mentioned it after the attempt on the gold-mine had failed. It had never been anything more than large talk.

Palace Yard, Westminster, where Ralegh was beheaded. Engraving by Wenceslaus Hollar

Almost for the last time, Ralegh was pleading a lost cause. On 24th October he was called before the Privy Council in Whitehall and informed that his execution had been ordered. He asked that he might be beheaded, and not hanged, drawn and quartered according to his original sentence.

He was taken back to his room in the Tower, shivering and sweating, with another bout of ague already coming on. He was still suffering from the fever when he was woken at eight o'clock on the morning of 28th October, and told that their Lordships required him to appear before them at Westminster.

Ralegh had grown careless of his personal appearance while in the Tower. The dandy who had once had six hundred thousand gold sequins sewn on to his shoes was now a tired, sick old man, shambling along the walks of the Tower on his stick, his white hair straggling and unkempt. Under Wilson's administration he had stopped having himself properly groomed. As he told Wilson sardonically, he would not take care over his head until he knew who was going to have it; 'he would not bestow so much cost of it for the hangman.' But as he was escorted along the corridor that morning he passed one of his old servants, Peter, who used to comb his hair and beard, and who was now horrified by his master's appearance. He asked Ralegh if he would allow him to comb his hair again. 'Let them kem it that are to have it,' Ralegh said, still capable of a flash of sombre humour. 'Dost thou know, Peter, of any plaster that will set a man's head on again when it is off?'

At nine o'clock Ralegh appeared before the bar of the King's Bench in Westminster Hall. Yelverton led again, opening with a speech which was a curious mixture of accusation and tribute to the prisoner.

My Lords, Sir Walter Ralegh, the prisoner at the bar, was fifteen years since convicted of high treason, by him committed against the person of his Majesty and the

331

state of this kingdom, and then received the judgment of death, to be hanged, drawn, and quartered. His Majesty, of his abundant grace, hath been pleased to show mercy upon him till now that justice calls unto him for execution. Sir Walter Ralegh hath been a statesman and a man who in regard of his parts and quality is to be pitied. He hath been as a star at which the world gazed; but stars may fall, nay they must fall when they trouble the sphere wherein they abide. It is therefore his Majesty's pleasure now to call for execution of the former judgment, and I now require order for the same.

Yelverton's speech made the investigation just concluded appear as a monstrous illogicality. Ralegh had been imprisoned, interrogated, accused and supposedly convicted for misdeeds he allegedly committed in Guiana. But these were now shown to be no more than cruel irrelevancies. He was to be executed, after all, on the old conviction.

The Clerk of the Crown, a Mr Fanshawe, then read out the conviction and judgment, and called to Ralegh to hold up his hand, which he did. He was asked if there was anything he wished to say why execution should not be awarded against him. Ralegh excused himself for his faint voice. He explained that he had been suffering from ague, and indeed was still sick. The Lord Chief Justice, Sir Henry Montagu, reassured him that they could all hear him.

So, for the very last time, Ralegh began to plead his case.

My Lord, all that I can say is this: that the judgment which I received to die so long since, I hope it cannot be strained to take away my life; for that since it was his Majesty's pleasure to grant me a commission to proceed in a voyage beyond the sea, wherein I had power, as marshal, on the life and death of others, so, under favour, I presume I am discharged of that judgment. For by that commission I departed the land and undertook a journey to honour my sovereign and enrich his kingdom with gold, of the ore whereof this hand hath found and taken in Guiana . . .

But even now, Ralegh was not to be allowed to finish. The Lord Chief Justice interrupted him to say that his speech was not to the point. He had not been pardoned. His pardon had not been implicit in his commission to go to Guiana. Unless he could say 'something else to the purpose', they would have to proceed to give execution.

At last, Ralegh gave up the struggle.

If your opinion be so, my Lord, I am satisfied, and so put myself on the mercy of the King, who I know is gracious; and under favour, I must say, I hope he will be pleased to take commiseration upon me, as concerning that judgment, which is so long past, and which, I think, here are some could witness, nay, his Majesty was of opinion, that I had hard measure therein . . .

Again the Lord Chief Justice intervened. 'Sir Walter Ralegh, you must remember yourself; you had an honourable trial, and so were justly convicted; and it were wisdom in you now to submit yourself.' The Lord Chief Justice summed up, and revealed that Ralegh's actions in Guiana had, after all, had a bearing upon the sentence of execution which was about to be carried out. Montagu seemed unaware of the legal absurdity of what he was saying. He, with the other Law Lords, had submitted that Ralegh was a dead man in law and could commit no further offence. Yet that same dead man in law had seemingly committed a string of further offences for which he was now to be beheaded.

> I am here called [said Montagu] to grant execution upon the judgment given you fifteen years since; all which time you have been as a dead man in the law, and might at any minute have been cut off, but the King in mercy spared you. You might think it heavy if this were done in cold blood, to call you to execution, but it is not so; for new offences have stirred up his Majesty's justice, to remember to revive what the law hath formerly cast upon you. I know you have been valiant and wise, and I doubt not but you retain both these virtues, for now you have occasion to use them. Your faith hath heretofore been questioned, but I am resolved you are a good Christian, for your book which is an admirable work, doth testify as much.

Montagu offered the oil of comfort, though, as an officer of the law, he admitted his balm might be mixed with vinegar. 'Fear not death too much, nor fear not death too little. Not too much, lest you fail in your hopes. Not too little, lest you die presumptuously.' Montagu ended with the words, 'Execution is granted.'

Ralegh had one final remonstrance. It was not a last argument for life. He had, he said, no desire 'to gain one minute of life, for now being old, sickly, in disgrace, and certain to go to it, life was wearisome to him'. But he did ask for a reasonable delay. This much favour he asked,

> that I may not be cut off suddenly. I have something to do in discharge of my conscience, and something to satisfy his Majesty in, something to satisfy the world in. And I desire I may be heard at the day of my death. And here I take God to be my judge, before whom I shall shortly appear, I was never disloyal to his Majesty, which I will justify where I shall not fear the face of any king on earth. And so I beseech you all to pray for me.

Ralegh was taken into custody by the Sheriffs of Middlesex, and lodged in the Gatehouse part of the old monastery of St Peter at Westminster, to await execution. King James signed the death warrant that day. Ralegh had won one concession; he was to be beheaded, as he asked, and not quartered.

King James had for some time been under discreet but insistent pressure from a number of sources to spare Ralegh's life. Some appeals were emotional, from Ralegh's family; from Lady Ralegh, from his son Carew, and from his cousin Lord Carew. These could be, and were, ignored. There were emotional appeals from James's own family, from the Queen, to whom Ralegh addressed poems of supplication. Though sick and suffering from dropsy, and with not long to live herself (some said she was crazy), Queen Anne roused herself to write to Villiers, as her 'kind Dogge', asking him to deal sincerely and earnestly with the King 'that

333

Sir Walter Ralegh's life may not be called in question'. This, too, was ignored. But there were other appeals, motivated by practical politics, from those who were described as being in great favour and esteem with the King. But James ignored them all. He was tired of it, tired of Ralegh, tired of hearing his name. He wanted an end to it. The execution was to be carried out on the very next day, 29th October, which was the feast of St Simon and St Jude. It was also the day of the Lord Mayor's Show. It was hoped that the majority of the London mobs would be drawn to the City for the processions and celebrations, and Ralegh's execution could be carried out with much less popular attention.

This unexpected concern for the effect of Ralegh's execution on public opinion is significant. It suggests that King James's government was already looking somewhat fearfully to the future. For, as it happened, King James would have done far better to have listened to those who asked for Ralegh's life. Spared to die a natural death, Ralegh would have eventually passed away in comparative obscurity, the last of the Elizabethans, remembered for a certain local notoriety. But by executing Ralegh, King James made sure he would be immortal. Ralegh had never been popular in his life-time, but after his death he became a national hero. Ironically, his death worked against the Spanish marriage which it was supposed to help bring about (and which, in the event, never took place). The people of England knew that Ralegh had been sacrificed to the Spanish faction. They remembered that the last survivor of '88, the living symbol of the old Merrie England, had been cut down for the sake of a foreign Catholic princess none of them had ever seen. As it was quite rightly said at the time, Ralegh's death 'will do more harm to the faction that procured it than he ever did in his life'.

As he was being taken across the courtyard from Westminster Hall to the Gatehouse, Ralegh saw an old friend, Sir Hugh Beeston of Cheshire, standing in the crowd, and he asked him to be present the next day. Sir Hugh said that he certainly would be there, if he could get a place to stand. Still in that sardonic mood, Ralegh said to him, 'I do not know what *you* may do for a place. You must make what shift you can. But for my part, I am sure of one.'

In the Gatehouse, he was able to receive visitors and say his last farewells to friends and relatives. He was so cheerful and so brave that a cousin, Francis Thynne, said to him, 'Do not carry it with too much bravery. Your enemies will take exception if you do.' Again, Ralegh was in that mood of grim humour. 'Do not grudge it to me,' he said. 'When I come to the sad parting, you will see me grave enough.' His demeanour fully lived up to the jaunty little couplet he is supposed to have written, 'On the Snuff of a Candle', the night before he died:

> Cowards fear to die, but Courage stout,
> Rather than live in Snuff, will be put out.

He had time to make his last dispositions, and settle his affairs. He had never, he wrote in a testamentary note, leased a parcel of land near Sherborne Castle, claimed by John Meere, to a Captain Thomas Caulfield. Meere's claim was false. But his conscience struck him over Henry Pyne, in Ireland. He asked that the evidence he had given be disregarded. He asked his wife to look after Christopher Hamon's wife, and to relieve John Talbot's wife 'who, I feare me – her sonn being deade – will otherwise perish'. (Talbot was his faithful servant in the Tower, who died in Guiana.) He remembered Stukeley, and asked that the money from the sale of the *Destiny's* tobacco be recovered from him, also the ten pieces he gave him 'the Sonday that wee tooke boate'.

Ralegh wrote a second note, which he left behind, in case he should be stopped from speaking on the scaffold:

'I did never receive advise from my Lord Carew to make any escape, neither did I tell ytt Stukeley.

'I did never name my Lord Hey (James Hay, Viscount Doncaster) and my Lord Carew to Stukeley in order words or sence then as my honourable freinds, among other Lords my honourable freinds.

'I did never shew unto Stukeley any letter wherein there were £10,000 named, nor ance one pound. Onely I told him I hoped to procure the paiment of his debts in his absence.

'I never had Commission from the French king. I never saw the French king's hand nor seale in my life.

'I never had any plot or practice with the French, directly or indirectly, nor with any other King, Prince, or State, unknowing to the King.

'My true intent was to goe to a Mine of Gold in Guiana. Itt was not fained, but is true that such a Mine there is, within three miles of St Tome.

I never had itt in my thought to goe for Trinidado, and leave my companies to come after to the Salvage Ilands, as hath by Ferne bine falsly reported.

'I did not carrie with me 100 peces (as I remember). I had with me 60 peeces, and I brought backe neare about the said somme.

'I did never speake to the French Mannering (Manourie) anie one disloyall word, or dishonorable word, of the King. Noe; if I had not loved and honored the King truly, and trusted in his goodnesse somewhat too much, I had not suffered death.

'These things are true, as there is a God, and as I am now to appeare before his tribunall-seate, where I renounce all mercy and salvacion if this be not a truth. Att my death, W. Ralegh.'

Late that night, Lord and Lady Carew brought Lady Ralegh to see him. She had spent most of the day trying to get the Lords of the Council to plead with the King. She had failed, but she did have permission to dispose of her husband's body. Even now, Ralegh's humour did not desert him. 'It is as well, dear Bess,' he said, smiling, 'that thou mayest dispose of it dead, that hadst not always the disposing of it when alive.'

After her last tears, and prayers, and embraces, Lord and Lady Carew took Bess home with them, where she wrote a letter to her 'best brother', Sir Nicholas Carew, at his house at Beddington in Surrey.

I desiar, good brother, that you will be plessed to let me berri the worthi boddi of my nobell hosban, Sur Walter Ralegh, in your chorche at Beddington, wher I desiar to be berred. The Lordes have geven me his ded boddi, thought they denied me his life. This nit hee shall be brought you with two or three of my men. Let me here presently. God hold me in my wites. E.R.

(But in this too Lady Ralegh was defeated. Her husband's body was buried in St Margaret's, Westminster.)

Meanwhile, after Bess had gone and he was left alone, Ralegh remembered a verse of a poem he had written to her, his dearest 'Serena', many, many years before. On the flyleaf of his Bible, he wrote another version of the verse, and added two more lines:

> Even such is tyme, which takes in trust
> Our yowth, our Joyes, and all we have,
> And payes us butt with age and dust:
> Who in the darke and silent grave
> When we have wandred all our wayes
> Shutts up the storye of our dayes.
> And from which earth and grave and dust
> The Lord shall rayse me up I trust.

Ralegh composed himself to sleep for three or four hours. He awoke, to prepare himself for the day. He had the company of Dr Robert Tounson, Dean of Westminster, and later Bishop of Salisbury, whom the Privy Council had sent to attend him in his last hours. In a letter written some ten days later to Sir John Isham, Tounson gave a most vivid account of Ralegh's bearing and state of mind on that last morning. Ralegh, to Tounson's mind, was almost unnaturally composed in the face of death.

He was the most fearless of death that ever was known [wrote Tounson], and the most resolute and confident, yet with reverence and conscience. When I began to encourage him against the fear of death, he seemed to make so light of it that I wondered at him, and when I told him, that the dear servants of God, in better causes than his, had shrunk back and trembled a little, he denied not, but yet gave God thanks, he never feared death; and much less than for it was but an opinion and imagination; and the manner of death though to others might seem grievous, yet he had rather die so than of a burning fever.

Ralegh was so fearless and confident, Tounson saw he would have to change his tack.

With much more to that purpose, with such confidence and cheerfulness, that I was fain to divert my speech another way, and wished him not to flatter himself; for this extraordinary boldness, I was afraid, came from some false ground. If it sprang from the assurance he had of the love and favour of God, of the hope of his Salvation by Christ, and his own innocency, as he pleaded, I said he was a happy man. But if it were out of an humour of vain glory or carelessness or contempt of death, or senselessness of his own estate, he were much to be lamented &c. For I told him, that Heathen Men had set as little by their lives as he could do, and seemed to die as bravely. He answered that he was persuaded, that no man, that knew God and feared Him, could die with cheerfulness and courage, except he were assured of the love and favour of God unto him; that other men might make shows outwardly, but they felt no joy within; with much more to that effect, very Christianly, so that he satisfied me then, as I think he did all his spectators at his death.

In the morning, Tounson gave Ralegh Holy Communion. Ralegh was very cheerful and merry, and 'hoped to persuade the world he died an innocent man, as he said'. This was a little too much for Tounson. He cautioned Ralegh about his speech. If he were too cheerful and brave, his very appearance would be a criticism of the Crown – 'men in those days did not die in that sort innocent, and his pleading innocency was an oblique taxing of the Justice of the Realm upon him'. Ralegh said that justice had been done, the law should take its course and he must die. But, he still said, he would stand upon his innocence. Tounson, a somewhat presumptuous cleric, told Ralegh the Hand of God had found him out, and ventured to remind the condemned man that some had thought him responsible for Essex's death. Ralegh told Tounson that Essex had been 'fetched off by a trick', but Tounson did not say what the trick was.

Ralegh ate his breakfast heartily, and took tobacco. He made no more of his death, in Tounson's phrase, than if he had been about to take a journey. 'He left a great impression in the minds of those that beheld him.'

At eight o'clock in the morning the Sheriffs came to take him to the Old Palace Yard of Westminster, where the scaffold was erected. Ralegh was ready. He was wearing a wrought nightcap under his hat, a ruff band, a black velvet nightgown over a hair-coloured satin doublet, a black wrought waistcoat, black cut taffeta breeches, and ash-coloured silk stockings. As he went somebody offered him a cup of sack wine. He drank it, and was asked how he liked it. 'I will answer,' said Ralegh, 'as did the fellow who drank of St Giles's bowl as he went to Tyburn: "it is good drink, if a man might tarry by it."'

Although, as John Aubrey said, Lord Mayor's Day had been chosen so 'that the pageants and fine shows might draw away the people from beholding the tragedy of one of the gallantest worthies that ever England bred', there was still a vast crowd in the Palace Yard. Wooden barricades had been set up to control the crowds but the Sheriffs still had difficulty in clearing a way. As he passed through, Ralegh caught sight of a bald-headed old man and spoke to him. The old man said he wanted nothing 'but to see you, and to pray God to have mercy on your soul'. Ralegh thanked him, took off the lace nightcap he was wearing under his hat and gave it to the old man. 'Thou hast more need of it now than I,' he said to him.

The crush was so great that Ralegh seemed out of breath and almost fainting when he climbed up on to the scaffold. It was a raw October morning and a fire had been lit beside the scaffold for the Sheriffs while they were waiting. They invited Ralegh to go down and warm himself, but he refused. If he delayed, he said, his fever might return, and people might think he was shaking with fear.

On the scaffold, Ralegh looked around and up, smiled and greeted his friends and acquaintances in the crowd. The Earls of Arundel and Oxford, and Viscount Doncaster, were at an upstairs balcony window of Sir Randall Carew's house overlooking the yard. Lord Sheffield and Lord Percy were there, on horse-back. Sir Hugh Beeston had found a place after all, with Sir Edward Sackville, Colonel Cecil, and Sir Henry Rich. Many of the noblemen had brought their ladies. Most of them were members of the old aristocracy of the Tudors, who had come to pay their last respects to their last champion. But also in that crowd were men of the future, such as John Pym, the great Parliamentarian, and Sir John Eliot, who was himself to die in the Tower under Charles I.

The officers called for silence. The murmuring hubbub of the crowd died down. Ralegh began to speak. He asked his audence's indulgence. He had just had two days of fever, which might return at any time. So if they saw any sign of weakness of voice or manner they must put it down to his illness and not to fear. He paused for a little while, and sat down. When he got up to speak again, he noticed that the lords in the balcony could not hear him very well and he said he would pitch his voice more strongly to reach them. Arundel told him not to do that. Instead, they would all come down and stand on the scaffold. When they arrived, Ralegh shook them by the hand, and began again.

As I said, I thank my God heartily that He hath brought me into the light to die, and hath not suffered me to die in the dark prison of the Tower, where I have suffered a great deal of adversity and a long sickness. I thank God that my fever hath not taken me at this time, as I prayed God it might not.

There are two main points of suspicion, that his Majesty hath conceived against me, and wherein his Majesty cannot be satisfied, which I desire to clear and resolve you of. One is that his Majesty hath been informed that I have had some plot with France, and his Majesty had some reason to induce him thereunto. One reason that his Majesty had so to believe was that when I came back from Guiana, being come to Plymouth, I had a desire in a small bark to pass to Rochelle, which was for that I would have made my peace, before I had come to England. Another reason was that upon my flight I did intend to fly into France, for saving of my life, having had some terror from above. A third reason was the French Agent's coming to my house here in London, and it was reported that I had a commission from the French King at my going forth. These are the reasons that his Majesty had, as I am informed, to suspect.

But this I say, for a man to call God to witness to a falsehood at any time is a grievous sin, and what shall he hope for at the Tribunal day of Judgment? But to call God to witness to a falsehood at the time of death, is far more grievous and impious, and there is no hope for such a one. And what should I expect that am now going to render an account of my faith? I do therefore call the Lord to witness, as I hope to be saved, and as I hope to see Him in his Kingdom, which I hope will be within this

338

Portrait and a later reconstruction of Ralegh's execution scene. The artist seemed to think that Ralegh was executed at the Tower of London

The History of the World

quarter of this hour; I never had any commission from the French King; neither knew I that there was an Agent, or what he was, till I met him in my gallery at my lodging unlooked for. If I speak not true, O Lord, let me never come into thy Kingdom.

The second suspicion was, that his Majesty hath been informed, that I should speak dishonourably and disloyally of him. But my accuser was a base Frenchman, a kind of a chemical fellow, one whom I knew to be perfidious. This fellow because he had a merry wit and some small skill in chemical medicines, I entertained rather for his taste than his judgment. He perjured himself at Winchester in my former troubles, in which my hand was touched, he being sworn to secrecy over night, revealed it in the morning.

But in this I speak now, what have I to do with kings? It is not for me to fear or to flatter kings. I have nothing to do with them. I have now to do with God, I am now the subject of Death, and the great God of Heaven is my sovereign before whose tribunal seat I am shortly to appear. Therefore to tell a lie now to get the favour of the King were vain. Therefore, as I hope to be saved at the last day, I never spake dishonourably, disloyally, or dishonestly of the King; neither to this Frenchman, nor to any other; neither had I ever in all my life, a thought ill of his Majesty. Therefore I cannot but think it strange, that this Frenchman being so base, so mean a Fellow, should be so far credited. So much for this point. I have dealt truly, and I hope I shall be believed.

I confess I did attempt to escape. I cannot deny it. I had advertisement from above that it would go hard with me. I desired to save my life. And I do likewise confess that I did dissemble and feign myself sick at Salisbury, but I hope it was no sin. The prophet David did make himself a fool, and did suffer spittle to fall upon his beard to escape the hands of his enemies, and it was not imputed to him as sin. I did it to prolong time till his Majesty came, hoping for some commiseration from him.

I forgive this Frenchman, and Sir Lewis Stukeley, and have received the sacrament this morning of Mr Dean, and I do also forgive all the world. But thus much I am bound to in charity to speak of this man, that all men may take good heed of him.

Ralegh might forgive Stukeley, but he also wanted to make sure that his treacheries were not forgotten. He dealt with Stukeley's false accusations and dealings one by one, answering them in turn. But he ended on a plea for forgiveness. 'Now God forgive him, for I do, and I desire God to forgive him. I will not only say God is the God of revenge, but I desire God to forgive him, as I hope to be forgiven.'

Ralegh looked over his 'note of remembrance'. 'Well, faith be,' he said, 'thus far have I gone, now a little more, and I will have done by and by.'

He touched next on the reports that he had never meant to come home after the failure of the Guiana expedition. He explained that, on the contrary, he had been threatened by the mutineers in the *Destiny* and he had to swear oaths, and use persuasion, bribes and promises of pardon, or they would never have allowed him to come home. He went on to deal with another slander.

'There was a report that I meant not to go to Guiana at all, and that I knew not of any mine, nor intended any such matter, but only to get my liberty, which I had not the wit to keep. But it was my full intent to go for gold, for the benefit of his Majesty and those that went with me, with the rest of my countrymen. But he that knew the head of the mine, would not discover it, when he saw that my son was slain, but made himself away.'

Ralegh turned to the Earl of Arundel and said, 'Being in the gallery in my ship at my departure, your Honour took me by the hand, and said you would request me one thing, that was, that whether I made a good voyage or bad, yet I should return again into England, when I made a promise and gave you my faith that I would.'

'So you did,' replied the Earl of Arundel. 'It is true. They were the last words I spake unto you.'

'Another slander was raised, that I would have gone away from them and left them at Guiana, but there were a great many of worthy men that accompanied me always, as my Sergeant Major George Ralegh and divers others [whom Ralegh then named by name] that knew my intent was nothing so.

'And these be the material points I thought good to speak of; I am now at this instant to render my account to God, and I protest as I shall appear before Him, this that I have spoken is true. I will speak but a word or two more, because I will not trouble Mr Sheriff too long.'

There was one more slander to answer, a very old one, which had perhaps wounded Ralegh more than any other.

Only I will borrow a little time of Mr Sheriff's to speak of one thing more, and that doth make my heart bleed to hear such an imputation laid upon me. It is said that I was persecutor of my Lord of Essex, and that I stood in a window over against him when he suffered, and puffed out tobacco in disdain of him. God I take to witness, my eyes shed tears for him when he died, and as I hope to look in the face of God hereafter, my Lord of Essex did not see my face when he suffered. I was afar off in the Armoury, where I saw him, but he saw not me.

I confess I was of a contrary faction, but I knew my Lord of Essex was a noble gentleman, and that it would be worse with me when he was gone; for those that set me against him, afterwards set themselves against me, and were my greatest enemies, and my soul hath been many times grieved that I was not nearer to him when he died, because I understood that he asked for me at his death, to be reconciled unto me.

Ralegh had spoken for nearly half an hour. He was near the end. He had had his wish, to be allowed to speak.

And now I entreat you all to join with me in prayer, that the great God of Heaven, whom I have grievously offended, being a great sinner of a long time and in many kinds, my whole course a course of vanity, a seafaring man, a soldier and a courtier – the temptations of the least of these were able to overthrow a good mind and a good man; that God, I say, will forgive me, and that he will receive me into everlasting life. So I take my leave of you all, making my peace with God.

The scaffold was cleared of spectators. Ralegh prayed, to prepare himself for death. He stood up, and gave away his hat, and some money he had on him. He shook hands and said goodbye to the Lords, knights, gentlemen, Tounson and the two Sheriffs. He took a special leave of the Earl of Arundel, thanking him for his company on this day, and asking him particularly to desire the King that no scandalous writing to defame him might be published after his death. He shook hands with Arundel and embraced him, saying, 'I have a long journey to go, and therefore I will take my leave.'

He took off his gown and doublet, and than asked to see the axe. The headsman hesitated but Ralegh said, 'I prithee, let me see it. Dost thou think I am afraid of it?' He ran his finger along the edge. 'This is a sharp medicine,' he said to the Sheriffs. 'But it is a physician that will cure all my diseases.'

He walked to one side of the scaffold and asked everyone if they would pray to God to help and strengthen him. He then walked to the other side and made the same request.

The executioner knelt and asked for forgiveness which Ralegh, laying a hand on his shoulder, gladly gave him. The man asked Ralegh if he would like a blindfold. Ralegh refused. 'Think you I fear the shadow of the axe, when I fear not itself?'

The executioner spread his own gown on the boards for Ralegh to kneel on. He knelt first with his head to the west. When somebody pointed it out, and found fault with it, Ralegh said 'So the heart be right, it is no great matter which way the head lieth.' But to satisfy them, he stood up and then knelt down again with his head to the east.

He told the executioner to give him a little time for prayer, and then, when he stretched out his hands, he should dispatch him.

Ralegh put out his hands once, and again. Still the headsman faltered.

'Strike, man, strike!'

The lips were seen to be moving in prayer. The first blow was mortal. The second took off the head, although the trunk did not shrink after the first.

The executioner lifted the head by the hair, and exhibited it on each side of the scaffold. A voice in the crowd said, 'We have not such another head to cut off!'

Sir Walter Ralegh had called himself Death's subject. He had himself described the features of his master.

It is therefore Death alone that can suddenly make man to know himself. He tells the proud and insolent, that they are but abjects, and humbles them at the instant; makes them cry, complain, and repent, yea, even to hate their forepassed happiness. He takes the account of the rich, and proves him a beggar; a naked beggar, which hath interest in nothing, but in the gravel that fills his mouth. He holds a glass before the eyes of the most beautiful, and makes them see therein, their deformity and rottenness; and they acknowledge it.

O eloquent, just and mighty Death! whom none could advise, thou hast persuaded;

what none hath dared, thou hast done, and whom all the world hath flattered, thou only hast cast out of the world and despised: thou hast drawn together all the far stretched greatness, all the pride, cruelty, and ambition of man, and covered it all over with these two narrow words, *Hic jacet*.

Sir Walter Ralegh's will

Bibliography

The bibliography on the Elizabethan Age in general, and on Sir Walter Ralegh in particular, is already huge and grows every year. Some of the more accessible sources are listed under headings below. Of the biographies, Stebbing (1891) is still one of the most useful; Philip Edwards (1953) is an excellent study of Ralegh as a writer; Norman Lloyd Williams (1962) is a good, crisp account of the man and his times. The standard edition of the Poems is Agnes Latham's (1951), and of the Letters, still Volume 2 of Edwards' Life of 1868. The 1829 Oxford edition of the Works, in eight volumes, and including the complete *Historie of the World* was reprinted in New York in 1962.

LIFE

Birch, Rev. Thomas, *Life of Sir Walter Ralegh*, in Vol. 1 of *Works*

Brushfield, Thomas, *A Bibliography of Sir Walter Ralegh Knt.*, (Exeter, 1908), and many contributions on Ralegh's life, family, writings and imprisonment in 'Raleghana' series in *Trans. of Devon Association*

Edwards, Edward, *The Life of Sir Walter Ralegh*, 2 vols. (London, 1868)

Edwards, Philip, *Sir Walter Ralegh*, (Longmans Green, London, 1953)

Fuller, Thomas, *History of the Worthies of England*, (1811)

Gosse, Sir Edmund, *Raleigh*, (Longmans Green, London 1888)

Hume, Martin A. S., *Sir Walter Ralegh*, (T. Fisher Unwin, London, 1897)

Irwin, Margaret, *That Great Lucifer*, (Chatto & Windus, London, 1960)

Lloyd, David, *State Worthies*, (London, 1766)

Naunton, Sir Robert, *Fragmenta Regalia* (1641), ed. E. Arber, English Reprints 1870

Oldys, William, *The Life of Sir Walter Ralegh*, (1735), in Vol. 1 of *Works*

Prince, Rev. John, *The Worthies of Devon*, (1710), Printed for Rees & Curtis, Plymouth, (London, 1810)

Rodd, Sir Rennell, *Sir Walter Raleigh*, (Macmillan, London, 1921)

Waldman, Milton, *Sir Walter Raleigh*, (Bodley Head, London, 1928)

Wallace, Willard, *Sir Walter Raleigh*, (Princeton Univ. Press, New Jersey, 1959)

Williams, Norman Lloyd, *Sir Walter Raleigh*, (Eyre & Spottiswoode, London, 1962)

Wood, Anthony A., *Atheniae Oxonienses*, (1691–1692), ed. Philip Bliss, 6 vols. (Oxford, 1813–1820)

LETTERS

Edwards, Edward, *Life of Sir Walter Raleigh*, Vol. 2

PROSE

Firth, Sir Charles, *Sir Walter Raleigh's "History of the World"*, (Essays Historical & Literary, Oxford, 1938)

Patrides, C. A. (Ed.) *Sir Walter Ralegh: The History of the World*, (Macmillan, London, 1971)

Ralegh, Sir Walter, *A Report of the Truth of the Fight About the Iles of the Acores* (1591), *The Discoverie of the Large, Rich, and Bewtiful Empyre of Guiana* (1596), in facsimile, (The Scolar Press, Menston, Yorks., 1967)

Ralegh, Sir Walter, *Works*, ed. W. Oldys, (Oxford, 1829; reprinted, Burt Franklin, New York, 1962)

Vol. I, *Lives* by Oldys and Birch; Vols. II–VII, *The Historie of the World*; Vol. VIII, Miscellaneous prose, letters and poems

POETRY

Black, L. G., "A Lost Poem by Queen Elizabeth I", *Times Lit. Supp.*, 23rd May, 1968

Davie, Donald, "A Reading of 'The Ocean's Love to Cynthia'", *Elizabethan Poetry* (Stratford upon Avon Studies 2, Arnold, London 1960)

England's Helicon (ed. of 1600 and 1614), ed. Hugh Macdonald, (Routledge & Kegan Paul, London, 1949)

Gosse, Sir Edmund, "Sir Walter Raleigh's 'Cynthia'", *Athenaeum*, 2nd and 9th Jan. 1886

Hannah, Rev. John, *Courtly Poets from Raleigh to Montrose*, (Bell and Daldy, London, 1870)

Latham, Agnes, *The Poems of Sir Walter Ralegh*, (Routledge & Kegan Paul, London, 1951)

Latham, Agnes, *Sir Walter Ralegh*, Writers and Their Work: No. 177, (Pub. for The British Council and the National Book League, Longmans Green, London, 1964). Also Chapters on Ralegh's prose

Oakeshott, Walter, *The Queen and the Poet*, (Faber & Faber, London, 1960)

Puttenham, George, *The Arte of English Poesie*, (1589), Ed. E. Arber, (English Reprints 1869)

Ure, Peter, "Two Elizabethan Poets: Daniel and Ralegh", (Pelican Guide to English Literature, Penguin, 1966)

UNIVERSITY

Emden, C. S., *Oriel Papers*, (Oxford, 1948)

FRANCE

Fisher, H. A. L., *A History of Europe*, Vol. II, (Eyre & Spottiswoode, London, 1935)

Thompson, J. W., *The Wars of Religion in France 1559–1576*, (Chicago, 1909)

IRELAND

Calendar of Carew MSS, Lambeth Palace, Ed. Brewer & Bullen, 1868

Calendar of State Papers (Ireland: Elizabeth)

Falls, Cyril, *Elizabeth's Irish Wars*, (Methuen, London, 1950)

Holinshed, Raphael, *Chronicles of England, Scotland and Ireland*, ed. John Hooker, Vols. III, IV and VI ed. H. Ellis, 6 Vols. (London 1807–1808)

Lismore Papers, ed. Dr Grosart, (1886)

Morton, Grenfell, *Elizabethan Ireland*, (Longman, London, 1971)

O'Connor, G. B., *Elizabethan Ireland*, (Dublin, 1906)

Pope-Hennessy, Sir John, *Sir Walter Raleigh in Ireland*, (London, 1883)

Spenser, Edmund, *A View of the Present State of Ireland*, (1633), ed. W. L. Renwick, (London, 1934)

VOYAGES

Betts, R. E., "The Lost Colony", *Cornhill Magazine*, July 1938

Gardiner, S. R., "Documents relating to Ralegh's Last Voyage", Camden Miscellany, Vol. 5

Hakluyt, Richard, *Voyages, Navigations, Traffics and Discoveries of the English Nation*, 8 vols. (Dent, Everyman's Library, London, 1907)

Harlow, Vincent, *The Discoverie of Guiana*, (Argonaut Press, London, 1928)

Harlow, Vincent, *Raleigh's Last Voyage*, (Argonaut Press, London, 1932)

Latham, Agnes, "Sir Walter Raleigh's Gold Mine: New Light on the Last Guiana Voyage", *Essays and Studies*, 1951

Purchas, Samuel, *Hakluytus Posthumus*, (1625) or *Purchas His Pilgrims*, 20 vols. (MacLehose, Glasgow, 1907)

Quinn, David Beers, *Raleigh and the British Empire*, (English U. Press, London, 1947)

Quinn, David Beers, *The Roanoke Voyages, 1584–1590*, 2 vols. (Hakluyt Society, London, 1955)

Quinn, David Beers, *The Voyages and Colonising Expeditions of Sir Humphrey Gilbert*, 2 vols., (Hakluyt Society, London, 1940)

Taylor, Eva G. R., "Hariot's Instructions for Sir Walter Raleigh's Voyage to Guiana, 1595", *Journal of Inst. of Navigation*, Vol. V. (1952)

Taylor, Eva G. R., *The Haven Finding Art*, (Hollis & Carter, London, 1956)

Taylor, Eva G. R., *Tudor Geography 1485–1583*, (London, 1930), *Late Tudor and Early Stuart Geography 1583–1650* (London, 1934)

NAVAL SERVICE

Mattingly, Garrett, *The Defeat of the Spanish Armada*, (Cape, London, 1959)

Navy Records Society, Vol. 40, (1912), *The Taking of the 'Madre Dios'*; Vol. 20 (1902), *The Voyage to Cadiz*, (Slingsby MSS)

Oppenheim, M. (Editor), *The Naval Tracts of Sir William Monson*, 5 vols., (Navy Records Society, London, 1902–1914)

Vere, Sir Francis, *Commentaries*, from Sir Charles Firth (ed.) *Stuart Tracts*, 1603–1693 (London, 1903)

MARRIAGE

Latham, A. M. C., "Sir Walter Ralegh's Will", *Review of English Studies*, XXII, No. 86 (May, 1971)

Rowse, A. L., *Ralegh and the Throckmortons*, (Macmillan, London, 1962)

Sorensen, J. W., "Sir Walter Raleigh's Marriage", *Studies in Philology*, 1936

SHERBORNE

Fowler, Joseph, *Medieval Sherborne*, (Dorchester, 1951)

Gentleman's Magazine, "Sir Walter Ralegh at Sherborne", 1853 Vol. II, 1854 Vol. I

ATHEISM

Boas, Frederick S., *Marlowe and his Circle*, (Oxford, 1931)

Bradbrook, Muriel, *The School of Night*, (Cambridge, 1936)

Hill, Christopher, *Intellectual Origins of the English Revolution*, (Oxford, 1965)

Lloyd, Rachel, *Dorset Elizabethans*, (Murray, London, 1967)

Shakespeare, William, *Love's Labour's Lost*, ed. Richard David, Arden Edition, (Methuen, London, 1956)

Shirley, J. W., "Scientific Experiments of Sir Walter Raleigh, the Wizard Earl and the Three Magi in the Tower 1603–17", *Ambix*, 1949

Strathmann, Ernest A., *Sir Walter Ralegh, a Study in Elizabethan Skepticism*, (Columbia, New York, 1951)

Tillyard, E. M. W., *The Elizabethan World Picture*, (Chatto & Windus, London, 1943)

Willobie, Henry, *Willobie His Avisa*, ed. G. B. Harrison, (John Lane, The Bodley Head, London, 1926) (Atheism Enquiry from Harleian MS.6849 BM printed as an Appendix)

CONTEMPORARIES, ELIZABETHAN & JACOBEAN

Aubrey, John, *Brief Lives*, ed. Oliver Lawson Dick, (Secker & Warburg, London, 1949)

Brooks, Eric St. John, *Sir Christopher Hatton*, (Cape, London, 1946)

Cecil, Algernon, *A Life of Robert Cecil, 1st Earl of Salisbury*, (London, 1915)

Chamberlain, John, *Letters during the Reign of Elizabeth*, (Camden Society, 1861)

Chamberlin, F., *The Private Character of Queen Elizabeth*, (London, 1922)

Chapman, George, *The Poems of George Chapman*, Ed. Phyllis Brooks Bartlett, (Oxford, 1941)

Clark, Eleanor G., *Raleigh and Marlowe*, (New York, 1941)

Dee, Dr John, *Private Diary*, ed. J. O. Halliwell, (Camden Society, 1842)

Devereux, Walter, *Lives and Letters of the Devereux, Earls of Essex*, 2 Vols. (London, 1853)

Gascoigne, George, *The Steele Glas*, (1576), ed. Edward Arber, (English Reprints, 1868)

Gilbert, A. H., "Belphoebe's Misdeeming of Timias", *Proc. Mod. Langs. Ass.* Vol. LXII (1947)

Goodman, Godfrey, *The Court of King James the First*, ed. J. Brewer, (London, 1839)

Handover, P. M., *The Second Cecil*, (London, 1959)

Harington, Sir John, *Epigrams* (1618), (The Scolar Press, Menston, Yorks., 1970)

Harrison, G. B., *A Jacobean Journal*, (London, 1941)

Harrison, G. B., *The Life and Death of Robert Devereux, Earl of Essex*, (London, 1937)

Howell, James, *Epistolae Ho-Elianae* (1645–1655), ed. J. Jacobs, 2 vols. (London, 1892)

Jenkins, Elizabeth, *Elizabeth the Great*, (Gollancz, London, 1958)

Jonson, Ben, *Discoveries: 1641 – Conversations with William Drummond of Hawthornden: 1619*, ed. G. B. Harrison, (John Lane The Bodley Head, London, 1923)

Jonson, Ben, *Poems of Ben Jonson*, ed. George Burke Johnston, (Routledge & Kegan Paul, London, 1954)

Koller, Katherine, "Spenser and Ralegh", *English Literary History*, 1934

Lacey, Robert, *Robert, Earl of Essex – an Elizabethan Icarus*, (Weidenfeld & Nicolson, London, 1971)

Neale, J. E., *Queen Elizabeth I*, (Cape, London, 1934)

Nichols, John, *The Progresses of Queen Elizabeth*, 4 vols., (London 1828)

Osborn, Francis, *Traditional Memoirs on the Reign of King James* (1658), reprinted in *Secret History of James I*, (1811)

Read, Conyers, *Mr Secretary Cecil and Queen Elizabeth*, (Cape, London, 1955)

Rowse, A. L., *Sir Richard Grenville of the 'Revenge'*, (Cape, London, 1937)

Rukeyser, Muriel, *The Traces of Thomas Hariot*, (Gollancz, London, 1972)

Sandison, H. E., "Arthur Gorges, Spenser's Alcyon and Raleigh's Friend", *Proc. Mod. Langs. Ass.* 1928

Shapiro, I. A., "The Mermaid Club", *Modern Language Review*, Vol. XLV (January 1950)

Spedding, James, *Sir Francis Bacon, Letters and Life*, Vol. VI of *Works* (London, 1872)

Spenser, Edmund, *Poetical Works*, ed. J. C. Smith and E. De Selincourt, (Oxford, 1912)

Statham, E. P., *A Jacobean Letter-Writer*, (Life and Times of John Chamberlain), (London, 1920)

Strachey, Lytton, *Elizabeth and Essex*, (Chatto & Windus, London, 1928)

Waldman, Milton, *Elizabeth and Leicester*, (Collins, London, 1944)

Willson, David Harris, *King James VI and I*, (Cape, London, 1956)

PARLIAMENT

D'Ewes, Sir Simonds, *Journals of all the Parliaments during the Reign of Queen Elizabeth* (1682). ed. Paul Bowes, (London, 1862)

Neale, J. E., *Elizabeth I and her Parliaments*, Vol. I (1559–1581) and Vol. II (1584–1601), (Cape, London, 1953 and 1957)

Neale, J. E., *The Elizabethan House of Commons*, (Cape, London, 1949)

Townshend, Heywood, *Historical Collections, An Exact Account of the Last Four Parliaments of Elizabeth*, (London, 1680)

STANNARIES

Hamilton, A. H. A., "The Jurisdiction of the Lord Warden of the Stannaries in the time of Sir Walter Raleigh", *Devon Ass. Trans.*, VIII, (1876)

Lewis, G. R., *The Stannaries*, (Cambridge, Mass., 1908)

JERSEY

Ahier, Philip, *The Governorship of Sir Walter Raleigh in Jersey 1600–1603*, (Bigwoods, St Helier, Jersey, 1971)

Eagleston, A. J., *The Channel Islands under Tudor Government*, (Cambridge, 1949)

TRIAL AND EXECUTION

"Declaration of the Carriage and Demeanour of Sir Walter Raleigh, A", Harleian Miscellany, Vol. III, 1809

D'Israeli, Isaac, *Curiosities of Literature*, (London, 1849)

Gardiner, S. R., "The Case against Sir Walter Raleigh", *Fortnightly Review*, Vol. VII (1867)

Howell, Thomas, Ed. of Cobbett's *Complete Collection of State Trials*, Vol. II, 1809

James VI of Scotland, Correspondence with Sir Robert Cecil and Others in England, ed. John Bruce, (Camden Society, London 1860)

Stephen, Sir Harry L., "The Trial of Raleigh", *Trans. Royal Hist. Soc.*, 1919

Stukeley, Sir Lewis, *Apology*, in Raleigh's *Works*, Vol. VIII

PORTRAITS

Black, J. B., *The Reign of Elizabeth 1558–1603*, (Oxford, 1959)

Bush, Douglas, *English Literature in the Earlier Seventeenth Century*, (Oxford, 1945)

Calendars of State Papers, *Domestic* (Elizabeth, 1558–1603, and James I, 1603–1618); *Ireland* (Elizabeth); *Venetian* (Elizabeth, and James); *Colonial*

Caraman, Philip, *The Other Face*, (London, 1960)

Castiglione, Baldesar, *The Book of the Courtier*, trans. George Bull, (Penguin, 1967)

Chambers, E. K., *Shakespeare's England*, 2 vols., (Oxford, 1916)

Collier, J. P., "New Materials for a Life of Sir Walter Raleigh", *Archaeologica*, Vol. XXXIV (1852), Vol. XXXV (1853)

Cust, Lionel, 'Portraits of Raleigh', *Walpole Society*, Vol. VIII, 1920

Dixon, William Hepworth, *Her Majesty's Tower*, Vol. I (London, 1870)

Egerton Papers, ed. J. P. Collier, (Camden Society, London, 1840)

Foxe, John, *Acts and Monuments*, (Martyrs), 1877

Fugger News-Letters, 1st and 2nd Series, Ed. V. von Klarwill, (London, 1924–1926)

Gerard, John, *Herball* (1597), arr. Marcus Woodward, (Thorsons, London, 1972)

Historical Manuscripts Commission Reports: *Allen George Finch* MSS; *Salisbury* MSS; *Lord De L'Isle and Dudley* MSS

Huizinga, Johan, *The Waning of the Middle Ages*, (Penguin, 1955)

Lewis, C. S., *English Literature in the Sixteenth Century*, (Oxford, 1954)

Privy Council, Acts, 1580–1604, *Registers*, Elizabeth and James I

Prothero, G. W., *Select Statutes and other Constitutional Documents*, Elizabeth and James I, (Oxford, 1913)

Rowse, A. L., *The Elizabethan Renaissance:* The Life of the Society, (Macmillan, London, 1971)

Rowse, A. L., *The England of Elizabeth*, (Macmillan, London, 1950)

Salaman, R. N., *The History and Social Influence of the Potato*, (Cambridge, 1949)

Scott, W. R., *The Constitution and Finance of English, Scottish and Irish Joint Stock Companies to 1720*, (Cambridge, 3 vols., 1910–1912)

Smith, Lacey Baldwin, *The Elizabethan Epic*, (Cape, London, 1966)

Stow, John, *The Survey of London* (1598), (Dent, Everyman's Library, London, 1956)

Strong, Roy, *Tudor and Jacobean Portraits*, (HMSO, London, 1969)

Tawney, R. H., *Religion and the Rise of Capitalism*, (Pelican, 1938)

Wilson, F. P., *Plague in Shakespeare's London*, (Oxford, 1927)

Wilson, John Dover, *Life in Shakespeare's England*, (Cambridge, 1911)

Index

Perrot, Sir John, 20, 24, 91
Perrot, Sir Thomas, 25, 71
Pett, Phineas, 281, 298, 302
Peyton, Sir John, 243, 245, 249
Philip II of Spain, 12, 27, 54, 68,
    77–8, 82, 99, 104, 138, 140, 160,
    179, 184, 195, 234, 252, 256
Philip III of Spain, 281, 293, 296,
    298, 306, 315, 320, 324, 329
Popham, George, 159–60, 162,
    222
Popham, Lord Chief Justice, 252,
    255, 257, 260, 262, 273, 279
Portugal, Don Antonio, Pretender
    of, 68, 82–3
Preston, Capt Amyas, 160, 162,
    174, 182, 228
Pyne, Henry, 137, 228, 305, 333

Ralegh, Sir Carew (brother), 13,
    19, 22, 62, 106, 136, 152, 154,
    156, 228, 270, 272
Ralegh, Carew (son), 272, 333
Ralegh, Damerei (son), 113–14,
    132
Ralegh, George (nephew), 304,
    311, 315, 341
Ralegh, Katherine (mother), 12–
    14, 34, 157
Ralegh, Margaret (sister), 13
Ralegh, Walter (father), 12–14,
    16–17, 19, 34, 157

RALEGH, SIR WALTER
family background, 12–14
birth, 13–14
education, 14, 16–17
to France (1569), 16–17
as poet, 11, 17, 19, 36, 42, 44, 46,
    60, 70, 72–3, 85, 90, 109, 111–
    12, 119–21, 124–7, 141, 151,
    210, 268–9, 282, 334, 336
and Leicester, 17, 25, 38, 62–5, 70
on threshold of Court, 19, 24–5, 38
appearance, 19, 36, 42, 52, 109,
    210, 240, 298, 331
personality, 11, 19, 25, 34, 36, 215
privateering (1578), 22, 24
Elizabeth first hears of, 22, 34,
    35–6
and Burghley, 24, 38, 42, 71
and Walsingham, 24, 38, 52, 56
to Ireland (1579–81), 25–35, 38
and favoured by Elizabeth, 36–44,
    48, 52, 54–5, 60, 62, 65, 69, 83,
    86, 88, 91, 104, 106, 136, 138,
    144, 156, 280

RALEGH, SIR WALTER continued
and property gifts, 39–41, 52, 69
and 'Farm of Wines', 39, 67, 211,
    242, 249–50, 262, 270, 272
Durham House, 40–1, 52, 96, 109,
    114, 116, 226, 239, 242
and wool cloth patent, 41–2, 67
spelling of name, 47
as explorer and coloniser, 11–12,
    47, 55, 73
first expedition to American
    coast, 49–50, 52
as parliamentarian, 11, 50, 52,
    137, 138–41, 212, 226, 230–4
knighted, 52
second expedition to Americas,
    50, 52–6, 58–9
as Lord Warden of the Stannaries,
    55, 61–2, 67, 114, 226–7, 231–2,
    249, 270
and tobacco, 60–1, 96, 240
privateering, 67–8, 73, 81–2
as Captain of the Guard, 69, 94,
    96, 109, 114, 119, 148, 194, 220,
    224, 227, 234, 242, 262
and Essex, 70, 72–3, 80–1, 114,
    152, 180–1, 194, 196, 201, 204,
    209, 214, 217–19, 224–5
expedition to Virginia (1587),
    73–7, 83
takes part in Armada, 76–8, 80
in the Portuguese invasion (1589),
    82–3, 85
out of favour with Elizabeth, 83,
    85, 90, 106, 108–9, 116, 118–19,
    121, 151–2, 158, 160, 177, 179,
    193–4
'Undertaker' in Ireland, 86, 88
lands in Ireland, 86, 88, 91–2
as botanist, 11, 88–9
Spenser and *The Faerie Queene*,
    89–91
The Ocean to Scinthia, 11, 90, 124–
    7, 151, 177
relief expedition to Virginia
    (1590), 96, 98
'A Report of the Truth Of The
    fight about the Isles of Açores,
    this last Sommer', 101–2, 104
in Tower of London (1592), 109,
    117–24
and women, 109, 112
and Bess Ralegh, 109, 111–14,
    116, 160–1, 246, 248, 266, 317,
    328
marriage, 11, 111–12
and Damerei, 113–14

RALEGH, SIR WALTER continued
and Cecil, 113–14, 118–19, 130,
    132, 194, 199, 211, 220–1, 233,
    248, 256, 259, 263
health, 119, 188–9, 193, 212, 230,
    234, 272–3, 295, 308, 310, 318,
    320–1, 328, 331
release from Tower, 127, 129, 132,
    158
Sherborne Castle, 109, 132, 134,
    137, 211, 226–8, 236, 249, 270,
    272–4, 292, 296, 302
and Wat, 134, 136, 142, 246,
    283–4
and falconry, 11, 136
The Phoenix Nest, 141
accused of atheism, 11, 142–8,
    152–6, 237, 248, 286, 290
death of mother, 157
first expedition to Guiana (1594),
    11, 158–77 c
illegitimate son, 160, 180
'The Discoverie of the Large,
    Rich and Bewtiful Empire of
    Guiana', 175
expedition to Cadiz (1597), 179–
    92
back in Elizabeth's favour, 195,
    210, 215, 225–6, 234, 236
will, 196, 210–11
Islands Voyage (1597), 196–209,
    288
illegitimate daughter, 211–12
as Governor of Jersey, 211–12,
    215, 221, 226, 242, 270
and Essex's rebellion and death,
    221–2, 224
relief expedition to Virginia
    (1603), 98, 227
Cecil's plot, 236–40, 242
death of Elizabeth, 239
and James's dislike of, 147, 240,
    242–3
stripped of favours, 242
*Discourse touching a War with
    Spain, and of the Protecting of the
    Netherlands, A*, 242–3
arrested, 243
suspected plot against James, 72,
    147, 234, 244–5, 249, 252
suicide attempts, 11, 245–6
indictment, 249, 252, 254
Winchester trial, 252–62
and Coke, 254–5, 257–60
sentenced for High Treason, 262
pleas for reprieve, 263
reprieved, 269